The Natural History of Moths

Dedication

For my family,

who have suffered the eccentricities
of my enthusiasm for moths with patience
and surprising good humour!

The Natural History
of
Moths

Mark Young

With illustrations by
Lyn Wells
and photographs by
Roy Leverton

T & A D
POYSER
NATURAL
HISTORY

First published in 1997 by T & A D Poyser Ltd
24–28 Oval Road, London NW1 7DX

Typeset by Phoenix Photosetting, Chatham, Kent
*Printed and bound in Great Britain by
the University Press, Cambridge*

*A catalogue record for this book
is available from the British library*

ISBN 0-85661-103-4

Contents

The colour plate section can be found between pages 146 and 147.

List of Colour Plates

1. Moths that rest on bark.
2. Moths that rest on foliage.
3. Moths that rest on rocks.
4. Moths that resemble specific plants.
5. Warningly coloured moths.
6. Moths that mimic other insects.
7. White and feather-like moths.
8. Caterpillars of various colours and shapes.
9. Eggs and caterpillars.
10. Caterpillars, pupae and parasites.
11. Emerging and mating moths.
12. Sexual dimorphism and melanism.
13. Variable and disputed species.
14. Moths at 'sugar' and variable species.
15. Migrant moths.
16. Colonists and rare species.

Preface

Moths are beautiful and mysterious creatures that, except for their predominantly nocturnal habit, are similar to butterflies, with which they comprise the great insect order the Lepidoptera. In the past 20 years, there have been many books on butterflies, and they have attracted great attention from naturalists and conservationists; moths, however, have been rather neglected. This is the first book that aims to cover the natural history of moths (as distinct from their identification and distribution), since E.B.Ford wrote his classic book in the 'New Naturalist' series in 1955.

I have tried to combine the enthusiasm and wide general knowledge of the amateur lepidopterist with recent scientific work on moths, to produce a book that will include something of interest to a wide spectrum of readers. I know from my own experience that amateurs are a mine of information on the life cycles and ecology of moths, often including knowledge that is laboriously 'rediscovered' by scientists later, but that there have also been some fascinating academic studies that will surprise and stimulate the amateur. Fortunately, the study of moths is a field where amateur and professional do still respect one another and I want to help to foster their mutual interest and understanding.

There are already excellent books for identifying moths, listing their larval foodplants and setting out their basic life cycles and so I have deliberately omitted these topics, except where necessary to illustrate my themes. I have also had to be selective in my coverage of a very large subject and so I have chosen a spectrum of material, based around my own pet interests, of course. I am sorry if your own particular interest receives less attention than it deserves! I have also used mainly British examples, with deliberate avoidance of the usual southern bias (!), but I have included world-wide studies wherever I can, when they are relevant.

Any book on the natural history of moths must expect unflattering comparison with Ford's outstanding book, but I have cunningly tried to avoid this by choosing to concentrate on subjects that he avoided, and omitting the genetics of moths, which was his special interest. His two books on butterflies and moths helped to change me from being a schoolboy collector to someone who studied moths and I should be very satisfied if I could prompt this progress in others. To help the enthusiast identify moths there are excellent recent guides and the multi-volumed *The Moths and Butterflies of Great Britain and Ireland* includes a wealth of fascinating detail about British species. I have referred to it often and use it as the standard source for the scientific names of moths used here, since it represents the most authoritative update of the last British check-list in 1972. I do differ from it consciously in one respect, however. I have bullied my editor into allowing me to use capital letters for the English names of moths – not to do so runs the risk of confusing a small Blood-vein (*Timandra griseata*) with a Small Blood-vein (*Scopula imitaria*), for example, and I am unrepentant for applying commonsense in this respect, instead of accepting traditional dogma!

I have had many happy hours in the company of fellow enthusiasts and they have welcomed me generously and tolerated my constant questions. I came to moths from general natural history and am constantly grateful to my parents for encouraging my interest in this. At the risk of unwittingly insulting those I omit, I must pay some tributes. Firstly, to my mentor, Michael Harper, who filled me with curiosity about moths and has remained many steps ahead of me in knowledge. Many others have helped stimulate my interest and have been frequent companions on field excursions. Early on Les Evans was very generous to a penniless student and more recently Bob Palmer welcomed me to Aberdeenshire and introduced me to Scotland's moths. He and David Barbour, John Langmaid, Keith Bland and many others have been excellent companions in the field and study. My students Neil Ravenscroft and Nigel Bourn have shown me what can be achieved by hard work and perseverance in all kinds of weather, and in this more academic vein Mark Shaw and Paul Waring have been most stimulating friends. Paul also provided distribution maps produced under contract for the Joint Nature Conservation Committee but the data for these have been provided by an 'army' of dedicated volunteer recorders. Special thanks are due to Roy Leverton, who not only provided his superb photographs, but has constantly forced me to justify my comments and theories by his sharp questions and healthy scepticism of received wisdom. Finally, all British moth enthusiasts owe a great debt to Maitland Emmet, who has done so much to encourage the rest of us with his own work, and I acknowledge a personal debt to the late Teddy Pelham-Clinton, who helped convert me to the study of the 'micro's' by the application of many hours of patient help. He was so modest and yet so knowledgeable.

CHAPTER 1

An Introduction to Moths

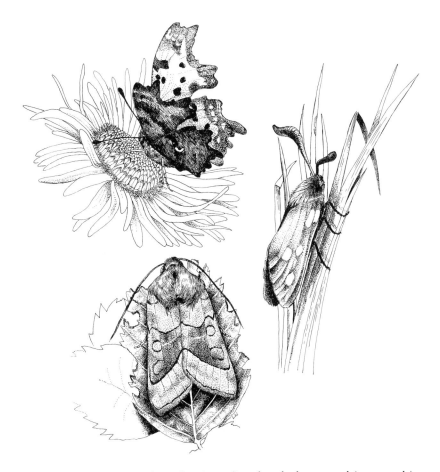

The contrast between a butterfly, a 'typical' moth and a burnet moth (not to scale).

MOTHS are members of the great insect order, Lepidoptera, which includes the more familiar butterflies – both have scale-covered wings, from which the scientific name is derived (Gk lepis=scale, pteron=wing). These scales are set like roof slates all over the wings and are the fine dust which rubs off so easily on to inquisitive fingers. Each scale is coloured and it is the mosaic of these myriad colours that gives butterflies and moths their fascinating and subtle patterns and colour schemes.

Butterflies have always received more notice than moths, no doubt because of their day-

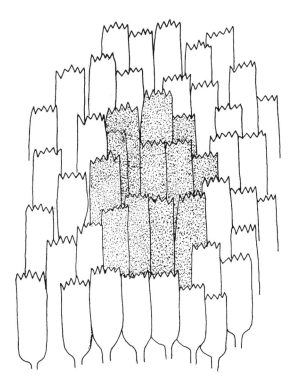

FIG 1   *Scales from the wing of a moth.*

flying habits and their generally more gaudy appearance, but I hope to convince you that moths deserve their share of attention too. They can be as brightly coloured – in fact many, like the 'burnets' (Zygaenidae) or the 'tigers' (part of the Arctiidae) are constantly mistaken for butterflies – and some of them are also day-flying, so that they can claim all the attractions of butterflies. In addition, moths have a wealth of extra features: such as the ability of some to detect bats' ultrasonic squeaks and either to take evasive flight or to produce their own confusing noises in return (see Chapter 8); or the well known trick of releasing powerful scent to attract potential mates from over a kilometre away (see Chapter 7). My purpose in this book is to review what is now known about these and many other exciting aspects of moths' natural history, illustrating this with information from recent scientific research.

A BUTTERFLY IS JUST A MOTH BY ANOTHER NAME

There is no proper answer to the question 'what is the difference between a butterfly and a moth?'. We have chosen to give the label 'butterflies' to members of a small number of related families within the order Lepidoptera. In these families the species generally share certain habits and features. They are day-flying; have colourful wings; hold their wings closed over their backs when at rest; have clubbed ends to their antennae: and by these combined characters we have come to know them. However, the 'skipper butterflies' hold their wings in various angled positions and have only moderately thickened antennae, whereas the 'burnet moths' (for example) are colourful, day-flying species, with well thickened ends to their antennae and we might well ask why they are not also called butterflies.

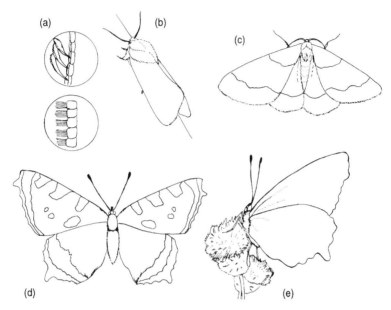

FIG 2 *Contrasting features of butterflies and moths. (a) Detailed structure of antennae; (b) a moth at rest, with 'roof-like' folded wings and simple antennae; (c) a geometrid moth at rest, with wings flat; (d) a butterfly, showing 'knobbed' antennae; (e) a butterfly at rest, with wings held above the body.*

COUNTING SPECIES

The Lepidoptera include about 130 000 known species, with an incalculable number still to be found and described, especially in the tropics (Groombridge, 1992; Nauman, 1994). Of these, the butterflies account for around 18 500 species, or only 12%; this alone indicates why there is so much to be gained from studying moths. Lepidoptera are one of the 'big four' insect orders, equalled or exceeded in number only by the true flies (Diptera), with 130 000 species; the bees, wasps, ants and saw-flies (Hymenoptera), with 130 000 species; and the beetles (Coleoptera), with 350 000 species. Together these four orders make up 80% of the insects and a staggering 33% of all known animals. The paltry tallies of mammals, 4000 species, and birds, 9700 species, are put into stark perspective by the richness of insect species. On average, around 700 new species of Lepidoptera are described each year, whereas only 5 or so new birds and about 25 new mammals are found.

TABLE 1   *The approximate numbers of different types of animals and plants.*

Types of animals	Numbers of described species	Estimate of total no.'s	Numbers currently being described each year
Viruses	5 000	500 000	?
Bacteria	4 000	400 000	?
Fungi	70 000	1 000 000	1 700
Higher plants	250 000	300 000	?
Protozoa	40 000	200 000	350
Nematodes	15 000	500 000	360
Molluscs	70 000	200 000	370
Fishes	19 000	24 000	230
Amphibians	4 200	5 500	}
Reptiles	6 300	7 300	} 105
Birds	9 000	9 300	5
Mammals	4 000	4 300	25
Arachnids	75 000	750 000	1 350
Crustaceans	40 000	150 000	700
Insects total	800 000–950 000	8 000 000 (5–30 million)	7 200
Insects other than top four	150 000	3 000 000	2 000
Hymenoptera	130 000	1 000 000	1 200
Diptera	130 000	1 000 000	1 000
Coleoptera	350 000	2 000 000	2 300
Lepidoptera	130 000	300 000	640

Source: Simplified with permission from Groombridge (1992).

Even in temperate regions, where insects might be expected to give way to warm-blooded mammals and birds, there are still many species – the lepidopterous fauna of Britain numbers around 2400, including the strays and regular migrants described in Chapter 3 (Emmet, 1991a). Although the 65 or so butterflies found regularly in Britain cover a wide range of habitats and show many interesting features, the moths are incomparably more widespread and varied in their occurrence, influence and behaviour.

MOTHS ARE FOUND EVERYWHERE

There are no marine moths, but on the autumn strand line of sandy shores in southern and eastern Britain, the eaten leaves of Sea Rocket (*Cakile maritima*) indicate the presence of the larvae of the Sand Dart moth (*Agrotis ripae*) in the sand beneath the plant. The moth itself can then be caught at 'sugar' (see Chapter 9) on the beach the following summer. Just above the high tide mark of rocky shores, the larvae of the Dew moth (*Setina irrorella*) feed on lichens splashed by the waves. There are no moths that live permanently on snow fields

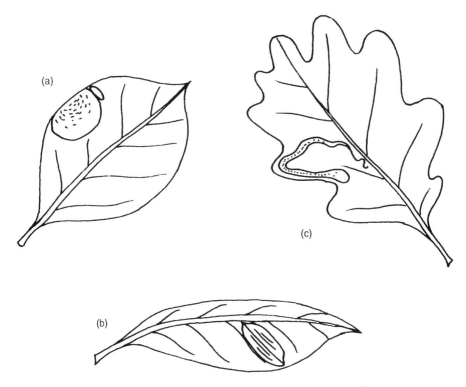

FIG 3 *Leaf mine patterns.* (*a*) Antispila *sp.* (*Heliozelidae*); (*b*) Phyllonorycter *sp.* (*Gracillariidae*); (*c*) Stigmella *sp.* (*Nepticulidae*).

either, but many can be found feeding on the sparse vegetation that is briefly free from snow on mountains in summer. Wherever there are plants, there are moths, but they also use a very much wider range of foodstuffs and turn up in the most unlikely places. One family, the Tineidae, specialises in feeding on fungus, or animal, or plant debris, and often shares human habitations. *Dryadaula pactolia*, now widespread but originally from New Zealand, has been found feeding on fungus in wine cellars; *Monopis weaverella* includes fox faeces in its diet; *Tinea pellionella* (amongst others) has moved from birds' nests to clothes; and *Myrmecozela ochraceella* eats debris in wood ants' nests.

The tiny size of the larvae of some moths also allows them to use highly restricted and specific food stuffs and there are many species whose entire larval life and growth takes place between the layers of one leaf (Hering, 1951). The family Nepticulidae shows this habit and, as the larvae feed, they slowly cut out a long mine in their leaf; since the mine is enclosed there is no exit for disposal of the faeces, which are piled behind the advancing larva, sometimes in intricate patterns. When the larvae are fully grown they bore out of the leaf and drop to the ground, forming a tough silken cocoon in which to pupate. Like most moths, leaf-mining species are usually restricted in their choice of foodplant and so the lepidopterist can find mined leaves and, knowing the foodplant, the shape and size of the mine, and the particular pattern of the faeces (usually called 'frass') can identify the species of moth that has done the damage. Other families of moths also make mines in leaves and this strategy, providing a sheltered environment and constant access to food, albeit on a very small scale, has clearly been a successful one (see Chapter 5).

Other moths, especially the Sesiidae, or 'clearwing' moths, feed inside the stems and trunks of trees and bushes, but as the nutritive value of wood is rather limited, the slowly growing larvae often spend two or more years feeding. Clearwings, as so aptly described by their common name, lack most of the scales on their wings and generally look more like wasps, bees or flies than moths. This is a defensive strategy similar to that of the wasp-mimicking hoverflies, and the resemblances can be striking and alarming (see Chapter 8).

MOTHS AS HERBIVORES

Most people are more familiar with the typical feeding habits of free-living larvae. Some of these larvae are so large that their depredations are clearly visible, in the form of extensive damage to leaves; this is obviously a potential problem to the larvae, which do not wish to advertise their presence to hungry bird predators. When lepidopterists search for larvae they often do so by looking for the feeding signs and there is clear experimental evidence that birds do the same (see Chapter 8). It is possible to find the finger-sized larvae of the Poplar Hawk moth (*Laothoe populi*) by noticing the dry, pea-sized black droppings on pavements beneath poplar trees, for even one larva eats a prodigious amount of leaf and produces a comparable amount of frass. Most larvae are much smaller but they may be so abundant that their presence is just as obvious as that of the Poplar Hawk moth. The Winter moth (*Operophtera brumata*) can be so common that it defoliates fully grown oak trees and the noise made by the frass pellets hitting the dry leaves on the forest floor can sound like heavy drizzle. This moth is an important pest and has been studied very extensively; therefore it appears in many places in the chapters that follow. In Britain, at least, this is one of the species that the gardener tries to foil by putting grease bands around the trunks of apple trees, for the females are wingless and have to crawl up the trunks on their way from their pupation sites in the soil to their egg-laying sites on the twigs of the trees (see Chapter 4).

There is another group of defoliating moths, whose larvae are prolific silk spinners, the 'ermine' moths of the family Yponomeutidae. In northern Britain, the Bird Cherry Ermine (*Yponomeuta evonymella*) often causes the complete defoliation of Bird Cherry (*Prunus padus*) trees for several years in a row (see Chapter 5).

Even the smallest urban garden provides a home for many species of moth, and in a suburban setting, with many nearby gardens and mature trees, the number of species runs into hundreds. They are accessible to everyone who is shown how to find them; that they are not always immediately visible is because they have to avoid predators.

THE CLASSIFICATION OF MOTHS

Moths are closely related to caddis flies (Trichoptera) but the latter are immediately separable by the presence of hairs on their wings (hence 'trichos' = 'hair' in their scientific name). Some moths have modified hair-like scales on parts of their wings but they always also have true scales; even so it is possible to mistake some small moths for caddis flies. In fact, there are over twenty characters that reliably differentiate moths and caddis flies, but the three most primitive suborders of moths have features that make them resemble the caddis.

So far, moth classification has depended on examination of morphological structures, occasionally including the egg, larval and pupal stages, but adult characters have been paramount. Different authors give different weight to a variety of morphological systems. The mouthparts have been used to help identify and differentiate the most 'primitive' groups of moths and the pattern of openings to the exterior of the female genitalia is generally used to separate the other main subgroups. Two other features have at times been used very extensively: the details of the branching pattern of the veins on the wings (e.g. Meyrick, 1928) and the fine structure of the male genitalia (e.g. Pierce and Metcalfe, 1938). Species that are small and have rather plain or variable wing patterns often require examination of the genitalia of preserved specimens to be sure of an identification, but the family arrangement usually depends on wing venation and an array of other features.

Scoble (1991) gives a comprehensive account of recent taxonomic arrangements and this topic is not covered here. However, Table 2 sets out the basic interrelationships between different suborders and families.

TABLE 2   *The subdivisions of the order Lepidoptera.*

Subdivision	Representative family or super-family	Features of each group
ORDER		
Lepidoptera		Scales on wings
SUBORDERS		
Zeugloptera	Micropterigidae	Pollen chewing; no proboscis
Aglossata	*Agathiphagoidea	Pollen chewing; non-functional proboscis
Heterobathmiina	*Heterobathmioidea	Pollen chewing; larvae mine leaves
Glossata		
INFRAORDERS		
Dacononypha	Eriocraniidae	No muscles in proboscis
Neopseustina	*Neopseustoidea	Two separate tubes in proboscis
Exoporia	Hepialidae	Separate oviduct and copulatory pore
Heteroneura		
'Monotrysia'	Nepticulidae – Heliozelidae	One genital opening
'Ditrysia'	All other families	Two genital openings

Source: Simplified from Scoble (1991).

* = no British representatives.

TYPES OF MOTHS

It is usual for lepidopterists to subdivide butterflies and moths into rather arbitrary groups, which are then studied separately. The butterflies comprise the ditrysian super-families the Hesperioidea and the Papilionioidea; in the UK there are about 65 species, which have a separate literature. The larger species of moths are collectively called 'macro-moths', (usually shortened to 'macro's') a division that includes not only the families Lasiocampidae to

TABLE 3　　*Examples of the main families of moths referred to in the text.*

Family	Comments
Micropterigidae	Tiny metallic moths; adults pollen feeders
Hepialidae	'Swifts'; larvae root feeders
Nepticulidae	Tiny moths; larvae in serpentine mines in leaves
Incurvariidae	'Longhorns'; day-flying with long antennae
Zygaenidae	'Burnets and Foresters'; day-flying with warning colours
Psychidae	'Bagworms'; larvae in cases
Tineidae	'Clothes moths'; larvae feed on organic material like bird's nests and fungi
Gracillariidae	Larvae in blister mines on leaves
Sesiidae	'Clearwings'; larvae feed inside stems
Coleophoridae	Larvae live on leaves and seeds in moveable cases
Elachistidae	Larvae mine in 'grass' leaves
Oecophoridae	'Flatbodies'; some larvae on wood or fungi, some on leaves
Gelechiidae	Very varied and numerous family
Tortricidae	'Leaf-rollers, tortrix moths'; many larvae live in folded or rolled leaves; some are pests
Pyralidae	'Grass moths, China Marks, Tabbys, Meal moths, Wax moths, Flour moths'; very varied family with some pests
Pterophoridae	'Plume moths'; dayflying moths with wings reduced to 'feathers'
Lasiocampidae	'Eggars, Lackeys, Lappets'; large moths with hairy larvae
Saturniidae	'Emperors, Silk moths'; large colourful moths
Endromidae	'Kentish Glory'; large colourful moth
Drepanidae	'Hook-tips'; larvae sit with tails raised
Thyatiridae	'Lutestrings'; some larvae in leaf-folds
Geometridae	'Emeralds, Waves, Carpets, Pugs, Beauties, Umbers, Thorns, (Spanners)'; larvae loop along with legs at front and back of body, some species are pests
Sphingidae	'Hawk moths'; large moths, larvae with 'horn' at tail
Notodontidae	'Prominents'; larvae have humps and adults hair tufts
Lymantridae	'Tussocks, Gypsy moth'; large moths with hairy larvae
Arctiidae	'Tigers, Muslins, Footmen, Ermines'; some warningly coloured, many with hairy larvae
Noctuidae	'Darts, Rustics, Underwings, Wainscots, Sharks, Chestnuts, Arches, Brocades, Sallows, Minors, Gems, Snouts, (Bollworms, Owls, Cutworms)'; very large family of typical nocturnal moths, some pest species

Noctuidae (placed at the end of the Ditrysia) but also the 'swifts' (Hepialidae), the Cossidae, the Limacodidae, the 'burnets' (Zygaenidae) and the 'clearwings' (Sesiidae). In the UK the 845 'macro's' are included in one identification guide (Skinner, 1984). Two other families are also often treated alone, namely the 'pyrales' (Pyralidae) and the 'plume' moths (Pterophoridae), leaving all the other generally smaller species as the 'micro-lepidoptera' (or 'micro's'). There are 1263 of these in the UK, with no single, modern identification text and they are rather neglected, although the Tortricidae are dealt with in two Ray Society volumes (Bradley *et al.* 1973 and 1979) and other families are slowly being included in the series '*The Moths and Butterflies of the British Isles*'. As far as possible, the examples used in this book range across all moth families, for the micro's are just as diverse, beautiful and interesting as the rest.

THE LIFE CYCLE OF MOTHS

Moths and butterflies share a common life cycle and the various ways in which this is adapted to differing climates, habitats and conditions are described and discussed in detail in Chapter 4. This account merely describes the basic pattern, as an introduction to Chapters 2 and 3.

Eggs

All adult female Lepidoptera lay eggs. In some species, mostly the largest, most specialised and longest lived, as few as 20–40 eggs are produced; more typically, medium and small species produce 100–200 or even more (although the tiny leaf-mining Nepticulidae produce only a few, relatively large eggs). This represents the potential egg production and it is probable that the actual number laid, before predation, starvation or another cause of death intervenes, is considerably less. Eggs are sometimes laid singly, spaced out over the potential foodplant, for example by hawk moths (Sphingidae), so as to avoid overcrowding; other species lay eggs in batches and the larvae must either live in communal groups, as in so many brightly coloured and distasteful species, like the Cinnabar (*Tyria jacobaea*), or must soon disperse themselves, like the larvae of the Vapourer (*Orgyia antiqua*).

Eggs are oval, round or dome shaped and most have a fine surface sculpturation. The only other obvious feature is a pore through which the sperm pass at fertilisation (the micropyle), and this often has an attractive radial pattern around it, perhaps to help guide the sperm to the opening.

Larvae

Larvae, commonly called caterpillars, are of a cylindrical shape, with a sclerotised head capsule, which has hard chewing mandibles, simple eyes and very small antennae. The first three segments of the soft, tube-shaped body correspond to the adult thorax, with one pair of small but clearly segmented 'true legs' on each. The rest of the segments comprise the abdomen and house the gut and digestive organs, with a terminal anus. The final segment usually has a pair of 'prolegs', which are basically outpushings of the body wall, different in origin and structure from the true legs, and in the commonest pattern there are another

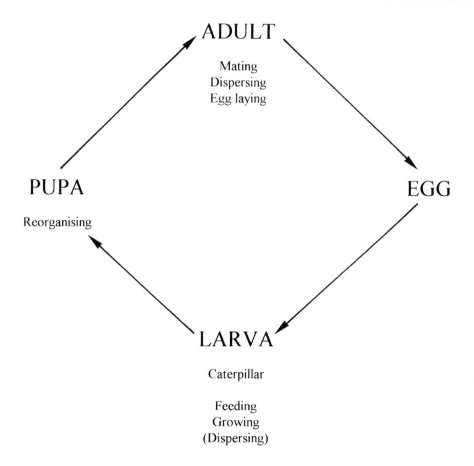

FIG 4   *The typical life cycle of a moth. In species that have wingless females the larvae may be the dispersive stage.*

four pairs of prolegs on central abdominal segments. A very characteristic variation in this pattern is for the middle legs to be absent but for there to be an extra pair on the penultimate segment. When these larvae move they loop along and so are familiarly called loopers (in Britain) or inch-worms (in the USA) and most belong to the numerous and very familiar Geometridae, whose scientific name reflects the larval habit of 'measuring' the ground. An odd feature is that whereas macro larvae can only crawl forwards, micro and pyrale larvae can also wriggle backwards.

Some larvae are virtually smooth but many have obvious hairs and in some cases they are densely hairy, or with thick tufts. They are often very colourful or patterned, either to provide camouflage or to warn of distastefulness and in some cases they also have a shape that amplifies this appearance. Some have 'lappets' which extend down on to the substrate to break up their shape; some are stick-shaped, with a rough surface to resemble bark; and some are coloured to match their background (such as the Emperor (*Pavonia pavonia*), whose basic colour is leaf green and whose pink spots on velvety black bands exactly match heather (*Calluna*) flowers). Others bend their bodies into un-caterpillar-like shapes, (such as many of the 'prominents' of the family Notodontidae), or have unlikely and startling features, with which to frighten would-be predators. The Puss moth larva (*Cerura vinula*) shows several of these features: it has a saddle-shaped blotch of colour to break up its shape; it sits with head and tail raised, to look unfamiliar, and it has prominent 'eye-spot' colours on inflated front body segments that it can expose threateningly, while from two spikes at its tail it waves pink threads, which are alleged to ward off parasitic wasps. The overall effect is bizarre but its effectiveness is unknown. Some Puss moth larvae become parasitised, so the strategy is clearly not infallible! A further unsolved mystery is why this and a few related species need such a spectacular defence, when so many equally large species survive with less extravagant measures.

Some larvae change substantially over progressive moults. Small Pine Hawks (*Hyloicus pinastri*) have longitudinal stripes like the needles of their host tree, whereas older larvae have a varied series of disruptive marks and streaks. There are many similar examples but a more profound change occurs in many leaf miners. These change their foodstuff as they grow, beginning by imbibing cell sap and having piercing and sucking mouthparts to accomplish this, and later chewing leaf tissue, for which they have mandibles. The early stages of these species are often flattened at the front, whereas the older larvae are more conventionally shaped. Such a significant change is referred to as hypermetamorphosis.

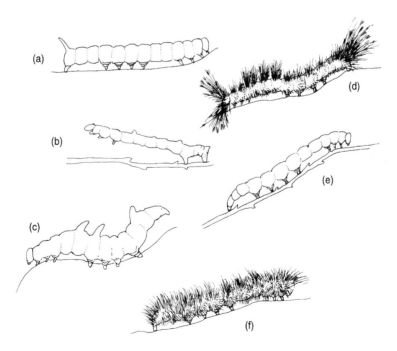

FIG 5   *Contrasting types of caterpillars. (a) A 'hawk' moth, Sphingidae; (b) a 'stick' caterpillar, Geometridae; (c) a 'promiment', Notodontidae; (d) a 'tussock', Lymantriidae; (e) a 'cutworm', Noctuidae; (f) a 'tiger', Arctiidae.*

The larvae devote their energies wholly to feeding and growing, except when they have to remain motionless to avoid being seen by potential predators. Growth takes place by a series of moults, when the old cuticle becomes too small and is sloughed off. This characteristic moulting cycle is one of the most significant features of the lives of insects. The activity of the larvae is dominated by whether they are just about to moult, have just moulted, or are feeding as rapidly as possible in order to reach the next moult expeditiously. If this were a book about the physiology of moths, it would have to be based essentially on this topic. During the moult, the larvae have to remain entirely undisturbed, with a secure foothold, so that they can safely pull themselves out of their old skin; even an unwitting collision from a harmless sibling can disrupt the process. Obviously, a moulting larva is very easy prey if it is found, so larvae choose a secluded and firm platform on which to moult.

The need to avoid being found by bird predators, which hunt mainly by sight, means that many free-feeding larvae have to hide by day and only come out to feed by night. This dramatically reduces their growth rate, which is also influenced by the quality of the material on which they are feeding and their body temperature. Consequently, the time taken to reach full size may extend to weeks, months or years, as in montane or wood-boring species. (Normally growth is as rapid as possible (see Chapter 4).) Once the final larval size is reached, the next moult produces the pupal stage, within which the larval body plan is reorganised to that of the adult, and since this stage is so vulnerable to predators, it is highly protected.

Pupae

Typical pupae have a sclerotised, smooth and shiny outer surface with a clearly identifiable thoracic region, with the wings, legs and antennae in thin cases glued on to the surface. The eyes are also usually obvious at the head end and the abdomen has a series of segments which have a limited ability to swivel. Some have warts, spines or other projections and in some the wings and legs are less firmly attached, but there is little real variety in the form of the pupal stage. There is a great variety in where the pupa is situated and how it is protected. Only a few species have an exposed and free pupa.

One of the commonest ways of protecting the pupa is for the larva to spin a silken chamber, the cocoon, within which to pupate. All larvae of Lepidoptera can probably spin silk to some extent, although for many it may be only to provide a small pad on which to attach while moulting, or as a single strand lifeline on which to descend from a leaf. A frequent use of silk is to draw together leaves to make a protected place within which to feed, but the most conspicuous is the spinning of a cocoon. Moths from several families do this, but it is the Saturnidae, often called the 'silk-moths', that produce the most voluminous silk and the most complex cocoons. The Silk moth itself (*Bombyx mori*) is now a wholly domesticated species, which has over generations been selected for the quality and quantity of its silk, but many wild species rival it in productivity. Most silk-moths are large and colourful, often with eye-spots on their wings, and the common and widespread European species the Emperor moth, (*Pavonia pavonia*), is a typical and excellent example. Its larvae spin a flask-shaped cocoon of brownish silk, with an opening at the narrow end closed by a ring of outwardly directed stiff hairs, which allow the newly emerged moth to push its way out but which prevent access from the outside. The outer layer of the cocoon is made of loose silk threads which entangle the whole construction amongst vegetation.

Other moths incorporate debris or chewed bark into their cocoons, to provide camouflage, or hide them under bark. Some cocoons are feeble affairs, others are extremely tough.

Many other strategies are used to protect the pupae. Sometimes the shape resembles a natural inedible object, or is so strange that the pupa passes unnoticed, but in many cases the larva hides in soil or leaf-litter before pupating, so that the pupa is protected there. In many of the Noctuidae, which include the large brown moths that come into houses, and in the Sphingidae, the hawk moths, this chamber may be several centimetres below the soil surface and its inner surface may be smoothed and strengthened by larval salivary secretions. In other species, the pupa merely lies amongst the soil and debris.

The pupal stage lasts long enough for the internal reorganisation to be accomplished; this may be only a matter of a few days in small species in warm weather, or all winter in others. In the last hours before the adult emerges the wing patterns and body colour are often visible beneath the pupal surface. Species that use cocoons may cut the silk with sharp projections on the pupal surface and wriggle so that the front of the pupa protrudes beyond the cocoon. The clearwing moths pupate in their burrows just beneath the bark of the tree trunk and their pupae also wriggle partly out of the burrow immediately before emergence. This often occurs in the early hours of the morning and most species have a characteristic time at which they emerge, presumably so that the adults can expand and dry their wings at a time which minimises predation risks and also prepares them for take-off at the first opportunity. At emergence the wings are crumpled and soft, but the moth soon finds a secure foothold and then forces a fluid through the veins in the wings, expanding them rapidly. Once they are at full size, the fluid is withdrawn and the wings dry and harden, before either being folded into the usual position at rest, or being used immediately for flight. Some species seem to have a wing pattern that is particularly visible during wing expansion, for example the eyespots on the Emperor moth's wings, and this provides protection at this most vulnerable time.

Adults

The adults of most species of moth are rather short-lived, a matter of days at most, and in their adult life they are preoccupied with the essential business of mating. A minority of species live for more than a week and some of these are adapted to particular life styles, such as hibernating or aestivating as adults (see Chapter 4).

Many adult moths disperse either within the habitat or to new suitable areas elsewhere. Although some larvae, for example those of the Vapourer moth (*Orgyia antiqua*), do disperse, it is usually the adults that do so and they can be dramatically good at it. We know conclusively, from captures on light ships, offshore oil platforms and from a wealth of records from light traps in out-of-the-way places, that many species disperse over great distances and often over the sea (see Chapter 3).

Some individuals of most species must occasionally fly or be blown beyond the limits of their preferred habitats and they then fly about until they either encounter another suitable area or they die. This 'random' dispersal is probably much more common than we think and anyone who has run a light trap for moths will immediately agree that you quite often catch stray specimens of species that certainly do not belong in the area of the trap. The biological significance of this undirected dispersal is difficult to judge, although it will certainly lead to some exchange of genetic material between semi-isolated populations of species, which may well be beneficial; and it may lead to the colonisation of 'vacant' habitat. There is considerable dispute about whether a new population could be founded successfully by a single female; if it could not, the odds against successful colonisation are dramatically lengthened, but there seems to be a slow acceptance that it may be possible, perhaps with further inputs of genes from dispersing adults in succeeding generations.

There are undoubtedly many species, however, which regularly disperse themselves beyond the limits of their current habitat and these are 'migrant' species. This is a generalised use of the term, compared with migration of birds. The great majority of migratory moths do not show a return flight by the same individual, or even by their offspring. Migrant moths may be very large and obvious, like the Convolvulus Hawk moth (*Herse convolvuli*), which is found throughout the tropical world, breeds successfully in the Mediterranean climates and then disperses far north and south of its usual breeding range. Oil platforms in the northern North Sea regularly attract migrating Convolvulus Hawks in autumn – presumably the flares and other lights draw them in, and the amazed oil men who find the giant moths often send them to the nearest museum or university for identification. Once this phenomenon was investigated further, it was found that not only strong-flying hawk moths were to be seen on oil platforms but many smaller moths, aphids, hoverflies, damselflies, lacewings and a host of other insects as well. The Diamond-back moth (*Plutella xylostella*), well known as a migrant species, is often found in great abundance. All have flown hundreds of kilometres to reach the platforms, without the chance to settle or feed on the way.

MATING IN MOTHS

For most adult moths, the immediate priority after emergence is to find a suitable mate; this poses a considerable problem for a relatively small organism in a large world. The opportunities for finding a mate by chance encounter are remote and most species have very effective mechanisms for locating the opposite sex of their own species. The obvious and indeed legendary way in which this is done is for the females to emit an attractive scent and, in some species, this plume of perfume is effective over a distance of several kilometres. This sort of attractive chemical, released by one individual and inducing a behavioural response in another, is called a pheromone. We have learnt to produce some of these chemicals artificially and to use them to attract the males of certain pest species to killing traps to control them (see Chapter 7).

The females have special organs on the abdomen from which the pheromones are released but, much more obviously, the males of many species have the surface area of their antennae increased by the presence of complex 'feathers' or pectinations, so that the number of receptive sensory cells on their surface can be greatly increased.

LAYING EGGS

Once a female moth has mated, she distributes her eggs at suitable places in the habitat. In most cases the eggs are mature at the time of adult emergence but in some species a brief period is required before they are ready to be laid and the moth will almost certainly use this time for feeding. Some male moths also feed and the predominant food resources for adult moths are nectar, other sweet plant exudates or the waste sugar, the honey-dew, produced by aphids. The exceptions are: the pollen-chewing Micropterigidae, already mentioned; a small number that do not feed at all as adults (such as the silk moths); and a very few species from Asia that have been found to feed on blood. Generally, the nectar provides sugars, which are used as the fuel for flight. Everyone who has kept adult moths knows that they need to be fed often on a dilute sugar solution if they are to remain alive and to lay their full complement of eggs.

The female moth may simply scatter her eggs, as do some of the swift moths (the Hepialidae), which lay a stream of eggs in flight. They can adopt this strategy because their larvae feed on the roots of plants which occur commonly together in great abundance, like

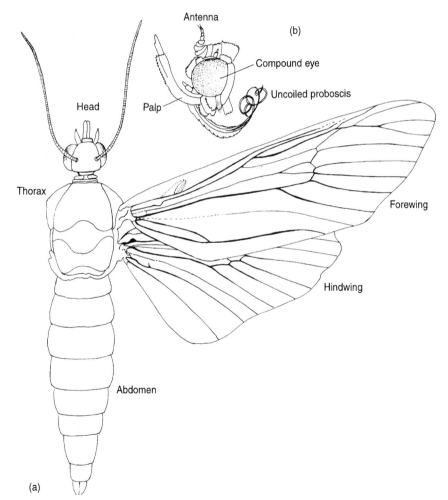

FIG 6   *The structure of an adult moth. (a) General view; (b) close-up of head.*

grasses or Bracken (*Pteridium aquilinum*), and so the scattered eggs are likely to land close to a suitable food source. In most cases, however, the foodplant is much more localised and the majority of moths are specialised in their choice of larval foodplant. So instead of using a wide range of foodplants (a strategy termed polyphagy), they use one or a few foodplants (oligophagy). These females must select the precise location for their eggs, placing them not only on or near the right foodplant, but on the part of the plant that is most suitable, and spaced out so that the emerging larvae will not suffer from a food shortage on a crowded foodplant. There is now much research on butterflies (for example Thomas, 1983) that shows that female choice of egg-laying site is one of the key factors that determines whether a butterfly thrives in a habitat or declines to extinction. Much less work has been done on this aspect of moth behaviour but the little evidence so far suggests that exactly the same applies. Barbour and Young (1993) found that female Kentish Glory moths (*Endromis versicolora*) will lay only at particular places on small birch bushes and that this restricts the species to young birch woodland (see Chapter 10).

THE STRUCTURE OF MOTHS

The structure of adult moths is clearly closely related to their function. The head has obvious sensory antennae, which may be extended by pectinations, and a pair of compound eyes, which allow even nocturnal moths to see sufficiently well to locate pale coloured flowers at night. It has also been shown that moths can navigate using either landmarks or a sun, moon or star compass and that the eyes are used for this. The other clearly visible structure on the head of most moths is a proboscis. When not in use, it is kept coiled under the head and between another pair of sensory appendages, the palps, which are also associated with the mouthparts.

The thorax is a muscular box, to which are attached three pairs of jointed legs; one pair to each segment. These are generally only sufficiently developed to allow the moth to hold firmly to a perch, or to walk rather feebly. Some species, however, including the wingless ones, have legs strong enough to allow a slow run. Typically, the legs have one or several stout spines on them, as well as some hairs. The thorax itself is also generally thickly covered with hairs, arranged as two lappets on the 'shoulders' and a further central band. Often the hairs are rather dark in colour and in temperate regions they may help the moth to absorb and retain heat.

The two pairs of wings are attached to the two rear thoracic segments and in the Heteroneura the front pair is longer and narrower than the hind pair. In flight, the wings beat synchronously and this is assisted by a small overlap and often by a stout hair from near the base of the hind wing, which engages in a catch on the front pair. In most species the wing is covered with overlapping coloured scales, whose patterns camouflage or emphasise the moth's appearance. In fact, there is a common set of markings, which recurs on the wings of many species and is broadly related both to the underlying venation pattern and to the way in which the wing pattern is controlled during development. Typical marks are shown on Figure 7. In some species the wings are either reduced or absent and in others they are highly modified. In the Pterophoridae, each wing is reduced to two or more fringed 'fingers' and the common name of the group, the plume moths, aptly describes their appearance. The fringes are actually present in most species but are generally less prominent. As a rule,

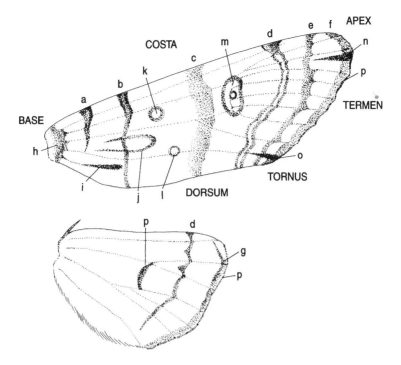

FIG 7   *The typical features of the wing patterns of moths. (a) Sub-basal fascia; (b) ante-median fascia; (c) median fascia: (d) post-median fascia; (e) sub-terminal fascia; (f) terminal fascia; (g) terminal shade; (h) basal spot; (i) basal streak; (j) claviform stigma; (k) orbicular stigma; (l) sub-reniform stigma; (m) reniform stigma; (n) apical streak; (o) tornal streak; (p) fringe of cilia. (Redrawn, with permission from Skinner, 1984)*

the smaller the moth the more obvious the fringes. Some moths lose their wing scales on first flight, or do not develop them fully; these species mimic wasps, bees or flies. The Sesiidae, or clearwings, are the prime example.

The abdomen is also usually hairy, except on the flexible joints between the segments. There are some species which also have sensory 'ear-drums' hidden under hairs at the side near the thorax, and others that have hair-pencils held in lateral grooves. The hairs are unfurled when the moth is releasing a pheromone. Otherwise the only obvious structures are the various parts of the external genitalia, which are on the terminal segments.

The relative sizes of the wings and the abdomen, together with the characteristic resting position, are often sufficient to differentiate the families. Experienced lepidopterists quickly come to recognise the broad wings and slim body of the Geometridae; the stout body and strong wings of the Noctuidae; or the strange upwardly tilted tail of some of the Yponomeutidae when at rest (for example the genus *Argyresthia*). Tweedie and Emmet (1991) illustrate the characteristic resting positions of most of the families found in Britain.

MOTHS AND MAN

Moths have frequently held our fascinated attention but it has to be admitted that the most common interaction between humanity and moths is when moths are acting as pests. Both in forestry and agriculture there are many species that cause very significant damage to our crops. A few examples show the extent of the problem.

The Gypsy moth (*Lymantria dispar*) was introduced to North America in 1869 from Europe, where it is a sporadic pest of various trees. It spread quickly over most of the north-eastern states and is now a serious defoliator of forest trees (Doane and McManus, 1981). The Pink Bollworm (*Pectinophora gossypiella*) is a pest of cotton, which has spread with the crop around the world and has been the subject of major control programmes (Campion *et al.*, 1989). The Winter moth (*Operophtera brumata*), which feeds on the leaves of a wide range of forest trees and shrubs, has spread widely in eastern North America, since its accidental release in Canada in 1930.

However, the vast majority of moths are not injurious in their effects and their beauty and interesting habits can be enjoyed with a clear conscience! Indeed, some species bring us a benefit, but only one does so on a grand scale. This is the domesticated Silk moth (*Bombyx mori*) (and one or two of its wild relatives on a much smaller scale). The silk produced by this species has been used in China since at least 2700 BC and the Silk moth itself is now found only in captivity. Centuries of selective breeding have left it unable to fly, with highly sedentary larvae and with an enormous production of silk in its cocoon. Even now China's production of silk, at around 42 000 tonnes in 1989 (Berenbaum, 1995), is much greater than that of any other country. In that year India produced 10 500 tonnes, Japan 7000 tonnes, the rest of Asia 7500 tonnes, USSR 4400 tonnes, Brazil 1900 tonnes and the rest of the world a few hundred tonnes at most. It is said that China guarded the secret of its domesticated silk moths on pain of death but that at last some eggs and seeds of its food-plant, the Mulberry tree, were smuggled out in a hollow walking stick. Although it would be nice to believe this, it cannot be literally true, for the trees would need to be established years before the moth could be reared on their leaves. Artificial silks and other fabrics cannot compete in value with real silk, the production of which remains of great importance.

If monetary benefits are not considered, then moths' main contribution to humanity is through the intense fascination they have engendered. Their nocturnal habits; their unexpected appearance in large numbers; their fatal and undeflected attraction to a candle's flame; their fantastic colours and shapes; as well as their sometimes unwelcome persistence in coming into our dwellings have all added to our interest. The common names we give them attest to this interest – the Ghost Swift, the Peach Blossom, the Shark, the Beautiful Gothic, the Scarlet Tiger, the Lace Border, the Argent and Sable, the Dusky Thorn. Most are clearly regarded as beautiful and mysterious, but some seem to be more dreadful. Perhaps the most dramatic and extraordinary example is the Death's Head Hawk moth, whose scientific name also reflects its appearance and our fear of it: *Acerontia atropos* from 'Acheron' – the river of pain in the underworld – and 'atropos' one of the three fates, who cuts the thread of life (Emmet, 1991b). This moth is the weight of a mouse and has a striking yellow pattern on its thorax, abdomen and hind wings, including the strangely coincidental death mask. To add to its fearful aspect it can produce a breathy squeak when disturbed, deterring human inquisitors as well as birds. The proboscis is short, stout and

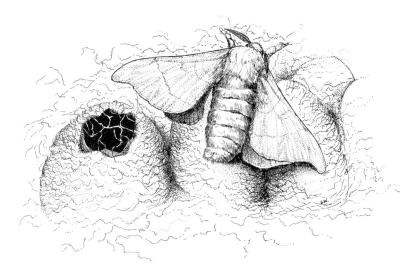

A newly emerged Silk moth (Bombyx mori) *and cocoons.*

pointed, and is apparently used to pierce the wax caps of honey cells in bee hives, which it then robs. Rothschild (1985) believes that the skull mark mimics a queen bee's face, so that the worker bees do not recognise the moth as an intruder. Its old English name is the 'Bee Tiger'. This species breeds in Mediterranean climates and occasionally migrates northwards. Before pesticides were widely used, its larvae were sometimes found in potato fields, for this is one of its foodplants.

THE STUDY OF MOTHS

Although illustrations of moths appeared in many of the very early books on the wild animals of Britain, there were no books that included a substantial amount of information on their natural history or ecology until the last century. Stainton (1857) began to introduce life history details into his books on the identification of moths, as well as charming accounts of his experiences when searching for them. He was unusual in that he paid great attention to the 'micro-lepidoptera', almost at the expense of the larger species; and in this he was followed by the most prolific of all authors on moths, J.W. Tutt. Tutt wrote many books on all aspects of moths, including voluminous detail of the distribution, life history and variation, as was then known, and his breadth of knowledge was astonishing. Many of the individual pieces of information relevant to the study and capture of moths (most of which were originally published in the *Entomologist's Record and Journal of Variation*, a journal which Tutt himself founded), he gathered in a set of three books, called '*Practical Hints for Field Lepidopterists*' (1901–05). The set's many nuggets of field craft are still a valuable source of natural history information not available elsewhere, so Tutt's influence endures.

Most early moth books were identification guides, mixed with some life cycle details, and perhaps understandably many authors repeated the same information, whether right or wrong. An influential set of books was produced by Barrett in 1892, providing a rich source of detail for the most long-lasting and successful of all moth books, which have only just been superseded; these are the two volumes produced in 1907 by Richard South called '*The Moths of the British Isles*'. They were essentially identification guides for the macro-moths,

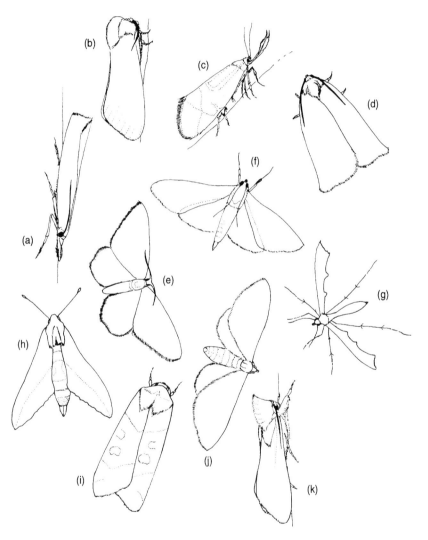

FIG 8   *Some contrasting types of moths. (a) Pyralidae; (b) Cossidae; (c) Oecophoridae; (d) Tortricidae; (e) Geometridae; (f) Pyralidae; (g) Pterophoridae; (h) Sphingidae; (i) Noctuidae; (j) Geometridae; (k) Noctuidae.*

with coloured photographs of the moths and the early printings, before the plates became slightly blurred, are still excellent guides to Britain's larger moths. Not until 1984 were new photographs produced, by David Wilson for Skinner's *'Colour Identification Guide to the Moths of the British Isles'*. Most intervening books, including later editions of 'South', used paintings, which were generally much less useful.

Meyrick (1928) included micro-lepidoptera in his unillustrated but useful identification guide, which is still the only book to include all British species, but is now very out of date and difficult to use. Equally useful in a different way is the series of volumes of drawings of the genitalia of moths by Pierce and Metcalfe (for example 1938), for these allowed surer identification of critical species. Nevertheless, natural history did not really feature in any books between those of Tutt and the iconoclastic New Naturalist book by E.B. ('Henry') Ford in 1955. This was totally unlike any previous moth book, for it ignored identification and concentrated on aspects of the biology of moths. It ranged over genetics, geographical variation, distribution, migration and a host of other exciting topics, but, regrettably, it was ahead of its time and did not immediately lead to an increase in the study of the ecology of moths.

However, one of Ford's contemporaries, H. Bernard Kettlewell, used moths in his studies on the effects of industrial pollution on the colours of insects, so-called industrial melanism, especially concerning the Peppered moth (*Biston betularia*). He also investigated the genetic basis for geographical variation and he has a great claim to be the father of the scientific study of moths. His only real competitor, apart from Ford, was George Varley, who studied the populations of Winter moths (*Operophtera brumata*) in Wytham Woods, near Oxford. His work is now regarded as a classic piece of ecological research, in many ways setting the whole subject of animal population dynamics on its way.

RECENT STUDIES

The amateur study of the natural history of moths remained in the doldrums, concentrating on the identification and distribution of the larger species, until A. Maitland Emmet began to publish widely on the micro-lepidoptera (especially leaf-miners), in the 1960s. The great increase in knowledge that he and others produced was one of the spurs to the start of the definitive series of volumes, collectively called *The Moths and Butterflies of Great Britain and Ireland* (MBGBI), which were initially edited by John Heath and now by Emmet and others. These volumes include all British moths and much information on the natural history of the species, as well as their identification and distribution. This last topic has been greatly assisted by the data gathered for the national distribution scheme and its successors, started by John Heath in the 1960s. Many amateurs have diligently and enthusiastically collected records of moths from all over Britain for this purpose.

Recently, butterflies have had much research effort aimed at elucidating their habitat requirements and ecology, prompted by worries about their decline. A few similar studies of moths have started in the last five years and it is to be hoped that more will follow. These are beginning to help conservation efforts for moths, as well as providing much information of general interest to ecologists.

THE CONSERVATION OF MOTHS

It is undoubtedly true that man's effect on moths has been immeasurably greater and more harmful than moths' effect on man. The advent of reliable recording schemes and the widespread use of light traps, which have allowed us to gain much more complete and accurate knowledge of moths' distribution and status, have clearly shown that many have become more localised and rare in recent years. Some species have become extinct in Britain and many have become restricted to a handful of sites. There are still many common and widespread species, however, and it might be argued that the local demise of a few is not of great significance. But this argument ignores the message that the losses bring. They are the symptom of changes in the countryside – the losses of semi-natural habitats, the pervasive influence of chemicals and the other adverse effects of mankind on the species that share his world. Moths also deserve conservation for their own sake and for the pleasure that their beauty and strange habits bring to those who observe them. After years of neglect, there has been some effort in the last few years to redress this balance and the conservation of moths has begun to be taken seriously (see Chapter 10).

Twenty years ago butterflies were nearly as neglected as moths are now, for nature conservation was dominated by birds, mammals and, to a lesser extent, rare plants. However, there are signs that the enthusiasm that has been generated for butterflies is spilling over on to other insects, equally deserving of attention, if less showy and obvious. In twenty years' time it would be splendid if moths had attracted their own army of enthusiasts eager to study and protect them.

CHAPTER 2

The Origins and Distribution of Britain's Moths

THE ORIGINS OF BRITAIN'S MOTHS

TWO main ideas on the origins of Britain's moth fauna have dominated in the last fifty years. The first systematic attempt to explain the present distribution of moths in terms of their origins was that of Beirne (1952), who produced a comprehensive theory at a time when there was only sketchy knowledge of the distribution of the moths and of the climatic events during and since the last Ice-age. His idea, endorsed by Ford (1945), was that there was an area of land to the west of the Scottish coastline that remained ice-free during the last ice-age, with a sufficiently temperate climate that some moths survived there, even during the full extent of the last ice sheets. Following the retreat of the ice, these species could have recolonised the western fringes of Britain, forming separate populations from those of the same species which recolonised from the south. This could explain the oddly disjunct distributions of species such as the Narrow-bordered Five-spot Burnet (*Zygaena lonicerae*), which is found throughout most of England and has isolated populations on Skye.

The currently accepted idea, which receives its most detailed and convincing exposition from Dennis (1977 and 1993), is that there could have been no land to the west of Britain that would have been suitable as a refuge from the fierce peri-glacial climate and so all re-colonisation must have taken place from the south. By this theory the current disjunct populations are the result of range changes since the recolonisation, with periods of more continuous distribution, which have since been fragmented. Dennis's ideas are supported by very much more detailed and reliable data than were available to Beirne.

THE LAST ICE-AGE

The furthest extent of the last Ice-age was around 18 000–16 000 years Before Present (BP). At that time there was a more or less continuous ice sheet covering Britain as far south as south Wales, through the central Midlands north to Lincolnshire and into northern East Anglia (see Fig. 9). In Ireland the same sheet covered the northern two-thirds and another, smaller sheet was present at the south-western point. Since sea levels were significantly lower then than they are now, all of Great Britain, including the Shetlands, Hebrides and

FIG 9   *The extent of the ice sheets and the position of the coastline at the fullest extent of the last Ice-age. (——— Coastline; – – – – Extent of the ice sheets). (Source: Dennis, 1993)*

Ireland, was united with the Continent, and much of the North Sea was also ice-covered land (Dogger Land). The mean temperatures experienced then in central England, just south of the ice sheet, were about 8°C during the warmest month and −26°C during the coldest month, but clearly there will have been great variations, depending on local topography and conditions, as there are now in areas close to ice sheets. Evidence for this comes from many sources, including planktonic remains in marine sediments; 0^{18} isotope proportions in ice cores; pollen and other plant fossil remains; beetle remains in dated sediments; and dendrochronology. The beetle evidence from the coldest times is that even species now found on the Arctic tundra were eliminated from Britain by the cold (Coope, 1995) and so it seems certain that all of our moths have recolonised Britain since the ice began to retreat.

At the glacial maximum there was also an ice sheet centred over the Alps and less extensive ones over the Pyrenees and in other mountainous areas of southern Europe (Denton and Hughes, 1981). There was also a steep climatic gradient in southern Europe, so that temperate conditions were available there, allowing many of our current fauna to survive. However, the winter sea ice and polar front is thought to have extended close to the north-western edge of Britain at that time (Ruddiman and McIntyre, 1981) and there would not have been a temperate climate on the land then exposed to the west of our current land mass.

THE VARIED CLIMATE AND VEGETATION SINCE THE LAST ICE-AGE

As Figure 10 shows, the climatic improvement that has led to our present inter-glacial climate began around 14 000–13 000 years ago and by 12 000 years BP the ice had retreated greatly and the climate had improved, so that central English mean temperatures in the warmest and coldest months were about 15°C and 0°C respectively. However, the ice re-advanced about 10 500 years ago, with evidence of ice sheets in parts of Scotland. This coincided with a central English climatic regime of 10°C and −24°C (as expressed above). Although this must have had enormous effects on our moth fauna, many species would have survived in Britain. The climate then improved again after 10 000 years BP at a rate that was remarkably rapid.

All the British land bridges were lost following the amelioration which began around 10 000 BP. It is likely that the connections between the British mainland and Ireland, the Outer Hebrides and Shetland were lost around 9500 BP; those to the Orkneys and many of the Inner Hebrides around 9000 BP; and by 8000–7500 years ago sea level had risen sufficiently to obliterate the last land bridge to the Continent.

By 6000 years BP the climate had improved and was significantly warmer than at present, with a mean central English warmest month temperature of about 18°C and a mean coldest month temperature of about 4–5°C. At this time the vegetation in Britain would have been largely dominated by forest, with more open habitats restricted to thin soils, coastal zones, exposed islands and some wetland areas. Therefore, although our moth fauna may have been favoured by the climate, and included species that have since retreated south, the balance of forest and grassland species would have been very different from now. Forest species of the south, such as the Crimson Underwings (*Catocala promissa* and its relatives), may well have been much more widespread. Species that have been able only to gain an occasional precarious foothold, such as the Lunar Double-stripe (*Minucia lunaris*), could have been permanent residents; whereas species of open habitats, such as the Square-spot Rustic (*Xestia xanthographa*), which is now so abundant everywhere, may well have been relatively scarce! Nothing certain is known of the climate on the Scottish mountains at that time but it is probable that the summer temperatures were higher than now and the winter snows less extensive or long lasting. This period is surely the time when some species that are now exclusively arctic were lost from Britain and when others that still survive were reduced to small relict populations on the high tops, which act as cool islands in a warm lowland 'sea'.

After the climatic optimum of 6000–5000 years BP, there followed a slow cooling, and it is also speculated that this was a cloudy and damp era (Dennis, 1993). Summer temperatures experienced a larger reduction than the winter temperatures and man's effect was

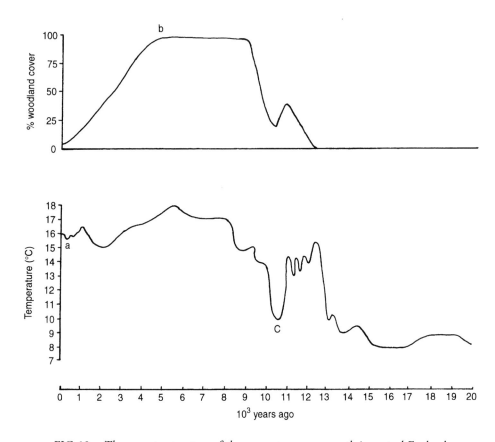

FIG 10   *The mean temperature of the warmest summer month in central England and the percentage cover of natural woodland in Britain since the maximum extent of the last Ice-age. (a) 'Little Ice-age'; (b) Start of man's clearance of forest; (c) Ice re-advance. (Source: Dennis, 1993)*

increasing with the onset of the first significant forest clearance (Atkinson *et al.*, 1987). Consequently there may have been a loss of those species that prefer more continental climates, with hot dry summers, and a slight reduction in forest species plus a progressive increase in open ground species. This period was also one of active peat formation; the extensive moorlands and peatlands of the north and west began to form, encouraged by forest clearance. This general climatic pattern continued with only rather gradual changes until about AD 1600 when a colder period began which lasted until around AD 1800–1830. This is usually referred to as the 'Little Ice-Age' and, even though it was not anything like as cold as during the real ice-ages, it is likely that there were small but active ice sheets on some of the Scottish mountains (Thomson, 1980). Evidence of the climate at that time is provided by the existence of regular ice fairs on the Thames! This cold spell would have had a profound but inestimable effect on Britain's moth fauna, additional to the continuing effect of human agricultural activities. No doubt some species that were lost then have recolonised since, but many others will not have done, partly because of the difficulties of crossing the Channel, and Britain's 'modern' moth fauna was surely set by this last major climatic episode. This would have been the time during which some continuous distributions of moths broke up, perhaps with north-western coastal refuges, leaving the current disjunct distributions. Unfortunately, although the first of the entomological authors were active during this period, the distribution of moths was so poorly known that there are no historical accounts against which to match our current knowledge.

We have climatic records for the last 150 years and know the temperature changes that have occurred. Broadly speaking there was a rather cool period until around 1910, followed by a gradual increase in temperature into the 1940s, fluctuation around that level until the 1970s and what seems to have been an increase since then. This last warming may have been due to the 'greenhouse effect' but this remains controversial. Since we also have better records of moth increases, reductions, extinctions and recolonisations in the last 100 years, it is possible to make closer to links to climate . However, other factors, involving dramatic loss of habitat and widespread use of insecticides, have been primarily responsible for the changes in distribution.

WHICH MOTHS INVADED BRITAIN FIRST?

Based on the account above, the simplified sequence of arrivals and departures of Britain's moths may have been as shown in Table 4.

WHAT DO WE KNOW OF THE CURRENT DISTRIBUTION OF BRITAIN'S MOTHS?

The earliest writers about Britain's moths were based in London and their knowledge of the distribution of any species was largely restricted to its environs. Consequently, we can learn little from their books except for odd snippets about some of the most showy species. Benjamin Wilkes (1747–49), for example, records that the Kentish Glory (*Endromis versicolora*) was then found near Westerham in Kent. During the Victorian period, when there was a tremendous upsurge in the study of wildlife, records began to come from more remote parts of Britain and authors were able to assess the distribution of moths from correspondence with other naturalists. Edward Newman (1874) was able to quote extensive lists of localities for most interesting species, including Irish notes that he derived from Edwin Birchall, and he was sufficiently confident of the general distribution of the commoner species that he provided comments that broadly agree with what we now know. Two factors combine to reduce the value of such records. First of all the coverage was still highly biased towards the south, so that the distribution of Scottish and Welsh species was patchy; secondly, some spurious records were introduced by dealers who made a trade by selling specimens of the most desirable species and encouraged this trade by 'finding' the species at various locations. Allan (1943) details the activities of some of these unscrupulous dealers. The White Prominent (*Leucodonta bicoloria*), for example, was recorded by Chappell from a Staffordshire wood in 1861 and he claimed to have found and bred 13 specimens and yet Allan records at least 60 bearing Staffordshire labels in collections in the 1940s. In a noto-

TABLE 4   *The changes in Britain's moth fauna since the last ice-age.*

Date	Changes in the fauna
13–14 000 yrs BP	Ice retreat and first climatic amelioration. First arrival of tundra spp. from south, followed by woodland spp.. Sequence of spp. of gradually more temperate climates.
10 500 yrs BP	Ice readvance. Retreat of southern spp.. Southern spread of northern spp. but no colonisation from north possible.
10–7000 yrs BP	Rapid climatic amelioration with forest closure to northern Scotland. Rapid recolonisation from south, latterly impeded by loss of land bridges. Forest spp. predominate. Upland and northern spp. retreat and become fragmented on isolated hills.
6000 yrs BP	Climatic optimum. Fauna includes many spp. now absent from Britain. Forest spp. predominate. Many northern and mountain spp. lost from Britain.
5500 yrs BP onwards	Climate slowly cools and becomes more oceanic. Loss of some 'continental' spp.. Man's influence increases with forest reduction. Peatlands in north. Some restriction of forest spp., extension of open ground spp..
AD 1600–1830	Little Ice-age. Ice fields in Scotland, cold winters in England. Forest destruction reaches peak. Man's influence overtakes climate. Fragmentation of some spp. with use of western refugia. Loss of southern spp.. Some extension of northern spp., but no gains from the north.
AD 1830–1940	Some recolonisation from south but man's influence on habitats paramount with loss of some species. Fauna similar to today.
1940–present	Climatic fluctuations and latterly warming. Some recolonisations but main influence is man's effect on habitats with some losses. Reality of warming and its effects still to be established.

rious case a Mr Raddon 'discovered' abundant larvae of the Spurge Hawk moth (*Hyles euphorbiae*) at Braunton Burrows and his records and specimens were accepted for many years before he was exposed as a fraud.

Although there was a bias towards the south, there were also some active collectors in the more remote parts of Britain and the discovery of most of the mountain and highland species dates from around 1850–80. The Mountain Burnet (*Zygaena exulans*), for example, was first recorded by Buchanan White in 1871 and the Northern Dart (*Xestia alpicola*) in the 1860s. Interestingly, this species was only found in its English localities in 1950 and in Ireland in 1972. The most active of the Victorian lepidopterists made strenuous efforts to discover the full extent of the distribution of Britain's moths, either by corresponding with workers from distant regions, and/or by making excursions to promising areas. Stainton (1854) recounts an expedition to Arran, Bute and the Clyde area in 1850 and his account makes very clear how difficult it was to travel and stay in such rural places in those days; he felt he was genuinely exploring a foreign country and he marvels at his catches, finding in abundance species that were virtually unknown in the south.

South (1907,1909) packed much information into a small space and distributions were often summarised as 'widely distributed over the British Isles' (as for the Wood Tiger (*Parasemia plantaginis*), for example). Often, as in this case, this bland statement hides a much more complex pattern of distribution, but for local species South often gave more detail. Overall, it was possible to gain a broad idea of the British distribution of moths, but the later editions did not really keep pace with the known updates of the range of moths and, by the 1960s, it was clear that our knowledge was seriously deficient. At this time the Biological Records Centre (BRC) had been established at Monkswood Experimental Centre, stimulated partly by the need to handle the detailed data sets of the plant recorders, whose pioneering atlas of British plants (Perring and Walters, 1962) showed what could be achieved using amateur recorders, and partly by the realisation within the Government conservation body, the Nature Conservancy, that it knew almost nothing about where Britain's rare plants and animals were found. The leader of BRC was John Heath, whose special love was moths (especially the Micropterigidae), and so he quickly planned a national recording scheme for the larger moths, to be based on their presence or absence in each of the 10 km national grid squares, the now very familiar dot maps of so many recording schemes.

Many amateur recorders were recruited to provide a wealth of records each year, which were then collated at BRC. By 1970, the first provisional maps were produced (Heath, 1970) and, although the initial rather limited coverage reduced their accuracy, it was quickly realised that some species were far less widespread and common than had been previously thought. Heath (1974) was able to illustrate this very clearly for selected species.

Generally, however, these maps showed that very local but easily recorded species were rather accurately known. The Grass Eggar (*Lasiocampa trifolii*), for example, was restricted to a few isolated coastal locations in East Anglia, Kent, Sussex, Hampshire, Dorset, Devon and Cornwall, with a separate set of colonies on the Lancashire coast. This is almost exactly as recorded by South. The Swallow Prominent (*Pheosia tremula*) was also 'pretty generally distributed throughout the country', as South said. The Wood Tiger has been mentioned above but the maps revealed that, although it was indeed found over a wide range in Britain, it was largely absent from the central English Midlands, south-west Wales, Cornwall, south-west Scotland and some other places, and had not been recorded after 1960 from south-east England, where it had previously been widely spread on chalk hills.

THE MOTHS AND BUTTERFLIES OF GREAT BRITAIN AND IRELAND

Unfortunately, only a small number of the largest moths were included in the published maps from BRC, although data continued to be collected until around 1980. The majority of maps were to be published in the multi-volumed *The Moths and Butterflies of Great Britain and Ireland* (MBGBI), the first volume of which appeared in 1976. So far seven out of a planned 11 volumes have been produced; the early volumes included the larger moths, except for the Geometridae. Despite all the efforts of the recorders, no maps of the Geometridae have yet appeared!

MBGBI includes the micro-lepidoptera and the editors realised that there were too few experts on these families to allow sufficient coverage for 10 km grid square recording. Consequently it was decided to base the maps on presence or absence in 'vice-counties', as

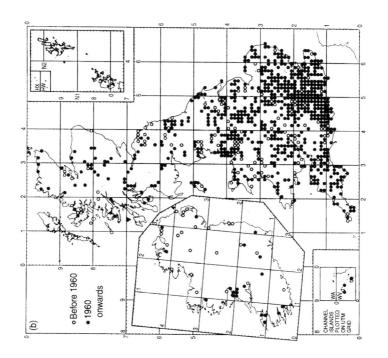

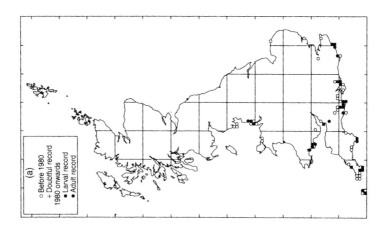

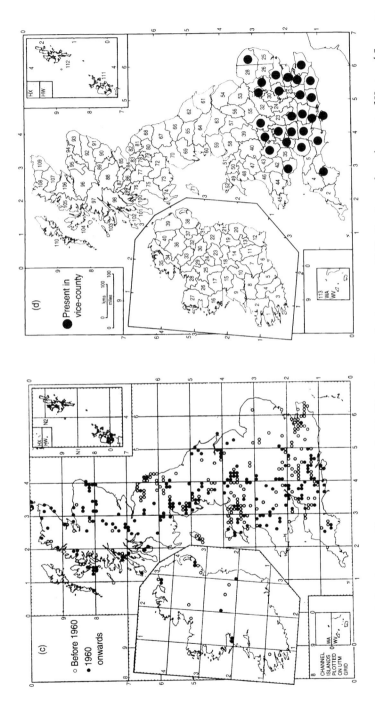

FIG 11   *The British distributions of four species of moths. (a) The Grass Eggar, Lasiocampa trifolii. Specimens from the coasts of Kent and Sussex are yellow, L. trifolii flava, as distinct from the brown specimens from other populations, L. trifolii trifolii. (b) The Swallow Prominent, Pheosia tremula. This species is widely distributed throughout Britain, but is more local in the north. (c) The Wood Tiger, Parasemia plantaginis. Although widely distributed this species is only locally present and is absent from many lowland areas. (d) A micro, Phyllonorycter lantanella. Like many other species, P. lantanella is widely distributed in the south but reaches a distinct northern limit. (Source: (a), courtesy of Waring, National Recording Network for the Rarer British Macro-moths; (b), (c) and (d) from Moths and Butterflies of Great Britain and Ireland, Harley Books)*

devised by Watson in 1852 for botanical records (Dandy, 1969). Watson divided the administrative counties into a series of 113 vice-counties, each of roughly equal size. Although the vice-counties include some anomalous boundaries and are too large to show proper associations with biogeographical features, they have been so widely used that they can be interpreted with some confidence. The maps of the micro-lepidoptera are of great use because there have been no previous attempts to summarise the distribution of these families in Britain and previously we have had to rely on the laconic comments of Meyrick (1928).

The 10 km square dot maps are of sufficient scale to allow very clear associations to be made with habitat features such as underlying rock type or altitude, but they do not identify the number of colonies present within any square, or the status of the colonies. A single stray specimen looks the same on the map as a series of strong populations.

THE ROTHAMSTED MOTH TRAP SERIES

There is a further data set that is greatly undervalued and underanalysed – the national series of standard design light traps run by Rothamsted Research Station, part of a government-funded agricultural research organisation. These traps are spaced around the whole of Britain, not placed on nature reserves but set in the more general countryside, and they have now been run for many years. They are operated every night of the year in a standard way and the catches are killed and analysed consistently. Although the traps are designed to be rather inefficient, and so catch and kill only moderate numbers of insects, the long-term information they provide is priceless for what has been revealed about the way in which common and widespread insect species have reacted to Britain's changing countryside. The results are set out each year in a brief descriptive way; Taylor *et al.* (1976) have used the data to illustrate theoretical patterns of abundance and diversity, and recently Woiwod and Harrington (1994), Luff and Woiwod (1995) and others have begun to compare the moth changes with climate and land-use patterns. However, much remains to be analysed.

BASIC PATTERNS OF DISTRIBUTION OF MOTHS IN BRITAIN AND THEIR POSSIBLE CAUSES

There are very few moths that occur everywhere throughout Britain. The oecophorid *Agonopterix heracliana* may be the most widely dispersed species, since it has been recorded recently from every vice-county, including all the main Scottish islands. Its larvae feed on a range of common umbelliferous plants, so that it is not limited by foodplant availability, and it can clearly cope with varied climates; however, it does not extend very high on to the hills. There are surprisingly few species that match *A. heracliana* but many that are found throughout southern Britain and then reach some sort of northern limit. This limit is often characterised by an area where the species is sparse and local, in contrast to the position in its central range, or by more northerly extension along the coasts, so it seems likely that climate is the controlling factor in these distribution patterns.

The effects of climate

Overall, there are perhaps 50% more species found in lowland areas of southern England, compared with similar places in the north. For many species, climatic factors probably limit distribution, as in the following examples.

The Small Angle-shades (*Euplexia lucipara*), is common throughout southern Britain, occurring on all soil types and at most altitudes and in Scotland it reaches Orkney and the Outer Hebrides. However, it is sparsely distributed in the northern half of Scotland and this is not merely because it avoids the hills. Even allowing for the fewer recorders in northern Scotland, it is less frequent there. The Cinnabar (*Tyria jacobaeae*) whose larvae feed on Ragwort (*Senecio jacobaea*) is abundant and ubiquitous in southern Britain but from Yorkshire northwards it becomes progressively more restricted to the coasts, so that in Scotland it is really only found in near-coastal areas, even though it extends to Skye in the west and Kincardine in the east. The Copper Underwing (*Amphipyra pyramidea*) is found in wooded country as far north as the north Midlands of England but there are only scattered records of strays from farther north and it has clearly attained a northern limit.

There are areas in the north of Britain where, for topographical reasons, the climate is atypically temperate in character, for example the Black Isle and inner Moray Firth. Some moths, which are otherwise more southern, have outlying populations in such places, including the Common Footman (*Eilema lurideola*) and the Least Black Arches (*Nola confusalis*).

Even moths that are widespread in the south are usually biased either to the south-east or, less commonly, to the south-west. The Least Yellow Underwing (*Noctua interjecta*) is very freely dispersed across southern England and Wales, extending to northern England but not Scotland. However, it is markedly more common in the south-east. The Scarlet Tiger (*Callimorpha dominula*) is more restricted, preferring damp river valleys, but it clearly shows a south-western bias, despite being recorded sparingly across the south. A similar example is that of the Red-necked Footman (*Atolmis rubricollis*).

Some species are found only at the extreme south-eastern fringe, perhaps confined by their need for the warmest and most continental climate available in Britain. The Scarce Chocolate-tip (*Clostera anachoreta*) breeds only at Dungeness in Kent and the Pygmy Footman (*Eilema pygmeola*) occurs there and along the easternmost fringe of Kent and Norfolk. A more extreme example is the Fiery Clearwing (*Bembecia chrysidiformis*), which is restricted to the suntrap of the slumped cliffs at the Warren at Folkestone.

Another location with an exceptionally continental climate, with cold winters and hot, dry summers is the Breck District, which is inland in East Anglia. This area also has freely draining soils and used to be covered in sparse grassy heaths, with many unusual plants. Much has now been planted with pine forests and some of the characteristic moths have been lost. However the Grey Carpet (*Lithostege griseata*) is one of the few species that remain, found nowhere else in Britain.

Many other species are less confined but are still primarily south-eastern. The Pine Hawk (*Hyloicus pinastri*), the Lunar-spotted Pinion (*Cosmia pyralina*) and the psychid *Proutia betulina* are excellent examples.

The climate in the south-west is a real contrast, being mild, damp and Atlantic, and this clearly suits some species. Some are coastal, like the Devonshire Wainscot (*Mythimna putrescens*) and Barret's Marbled Coronet (*Hadena luteago*). The latter extends to the Welsh and Irish coasts. The Jersey Tiger (*Euplagia quadripunctaria*),

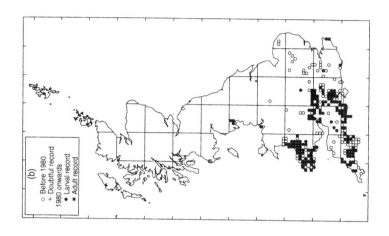

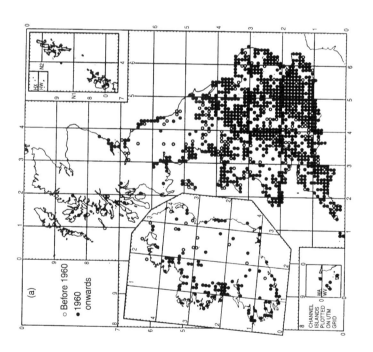

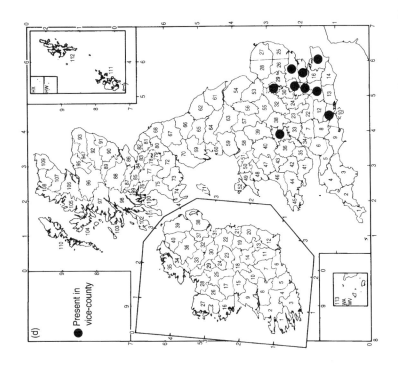

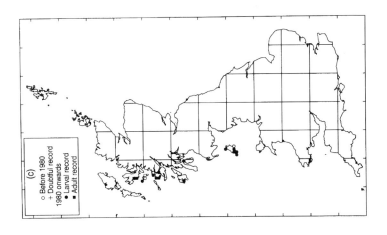

FIG 12   *The British distributions of four species of moths. (a) The Cinnabar, Tyria jacobaea. Although widespread in southern Britain, this species becomes mainly coastal in the north. (b) The Scarlet Tiger, Callimorpha dominula. An example of a species which is primarily south-western in its British distribution. (c) The Grey, Hadena caesia. This species is found only on north-western rocky coasts, mainly on islands. (d) A micro, Proutia betulina. The distribution of micro's is often poorly known but this species is clearly restricted to the south-east. (Source: (a) and (d) from Moths and Butterflies of Great Britain and Ireland, Harley Books; (b) and (c), courtesy of Waring, National Recording Network for the Rarer British Macro-moths)*

which originally invaded Britain in Devon, has not managed to extend far inland or east along the coast. The Marbled Green (*Cryphia muralis*) is also more widespread in the south-west.

The extreme Atlantic climate extends along the western fringe of Britain, providing conditions suited to other species. The Burren Green (*Calamia tridens*) occurs in the British Isles only in the Burren district of western Eire; the Belted Beauty (*Lycia zonaria*) only in the Hebrides and a very few sites on the extreme western fringe of the mainland, and the Grey (*Hadena caesia*) only on coasts in the Hebrides and the Isle of Man. Several of the burnet moths fall into this category (see Chapter 10).

Cold climates and high altitudes

It is much less common for species to be generally northern in their British range but there are several examples that reflect this to different degrees. The Gold Spangle (*Plusia bractea*) extends from Scotland well down into England and Wales, being absent from only the most southern areas, as does the Chi moth (*Antitype chi*), but the birch feeding micro *Parornix loganella* is more restricted and the Cousin German (*Paradiarsia sobrina*) is found in only a few highland valleys. A small number of species share these valleys, including the micro's *Bucculatrix capreella* and *Depressaria silesiaca*, both of which feed on Yarrow (*Achillea millefolium*), a plant common throughout Britain. All of these species seem to be favoured by the northern climate.

Other northern species are found only at various altitudes on the mountains, ranging from those using the lower and middle slopes (such as the Small Dark Yellow Underwing (*Anarta cordigera*) and the micro *Callisto coffeella*), to those of the summit plateau (such as the 'grass' moth *Crambus furcatellus,* the Broad-bordered White Underwing (*Anarta melanopa*) and the Black Mountain moth (*Psodos coracina*). Several of these, such as *C. furcatellus,* are also found in the Shetland Islands, where they live at relatively low altitudes. The same can apply on the north coast of the mainland, as exemplified by the leaf-miner *Stigmella dryadella.* This species mines the leaves of Mountain Avens (*Dryas octopetala*) and is found on the coastal heaths of Sutherland. Farther south in the Highlands both the plant and the moth are confined to high altitudes in the mountains.

It is difficult to see why moths should apparently prefer cold climates, their developmental rates will be lower in such conditions and this would be detrimental. The standard explanation is that they are taking advantage of the lower competition offered by the smaller number of species in the north, but this is purely speculation.

Strangely, a few species are confined to the central area of Britain, for example the Least Minor (*Photedes captiuncula*), (although this also occurs in the Burren area of Ireland) and, to a lesser extent, Lempke's Gold Spot (*Plusia putnami gracilis*). However, it is difficult to define the set of environmental conditions which might lead to this pattern.

Lennon and Turner (1995) have recently provided a very detailed series of maps of the temperature regimes that apply throughout Britain in different seasons, using topographical features combined with data from weather stations, so that the temperatures reflect local conditions more closely than has been achieved before. These maps are to be used to compare with those of the distributions of Lepidoptera, but it may be that other climatological factors, such as rainfall or exposure, are also important, either singly or in combination.

Availability of foodplants

Surprisingly few species of moth are restricted in range by their foodplant. In fact the vast majority of moths, including the rarest species, use foodplants that are comparatively common and widespread. What may be the rarest British moth, the New Forest Burnet (*Zygaena viciae*), which has only one known breeding site, feeds as a larva on one or two very common vetches and the almost equally rare Reddish Buff (*Acosmetia caliginosa*) feeds on Saw-wort (*Serratula tinctoria*), which is reasonably widespread in southern and south-western Britain.

A few species are dependent on a very localised foodplant; good examples are the leaf miner *Phyllonorycter staintonella*, found only in the extreme south-western tip of Britain, one of the few places that its foodplant, *Genista pilosa*, occurs; and Fisher's Estuarine Moth (*Gortyna borelii*), restricted to the Essex coast, although its foodplant, Hog's Fennel (*Peucedanum officinale*), is also found on the Kent side of the Thames estuary. However, in most cases where the foodplant limits the moth, both are moderately widespread, for example, the pyralid moth *Mecyna asinalis* feeds only on Madder (*Rubia peregrina*) and both extend up to the southern edge of the English midlands.

Even species restricted to a major climatic zone that has specialist plants found in it, such as the mountains in Scotland, seem to use foodplants that are much more widespread than the habitat. Typical of this is the Mountain Burnet (*Zygaena exulans*), which feeds on Crowberry (*Empetrum nigrum*), a very common and widespread plant, whereas the moth is restricted to three sites near Braemar. Possibly *Callisto coffeella* is an exception, since it seems to be mainly associated with *Salix myrsinifolia*, which is itself an upland species.

Geological factors

Some moths are found only where their foodplants are growing on chalky or limey soils, despite the fact that the plants extend on to other soil types. The Straw Belle (*Aspitates gilvaria*) occurs only on the chalk of the North Downs and yet feeds on a variety of plants that are found on several soils. The Maple Prominent (*Ptilodontella cucullina*) is also restricted to chalk soils in the south-east, despite the fact that its foodplant, Field Maple (*Acer campestris*) is scattered across much of southern and midland Britain. This is a more common feature in the distribution of moths than might be expected, for it is difficult to see how it works. Presumably there is an effect of the soil type on the chemical composition of the plant and this is what the moth is responding to. It is not known what this chemical factor is and yet it must be not only subtle but also powerful, because of the many examples that occur.

In one extraordinary case a tortricid moth *Periclepsis cinctana*, thought to be found only on the chalk downs near Brighton despite using a wide range of foodplants not restricted to chalk, was discovered on the inner Hebridean island of Tiree, where it was found only on the few, small outcrops of dark hornblende (Harper and Young, 1986). There is no chalk or limestone on Tiree but hornblende is a rich rock and so presumably it releases chemicals that leach into the soil and thence to the moth's foodplants.

Some species favour basaltic rock types. The Slender Scotch Burnet (*Zygaena loti*), which occurs only on the coasts of Mull, certainly seems to be found only on such rock (Ravenscroft, 1994). Although basalt is also rich in minerals and so may have an effect through the soil which results from its weathering, it is also very dark in colour and it, and its dark soil, may provide a substrate that warms up very quickly in sunshine. In the cool

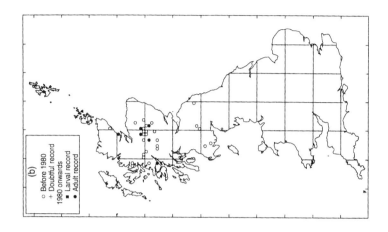

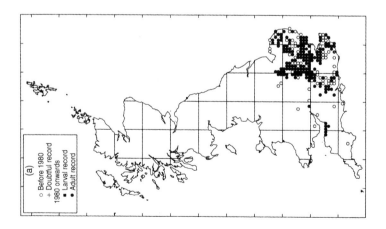

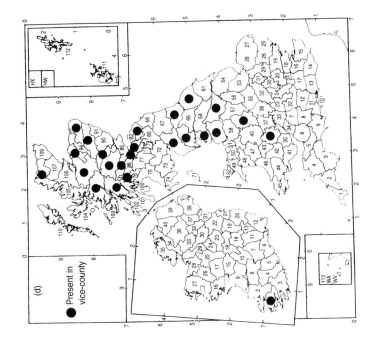

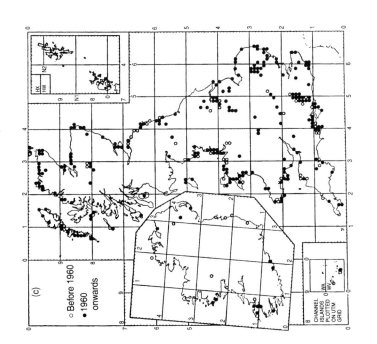

FIG 13   *The British distributions of four species of moths. (a) The Maple Prominent, Ptilodontella cuculina The Maple Prominent is restricted to chalk soils in south-east England. (b) The Broad-bordered White Underwing, Anarta melanopa. This is mountain species, rarely found below 600 m and most frequently found in central Scotland. (c) Archer's Dart, Argotis vestigialis. This is a classical coastal species, inhabiting sand-dunes, but is also found at some inland sites on shingle or sandy soils. (d) A micro, Parornix loganella. A northern species with an obvious southern limit. (Source: (a) and (b), courtesy of Waring, National Recording Network for the Rarer British Macro-moths; (c) and (d), from Moths and Butterflies of Great Britain and Ireland, Harley Books)*

northern locations in the Hebrides this may be an important advantage to the moths concerned and their larvae.

In other cases, the geological features involved are more obvious in their action and this is to do with the surface features. Several species, notably Archer's Dart (*Agrotis vestigialis*), are found only on sand or shingle and follow this soil type inland, such as on to the Spey shingles. Other examples are where moths are found only on cliffs or where there is exposed rock. In these cases the limitation often seems to be that the adults choose to sit on the rock and it is very rare to find *Eana penziana* or the Northern Rustic (*Standfussiana lucernea*) resting anywhere else. It is well known that some species occur in colour forms that match the rock in each of the regions that they inhabit. The classic example is the Tawny Shears (*Hadena perplexa*) but another good example is that of the Annulet (*Gnophos obscuratus*). Both these species have pale wings in chalky areas and dark wings where the prevailing rock types are dark.

A female Belted Beauty (Lycia zonaria) *on the stem of a boat. Could they be carried like this to new island habitats?*

Natural barriers

The most obvious natural barriers that will influence the distribution of moths in Britain are the various sea channels that isolate the many islands. It is difficult to be sure of the influence of these channels, however, because there are other factors that confound the analysis. Firstly, most of the islands are to the west or north of Britain and so have a relatively cool and wet climate, which will lead to them having fewer species for climatic reasons. Secondly, they also have little woodland and, since this is the mainland habitat with the largest complement of species, this reduces the number of island species. In general, the islands also seem to have a smaller range of habitats and so have less scope for species. Thirdly, their size will limit the number of species they can harbour, for it has long been known that small habitat units retain fewer species. This central tenet of the 'island biogeography theory' derives from the observation that the smaller populations on small islands tend to become extinct more quickly than the larger populations on larger islands and this loss is not made good easily, because immigration to the smaller islands takes place relatively slowly (Gorman, 1979). The farther an island is from the mainland, the greater the barrier presented to colonisation.

Despite this, many moths do fly to Britain from the continent and do reach even the outer islands, as evidenced by the many vagrants reaching Shetland (Pennington, 1995), and the frequent sighting of moths on oil platforms (Young, 1984).

Nevertheless, some species seem to have an almost inexplicable relationship to the potential barriers. The Belted Beauty (*Lycia zonaria*) is found only on the extreme western fringe of Britain and is at its commonest in the Hebrides, where it occurs on most of the larger islands. This is despite the fact that the female is wingless and so the dispersive potential of the species is small. The larvae do not disperse freely but crawl slowly about on their foodplants, generally near the sea-shore. Neither do the males carry the females when mating, as happens to a limited extent in many moths and butterflies, for the female is large and heavy bodied. Various potential explanations have been proposed in the past. Possibly the flightlessness has evolved only recently, following the dispersion to the islands. This seems quite unlikely, for the time available since the islands were available for colonisation after the last Ice-age is merely 10 000–12 000 years and this seems far too short a time for complete winglessness to evolve. Surely it is not possible that the species followed the retreating ice so closely that it reached the islands before they were fully isolated. It is now so restricted to areas of temperate climate that this explanation seems impossible. It must be true that the species has managed to disperse across the sea somehow. Perhaps the females, the larvae, the pupae or the eggs have sometimes become attached to debris or grass-tussocks and have floated to the islands, in the way that has certainly happened with the Icelandic volcanic island of Surtsey. Pelham-Clinton (personal communication) even suggested that the females may occasionally cling to the outsides of fishing boats and be transported from island to island!

HABITAT PREFERENCES OF MOTHS

It seems simplistic to comment that most species of moth show a preference for one habitat type. In many cases the reason for this is obvious; for example, the Heath Rustic (*Xestia agathina*) feeds as a larva on Ling (*Calluna vulgaris*), which more or less defines the habitat, and the Shore Wainscot (*Mythimna litoralis*) feeds on Marram Grass (*Ammophila arenaria*) and is confined with its foodplant to sand dunes. However, there are some species that are found only in one habitat type and yet feed on a plant that is much more widespread. This is most notable with woodland species, or more strictly woodland-edge species, rather few of which actually feed on the trees themselves or on plants restricted to woodlands.

There are many examples that could illustrate this but the Plain Clay (*Eugnorisma depuncta*) feeds as a larva on almost any herbaceous plants and yet it, and many grass feeding species, such as the Clouded Brindle (*Apamea epomidion*), are commonest in woodland. In such cases it must be the structure of the habitat that is the controlling factor and perhaps the shelter provided by trees is the key feature. Corroboration of this is that such species are most freely found in clearings or woodland edges, rather than inside the woods and the warmer southern facing edges are those most often used by the moths.

Wetlands also have their own characteristic species and this applies especially to the extensive fens of East Anglia. A large number of species are found only there, often using the Common Reed (*Phragmites australis*) as their foodplant. Several are called 'wainscots' and classic examples are Fenn's Wainscot (*Photedes brevilinea*) and the Reed Leopard (*Phragmataecia castaneae*). Others live on the edges of these wetlands, taking advantage of the fringe of semi-natural vegetation that has survived there. The Marsh Carpet (*Perizoma sagittata*) feeds on Meadow Rue (*Thalictrum flavum*) in damp meadows and the Marsh Moth (*Athetis pallustris*), an elusive species, also lives on these wet fringing habitats along the east coast.

An intriguing feature is that very few of the moths that feed on the Common Reed extend to the other major fenlands in Britain. Perhaps most of these are distinctly farther north or west than East Anglia, so that their climate is different, but the extensive reedbeds along the River Tay in Scotland, for example, harbour only the pyralid *Chilo phragmitella*.

ANOMALOUS DISTRIBUTIONS AND THEIR CAUSES

There are some examples of moths that show anomalous patterns of distribution, with apparently contradictory or inexplicable features. Finding explanations for these may help our understanding of other cases but occasionally it is clear that random influences have left a species occupying a genuinely anomalous position.

A common form of anomaly is where a species now has a disjunct distribution, with obviously different habitat requirements in each of its locations. The Dew moth (*Setina irrorella*) is found rather uncommonly on chalk and limestone grassland across southern England but is also present in some coastal areas as far north as Skye. Although one or two of its coastal sites, in Kent, share the warm, dry climate of its inland grassland locations, those on the west of Scotland are very different, being mild and damp. It is also widespread in the Burren district of western Eire, where the limestone pavement could be considered rather intermediate, being freely draining and warm in sunny weather but with an Atlantic climate.

Mention has already been made of the discovery of *Periclepsis cinctana* on Tiree, in contrast to its previous sites near Brighton. Odd though this is, Tiree is the sunniest part of Britain and, despite being a Hebridean island, it is also very dry, because it extends beyond the coastal area where the first of the western Scottish mountains encourage the Atlantic rain to fall. You could therefore claim that both of the moth's locations are sunny and dry.

The same cannot be said of *Aethes rutilana*, which feeds on Juniper (*Juniperus communis*) as a larva and was once found on chalk downs in south-eastern England. Recently this species was found feeding on prostrate Juniper at about 600 m on Beinn Eighe in Wester Ross (Agassiz, 1984). Morphologically both adult and larva appear just like the southern form but physiologically they must surely be different, for the climate on Beinn Eighe is dramatically different from that of the South Downs, being wet, cold and windy. The only common feature is Juniper but that certainly differs itself between the two locations, its prostrate form being an obvious response to the mountain climate.

Some of the anomalous distributions are merely unexpected restrictions. Ashworth's Rustic (*Xestia ashworthii*) lives amongst the rather grassy heaths of the Welsh mountains, including much of Snowdonia and just extending down to Cader Idris. Its larva is polyphagous and its altitudinal range is wide. There seems no reason why it is not more widespread in Wales, let alone on the much more extensive mountainous areas throughout the rest of western Britain. There is another more dramatic Welsh example, for the Silurian (*Eriopygodes imbecilla*) is found only in one small area of Monmouthshire. Its larvae feed on Bedstraws (*Galium* spp.) and its habitat is just the sort of grassy gully that is found in many hilly areas of south Wales. There are no rational explanations for its extreme localisation. Both species are much more widespread in Scandinavia (Skou, 1991).

RECENT CHANGES IN DISTRIBUTION

Extensions of range

There have been many changes to the British landscape, the habitats within it and the climate in the last decades. These have been influential in causing changes in the moth fauna.

Some species have changed their range considerably in recent years, although sometimes it is difficult to be sure that this has happened. For example, the previously common Cabbage moth (*Mamestra brassicae*) has hardly been seen in north-east Scotland for some three to four years and it may either have retreated south, or have become very scarce. All or most species of moth undergo similar variations in abundance and these may not necessarily be accompanied by range change. There is no doubt, however, that the Golden Plusia (*Polychrysia moneta*) made a great northern extension in range following its colonisation of Britain in 1890, followed by a substantial reduction in the last 35 years (Heath, 1974). It invaded gardens, where it feeds on *Delphinium* and its relatives, and reached as far north as Inverness-shire by 1938 and Aberdeenshire in 1945. Since 1958, however, it has retreated, so that its northern limit is currently the central belt of Scotland.

A more recent example is that of the Dotted Rustic (*Rhyacia simulans*). This species probably feeds as a larva on a variety of low plants and it is certainly not restricted to one habitat type. Historically, it has always been known to vary greatly in abundance from time to time but it has generally been found in south central England and separately in the Hebrides and Orkney (with odd strays in the Highlands). Specimens from the north are distinctly darker and more suffused than those from the south. In the late 1970s, this species began to be found outside its usual range and in particular the southern population began to spread north rapidly, so that by the mid-1980s Scotland was reached, with the first recorded Aberdeenshire specimens found as wings in a spider's web in 1988. The specimens

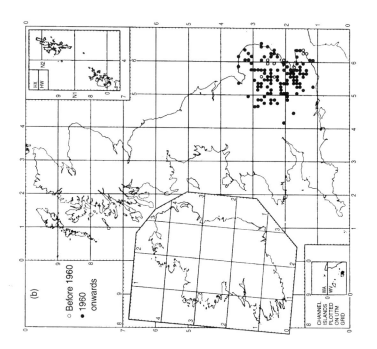

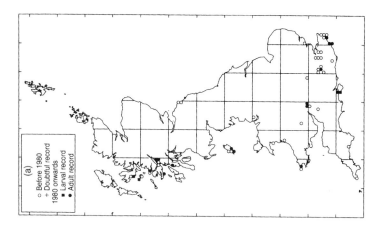

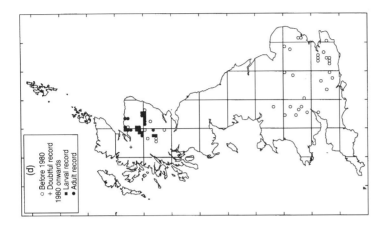

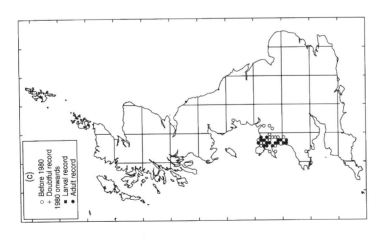

FIG 14   *The British distribution of four species of moths. (a) The Dew Moth, Setina irrorella. This species has a markedly disjunct distribution, found on downs in south-eastern Britain and coasts in the north and west. (b) The Varied Coronet, Hadena compta. Since 1948, when it was first found in Kent, this species has established itself widely in south-eastern Britain. (c) Ashworth's Rustic, Xestia ashworthii. For unknown reasons this hill and mountain species is restricted to north Wales. (d) The Kentish Glory, Endromis versicolora. Once this was found in birch woods in England and Scotland, but it became progressively more restricted in England, before finally becoming extinct there in 1969 or 1970. (Source: (a), (c) and (d) courtesy of Waring, National Recording Network for the Rarer British Macro-moths; (b), from Moths and Butterflies of Great Britain and Ireland, Harley Books)*

found widely during the extension of range have all been 'southern' in appearance and the Orkney population showed no signs of increase.

A more explicable extension has been shown by the Juniper Carpet (*Thera juniperata*). Before 1970, this species had a disjunct distribution, with one centre associated with the Juniper that grows on the limestone and chalk hills of the south-east and one with Juniper in the highland valleys. Since then, it has been found commonly in gardens throughout the English Midlands and extending northwards towards Scotland, so that the two original populations are now nearly linked (Waring, 1992c). This spread seems to have followed the increased popularity of ornamental Junipers in gardens, for the moth has been able to breed successfully on these. It has been accompanied by some other Juniper-feeding species, such as *Argyresthia dilectella*.

The northern edge of a moth's range is the best place to observe changes. Recently the Clouded Border (*Lomaspilis marginata*) has extended from Angus into Kincardineshire, Aberdeenshire and Banffshire. It is an easily recorded day-flying species and we can be quite sure that it was not present previously (apart from an old record in 1890), but we cannot say what has led to the extension. There are records to show that it gradually spread from the south over a four-year period, covering about 130 km in that time. Welch (1992) has recorded the gradual uphill spread by the case-bearing moth *Coleophora alticolella* in the northern Pennines in recent years, perhaps indicating an amelioration of the climate there, but the moth already extends to the north of the Scottish mainland and so no northward trend is possible.

Recent colonists and their rate of spread

Sometimes species suddenly appear in the British Isles but in places and circumstances that make one think that they may have been present for many years, rather than being recent arrivals. The Irish Annulet (*Odonthognothos dumetata*) is one. It was first found in Co. Clare in Ireland and the Irish specimens are distinctly blue-grey rather than brown, as is normal on the continental mainland, and this suggests that they are long-established inhabitants, which have evaded detection, rather than new colonists (Forder, 1993). The foodplant is *Rhamnus*, a long-standing Irish tree.

Perhaps the same applies to the Southern Chestnut (*Agrochola haematidea*), which was found in 1990 on a Sussex common (Haggett and Smith, 1993). This moth flies in October and the discoverers believe that it is a long-established resident that has merely been missed in the past. Its foodplants, *Erica* spp., are certainly widespread and native but the moth cannot be widely distributed in southern Britain, for no extra sites had been dis-covered by 1995.

The spread of other species subsequent to their original discovery makes it very clear that they are genuine colonists. The Varied Coronet (*Hadena compta*) was found as an occa-sional stray migrant until 1948, when several adults and larvae were found in and near Dover. It has since spread northwards and a little westwards from there, so that it is now found throughout East Anglia and across to Herefordshire and Leicestershire (Skinner, 1984). The larvae feed on the seeds of Sweet William (*Dianthus barbatus*), which has long been a common garden plant all over Britain, so that it was not the sudden availability of its foodplant that initiated the spread. Perhaps it has responded to some long-term climatic change and any further spread will be dependent on future climatic conditions.

Blair's Shoulder-knot (*Lithophane leauteri*) was almost contemporary with *H. compta* in its first appearance, in 1951 on the Isle of Wight. It may also have invaded Sussex and Devon at around the same time, for the subsequent rapid spread was broadly based around all three of these areas. The extension has been inexorable, especially since the 1970s, and it now occurs commonly as far north as the north Midlands and it ranges fully from east to west. It will be most interesting to see how far it can now spread northwards for its food-plants are very widely planted in gardens throughout Britain. The original foodplants on the continent are Juniper and the Common Cypress (*Cupressus sempervirens*) but it now uses widespread garden conifers in Britain. Possibly the spread of the moth was initiated by a physiological change, allowing the larvae to feed successfully on an extended range of trees.

Several micro-lepidopterans have invaded Britain recently and their spread has been observed closely. *Caloptilia rufipennella* makes conspicuous and characteristic leaf cones on Sycamore trees (*Acer pseudoplatanus*) as a larva, enabling the presence of the species to be easily and reliably plotted. It was first recorded in Britain in 1970 but was even then clearly well established. Since then, it has spread in two main areas, possibly indicating two original invasions. In Scotland and northern England the species is now found throughout the mainland even to the north coast of Sutherland; from eastern England it has spread from East Anglia across the Midlands and down to the south coast in Devon. At the current rate of spread, with the obvious tolerance of the species to different climatic zones and with the universal range of its foodplant, there seems no limit to its eventual extent. Perhaps the recent arrival of this species from more southern and eastern areas of Europe, and its rapid spread, has been facilitated by the continued increase in sycamore, although this tree has been in Britain for centuries and it is a puzzle why the moth should arrive only now.

In 1989, the blister mines of *Phyllonorycter leucographella* were noticed in Essex, on the outskirts of London on *Pyracantha* and the species has since spread as far north-west as Leicestershire, although its centre of abundance is still London and the Thames valley. *Pyracantha* is also a very widely distributed plant in gardens throughout Britain, so the foodplant is not going to limit the moth. However, this was a rather southern species on the Continent until recently and it has shown some fluctuations in abundance in Britain, per-haps partly associated with cold weather. This, and its current restriction to the warm and low-lying Thames valley, may indicate that it will remain a species of the relatively warm south-east, in contrast to *C. rufipennella*.

Nash *et al.* (in press) report that *P. leucographella* has been spreading at a rate of 10.3 km per year and that a similar new arrival *P. platani*, which feeds on Plane trees and was first found in London, has managed 8.6 km per year. Lawton (1995) and Agassiz (1996) note that almost all invading moth species spread at more than 2 km per year.

Reductions in range

Unfortunately, many more species have reduced in range in the last decades than have extended. Often the reasons for the decline can only be guessed at but there is no doubt that loss of habitat has been the primary factor. Perhaps climatic changes are also important but different species have changed their range at different times and so this link is difficult to make. Reliable data on the reductions have been available only since the advent of the recording schemes but there are a few examples of very conspicuous species that date from earlier times. One of these is the Kentish Glory (*Endromis versicolora*), which was first recorded from Kent in 1741 by Wilkes. In the succeeding century it was also found across central and south-eastern England, always in commons and woods where its foodplant, Birch (*Betula pendula*), was common. The western limits were Somerset and Worcestershire and it extended up to Northamptonshire. In the mid-1880s it was also discovered in the central and eastern highland valleys of Scotland.

By the 1860s it was apparent that the species was less common than previously and it was last seen in Kent in 1868, following which it vanished from Sussex in 1892, Berkshire in 1919, Norfolk in 1925 and the Wye Valley in the 1940s. The only surviving English colony was then in the Wyre Forest on the border of Worcestershire and Shropshire but the last specimens were seen there in 1969 or 1970. Meanwhile in Scotland there have been some fluctuations but the species is still found throughout its historic range. The reason for the English decline is probably that the moth needs extensive areas of regenerating birch, which became progressively less common as woodland management changed, with a reduction in coppice and the 'weeding' out of birch in the period 1850–1930, so that many woods grew to maturity (Young, 1991).

Several species that have declined have shown a loss of records from throughout their previous range but it is also usually possible to detect something of a retreat towards an apparently favoured area. For example, the Narrow-bordered Bee Hawk (*Hemaris tityus*) has declined dramatically throughout its range but the remaining locations are predominantly in the west. In contrast, the Broad-bordered Bee Hawk (*H. fuciformis*), which has also lost most of its pre-1980 records, has remained more common in the south-east.

The Broom Tip (*Chesias rufata*) also appears to have become much less common since 1980 but in this case it still has some colonies in every part of its previous range. This species feeds as a larva on Broom (*Cytisus scoparius*), which remains abundant in marginal habitats throughout Britain, and so it seems unlikely that there has been a significant loss of foodplant or habitat. However, the continued presence of the moths throughout Britain suggests that the cause of decline is not likely to be climatic.

Waring has put forward persuasive arguments that the Buttoned Snout (*Hypena rostralis*) has retreated to relatively warm areas in its former range (Waring, 1993b). Its foodplant, Hop (*Humulus lupulus*), remains much more widespread than the moth, which is now found either on south-eastern coasts or more commonly along the course of the river Thames and its main tributaries, as far west as Oxfordshire. The moth does not hug the actual water course but is confined to the nearby countryside; Waring suggests that the important factor may be the need for suitable adult hibernation sites.

The decline of the Double Line (*Mythimna turca*) and its retreat to the south-west may be associated with a loss of habitat, for Waring (1993c) believes that the species is found in areas of rough unimproved pasture, which has become progressively less frequent in agricultural areas, but is still present in marginal ground in Wales and the west country.

Extinctions

Unfortunately, there are a number of species that have become extinct in Britain since 1900. Some of these have disappeared without being studied or understood and we can only speculate on the reasons for their demise. The Union Rustic (*Apamea pabulatricula*) originally had an oddly restricted distribution in central eastern areas of England, with isolated colonies in the Scottish central belt, East Anglia and the west Midlands. The last records from Yorkshire and Lincolnshire date from around 1920 and from Scotland in 1902. Stray records since then may refer to migrants and the moth certainly seems to be extinct. Another species that disappeared at about the same time is the Orache moth (*Trachea atriplicis*) but in this case the cause of the decline is more certain. This species inhabited the margins of the fens and drains in Cambridgeshire and Huntingdonshire and it may be that the progressive drainage of these areas led to the loss of the moth by 1915. This is a familiar story, for the drainage in East Anglia and the fens has led to many extinctions amongst the moths and butterflies, including the notorious case of the Large Copper butterfly (*Lycaena dispar*) as well as other moths such as the Marsh Dagger (*Acronicta strigosa*), last found in 1933 (Heath, 1974).

The Breck district in Suffolk is still the only locality for several moths but it has also lost the Spotted Sulphur (*Emmelia trabealis*), not seen since 1960; and more recently the Viper's Bugloss (*Hadena irregularis*), which has not been seen since about 1985, despite extensive searches for the larvae, which feed on Spanish Catchfly (*Silene otites*) (not Viper's Bugloss!). In general, the thin well drained soils of the Breck have been used for extensive plantations of Scots Pine (*Pinus sylvestris*) and the characteristic open grass/heaths have declined dramatically in the area. These are now being conserved more effectively and so it is hoped that future declines can be avoided.

The most recent extinction has been that of the Essex Emerald (*Thetidia smaragdaria*), which has not been seen in the wild in Britain since 1991, when the last few larvae were found on the Essex saltings.

RACES, CLINES AND SUBSPECIES

The presence of many islands around the British coast, as well as the existence of isolated lowland areas in the north, means that there are many populations of moths that are isolated from one another. Furthermore, these populations experience very different conditions in these various places. Until recently it was thought that such isolation was a prerequisite for the evolution of races, subspecies and/or species. It has now been discovered that such differentiation can occur even when populations are still in contact, provided that there is some restriction in gene flow between populations. Nevertheless, the islands and isolated areas provide fertile ground for such evolution.

It is very difficult to define what is meant by a race or a subspecies (even more than to be sure what a 'species' really is) and the concepts have caused much confusion in the past. The most widely accepted definition of a 'species' is that it is a set of populations of organisms that are all potentially capable of interbreeding to produce fully fertile offspring (Naumann, 1994). This is a biological definition and there is often a morphological addendum which says that the individuals in a species share an appearance, so that the variation within the species is less than the variation between it and individuals of other species. There are many difficulties in this definition, often caused by a lack of knowledge of exactly which populations can interbreed with which other ones. We do not know enough to apply the biological definition in most cases and so rely on the morphological similarities, which fortunately often seem to correspond to the 'biological' situation.

In this context the general concept of a 'subspecies', which would be recognised by most lepidopterists, is that of a population or set of populations within a species that share an appearance recognisably and consistently different from that of the 'parent' species. It is often speculated that such subspecies will have only limited genetic contact with the parent species. Unfortunately, there is no agreement about how different the morphological differences have to be, with resultant confusion. A 'race' would have precisely the same definition as a subspecies, except that there is usually an additional stipulation that each race inhabits a defined geographical area (but this usually applies to subspecies too). Some lepidopterists prefer to describe geographic 'forms' as races but others prefer to describe them as subspecies and there is no law to say which is right! A significant difference in formal taxonomic terms is that a subspecies is assigned an extra taxonomic name, becoming a trinomial, with the appropriate authority, whereas a race is given no taxonomic status. An extraordinary consequence of this is that, in these days of biodiversity conservation, Governments are formally charged with a duty to conserve all separate subspecies within their jurisdiction, but can ignore races. Hence a taxonomic accident theoretically protects the British subspecies of the Ingrailed Clay on Orkney (*Diarsia mendica orkneyensis*), whereas the Scottish race of the Grey Pine Carpet (*Thera obeliscata*) has no such protection. Fortunately, neither of these needs protecting. If a subspecies is endemic to a country, it receives even more attention.

In many cases there is a more or less gradual change in morphology along the range of a species, or a gradual change in the proportions of different forms and this continuous change is described as a 'cline'. There are clines, subspecies and races amongst the moths of all countries but the terms have been used so inconsistently that their interpretation is difficult. Interpretation might have been easier had there been more work either on the detailed genetics or on the interbreeding capabilities of moths, as pleaded for by Ford (1955). However, apart from the continued work on the Peppered moth (*Biston betularia*) and the start of some work using the very recent techniques of DNA analysis, there has been nothing to elucidate the situation.

THE NUMBERS OF SUBSPECIES IN DIFFERENT FAMILIES OF MOTHS

To illustrate the arbitrary nature of the use of the 'subspecies' category, it is interesting to compare the numbers identified for each of a sample of the families of moths found in Britain. The figures in Table 5 are taken from Emmet (1991a).

These figures can be interpreted in various ways. It may be that families of moths genuinely differ in the extent to which they can differentiate into subspecies; however, there is no biological basis for this assertion – all show the same mating systems. Alternatively, those families with a small proportion of recognised subspecies may have received less taxonomic attention. There may well be some force in this argument for it is true that the Zygaenidae (a small family of very visible and charismatic species) have been very well studied, whereas the Oecophoridae, for example, have been little studied. This is problematical, however, for the Nepticulidae have just been the subject of a detailed taxonomic revision which resulted in no recognised subspecies (Johannson *et al.*, 1990). Possibly more subspecies have been described in those families whose members are large and have complex wing patterns. If so, it is odd that the Notodontidae, a family of large and well patterned species, has so few sub-

TABLE 5 *The total number of species within certain families of moths and the number of those for which one or more subspecies are listed in the current British check-list.*

Family	Total number of species	Number of subspecies	Proportion (% of total no. of species in families)
Zygaenidae	10	7	70
Nepticulidae	98	0	0
Oecophoridae	89	0	0
Gelechiidae	149	2	2
Tortricidae	363	4	1
Pyralidae	189	2	1
Geometridae	309	48	17
Notodontidae	26	1	4
Noctuidae	415	45	11

species. Overall the differences seem to be more of a taxonomic 'accident', depending on the predilections of the taxonomists who happened to work on a particular family. If this is true, it does not bode well for finding interesting biological features by the study of sub-species of moths in Britain and the subspecies themselves appear to have a doubtful valid-ity.

For the remainder of this chapter I shall use the term 'race' (with the meaning set out above) to include all recognisable geographical forms, regardless of whether they have pre-viously been called races or subspecies.

COASTAL RACES

Several species with isolated colonies at different coastal locations show distinct geographi-cal differentiation and this is often clear cut. For example, specimens of the Grass Eggar (*Lasiocampa trifolii*) from the Lancashire, Devon and Hampshire coasts are of a definite reddish-brown hue, whereas those from Kent are yellowish and distinctly different. In this case the real interest is not in why the Kent specimens are different but why the other pop-ulations, which are certainly just as isolated, are so similar. This species does not rest on rocks and so it is probably not affected directly by the paler rock type in Kent and there is no obvious adaptive value to the colour of the wings. The Sandhill Rustic (*Luperina nick-erlii*) demonstrates an analogous but more complex situation. This species has several highly localised and isolated populations on sand dunes. In south-western Ireland the forewings are dark and not very strongly patterned – this race has been named *L. nickerlii knilli*. In Essex and Kent specimens have been found that are also quite dark but with a slightly more variegated forewing pattern; these approach the typical race, *L. nickerlii nick-erlii*. Along the North Wales coast (and previously just into Lancashire) are populations of the rather pale and weakly patterned race called *L. nickerlii gueneei*. Finally, there is a single population in Cornwall that is pale but also strongly patterned on the forewings called *L. nickerlii leechi*. No-one knows whether the differentiation has been due to evolutionary divergence from a common type, to adaptation to local conditions, or whether there were differences in the founder individuals. Also no-one knows how long the populations have been isolated or from where they originated and no-one has tried to cross breed the races, to see whether there is still full fertility in their offspring.

A Sandhill Rustic (Luperina nickerlii) *at rest.*

Specimens of the Grey (*Hadena caesia*) from the south-west coast of Ireland and from Islay have a definite bluish tint to their forewings, as do those from the Isle of Man (although perhaps to a slightly lesser extent), whereas the other Scottish specimens, which are mostly from the Inner Hebrides, are more black than blue and have less of an irrorated appearance. Surprisingly, the Scottish and Irish populations are described as one subspecies, distinct from the paler continental nominate subspecies, but this subspecies was established before the Scottish specimens were properly known.

ISLAND RACES

On the Isle of Skye is a race of the Narrow-bordered Five-spot Burnet named *Zygaena lonicera jocelynae*, which has larger and more confluent wing markings than the usual British speci-

TABLE 6   *Examples of moth 'subspecies', races and clines described in the text.*

Type of race or variation	Example
Generally variable	*Hydriomena furcata* July Highflyer
	Noctua pronuba Large Yellow Underwing
Cline	*Xanthorhoe fluctuata* Garden Carpet
	Spilosoma lubricipeda White Ermine
Habitat 'race'	*Entephria flavicinctata (ruficinctata)* Yellow-ringed Carpet
	Lasiocampa quercus (callunae) Oak/Northern Eggar
Northern race	*Tethea or (scotica/hibernica)* Poplar Lutestring
	Rheumaptera hastata (nigrescens) Argent and Sable
Island race	*Epirrhoe alternata (obscurata)* Common Carpet
	Camptogramma bilineata (atlantica/hibernica/isolata) Yellow Shell
Coastal race	*Lasiocampa trifolii (flava)* Grass Eggar
	Luperina nickerlii (gueneei/ leechi/knilli) Sandhill Rustic

mens. It is easy to produce hybrids between the two races, with no apparent loss of fecundity or vigour, but no-one has yet assessed the fertility of the hybrids themselves. These are intermediate in appearance between the two parent races, with a continuously varying degree of spot size, suggesting that the wing pattern is the result of several genes.

The Hebrides harbour a number of races of which the highly variegated form of the Common Carpet (*Epirrhoe alternata*) and a pale form of the Barred Rivulet (*Perizoma bifaciata*) are good examples. One of the most striking, however, is the dark form of the Yellow Shell (*Euphyia bilineata*). This species is prone to produce dark specimens, even on the northern mainland, but such forms predominate on the Hebrides; there is an even darker race on the Shetlands (*E. bilineata atlantica*); the Irish race is also particularly dark but with rather distinct markings (*E. bilineata hibernica*); and finally there is an almost black race on two of the Blasket Islands of Ireland's west coast (*E. bilineata isolata*).

Strangely, the almost black form of the Rustic (*Hoplodrina blanda*), which occurs on many of the Hebridean islands, has not been given an official subspecific name.

The Shetlands are also well known for the distinct forms that occur there, of which the most famous are the almost black form of the Autumnal Rustic (*Paradiarsia glareosa edda*), whose occurrence was studied by Kettlewell, and the yellowish form of the Ghost Swift (*Hepialus humuli*).

NORTHERN RACES

Amongst those species which have separate northern populations, it is common to find that these are distinct morphological races. Sometimes they are immediately recognisable but rather undramatic, such as the northern race of the Yellow-horned (*Achyla flavicornis*), which is larger and slightly bluer than the usual southern race, or the Poplar Lutestring (*Tethea or*), which has more distinct cross-lines and a paler ground colour.

A most interesting example is provided by the Argent and Sable (*Rheumaptera hastata*), for the difference between the northern and southern subspecies is also associated with a difference in habitat. In the north, specimens are slightly smaller and have many more dark cross-lines but they also feed on Bog Myrtle (*Myrica gale*) on damp moorland, whereas the southern specimens are pale and the larvae feed on birch in light woodland. The boundary between the two races is confused but, regrettably, there is no clear information about the foodplants used in the crucial marginal areas.

Some of the populations of the single brooded race of the Common Marbled Carpet (*Chloroclysta truncata*), which occurs in the north, have been designated as a separate species, given the name *C. concinnata*. These are the populations found on the island of Arran and one or two other sites in south-west Scotland and the Hebrides; they have a particularly striking and irregular pattern on the forewings. However, this species is variable, especially the northern populations, which are always more colourful and variegated, and it is certainly unrealistic to try to put definite boundaries between groups of populations of this species.

RACES ASSOCIATED WITH SPECIFIC HABITATS

Some species have different races associated with different habitats. An excellent example is provided by the Yellow-ringed Carpet (*Entephria flavicinctata*). This species is found from Yorkshire up into Scotland, although there are old records from Wales and the border counties and it may well be more widespread than is currently confirmed. In England, the larvae are said to feed on Mossy Saxifrage (*Saxifraga hypnoides*) and on the west coast of Scotland they feed on English Stonecrop (*Sedum anglicum*), occurring down to the shore-line rocks in places. Specimens from these locations are a rather pale grey, with pale yellow markings, *E. flavicinctata flavicinctata*. Those from the Scottish mountains, however, where they live in gullies and rocky places and feed on Yellow Mountain Saxifrage (*Saxifraga aizoides*), are distinctly darker and have rather orange-yellow markings. These are referred to as a separate subspecies, *E. flavicinctata ruficinctata*. The form found on the north coast of Scotland is *flavicinctata* but the foodplant is *S. aizoides*. One is left with the suspicion that when a fuller picture is available for more populations, the distinctiveness of the races may be less certain.

In Scotland, the Northern Eggar (*Lasiocampa quercus callunae*) has a two-year life cycle, emerges as an adult in May and June and feeds as a larva on Ling (*Calluna vulgaris*), heather (*Erica* spp.), or Blaeberry (*Vaccinium myrtillus*). Specimens from this race are also morphologically different from those from lowland England, with darker females and a slightly different extent to the yellow markings of the male. This race ranges south on to the moors of the Midlands, south-west England, northern England and Wales. In all these areas it retains its two-year life cycle. In the rest of England the Oak Eggar (*L. quercus quercus*) has a one-year life cycle, emerges as an adult in July and August and feeds as a larva on many shrubs and trees, especially including Bramble (*Rubus* spp.). The different races can clearly retain some degree of separation by virtue of their different emergence time, even where they live close together, as they do in south-west England and Wales, and their differences are principally related to their habitat and larval foodplant. It has been customary to regard the two races as separate subspecies but this idea is abandoned in Emmet and Heath (1991), because more careful investigation has revealed some '*callunae*' populations from south-west England that have one-year life cycles, and some broods of larvae from females from the English Midlands and Wales have been found to segregate into groups that spend either one or two years feeding. This example shows how proper study of apparently distinct races may reveal that the conventional distinction is not sustainable.

The Small Square-spot (*Diarsia rubi*) is almost always univoltine in Scotland and bivoltine in southern Britain but there are populations from East Anglia, Lincolnshire, Yorkshire and Borth Bog in Wales, which inhabit fens and marshes, and which are univoltine and generally larger and paler than the typical southern bivoltine form. It is also claimed that the marshland form flies later in the night than the dry ground form. It is referred to as *D. florida* but no-one is yet really sure whether it is a genuinely separate species, or a subspecies, or race, mainly because the differences seem to be less in the north, where the forms overlap in appearance and habitat and where all are univoltine. Fertile hybrids have been obtained in captivity and it is not true, as sometimes claimed, that the larvae of the univoltine marshland race cannot be persuaded to feed up quickly, so as to produce a second brood in captivity. What remains is a most interesting biological situation, in which a marshland race shows phenological and morphological differences from the dry ground race nearby, but for which it is not correct to impose an artificially tidy taxonomic distinction.

CLINES

Many species of moth show great morphological variation over their British range and, whereas the full set of variation is frequently shown everywhere, as for the Large Yellow Underwing (*Noctua pronuba*) or the July Highflyer (*Hydriomena furcata*), there is often a tendency for the variation to be arranged along a geographical gradient. This is referred to as a cline. The underlying genetic situation is that there is a gradual change in the frequency of one or more genes along the geographical gradient and this may result either in a gradual change in appearance (for example a gradual darkening), or in a gradual change in the frequency of a recognised form (for example a change in the frequency of melanic specimens). The cline may also be continuous or it may have areas where the rate of change is either greater or less than over most of the range and/or it may have discontinuities, sudden rather than gradual changes. A common situation is for there to be little change over much of the geographical range but then a rather rapid cline over a short distance. Unfortunately, our knowledge of the underlying genetics of moths showing clines has not improved since Ford (1955) had to use a butterfly example in his book on moths!

Many species show clines within Britain, often of the type where there is an increasing frequency of dark specimens as one moves north. The Blue-bordered Carpet (*Plemyria rubiginata*) is rather uniform in appearance in southern Britain but from the north of England northwards there are increasing numbers of dark specimens and the degree of darkness also increases. Even in northern Scotland some typically pale forms are found but the majority are dark. Almost the same applies to the Garden Carpet (*Xanthorhoe fluctuata*), which has increasing numbers of semi-melanic forms in the north, although there are also melanic specimens in some urban areas in the south. The Silver-ground Carpet (*X. montanata*) shows variation throughout the British Isles in the intensity and clarity of the dark cross-band on the forewing but from northern England northwards there is an increasing tendency to find specimens in which this band is broken and indistinct, so that the overall appearance is lighter and more variegated. The northern specimens also tend to be rather smaller than those in the south.

The Lesser Yellow Underwing (*Noctua comes*) not only shows more black specimens (form *curtisii*) in Scotland but also many more that are dark red and dark brown, whereas the southern populations are more inclined to be a pale grey or brown on the forewings. The White Ermine (*Spilosoma lubricipeda*) shows an increasing tendency for a buff rather than white ground colour to the forewings in the north and west but also for there to be more dark marks and for these to be more streaky.

Finally, the Hebrew Character (*Orthosia gothica*) is more variable in the north of its British range, with every aspect of its coloration being affected.

Recently, it has been shown that there may be distinct changes in the frequency of different forms in many moths over a matter of tens of metres (Kearns and Majerus, 1987; Aldridge *et al.*, 1993; Fraiers *et al.*, 1994) (see Chapter 8). This puts a dramatically new perspective on our understanding of the selective forces that are acting on the wing patterns of moths. They are clearly both stronger and more discriminating than was previously thought. Regrettably, there has been very little study of the genetics of moths, except with reference to melanic forms. Consequently we can describe the situations found but cannot explain them!

CHAPTER 3

Dispersal and Migration of Moths

MOVING ON OR STAYING PUT?

The benefits of a sedentary life

SOME moths spend their entire life within a few metres of where they were laid as an egg. This can continue for many generations, as long as local conditions and resources remain. If the area of suitable habitat for a colony is small and isolated, so that the chance of finding somewhere else to survive beyond its boundaries is slim, there is nothing to gain by moving on and natural selection will favour sedentary individuals. A moth that inhabits a small 'island' which is a long way from others will not be likely to move away from its island across the surrounding 'sea' of unsuitable terrain. The leaf miner *Stigmella dryadella* feeds as a larva inside a leaf of the Mountain Avens (*Dryas octopetala*), which is confined in central Scotland to a small number of isolated locations near the summit of mountains that have lime-rich soils. No-one has ever studied the movement patterns of these tiny moths but they must adopt a stay-at-home approach, if they are to survive. Although it has less restricted foodplants, the mountain top grass moth *Crambus furcatellus* is found only on small patches of suitable habitat on mountains and its short flights rarely take it beyond their borders.

The Sand Dart (*Agrotis ripae*) presents a slightly different example. It feeds only on plants at the high tide mark on sandy shores and so its habitat is very limited in area but is long and thin. Furthermore, its foodplants are affected by blown sand and so are displaced short distances along a shore line and it can be speculated that the moth must be able to move small distances within a tightly bordered area, but will be unlikely to move beyond it. This species and several others that live on the seashore, such as the Lyme Grass (*Photedes elymi*), are hardly ever caught in moth traps that are even tens of metres behind it, and the Sand Dart is most often seen visiting entomologists' 'sugar', when this is painted on jetsam on the sand. The most extreme example is the race of the Sandhill Rustic (*Luperina nickerlii leechi*) that is found only on one beach in Cornwall; Spalding (1994) failed to find any at light traps even on the beach, at times when the moths were easily seen sitting on the stems of their foodplant, the Sand Couch-grass (*Elytrigia juncea*), and he has only ever seen one female in flight but has often seen females crawling slowly over the sand to neighbouring grass stems to lay their eggs.

The advantages of moving on to find new resources

Moths that depend on shifting resources, however, must move on to find the new locations of these resources. Thus, species whose larvae feed on weeds, or on plants of temporary habitats or transitory stages in vegetation succession, must be mobile and effective at locating their resources. The ultimate examples are probably the Tineidae, whose larvae feed on corpses or other rotting organic matter. There is no predicting where the next corpse will be and each one is a minute speck in the general area of habitat where the moths live. Such moths, for example *Monopis weaverella*, are often encountered fluttering about at dusk, presumably searching for food. Other examples are the few species that feed on weed species. The tortricid moth *Eucosma campoliliana* feeds on Ragwort (*Senecio jacobaea*), which is a biennial that invades freshly disturbed ground and is constantly establishing new locations. The moth is a regular visitor to moth traps, even far from Ragwort plants, and it obviously strays freely, searching for new foodplants. The same applies to the Mullein Shark (*Cucullia verbasci*) which feeds on Mullein (*Verbascum thapsus*), a very transient plant.

Choosing whether to move on or stay put

The moths mentioned above have become adapted to a particular dispersal pattern, but no doubt even the most sedentary species of moth has some individuals that disperse and the most mobile has some sedentary individuals. The species will succeed only if the pattern is adapted to the circumstances of its habitat. Dempster (1991) suggests that, as the fenland habitats of the British race of the Swallowtail butterfly (*Papilio machaon*) became smaller and more isolated, the butterflies came to have relatively smaller wings and wing muscles, implying that the race as a whole was becoming less mobile. There has been no equivalent research done on recently isolated moths but the same selection pressures will apply. Each species will become adapted to the habitat features that apply to it and individuals will typically use a pattern of dispersal that suits survival in those circumstances. Moths that are found on islands are prone to have wingless females (Wagner and Liebherr, 1992). The path that each individual follows in its life is referred to as its 'lifetime track' and successful individuals follow a track that locates the resources required, such as a mate or a foodplant, more effectively than an unsuccessful individual. This chapter considers the many different types of lifetime track followed by moth species with different degrees of mobility.

DISPERSAL

Defining terms – dispersal or migration

Those familiar with the migration of birds or whales will not have recognised the sort of dispersal noted above as true migration. Nevertheless, some workers use the word to include it, so it is necessary to define the terms to be used here. The problem is setting the limits of different sorts of movement, for in practice there is no sharp dividing line.

The Monarch butterfly (*Danaus plexippus*), carries out a movement pattern that everyone would recognise as true migration. In this species individuals which emerge in the late summer in the more northern states of the USA move southwards until they reach restricted hibernation sites, typically groups of trees on lower mountain slopes in Mexico or California. There they stay, in huge assemblages, until the spring when they fly north again, eventually laying eggs in the northern states from which they came. Such movement involves all of the attributes that are reserved for true migration. It is long distance; directional; undistracted by local needs for long periods; includes a return movement; and is over unsuitable territory. During the migration the butterflies show clear and consistent orientation. If this is true migration, then what should one call the movement of the Silver Y moth (*Autographa gamma*)? In the spring, individuals of this species that have emerged in southern Europe fly northwards, showing consistent orientation, for long distances, often over unsuitable territory, and rather undistracted by local needs. These individuals lay eggs in northern Europe and then die. Their offspring emerge in late summer and some show a tendency to return southwards, although it is only a tiny minority that reach equable climates and survive the winter. The essential difference is that it is not the same individual that returns south but the functional result is the same. What of the Small White butterfly (*Pieris rapae*), studied by Baker (1978)? He found that individuals moving north in Britain in August, showing long distance, oriented flight, then change direction completely and begin to return south again. In this case the same individual undertakes the return journey. Neither of these

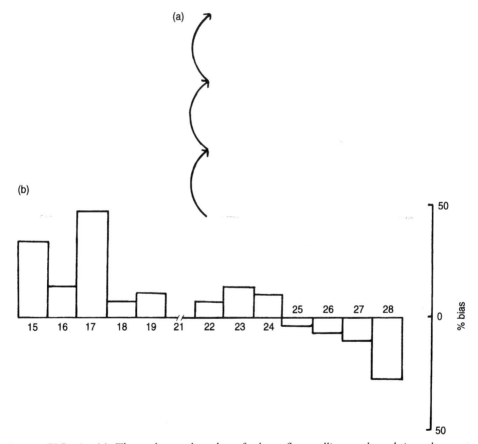

FIG 15 (*a*) *The track over three days of a butterfly travelling northwards in early summer using an uncorrected sun compass.* (*b*) *The percentage bias towards the summer mean angle and the autumn mean angle at dates between 15 and 28 August 1973.* (*Source: Baker, 1982*)

examples show all of the features of migration shown by the Monarch butterfly but both do much more than would normally be included in the term 'dispersal'. The latter term would usually be reserved to describe the movement patterns of individuals that moved away from their emergence site for a relatively short distance, perhaps even within the same habitat patch, such as when a Poplar Hawk moth (*Laothoe populi*) flies off to find a new poplar on which to lay eggs. Where is the boundary to be drawn between these types of movement?

The difficulty of finding a suitable place at which to draw the line has led some authors, such as Baker (1982), to include all movements within the term migration in a wide sense, namely 'any movement from one spatial unit to another'. This is the prudent use of the word, for it acknowledges that there are no clear boundaries available, but it is not very useful, for it does not allow easy differentiation between what are obviously functionally different movement patterns.

In this book I use the term 'migration' as defined by Kennedy (1985), that is 'persistent and straightened-out movement effected by the animal's own locomotory exertions. It depends on some temporary inhibition of station-keeping responses but promotes their eventual disinhibition and recurrence'; furthermore I shall not require a return by the same individual. 'Dispersal' I take to be more short distance and less directional, but I acknowledge that there is no absolute division between the two. I include the Silver Y and the Small White butterfly as migrants but not the Poplar Hawk.

Patterns of Movement within Suitable Habitats

All individual moths disperse to some extent and the advantage of this is clearly to make full use of the habitat space that is available. Since this space will change from time to time, some exploration is necessary. As the summer develops in high latitudes suitable habitat becomes available and so a species that moves north finds a resource not available to those that do not move. Alternatively, a woodland may expand as seedlings grow up around its edges, or an open habitat may appear where a tree has blown over, or a fire has been. If a moth can find this new habitat before others do, it has a valuable resource that will allow it to reproduce successfully and, in the leaving of more offspring, succeed in an evolutionary sense. However, if an individual flies beyond the bounds of suitable territory without finding new resources, it will fail. If one watches a colony of moths, which is easiest to do with day-flying species such as burnet moths (Zygaenidae), it is possible to watch these conflicting strategies at work.

Most burnet moth flights are short and aimed at a definable local resource, such as a mate, a flower or a foodplant, well within the obvious boundaries of the colony. Some flights take an individual to the colony boundary and the moth often then veers back into the suitable habitat. If the boundary is a woodland edge this is clearly recognisable but the same can happen when an area of unsuitably short or long vegetation is encountered. Most individuals stay within the colony boundaries but occasionally an individual strays. Sometimes this seems to be involuntary, perhaps a strong breeze suddenly blows the specimen away, but often the individual just seems to 'choose' to ignore the obvious boundary and fly beyond it. Mark/release/recapture by Bourn (1995), at a site where the Narrow-bordered 5-spot Burnet (*Zygaena lonicerae*) inhabits a series of vegetated slopes, each separated by uninhabitable rocky areas some tens or hundreds of metres across, has shown that gen-

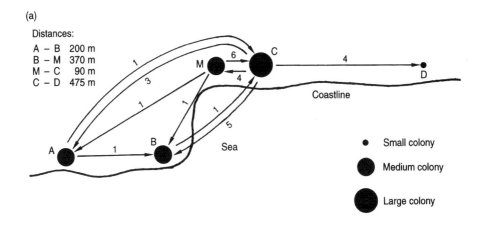

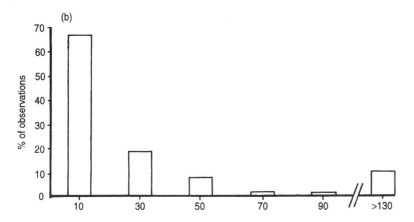

FIG 16 *Dispersal in Six-spot Burnet moths* (Zygaena filipendula). (*a*) *Movement between colonies on the coastal fringe of the Sands of Forvie NNR, Aberdeenshire in 1995.* (*b*) *Distances moved by individual moths as judged by the distance between first and last captures.* (*Source: unpublished data from Huai-Jung Chang*)

erally 90% of individuals stay on their original patch. If males disperse to a neighbouring colony they may transfer their genes but for a newly vegetated rock fall to become inhabited, one or more females must reach it. Similar work at an adjacent grazed slope, where the Transparent Burnet (*Zygaena purpuralis*) occurs in a series of close sub-colonies, suggests that females tend to remain close to their emergence point to lay their first egg batches but may disperse significantly farther later in their lives before laying their last eggs. This appears to be a hybrid strategy that allows both continuation on the original colony area and some chance of locating and using new areas. Perhaps if more moth species were studied it would be found that this is a common occurrence. It is generally thought that the same effect is achieved for a population by some individuals being sedentary and a varying proportion being dispersive. Horton (1977) reports such local dispersal from grassland habitats on Salisbury Plain, even by species like the Narrow-bordered Bee Hawk (*Hemaris tityus*), in the warm summer of 1976.

WHICH STAGES ARE DISPERSIVE?

Cinnabar moth (*Tyria jacobaea*) larvae live communally and almost always find that they need to move from their original individual foodplant of Ragwort, because even the largest plant is hardly big enough to support a brood of the larvae. Consequently, the larvae crawl off to find another plant and, although they tend to do this as a group, many get separated and the group size for final instar larvae is usually less than for young larvae. However, if the plants are scarce or the moths numerous, the reverse may occur, with huge groups of larvae on the few remaining plants. In any case such dispersal by the larvae only involves crawling over a few metres of space between the plants, which tend to be clumped because, when possible, female moths choose to lay eggs on large individual foodplants occurring in groups (Crawley and Pattrasudhi, 1988). Overall, in this species, the females disperse widely to find new Ragwort clumps and the larvae disperse locally to find new individual foodplants.

The Kentish Glory (*Endromis versicolora*) female is large-bodied but can fly to disperse her eggs. She lays a series of batches of typically about 12 eggs, moving on to lay up to 200 if she survives long enough, and the larvae initially feed in a group at the tip of a twig. They are believed to gain an advantage by living in a group, either because they look like a bundle of buds, or because they resemble the clustered larvae of a distasteful species of sawfly. When half-grown, the larvae move away from their groups and eventually live separately but they do not spread beyond their initial tree. The final dispersal of individuals results mainly from movement of the females and only a little from the larvae (Young, 1991).

In a species like the Pebble Prominent (*Notodonta ziczac*), which lays its eggs singly and widely separated on leaves of the host tree (de Worms, 1979), it is also the female that is dispersive and the larva moves very little in its life, except to find new leaves on which to feed and to move away from the signs of damage that it has left.

Wingless females

Where the female has no wings or has reduced wings, however, a different strategy is needed. Less than 1% of Lepidoptera are wingless, compared with around 10% of beetles (Coleoptera) and around 50% of grasshoppers and crickets (Orthoptera) (Wagner and Liebherr, 1992). Most of that 1% live either on islands or in places where the climate is cold, or they emerge as adults in the cold seasons of the year. It is energetically costly for a large-bodied female to fly in cold conditions and risky for an individual that lives on an island.

The Belted Beauty (*Lycia zonaria*) has a completely wingless adult female and it is the larvae that disperse. However, they do not move far and the pattern of dispersal is as follows. The female crawls around in the habitat, so spreading out the eggs to some extent; the larvae then also crawl about, achieving a further dispersal; but the final effect is not great. What is important is that the larvae must be able to feed on a wide range of foodplants, for the rather feeble larval dispersal cannot ensure that new examples of one foodplant will be reached (see Chapter 5).

The Winter moth (*Operophtera brumata*) has a wingless female, which climbs up the trunks of deciduous trees and lays its eggs on the twigs and buds. The larvae either burrow into the opening buds or the newly spread leaves of the trees or, if these are not yet available when the larvae hatch, they try to find an alternative host by spinning a very fine thread of silk, which acts as a parachute. When the floating thread is sufficient to lift off the larva, it lets go and drifts off with the wind until it becomes entangled around another branch. This is a haphazard process and the Winter moth can feed on almost all species of tree.

Another example is provided by the Vapourer moth (*Orgyia antiqua*). The wingless female lays all its eggs on its cocoon and so achieves no dispersal at all. The larvae spin their silk parachute immediately on emergence and float off into the distance. The larvae are able to feed on most potential host plants and become very widely spread around the general habitat. There are few species in which all the dispersal is carried out by the larvae, but Wagner and Liebherr (1992) report that wingless females are generally more fecund than their winged relatives, as partial compensation for the risky larval dispersal method.

An extreme example is the psychid *Acanthopsyche atra*. Hattenschwiler (1985) reports a previous study which found that when mated females were fed to robins their eggs appeared in the birds' droppings and then hatched successfully! By this method, it is suggested, the species is dispersed.

The results of these movements are that potential habitats become colonised in time and that species spread themselves within each location, optimising their use of the habitat available. Furthermore, dispersal also discourages mating with close relatives, so offering a genetic advantage.

WHAT STARTS MIGRATION?

Migration only pays if the possible benefits of moving outweigh those of remaining sedentary. It follows that migration is frequently prompted when the local environment has become unsuitable (Gatehouse and Zhang, 1995). However, some species, like the Diamond Back moth (*Plutella xylostella*), almost always seem to migrate, regardless of local suitability. Typically, such species use weeds or short-lived plants as food, so that their habitat patches are short-lived.

Habitats may become unsuitable for several reasons. If there is a drought, the food-plants may die or wither, and migration has been found to follow such food shortages. If the local population of a moth has increased so that there is crowding and food shortage, then the emerging moths may migrate away. Gunn and Gatehouse (1987) found that the African Army Worm (*Spodoptera exempta*) responds to larval crowding by producing adults that are more adapted to migration. They fly longer distances, contain more glycerides (the fuel used on long-distance flight) and develop more eggs than sedentary adults, although long flights tended to use up resources so that the full fecundity is not realised.

Owen (1987a) reported that the Painted Lady butterfly (*Cynthia cardui*) may migrate away from areas where parasite numbers have built up. He found movement away from a site where almost all larvae were parasitised by an *Apanteles* wasp and subsequent breeding at a place where no parasites were present.

Most species that migrate remain in a pre-reproductive state until after their migration. Their energy resources are directed at first to their flight requirements and lipids are stored to provide essential fuel (Dudley, 1995). This allows their migratory range to be greatly increased, as does the ability to fly high up, where the airstream is flowing strongly in the appropriate direction. The Oriental Armyworm (*Mythimna separata*) in China and Japan usually flies at an altitude of between 200 and 1000 m but has been recorded at 1500 m (Chen *et al.*, 1995)!

WHAT STOPS MIGRATION?

Many migrant moths continue to fly on, even when they have reached an area where there is suitable habitat available. They seem to be 'programmed' to use up their metabolic resources before they stop. For this reason some Silver Y moths (*Autographa gamma*) fly to northern Britain to breed, passing over territory where other Silver Y's have stopped and successfully laid eggs. However, the final stop is usually at a place which offers suitable habitat, at least for a while.

WHAT GUIDES MIGRATORY MOTHS?

It used to be thought that moths could migrate only with the wind (Johnson, 1969) and it is possible to back-track airstreams and retrace the path of migrants, sometimes to as far as North Africa. More recently it has been claimed that moths can control their flight path to a much greater extent – not against strong winds but adding their own vector, so that the eventual destination is not merely downwind (Baker, 1978). It is a common observation that migrants from eastern Europe reach Britain only when there have been easterly air-flows, but migrant moths can then spread out in Britain partly independently of local winds.

By taking off when wind and weather are favourable, moths begin the process of determining their destination, but it is likely that the final track is partly due to prevailing winds and partly to the orientation ability of the moths. For this to work, moths must judge and control their direction of flight, even if they are not navigating in the true sense of the word.

DEFINITIONS OF ORIENTATION AND NAVIGATION

There is an essential difference between orientation and navigation that can best be explained by use of a simple example. Imagine a moth flying along a reasonably straight track. If this moth is captured and displaced laterally for some distance and then released it may resume its direction of flight, roughly parallel to the original track. If it does this, it may be said to be using *orientation* to maintain it direction. If, when released, it moves in such a way as to head back towards its original destination, taking a new heading to compensate for its displacement, then it can *navigate* towards a goal (provided the goal is not in sight, so that the moth is not just flying to a landmark).

Can moths orientate? If a short perspective is used then this is a trivial question. Of course moths are able to move in reasonably straight lines towards clearly defined goals; everyone who has ever watched them will have seen this. This sort of flight is presumably accomplished by using local landmarks – the moth can see its goal and can fly directly to it. What is not quite so clear is whether moths use long-distance orientation, but in some situations this must occur.

When a male Emperor moth (*Pavonia pavonia*) searches a moor for a mate the main strategy is to fly in an erratic fashion, until it encounters a female's pheromone; the male then turns to fly upwind in a reasonably straight line, which leads towards the female. Even if this straight flight involves the use of a series of landmarks, or the ability to fly steadily into the wind, it still represents orientation. If a large number of Convolvulus Hawk moths (*Herse convolvuli*) successfully fly north into Britain, they must have used some orientation

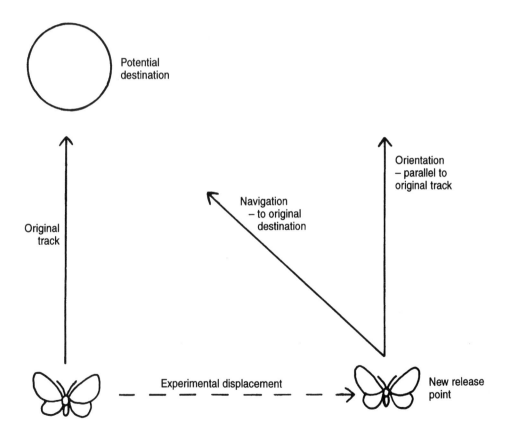

FIG 17   *Orientation and navigation patterns. In orientation, the moth continues on its original direction after displacement and release. In navigation, the moth alters its direction of movement and heads for its original destination.*

skills to convert random directions into northward travel. Moths obviously do not use a vague random motion to disperse themselves across suitable habitats – they use orientation. The question is, how do they achieve this?

CUES USED IN ORIENTATION

Landmarks

Landmarks have already been referred to and, in the hierarchy of moth orientation cues, are the simplest and probably the most often used, at least for routine flight about the neighbourhood. This can be observed in action. Day-flying moths, like the more familiar butterflies, can be watched as they fly with clear purpose directly to a nectar source, a roost, a mate or other features in the landscape. Night-flying moths may at first seem to have a more difficult task but nights are rarely so dark to the dark-adapted eyes of moths that landmarks cannot be seen. On slightly brighter nights, when we can also see the vague outlines of objects and the pale shapes of moths, we can also see them unerringly pick out nectar plants.

Sun compass

A more interesting question is whether moths can also use the sophisticated variety of cues that are available to more well known travellers, such as homing pigeons. This topic has been studied in both butterflies and moths by Baker and others, with conclusive and startling results. The Small White butterfly can be tracked along its path individually, or successive specimens can be observed and their direction noted as they pass an observer during the course of a day. When this is done in the early summer, the majority of specimens move in a roughly north-westerly direction in the early part of the day, gradually swinging through a northerly to a more north-easterly path in the afternoon. This is the characteristic track of a migrant using what is best called an 'uncorrected sun-compass'. In the butterfly's case, it can detect the position of the sun and can fly more or less directly away from it, without allowing for the movement of the sun across the sky. The result is a series of wide daily arcs, which tend to move the butterfly generally northwards (which is advantageous), without letting it recross ground that it has already passed (again advantageous). An exact north path is not needed and so the lack of correction is not a problem. In the autumn the butterflies tend to fly towards the sun in a similar way. Butterflies and day-flying moths, like bees on which so much of the early research was done, can detect the plane of polarised light and so can place the sun in the sky, even when clouds obscure it (Wehner, 1984). Thus, a sun-compass is an effective device in most conditions when a moth might find the weather good enough to fly. It may be that no-one has specifically observed the use of an uncorrected sun-compass in moths but it has been shown that night-fliers use an uncorrected moon-compass.

The moon and stars

The Large Yellow Underwing (*Noctua pronuba*) has been experimented on extensively and it has been shown that individual moths tend to move in a specific direction in relation to the angle they subtend to the moon (Sotthibandhu and Baker, 1979). This is confirmed experimentally by using mirrors or artificial moons, to move the apparent position of the moon, with the result that the moths then re-orientate to take up the same direction with respect to the 'new' moon.

Moths flying in moonlight.

The moon moves more quickly across the sky than the sun, and not over such a simply described arc, and so it would be less suitable as a reference point for long-distance orientation, but it serves very well for maintaining a steady path over the sort of distances and times that are used by moths in all but long-distance migration. If the moon has not risen but stars are visible, Large Yellow Underwings can orientate to the position of the stars. By painting over different parts of the moths' compound eyes, Sottibandhu and Baker (1979) showed that they use a set of ommatidia near the top and rear of the eye to detect the stars. By altering the pattern of stars in an artificial display, they found that a group of stars near the pole star is used by this species of moth in the northern hemisphere. It has not proved possible to demonstrate the effect in wild-caught moths but only in those reared in captivity, whose only experience was the artificial sky provided by the experimenters. It has also been claimed that the eyesight of moths is not sufficient to detect detailed patterns of small stars (Wehner, 1984), but detailed recognition is clearly not needed, merely the ability to detect a similar general pattern and to fly relative to that.

A geomagnetic sense

When Baker and Mather (1982) enclosed many specimens of the Large Yellow Underwing (*Noctua pronuba*) in a closed box, they found that most tended to move consistently to one side of the box, as if trying to maintain a particular direction. This happened even when no lights or landmarks were visible and, when the box was rotated, the orientation was retained relative to the outside world rather than to the box! Baker's work on pigeons and university students(!) had shown that these subjects could detect the directionality of the earth's magnetic field, and so the box was surrounded with electrical coils, arranged so as to reverse the direction of polarity within it. When this was done, the moths changed their orientation to one directly opposite to the original. This seems to be conclusive evidence that they

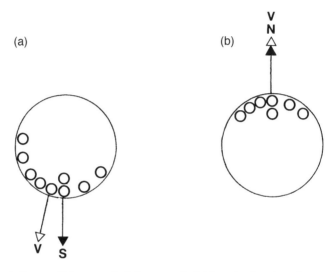

FIG 18 *The influence of the reversal of the magnetic field on the direction of movement of the Large Yellow Underwing* (Noctua pronuba). *The small circles represent mean directions of individual moths overnight and the arrows, V, show the mean vector for all moths. The arrows, N and S, show the approximate direction of magnetic compass points. The magnetic field was reversed between large circles (a) and (b). (Source: simplified from Baker and Mather, 1982)*

can detect a magnetic field and orientate to it. How they do so is not yet properly understood, for even in pigeons it is only recently becoming clear how this detection may be achieved, using cells containing minute metallic elements which could respond to magnetism.

It is probable that moths, just like us, use a hierarchy of methods, choosing the easiest in any given circumstance. Landmarks will suffice for short flights, or light source cues for longer straight flights, with magnetic senses only being used when the others are not available. For long-distance migrants the weather systems may then have a moderating effect and determine the final direction of flight.

CONFUSING ORIENTATION – MOTHS AND CANDLES

The attraction of moths to candles is proverbial and explanations for this behaviour range from the supernatural to the scientific! Generally, however, there seem to be two main theories.

The traditional view about why moths are attracted to lights is satisfyingly logical but probably wrong. This suggests that a light source is mistaken by a moth for the moon, or a similar very distant orientation beacon. Normally a moth will keep a set angle between its path and the beacon, so as to fly on a straight path, but if this is done with a relatively close light it will result in a spiral path, bringing the moth towards the light in an ever tightening circle. This seemed so probable that for a long time it was not challenged critically, but even a brief period of observation will show that moths do not behave like that with lights; they do not spiral in but zoom about in erratic and wild loops, often settling well away from the light or approaching and then flying away. If this is the explanation, it must be modified by many other factors (Waring, 1994). However, Baker and Sadovy (1978) provide some supporting evidence. They found that the distance over which attraction occurs increases from 3 to 10–17 m when a light is raised from ground level to a height of 9 m. They suggest that this is because the light is then being viewed by the upper part of a moth's eye, mimicking the moon.

Hsiao (1972) proposed an alternative explanation. He studied the effect of bright light on the insect's compound eye and suggested that the peripheral ommatidia of the eye experience inhibition, so that the moth perceives a very dark area around the light source and is trying to fly into that as it approaches and closely passes the light. As the position of the light constantly changes, (with respect to which ommatidia are illuminated), there is constant shifting of the moth's flight path to aim at the dark zone, and this results in the erratic flight. Moths often settle in and around light traps in shadows just out of the beam of the light, and these places can be interpreted as being the dark zones, so this theory seems to bear some relationship to reality.

The behaviour of moths at lights

Studies of the behaviour of moths around lights have been summarised by Muirhead-Thomson (1991). Many originate in efforts to increase the effectiveness of the traps, so that pest species may be trapped more efficiently. Such studies have been carried out in tropical countries, where pest problems are greatest. By varying the design of the traps, the types and powers of lights, the direction of the light beams, the position of the traps and so on, it has become clear that different families of moths tend to fly at different heights and speeds and so are caught preferentially by different designs of trap. The Pyralidae fly low down and are attracted well to traps with a horizontal 'throw', whereas Noctuidae tend to fly higher and faster and often shoot past the traps. McGeachie (1988) used a large series of water traps, set out concentrically around light traps, so as to catch individuals that approached but landed before entering the light traps. This procedure is similar to earlier American work by Hartstack *et al.* (1968), who wished to test the efficiency of such traps. They found that *Heliothis* spp. (Noctuidae) frequently settle on the ground short of the traps, so that the actual trapping efficiency was as low as around 10%; however, the Cabbage Looper

(*Trichoplusia ni*) was more inclined to fly right to the trap, resulting in a higher trapping efficiency. These calculations are complicated by the fact that they do not allow for the moths taking off again from the ground and so eventually reaching the trap, but they do at least confirm the moth-trappers' general experience that light traps are not very efficient and that some species are trapped more than others. Micro-lepidoptera are less common in traps than larger species, for example, but this could be because their slower flight allows them to veer off before they reach the point of no return, or because they can fly out of the trap openings at dawn more easily than larger species, or that they find more effective shade in small crevices around traps.

The trapping range of light traps

McGeachie (1988) studied mainly the directionality of the catches but he also noted the zone of effective catch and estimated this as no more than 10–25 m (similar to Baker and Sadovy, 1978 and Roberts, 1996). This corresponds well with the practical experience of trappers, that moths have to be close to a trap before they seem to be attracted, but it does not confirm a further speculation that there is a zone of repulsion around the zone of attraction and that this varies with the type of bulb used. Different types of bulb vary in efficiency but the evidence suggests that this results from differences in their brightness to the moths; the brighter and the more contrasting with the background the better. Consequently, lights that produce high quantities of the wave-lengths that are perceived by moths' eyes, i.e. ultra-violet, are the most effective (Waring, 1994).

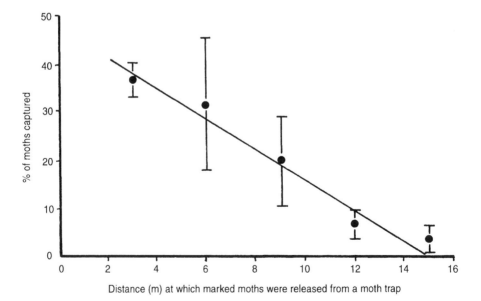

FIG 19   *The relationship between the recapture rate of marked moths and the distance from a light trap at which they were released on calm nights in July 1995. (Best fit line and 95% confidence limits.) (Source: Roberts, 1996)*

McGeachie found that the wind speed and direction affected the 'catch' pattern around the trap, with a downwind displacement, so that, if two traps are set near to one another, the downwind trap catches most moths and to avoid 'interference' traps need to be at least 200 m apart. He also noted that different groups are caught with varying efficiency and that the overall catch was less than 30% of those which approach the lights.

TABLE 7   *Factors that influence the catches of moths by light traps.*

Factors favouring large catches	*Factors leading to low catches*
High night temperatures	Low night temperatures
Low wind speeds	High wind speeds
Winds from S or W in UK	Winds from N or E in UK
High humidity	Low humidity
?Steady barometric pressure	?Dropping barometric pressure
Low moonlight levels	Full moon conditions
High UV light levels	Low UV light content
High contrast with background	Low contrast with background
No other lights nearby	Interference from lights
Light held above ground level	Inappropriate light height

Gaydecki (1984) confirmed a widely recognised observation, that catches are positively correlated with night-time temperature (especially soon after dusk, which he found to be the time of greatest catch), and negatively correlated with wind speed. In his studies these two factors accounted for at least 90% of the variation in catch numbers. He also corroborated the earlier findings of Hsiao that there is a pattern to the numbers of moths that settle at varying distances from the light, with a maximum around 30–40 cm from the light (depending on species) and a decline from that point both outwards and inwards.

Light catches and lunar cycles

Another frequently observed feature of the effectiveness of light traps, that they are least effective at full moon, has been extensively studied, especially in Africa where the path of the moon across the sky and its interruption by cloud is less complicated than in higher latitudes. Bowden and Church (1973) showed that catches may be three or four (sometimes as much as 10) times greater at new rather than full moon. Siddorn and Brown (1971) also showed a difference between catches at different times of the night, with greater catches of *Spodoptera* spp. at dusk and thereafter, when the moon rose late, and at dawn and just before, when the moon rose and set early. The question is why this should be; the two possible alternatives are that the traps are less effective in brighter sky conditions, or that fewer moths are flying then. Male and female moths may vary in their response, as may different species, but generally a bright night deters moths from flying. Even within a genus this can vary, for *Heliothis armigera* was less common on moonlit nights but *H. punctiger* was unaffected (Morton *et al.*, 1981). Such differences in flight activity have been corroborated by studies of the numbers of eggs laid by *Heliothis zea* in cotton fields on nights that differed in brightness, with fewest found after moonlit nights (Nemec, 1971) but it can also be shown by observing the relative proportions of active moths in cages exposed to different light levels. Since it has been shown that the effectiveness of light traps is dependent on the contrast that they make with their background, it is clear that there is both a variation in the numbers of flying moths and the relative proportions caught, in different phases of the moon. For some species the position is even more complicated. The Diamond Back (*Plutella xylostella*), for example, may show three peaks of abundance in the lunar cycle, two between the new and full moons and one at the full phase. Such a pattern is disguised by the results of light trap catches, owing to their lower efficiency at high light levels, but is clear from suction or pheromone trap catches.

DO MOTHS EVER NAVIGATE?

True navigation in butterflies has been observed operating over short distances, where territorial males may show a very clear ability to navigate around their territory, presumably using a map that they have 'constructed' following exploratory flights (Baker, 1972; Shreeve, 1987). They often return directly to a perch, following an erratic chase of a rival male, presumably having 'computed' the correct course from their map. Navigation has not so far been shown over long distances. No moths have yet been shown to be territorial, but there seems to be no rational reason why they should not be. The obvious place to look for territoriality, and hence navigation, is amongst the diurnal species, but those that have been studied, such as the burnet moths (Zygaenidae), do not show it. There is meagre evidence for moth navigation in that the same individual moths can sometimes be seen repeatedly visiting a series of nectar-bearing plants or 'sugar' patches, over several days (or nights), implying that they have at least some 'map' of the area in which the plants occur. However, this repetition could be explained by the moths responding to the attractive perfumes or appearances of the plants, rather than the use of a map.

EVIDENCE FOR MIGRATION IN MOTHS

When Williams first published his papers on migration (in the 1930s) and even when he wrote his pioneering book on insect migration in 1958, he had to persuade his readership that insects did actually migrate in significant numbers. Many still believed that, except for a few, exceptional species such as the Convolvulus Hawk (*Herse convolvuli*), most moths did not stray far from their place of emergence. When occasional specimens did turn up beyond their normal range, they were regarded as representatives of very low density breeding populations or to have been carried by humans, or to be of no biological significance. This was not true of all workers, for by 1931 there was an organised effort to collate records of insect migrants in southern Britain and summaries of these collations were published in *The Entomologist*. Williams (1958) set out to show that many specimens will disperse away from the home colony, even in species thought to be generally sedentary in their habits. He and others, like Johnson (1969), were so successful that now it is accepted that there are many species that regularly disperse in this way. Bretherton (1983) sealed this debate and Drake and Gatehouse (1995) have recently produced an extensive review of the topic. The evidence comes from several different sources.

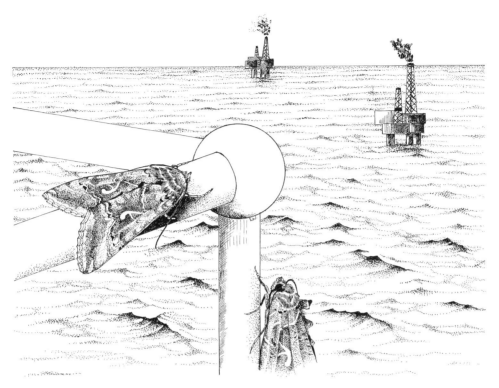

Migrant Silver Y moths (Autographa gamma) *resting on an oil platform in the North Sea.*

Moths at sea

There are now extensive records of moths from lightships and more recently from oil platforms that are well out to sea (e.g. Young, 1984). The numbers recorded and the range of species involved have been surprisingly large, so that we have a better appreciation of the volume of migration and of the fact that normally sedentary species are included. The Brown-spot Pinion (*Agrochola litura*), for example, has been found on an oil platform right in the middle of the North Sea, despite being regarded as a non-migratory species. It is not a regular find, however, and is probably a species in which only a few individuals move a significant distance. The moths on platforms tend to arrive in batches, usually at times when many other insects such as hoverflies (Syrphidae) and lacewings (*Chrysopa* spp.) are also present and bird migrants are arriving at the same time. Such records are incontrovertible evidence for insect migration, for we can rule out the possibility that they have been carried there by human means.

Evidence from light traps

Some moth traps are run directly on coasts known to be the regular landfall sites for migratory birds. Occasionally they attract large numbers of presumed migratory species of moth;

often several species arrive together and may be recorded at other traps set progressively farther from the coast. At times these migrations are sufficiently large for individuals to be seen coming ashore and even for groups to be visible on radar.

The series of traps run by the Rothamsted Insect Survey are well suited for showing the spread of migrants through the country. This has been best demonstrated with abundant migratory species such as the Silver Y (*Autographa gamma*) and the Diamond Back (*Plutella xylostella*). Both of these species are occasionally also crop pests and so the information from the traps provides welcome early warning.

The most voluminous evidence is the accumulated records of specimens well away from their usual habitats, often in association with other apparently migratory species. Bretherton (1983) notes the finding of the first British specimens of Lorimer's Rustic (*Caradrina flavirena*) and the Egyptian Bollworm (*Earias insulana*) on 8/9 October 1967 in different places in England, on a night when many other migrant species were also found. Often the specimens are of a form that only breeds abroad. For example, the Great Brocade (*Eurois occulta*) is an almost black species in its British breeding range in central and western Scotland but migratory specimens, which usually appear in August or September in eastern areas, are pale grey. Similarly, the Rannoch Looper (*Semiothisa brunneata*) is much paler and slightly larger, when a migrant in southern England, than in its breeding range in Scotland.

This evidence has grown to such an extent that nobody now doubts that many species regularly migrate (in the wide sense of the word) and that most species have occasional wanderers. A series of collations of yearly moth migrants in the *Entomologist's Record* in recent years, produced by Chalmers-Hunt, Bretherton and latterly Skinner, has allowed a worthwhile analysis of the underlying patterns of migration and its frequency.

WHICH SPECIES MIGRATE?

Moths from many families migrate but the larger size of some ensures them disproportionate attention. Table 8 sets out the numbers of regular migrants, excluding strays, found in Britain. The data for this table are taken from Emmet (1991a) and include all species that he has listed as 'M' – migrant; 'MB' – breeding migrant that arrives in the spring and then breeds over the summer; and 'ER M' – extinct species that was formerly a resident but is now merely a migrant. This list updates that of Bretherton (1983).

Such data present many uncertainties, principally how to interpret occasional occurrences and whether some species have been inadvertently moved through human activity. Nevertheless, it is immediately clear that there are enormous differences between families. To some extent it is true that it is the large species that migrate but this must be considered against the background that many observers either do not notice or do not record the micro's. That small species can migrate is attested by the Diamond Back (*Plutella xylostella*), which is a world-wide and long-distance migrant of great abundance. However, the almost complete lack of migrants amongst micro's is probably genuine.

Amongst the larger species there are also great differences, for some families and subfamilies, such as the Plusiinae, seem to have a disproportionately large number of migrants. Some divisions of the Pyralidae, Sphingidae, Plusiinae and Heliothinae also seem to have a high proportion of migrants; with significant numbers amongst the Lymantriidae, the Arctiidae and the other Noctuidae.

TABLE 8 *The numbers of migrant species among British moths (excluding occasional strays).*

Families	Number of migrant species (% of overall number of species in family)	Overall number of species
Micropterigidae – Sesiidae (18 families)	0	384
Choreutidae	1	6
Glyphipterigidae – Heliodidae (3 families)	0	10
Yponomeutidae	2 (4%)	75
Epermenidae – Elachistidae (4 families)	0	157
Oecophoridae	?2	90
Gelechiidae – Scythriidae (5 families)	0	199
Tortricidae	1	366
Alucitidae	0	1
Pyralidae	31 (14%)	190
Pterophoridae	?1	38
(Next 5 families butterflies)		
Hesperidae	0	11
Papilionidae	3 (43%)	7
Pieridae	10 (71%)	14
Lycaenidae	6 (21%)	28
Nymphalidae	12 (25%)	48
Lasiocampidae	1	12
Saturnidae – Endromidae	0	3
Drepanidae	1	7
Thyatiridae	0	9
Geometridae	25 (8%)	310
Sphingidae	10 (43%)	23
Notodontidae	4 (15%)	27
Lymantridae	3 (27%)	11
Arctiidae	9 (26%)	35
Nolidae	1	5
Noctuidae	93 (39%)	415
(Heliothinae	6 (75%)	8)
(Plusiinae	12 (52%)	23)

It is difficult to be sure why this should be. It is possible to claim that only larger species have the muscle power to travel great distances, although aphids somewhat belie this, and the micro *Plutella xylostella* travels to Britain from the Baltic states and may cover 1000 km a day without feeding! It is also noticeable that there are very few migrants amongst tree-feeding species, such as the leaf-mining Nepticulidae, whereas many exist among species that feed predominantly on grasses and low-plants (that might be claimed to include many 'weed' species), such as the Noctuidae.

WHERE DO MIGRANTS COME FROM?

Only rarely do observations from abroad about the departures of migrants coincide with observations of subsequent arrivals in Britain. (This is more common with the day-flying butterflies.) More often migrants are tracked back along air streams, relying on the generality that they travel mostly down-wind. Further evidence of origin is the usual breeding distributions of the species concerned, or more usefully the particular form of the species that is migrating. Putting these pieces of evidence together there is little doubt about the usual origin of many species (Bretherton, 1983). Most regular and common migrants, such as *Udea ferrugalis*, the Dark Sword Grass (*Agrotis ipsilon*) or the Gem (*Orthonama obstipata*), come from the south, including the Mediterranean, Spain and North Africa. A small number, illustrated by the Eastern Bordered Straw (*Heliothis nubigera*) or the Scarce Bordered Straw (*H. armigera*), come from the south-eastern Mediterranean (Pedgley, 1985), but more, such as the Great Brocade (*Eurois occulta*) or Eversmann's Rustic (*Ochropleura fennica*), come from the Baltic or eastern European states. Some, like the Purple Cloud (*Actinotia polyodon*), may be strays from immediately across the Channel. The most intriguing are the very few that have come from North America; Stephen's Gem (*Autographa biloba*) is the only one likely to have come under its own power. The two specimens so far recorded were found in Devon and west Wales; one was coincident with several American bird migrants. Other American species, such as the Giant Leopard (*Hypercombe scribonia*) that was found on the outer wall of a warehouse in Aberdeen the day after some containers from Texas were unloaded, seem to be accidental importations (Young, 1995).

The 'classic' migrants to Britain include several hawk moths. The day-flying Hummingbird Hawk moth (*Macroglossum stellatarum*) is seen somewhere almost every year, as is the more common Convolvulus Hawk (*Herse convolvuli*). Less frequently, the Death's Head Hawk (*Acherontia atropos*) visits Britain and it has frequently been found on oil platforms (unfortunately often in sad condition, because its startling appearance has led to it being swatted).

The general annual pattern is that some individuals of many species arrive in Britain in the spring and early summer but not generally in the masses that are seen later. There is something of a lull in mid-summer and then many species arrive in late summer and autumn, although these may be mixed with the offspring of the spring arrivals. In 1994, there was a small migration of Silver Ys in May/June and their resultant larvae were reported as a pest on various crops, including carrots and oil-seed rape. These emerged as adults in August and September and produced the largest numbers of specimens ever seen in Scotland.

No satisfactory explanation has been produced for why northerly migration continues into the autumn, often at a time when there is also some slim evidence of a southern movement by the offspring of the summer migrants. The many Convolvulus Hawks that appear in October must surely die in the first frosts and so the behaviour does not seem to be adaptive. When specimens reach oil platforms at that time the wind directions usually suggest that these have moved out in a north-easterly direction from the British mainland, rather than north-westerly from the Continent. Similar losses of northerly migrants occur in all areas; for example, in the USA many moths make long-distance northerly migrations in the spring and early

FIG 20   *Backtracks of the Cotton Bollworm* (Heliothis zea) *from the Gulf of Mexico to Arkansas and Tennessee in March 1981, in relation to a typical weather pattern, a mid-latitude depression. Solid line arrow – high altitude; dashed line arrow - surface.* (*Source: Johnson, 1995*)

summer, typically following the prevailing airstreams between low pressure in the centre of the continent and high pressure over the western Atlantic. The Cotton Bollworm (*Heliothis zea*) frequently spreads north from central America in this way (Johnson, 1995).

MASS ARRIVALS AND YEARS OF ABUNDANCE

Often large swarms of individuals arrive together and Bretherton (1983) records an occasion when hundreds of Silver Ys settled together on a lighted sheet near the south coast, only for almost all of them to fly off later, moving inland. Another common feature is for several species to arrive in Britain on the same nights. Some years seem to be good for several species but Bretherton listed the years in which various species have been most abundant and these do not necessarily coincide. For example, over 500 Striped Hawks (*Hyles lineata*) were seen in 1943 but few other species were common; over 400 White-speck (*Mythimna unipuncta*) were recorded in 1966, with no other species in attendance; whereas in 1982 seven species all had an atypically abundant year. The most regular migrants seem to share years of abundance but the scarcest species seem to have their own particular years of abundance, unrelated to most others.

RETURN MIGRATION – DOES IT WORK?

As noted above, there is evidence that some species of moth migrate southwards in the autumn, at least in small numbers. Silver Ys have been seen moving offshore from the south coast but most other migrant species are not in sufficient numbers to allow this sort of observation. Baker (1978) provides a similar example from China, involving the

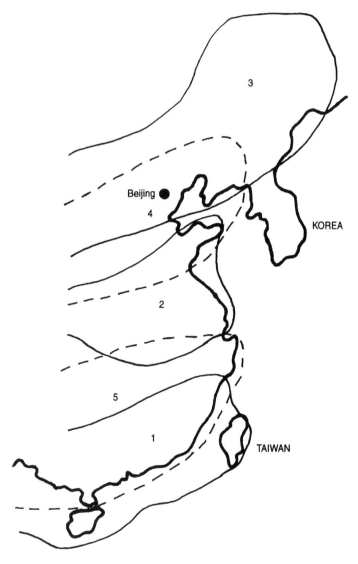

FIG 21   *The regions where successive generations of Oriental Armyworm moths* (Mythimna separata) *breed in China each year. 1 January/March; 2 April/May; 3 June/July; 4 August/September; 5 September/October.* (*Source: Chen et al., 1995*)

mark/release/recapture of the Oriental Army Worm (*Mythimna separata*) (also described in detail by Chen *et al.*, 1995). This species was shown to move northwards in the period from March to July and then there was a smaller southward return in August and September. However, as suggested above for the hawk moths that appear in Britain in the autumn, some specimens are still moving northwards then and as it is certain that they will not survive to breed, they represent a 'loss' to the species. How is such migration favoured by natural selection, since the individuals involved in the movement do not survive to pass on their 'migratory' genes – the 'pied piper' effect?

The answer to this puzzling question must be sought in the wider context of dispersal around a whole range of areas, at many latitudes, rather than just at the extreme northern edge of the migratory range. In the more central parts of the range of a migratory moth there may be many incidences of individuals reaching newly suitable habitats, both in northward movement in the spring and during southward movement in the autumn. These migrating individuals would gain a selective advantage. At some latitude to the north there will be a zone where the advantage can be gained only in climatically favourable years. Usually, individuals that arrive there will be lost but, in periods when climate is warming, this zone may be moved slowly northwards and there will be a great advantage to those individuals that are available to use the newly suitable areas. There is no obvious example involving a moth in Britain but currently there is much debate about whether the Red Admiral butterfly (*Vanessa atalanta*) has overwintered successfully in southern Britain in recent years.

COLONISATION FOLLOWS MIGRATION!

The ultimate evidence of success as a result of migration is the colonisation of new areas, of which there are now many examples in Britain. In some cases the colonisation has been been only temporary and the species have subsequently returned to the status of being irregular migrants. Emmet (1991a) lists six species in this category and they are shown in Table 9; micro's have been omitted because of the greater uncertainty surrounding their records.

These species mostly occurred in south-east England and, since this corresponds to the most continental climate in Britain, this is not surprising. Hamstreet Woods are extensive and unusual in having a high proportion of aspen, which favoured the Clifden Nonpareil (*Catocala fraxini*). Chalmers-Hunt suggests that the Lunar Double-stripe (*Minucia lunaris*) became resident just after the 1939–45 war when young foliage was available in abundance on newly cut oak stools, but then disappeared as this favoured foodplant declined as the oaks grew up again.

Bruun (1992) has made a study of the changes in the Lepidoptera of a group of islands off the Finnish coast, between 1954 and 1989, using many different trapping techniques in a standardised way. Of the 513 species of butterflies and moths recorded in 1954, 58 have become extinct; 33 previously common are now threatened; 73 migrant or stray species have been found; and 10 species have colonised. This illustrates clearly the changeability of the fauna. Most of the losses were in the 1970s, among species that overwinter as larvae, perhaps for climatic reasons, but radioactive dust from Chernobyl in 1986 led to significant declines in 1986 and 1987. This was complicated by a cool summer in 1987, which did not allow sufficient development time for some species which feed up as larvae in the summer

TABLE 9   *Species of larger moth that were once colonisers in Britain but are now occasional migrants.*

Species	Date of residence	Area of residence
Arctornis l-nigrum Black V moth	1947–60	Bradwell-on-Sea, Essex
?Lithophane lambda Nonconformist	?1865–1938	Surrey & Cambs
?Blepharita satura Beautiful Arches	19th century	East Midlands
Trigonophora flammea Flame Brocade	1855–92	Sussex
Catocala fraxini Clifden Nonpareil	early 1930s 1935–64	Norfolk Hamstreet, Kent
Minucia lunaris Lunar Double-stripe	1942–58 early 1950s	Hamstreet, Kent Laughton, Sussex

FIG 22   *The northern limit of the area in Europe where the European Corn-borer* (Ostrinia nubilalis) *can achieve two generations. —— climate 1951/1980; – · – · – · climate 2020, assuming a rise of up to 1.5°C; – – – – climate 2020, assuming 1.5–2.5°C rise.* (*Source: Porter, 1995*)

and emerge as adults in autumn. Migrants to Bruun's islands were frequently back-tracked to Britain and France but there were some from the south-east as well.

MOTHS AND CLIMATIC WARMING

Porter (1995) has modelled climatic warming and its potential effect on the European Corn-borer (*Ostrinia nubilalis*). He predicts that the most likely increase in temperature may result in the spread of the species into Britain, perhaps as far north as the Midlands. The crop that is its foodplant, Sweet-corn (*Zea mays*), is already grown to a small extent in south-eastern Britain and will probably become more common if the climate warms. Williams and Liebhold (1995) make similar predictions for two forest pests in North America, namely the Gypsy moth (*Lymantria dispar*) and the Spruce Bud-worm (*Choristoneura occidentalis*). If both the ambient temperature and precipitation increase, the outbreak areas will extend dramatically, whereas if only temperature increases there may be a decrease in outbreaks.

It is the ability of a moth to make the changes described above, so that it constantly extends or retracts its range to match the extent of suitable environment, that is the real test of migration. All species have some ability to spread to new sites but some are so sedentary that this process is very slow.

CHAPTER 4

Life Cycles and Hibernation

WHAT IS A LIFE CYCLE?

THE success of any animal's life is judged by the number of offspring that it produces. Successful individuals place more copies of their genetic material in the next generation than do the unsuccessful; they are favoured by natural selection in the process of evolution. Consequently, the preoccupation of all species, including moths, is to reproduce as freely as possible and the early stages of their lives are merely devices to ensure that the reproductive stage is reached quickly. All of the specialised and intricate structures of the eggs, larvae, pupae and adults are really servants to the eggs and sperm that will combine to form the next generation.

The life cycle of a moth represents the time-scale for development of the various stages between hatching and final reproduction. The life cycle strategy is the characteristic pattern of development of the species in relation to the external environment, which serves to complete the development effectively. The best solution is not necessarily to mature as soon as possible, for the adult moth may then be very small and will produce relatively few eggs. A larger moth, which will take longer to mature, may also contain more eggs, or the same number of larger eggs, and each species reaches a different compromise between adult size and generation time. Some have short generation times, others lay many eggs. Another compromise is the size of each egg. Large eggs have large food stores and the resultant larvae are better able to establish themselves in the environment; however, a moth can produce only a relatively small number of large eggs. Small eggs result in small and vulnerable larvae but can be carried in large numbers. The Sword-grass (*Xylena exsoleta*) is a large moth but lays many small eggs; some Hepialidae produce up to 18 000 (Thompson and Pellmyr, 1991), whereas the Small Elephant Hawk moth (*Deilephila porcellus*), which is more or less the same size, lays many fewer (c. 80–100) but much larger eggs.

CONTINUOUS DEVELOPMENT OR SEASONAL PATTERNS?

If food resources were unlimited, if there were no predators or diseases, and if the climate was constantly warm and moist, there would be no reason why moths should not proceed through a series of short, unhindered generations rapidly, but such Utopian conditions do not apply. The climate is rarely equable for long; food resources are often in short supply

82

Egg-laying by a Kentish Glory moth (Endromis veriscolora).

and many diseases and predators assail all stages of a moth. Consequently, each life cycle is compromised in many ways and cannot continue unchecked. This chapter considers the various ways in which moth life cycle strategies work, to allow moths to adjust to different environmental situations.

There are hardly any places that have truly aseasonal climates, for even in stable tropical areas there are often slightly drier or wetter seasons. However, even if there were fully aseasonal conditions, it might be advantageous to have synchronised life cycles. For example, if adult appearance is synchronised, mate-finding is facilitated. Consequently, moths generally show cyclical periods of adult occurrence, with concomitant larval seasons. If there are species that feed as larvae on food resources that are genuinely available throughout the year, scattered so that there is little reliance on a specific habitat, then perhaps there may be moths with continuous, asynchronous broods. By analogy to house flies (*Fannia* and *Musca* spp.), which feed on randomly and unpredictably scattered corpses and caches of decaying organic material and have little organisation in their life cycles, one finds such moths among the Tineidae (many of which are continuously brooded and feed in old nests and on old fungi even in seasonal climates), and among the pests of stored grain (such as the Gelechiid *Sitotroga cerealella*) but such examples are rare. Most moths are seasonal to a greater or lesser extent.

LIVING IN A SEASONAL ENVIRONMENT

The great majority of moths live in climates that show variation, and on foodplants that are also affected by the climate and so show their own seasonality. Although extreme heat and excessive rainfall can be disadvantageous, generally it is cooler or drier weather that presents more problems for moths. Because they are ectotherms (that is they rely on external heat sources), moths have to use behavioural methods, such as basking in the sun, to warm up to ideal body temperatures, and this may be difficult in cool weather. They also usually depend on plants for their source of water; in dry weather this may be limited and they will also lose more water themselves into the dry air. The respective life strategy responses to severe periods of cold or drought are hibernation and aestivation.

HOW MANY GENERATIONS IN EACH SEASON?

Usual patterns in temperate climates

In southern Britain, which might be said to have a typical temperate climate, with cool wet winters and mild, rather drier summers, there are two almost equally common life cycle types amongst moths. Some species have only one generation each year, such as the Peach Blossom (*Thyatira batis*) (Emmet, 1991a). The adults of this species emerge in early- to mid-summer, often in June, and feed, mate and lay eggs in a brief adult life of perhaps 5–10 days. The eggs also have a short life before the larvae hatch in July to feed on Bramble (*Rubus fructicosus* agg.), reaching full size and pupating in September or even October. The moths overwinter as pupae, adults emerging the following June. Presumably the temperature of normal British summers is not sufficiently high to allow the larvae to develop in time to produce a second generation in the same year. A great many species share this univoltine habit, from some small micro's, such as the Gelechiid *Teliodes proximella* to the hawk moths (e.g. Pine Hawk *Hyloicus pinastri*).

In this typical life cycle, the adult emerges at a time of year when it is sufficiently warm to allow economical flight and when flowers are available to provide nectar as fuel. The larvae also feed at a temperature that permits digestion to proceed fast enough to keep the larval growing season reasonably short. The limitation on the growth rate of a larva is probably the rate of digestion. Larvae can pack food into their gut rapidly, as anyone watching a hawk moth larva systematically devouring a leaf will know, but since larvae are cold-blooded the digestive enzymes have to operate at the ambient temperature. Most enzymes work at maximum speed at around 35°C, but this temperature is never reached in the shade in a British summer and so digestion will be slower than it could be. To speed things up and shorten larval growth periods, many larvae bask in the sun (if, like burnet larvae they are protected from visual predators in some way). Those that have to remain hidden in shade by day can grow only rather slowly. Butterfly larvae, such as the High Brown Fritillary (*Argynnis adippe*) (Warren, 1995) have been shown to increase their rate of digestion dramatically by basking in sheltered sunny locations. In the typical univoltine moth life cycle the pupa then overwinters, completely immobile during the cold months, thus each stage is appropriately timed to match environmental conditions.

If the summer weather is particularly warm, a few larvae of the Peach Blossom feed up rapidly and produce pupae in August; from these hatch a second generation of adults in August or September. The adults mate and lay eggs but it is not certain how many of the resultant larvae complete their feeding in time to avoid the cold weather of winter. Perhaps the second generation is a loss in this species. However, there are many species that routinely produce two broods of adults in each year, ranging from tiny leaf miners such as *Phyllonorycter rajella*, which lives as a larva in blister mines on Alder (*Alnus glutinosa*), to noctuids like the Small Square-spot (*Diarsia rubi*). Typically these species have an adult emergence in spring or early summer, followed by a second in late summer.

Mediterranean life cycles

Yela and Herrera (1993) have studied the life cycles of moths in the Mediterranean area. Typically there is a mild and damp winter period with a rigorous hot and dry summer and in these circumstances the main problems for plants and moths come in the summer, when water is in short supply.

Larvae of moths are most abundant in spring and early summer, when the plants are growing vigorously. There are then two peaks of adult occurrence, in early summer and in early autumn, with a distinct trough in mid-summer; the peaks correspond to the emergence of 'short duration' and 'long duration' pupae. Species emerging in early summer either mate and lay eggs, which then delay hatching until the autumn, or aestivate as adults, before re-emerging and mating in late summer. The 'long duration pupa' species emerge and mate in early autumn. Larvae then feed in autumn and winter, but especially in the spring, so taking advantage of the main period of plant growth. Although there are many evergreen shrubs in Mediterranean plant communities, larvae tend not to feed on them during the summer, when the plants are drought-stressed.

Adult moths that emerge in winter

A most interesting variation on the first of the life cycle patterns is shown by a group of Geometridae species that emerge as adults in the winter. There are species that emerge in late autumn, like the 'November' moths, which include the Autumnal moth (*Epirrita autumnata*), emerging in September and October; the Pale November moth (*E. christyi*) in October and early November; and the November moth (*E. dilutata*) in November. These have to cope with very cool and wet conditions, as do the two 'Winter' moths, (*Operophtera brumata* and *O. fagata*). The Mottled Umber (*Erannis defoliaria*) may emerge as a moth in December and the Pale Brindled Beauty (*Apocheima pilosaria*) is the first of the new season's moths, emerging as an adult in mild spells in January and February. A small succession of other species follows through into the spring. These may

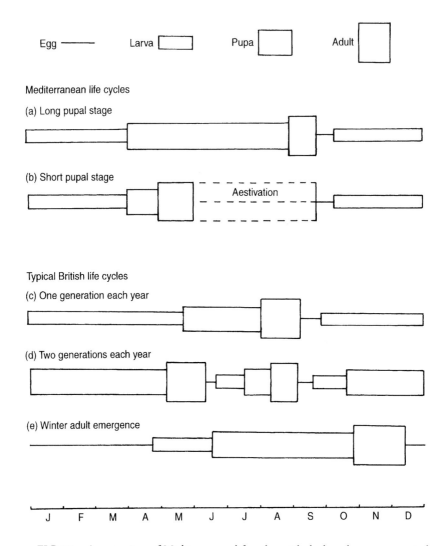

FIG 23   *A comparison of Mediterranean life cycles, with the hot, dry summer period passed as a pupa or an aestivating adult, with typical British life cycles.*

all share the benefit of the relative shortage of predators active in the winter, migratory insectivorous birds being absent and bats and spiders largely quiescent, but there is little nectar and the air temperatures are very cold for flight. Most of these species do not feed as adults and a common occurrence is for the heavy-bodied females to be wingless and for the males to fly slowly to the females on atypically mild or still winter dusks. Sattler (1991) notes that most wingless species are cold season species from northern temperate regions, although there are also such species on small islands, where flightlessness is associated with avoiding the problem of being blown off the island! There are also some wingless species in mountainous places, where cold conditions make flight energetically inefficient.

The effects of latitude on moth life cycles

Even in southern England univoltine species outnumber those that are bivoltine, but in Scotland there are very few moths that can complete two generations in one year. Some of the leaf mining *Phyllonorycter* species are double-brooded but almost none of the macro's achieves it, with the exception of the Garden Carpet (*Xanthorhoe fluctuata*) and the Grey Pine carpet (*Thera obeliscata*). Even the Brimstone moth (*Opisthograptis luteolata*), which apparently manages three overlapping generations in southern England, is almost always univoltine in Aberdeenshire, and on Shetland none of the larger moths is bivoltine (Pennington, 1995). It is a very common observation that species which are bivoltine in the south of Britain are univoltine in the north. Good examples are the Small Square-spot (*Diarsia rubi*), the Common Wainscot (*Mythimna pallens*), the Swallow Prominent (*Pheosia tremula*), the Common White Wave (*Cabera pusaria*), the Common Carpet (*Epirrhoe alternata*) and the pyralid *Pyrausta purpuralis*. The real interest lies at the transition band for these species. How is the switch achieved?

WHAT CONTROLS THE START OF OVERWINTERING?

The control of whether development will proceed, or whether an overwintering stage will be entered, has been studied extensively in butterflies but only a little in moths. The most common cue that stimulates a larva to enter its overwintering state is photo-period, but this may interact with temperature. Tauber *et al.* (1986) review the evidence and conclude that in general, if a larva of a bivoltine species experiences a declining day-length, which passes below a certain level, then it proceeds to overwinter. This applies to the Comma butterfly (*Polygonia c-album*) in Sweden, for example (Nylin, 1989). However, temperature may interact with day-length, either indirectly, whereby high temperatures allow a larva to develop quickly and so pass the critical developmental stage before minimal light levels are reached, or directly, so that the lowering light level will have no effect unless the temperature is also below a critical level. By such means the bivoltine species 'control' whether they proceed rapidly into the next generation or move to an overwintering stage. In species of moths that sometimes have a partial second generation, it is probable that the indirect effect of temperature, allowing some larvae to grow beyond the light sensitive stage, produces the extra brood.

Possibly, as one proceeds north in Britain, with gradually cooler summer temperatures, progressively fewer larvae grow beyond the light sensitive stage and so the second generation is gradually lost. Evidence for this theory is the appearance in unusually warm summers of occasional examples of second brood individuals of species that are usually univoltine in an area. In late 1994 and 1995, for example, a few Small Square-spot (*D. rubi*) and Brimstone moths (*O. luteolata*) were caught in Aberdeenshire. Unless these were strays from farther south, (which is unlikely for the Small Square-spot at least, for they were of the typically large Scottish form, rather than the smaller second brood English type), they argue for the possibility of flexible control of voltinism, with the bivoltine habit spreading north in warm years.

However, Pullin (1986, quoted in Dennis, 1993) has shown for the Small Tortoiseshell butterfly (*Aglais urticae*) that, although southern British populations show a typical response to declining photo-period, northern populations invariably produce only one generation. (In this species the adult overwinters and all adults from Aberdeenshire hibernate before reproducing.) Similarly, Lees and Archer (1980) found that all mid-summer adults of the Green-veined White butterfly (*Pieris napi*) in Scotland produced offspring that proceeded to overwinter, whereas only some of those in southern England did so. These cases show that some populations from Scotland may not have the capacity to produce two generations. Presumably they differ genetically from individuals from farther south and even warm summers will not induce the production of a second brood.

BOUNDARIES BETWEEN SINGLE AND DOUBLE BROODED RACES OF MOTHS

The boundary between single and double brooded races of moths is never easy to fix. 'Northern England' is the nearest that can often be applied but this is confounded by altitudinal and habitat effects. For example, the Small Square-spot (*D. rubi*) has either a separate race, or a sibling species, the Fen Square-spot (*D. florida*), that is invariably univoltine, even in East Anglia, where it lives in fens and marshes. *D. rubi* is wholly bivoltine in the drier parts of East Anglia, as it is up into Northumberland, on low ground, but it is usually univoltine in all of Scotland and on the Pennines in northern England. The univoltine Scottish race has the larger and paler appearance of the Fen Square-spot – is it conspecific with the Fen Square-spot as a distinct species, or are the Fen Square-spot and the Scottish individuals merely univoltine examples of the same species as the bivoltine Small Square-spot? Cross breeding would help to resolve this problem.

If the control of the number of generations per season were purely the result of temperature effects on larval growth rate, there would seem to be great risk of species producing partial broods and of losing many larvae that had been left with too little warm weather in which to feed and grow. By analogy with Pullin's work on Small Tortoiseshell butterflies, there may be a gradual increase in the day-length required to lead to a second brood at increasing latitudes. In Scotland even 24 hours of daylight does not induce direct development in this butterfly, whereas in central England 18 hours permits direct development and in southern England even 14 hours will do so. Unfortunately, no-one knows how all this is controlled in moths.

If climatic warming is a reality, it can be predicted that there will be a shift northwards of the zone where single and double brooded populations of moths occur.

SPECIES REQUIRING MORE THAN ONE YEAR FOR EACH GENERATION

In Britain some species take longer than one year to complete their life cycle. The Pine Gall moth (*Retinia resinella*) emerges in summer and lays eggs, which hatch soon afterwards. The larvae then feed in a pine twig, inducing a resinous gall that gradually increases in size. The larvae overwinter and then continue to feed throughout the next summer; they overwinter

FIG 24   *The approximate current boundary between the univoltine and bivoltine races of the Small Square-spot* (Diarsia rubi). *The main division is between the northern and upland univoltine populations and the southern and lowland bivoltine populations.* 'D. florida' *is a disputed univoltine taxon, which has been found in marshy ground in Yorkshire, Fenland and some localities in Wales and Cumbria (not all shown). (Source: Bretherton et al., 1979)*

again before pupating in the gall in the spring, followed by the emergence of the moth two years after its parents. A similar life style and two-year cycle is followed by *Cydia millenniana*, which forms galls in Larch (*Larix* spp.) twigs. The Reed Leopard (*Phragmataecia castaneae*) does more or less the same, feeding inside a reed stem, as do some clearwings (Sesiidae), which feed on wood. The larva of the Goat moth (*Cossus cossus*) also feeds in the trunks of trees and may overwinter four times. In these cases it seems to be the poor nutritional quality of the foodstuff that dictates the slow growth rate. The larvae, however, are in a protected environment, where predation and parasitism may be lower than normal.

NORTHERN AND MOUNTAIN SPECIES

Northern and mountain species may also have multi-year life cycles but in this case the limiting factor seems to be the cool temperatures and so the length of the growing season. The extreme example seems to be the lymantriid *Gynaephora groenlandica*, which is found in

Greenland and takes up to 14 years to complete development. It emerges and lays eggs in one year, larvae hatch and by the end of the second year they have reached the third instar. Each succeeding instar then takes up to three years to complete, before the larvae are fully grown and pupate. The larvae can feed for only a matter of a few weeks in mid-summer and each day the air temperatures only allow them to begin feeding towards midday. They then feed a little before basking in the afternoon sun, during which their body temperature rises to 20°C, allowing the digestion of that day's very small meal (Bale, in press).

This example is an extreme one, but there are many arctic and montane species that take more than one year to complete their growth. In Britain, this applies to the Black Mountain moth (*Psodos coracina*), the Mountain Burnet (*Zygaena exulans*) and the Northern Dart (*Xestia alpicola*), for example. The last species belongs to a genus that is typically northern in distribution. The life cycles of *Xestia* species have been studied extensively in Scandinavia by Mikkola (1976) and others. They found that most species showed a multi-year life cycle, usually with a two-year pattern, but occasionally with three. This resulted from the same problem that afflicts *G. groenlandica*, namely that there is insufficient time during the cool summer for full growth to take place in one season. In a general way this can be expressed as the number of days available with a temperature above a certain level, or as the product of degrees temperature and days (degree-days). Each species requires a given number of degree-days for full growth by its larvae and, if the summer season does not supply this, the life cycle extends to a second year.

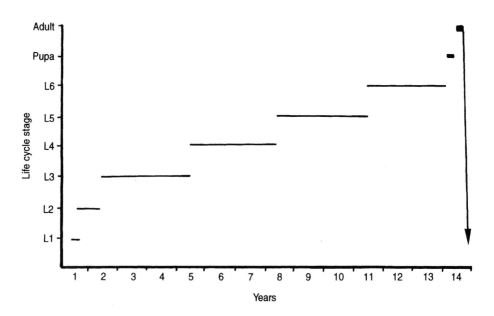

FIG 25   *The life cycle of* Gynaephora groenlandica (*Lymantriidae*) *in Greenland. The adults emerge, lay eggs which hatch and the larvae moult once in the first year but later larval stages take several years for completion. (Redrawn from Bale, in press, with permission from Blackwells Scientific)*

SYNCHRONY OF EMERGENCE IN MULTI-YEAR LIFE CYCLES

If the climate in a northern or montane zone results in some years not being really suitable for adult moths, it could be highly advantageous for some adults to appear each year, rather than all appearing synchronously in a year that happened to be climatically unsuitable. However, there are contrasting advantages to synchronised emergence, as reviewed by Heliovaara *et al.* (1994). It helps assure mating; it may reduce parasitism (if large larvae are not present every year, although parasites could surely adopt suitably synchronised life cycles); and it may reduce predation. A predator of either the adults or the larvae would find a superabundance present one year, perhaps swamping its ability to harvest them all, but a dearth the following year. In Scandinavia, several species cycle together, as shown for *Xestia* species in Figure 26; this tends to exaggerate the swamping effect on predators, but there is no direct evidence that it is really important and in some areas the multiple synchrony breaks down. Interestingly, the Pine Gall moth (*Retinia retinella*) has a three-year development period near the northern limits of its distribution in Scandinavia and there the usual synchrony of adult emergence also fails. Perhaps it is a combination of factors that leads to synchrony.

Why should synchrony be so strictly maintained? If some moths emerged in the 'wrong' year, why would this not lead to an eventual breakdown of the regularity? Of course, it could easily be that such irregular emergers would merely fail to find mates but Heliovaara and Vaisanen (1988) have suggested an alternative explanation in the case of *R. resinella*, which might also apply to other species. They wonder if the presence of actively feeding and large larvae in one year, leads to the development by the host plant of induced chemical

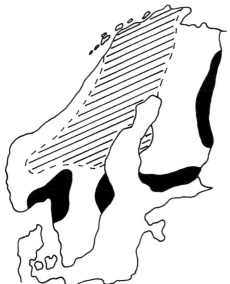

FIG 26 *The distribution of even-year and odd-year broods of* Xestia *spp.* (Noctuidae) *in Scandinavia. At least 10 species are synchronised in most of these areas.* ■ *odd-year broods;* ▨ *even-year broods;* ☐ *mixed broods.* (*Source: Heliovaara et al., 1994 with permission from Elsevier Press*).

defences (resins) that render the plant unpalatable in the following year, followed by a decline in resins, so that the tree is again usable in the next year. If this were so, the larvae of any moths from the 'wrong' year would not be able to feed successfully. This speculation has not been tested.

Whatever the cause, it is well established that adults of the Northern Dart (*Xestia alpicola*) are more common in even years, and the Black Mountain moth (*Psodos coracina*) in odd years, in the central Highlands of Scotland. However, it seems that *X. alpicola* is an 'odd year' species on the northern Pennines in England.

DELAYED EMERGENCE FROM PUPAE – BET-HEDGING

In the section above it was suggested that for all the population to emerge in one year in an area where the climate was unreliable might be a risky strategy. If the entire emergence period of the species was too cold and/or damp to allow mating and egg-laying, the species would be in severe trouble. The only way to avoid this is for some individuals to lie over to succeeding years – this strategy is known as 'bet-hedging'.

This can take different forms, but the most common is for the moth to remain for more than one year in the pupal stage. In northern Britain and in other cool countries this is a common strategy. Smaller species, micro's, do not seem to use it and there seems to be a greater tendency for it to happen as the size of the moth increases. The large Kentish Glory (*Endromis versicolora*) is very well known in this respect. The pupae are formed in loosely woven cocoons among the litter at the soil surface and just before emergence the moth in the pupal case forces its way through the silk of the cocoon, so that the adult can escape easily. Many pupae produce moths in the first year after they are formed but a significant number emerge either in the following year or up to four years later (Young, 1991). Leverton (1994) believes that this behaviour is found at least occasionally in most large Scottish species – perhaps the Scottish weather is rightly not to be trusted. Certainly the Kentish Glory emerges in late spring and there are years in which this can be very cold and wet in the Highland valleys, where the species is found. The Rannoch Sprawler (*Brachionycha nubeculosa*) is another large species that also lives in the Highland valleys and emerges even earlier in the season than the Kentish Glory. It too may spend several years in the pupal stage. Several of the Acronictinae, including the Miller (*Acronicta leporina*), also frequently pass two or more years in the pupal stage.

The Small Eggar (*Eriogaster lanestris*) is found sporadically across central and south-western Britain, where its larvae live in communal nests on hedges and bushes of Hawthorn (*Crataegus* spp.) or Sloe (*Prunus spinosa*). They are interesting partly because they will only feed and thrive when in groups in full sunshine. Once they are full-fed, they disperse before spinning tough, brown cocoons and sometimes stay in these for up to seven years, although most hatch after two years. Hatching can be encouraged by putting the cocoons in sunshine at the time of normal emergence. Obviously, the adult moth is formed up in the pupa, ready to emerge, and the wait is spent in this stage. This moth is found in southern areas, but the adults emerge in February and March, when it is frequently snowy and cold. Thus, the moth has to contend with unpredictable weather.

SPECIES ON THE ATLANTIC FRINGE – LARVAL DIAPAUSE

A very unusual form of bet-hedging is found amongst the burnet moths (Zygaenidae) that live along the Atlantic coast of Britain. Although the climate they encounter is very mild, it is also very wet and there are frequent cloudy spells, even in mid-summer when the adult moths fly. These species are essentially sun lovers, flying only when the sun shines, and so some years they may fare very badly.

The way they overcome such problems is not by pupae lying over – perhaps their papery cocoons, which are generally exposed and not very robust, would not survive this. Instead, the larvae may spend additional seasons in diapause. The larvae enter their first hibernation in an early instar and then the following spring they emerge and moult. Some then begin feeding but others immediately return to diapause and do not emerge again until the following spring. This may even be repeated more than once. The result is that not all of the population will fly in any one season and so inclement weather may be survived (Tremewan, 1985).

MICRO-CLIMATE EFFECTS

Burnet moths also show a very pronounced preference for particular micro-habitats. The Slender Scotch Burnet (*Zygaena loti*) lives only on steep and unstable slopes very close to the sea in western Scotland. This on its own assures relatively warm conditions, for the closeness of the sea prevents frosts and the slope, which tends to be perpendicular to the sun, ensures that the place will be warm when the sun is shining. In addition, the female lays her eggs only where the foodplant, Bird's-foot Trefoil (*Lotus corniculatus*), grows adjacent to an eroded patch or hollow of bare soil. This hollow offers shelter and warmth, accentuated by the dark basaltic colour of the soil. This warms up easily and the larvae spend much of their time basking on the hot surface, digesting their meals. Although the species occurs so far north and west, the micro-climate that it experiences may well resemble that of much more southerly zones (Ravenscroft, 1994).

Wherever moths are found they show similar, if less pronounced preferences for favourable micro-climates. This is most obvious for species that reach the northern edge of their range in Britain, such as the Fiery Clearwing (*Bembecia chrysidiformis*), which is found only on the sheltered and sunny undercliff of parts of the south coast, despite the fact that its foodplants, docks and sorrels (*Rumex* spp.) are very widespread.

AESTIVATION

In many places, such as the Mediterranean, where the year-round climate is warm enough for continuous activity, there is a distinct wet and dry season and the problem of desiccation during the dry phase may be as acute as that of overcoming cold conditions in higher latitudes. Many moth species aestivate to avoid this problem, a famous example being the Bogong moth (*Agrotis infusa*), whose adults migrate in huge numbers from their breeding grounds in south-eastern Australia to caves in the nearby mountains (Williams, 1958). There they aestivate colonially during the driest months of the year. Many Jersey Tigers

(*Euplagia quadripunctaria*) aestivate clinging to cool rocks in damp, wooded valleys in the hills of the island of Rhodes, before returning to the lowlands to breed.

Aestivation is not confined to sub-tropical or Mediterranean countries, however, for even in Britain some species are known to become inactive during summer. The Dotted Rustic (*Rhyacia simulans*), the Copper Underwing (*Amphipyra pyramidea*) and the Lunar Yellow Underwing (*Noctua orbona*) emerge as adults in July. Although they are occasionally caught then, they mostly disappear until late August and September, when they reappear and start feeding on nectar. In the intervening time they are inactive and some specimens of *R. simulans* have been found in sheds and outhouses (usually as wings in spiders' webs!) and *A. pyramidea* has been found in cellars, so presumably cool, dark sites are favoured. Dacie (1985) reports finding up to 24 Old Lady moths (*Mormo maura*) aestivating in an old air-raid shelter in London during July and August. These months cannot usually be described as hot and dry in Britain and so perhaps this behaviour is really a response more appropriate to specimens farther south in the range of the species.

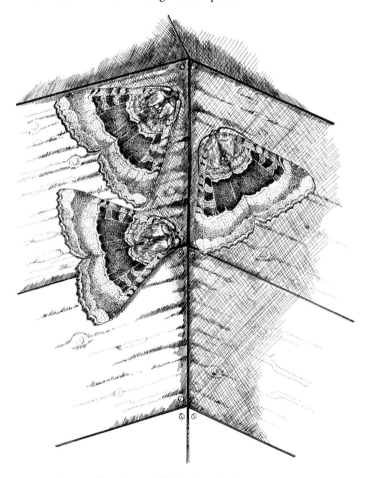

A group of aestivating Old Lady moths (Mormo maura).

PASSING THE WINTER

The advantages of passing the winter as an egg, a larva, a pupa or an adult

In winter a number of adverse factors coincide. The temperature is generally lower, and may include periods below freezing; it is often more windy; rainfall or snow-fall are more frequent; the day-length is much shorter; many foodplants are dormant and unavailable; all factors may combine to make it an unsuitable time for the active stages of a moth's life cycle. It makes one wonder why any species remain in areas where the winter weather is so unfavourable, but if they are to take advantage of the summer conditions in these areas, then they must either overwinter or rely on migration, which obviously carries its own costs.

Not all species of moth will be affected in the same way, for some feed as larvae internally on wood, or inside an old nest or a large bracket fungus, and, although the temperature may drop, the foodstuff is still available and there is no penalty for moving and feeding very slowly. Such species continue feeding throughout the winter.

Most species will not be able to do this and so must find a protected place within which to remain quiescent. Whatever stage they are in over the winter, they must remain largely immobile and must be sheltered from predation and perhaps from the extreme low temperatures. It is interesting to see which stage is present during the winter and to relate this to the life style of the species concerned. Table 10 lists the numbers of species in each family of British moths that pass the winter in each stage of the life cycle. The data were extracted from Emmet (1991a) but continuously brooded species were omitted, as were migrants to Britain, and there are also still many species of micro for which this information is unknown (which is why the final total number of species is only 1777, whereas 2391 are listed by Emmet). For convenience, the overwintering stage was taken as that found during January, as this is the coldest month.

These figures may be compared with those of Seppanen (1969), as quoted in Leather *et al.* (1993), for macro-lepidoptera in Finland. He found that of the 718 species resident (including butterflies), 16% overwintered as eggs, 35% as larvae, 43% as pupae and only 4% as adults. This almost exactly matches the respective figures for British macro-lepidoptera of 17%, 39%, 41% and 3% – an amazing agreement, considering that Finland is so much farther north. A feature of both lists is that there is often great uniformity within one related group, with all but two of the Notodontidae overwintering as pupae, for example, and all the *Mythimna* spp. (Noctuidae) as larvae.

Since the overwintering phase is essentially quiescent, it seems logical to expect that either of the two immobile life cycle stages, the egg and the pupa, would be the predominant overwintering stage. However, this is clearly not the case. Relatively few eggs overwinter, although substantial numbers of pupae do so. If all moths are considered, the main overwintering stage is the larva, suggesting either that there are opportunities for feeding during the winter, despite the obvious lack of green tissue available then, or that it is advantageous to be able to move about a little. Perhaps it helps to be able to adjust position slightly if conditions change. After all, if a secluded overwintering site were accidentally exposed by strong winds, or by inquisitive animals, it would be beneficial to be able to move to a new site. The same could be said for the adult stage but wings are not really useful in winter and it is difficult to envisage adults being able to burrow into sheltered hollows as easily as larvae.

Overwintering as an egg

Eggs are tiny, easily hidden in crevices, so as to reduce predation risks over the winter. However, they can contain only very small food reserves and so may be especially susceptible to running these short during mild spells in winter. If moths are active earlier than autumn, it might be expected that their eggs would hatch after a short time, so that the larvae could take advantage of the feeding period that leads up to winter. (The Dark Bordered Beauty (*Epione paralellaria*) is an exception here; it flies in late July and early August but its eggs do not hatch until the following May. The Rannoch Looper (*Semiothisa brunneata*) also has the same phenology.) Normally only 'autumnal' moths lay eggs that then overwinter and there are relatively few moths that are active so late in the year. Furthermore, a significant proportion of these overwinter as adults, which may help account for the small number of species that overwinter as eggs.

Overwintering larvae

Many of the larvae that overwinter either feed on roots (such as the Orange Swift (*Hepialus sylvina*) which feeds on Bracken (*Pteridium aquilinum*)); or within stems, (such as the Orange-tailed Clearwing (*Synanthedon andrenaeformis*), which feeds on *Viburnum* spp.); or

TABLE 10   *The numbers of species of each family of British moths that overwinter in each life cycle stage.*

Family		Overwintering as:			
	Eggs	Larvae	Pupae	Adults	Note
Micropterigidae		5			
Eriocraniidae			8		1
Hepialidae		5			2
Nepticulidae		10	82		
Tischeriidae		3	2		
Incurvariidae		22	2		
Heliozelidae			5		
Cossidae		3			
Zygaenidae		10			
Limacodidae		2			
Psychidae		17	1		
Tineidae		18			3
Ochsenheimeriidae	1	1			
Lyonetiidae		1	7	3	3
Bucculatricidae		1	7	1	1
Gracillariidae		12	61	17	4
Sesiidae		14			5
Choreutidae		1			1
Glyphipterigidae		3			
Douglasiidae		2			
Helionidae				1	
Yponomeutidae	8	21	8	13	6
Epermeniidae			3	1	
Schreckensteiniidae			1		
Coleophoridae		101			7
Elachistidae		21	1		
Oecophoridae		19	11	28	8

TABLE 10 – *continued*

Family			Overwintering as:		
	Eggs	Larvae	Pupae	Adults	Note
Gelechiidae	1	28	15	4	9
Blastobasidae		2			
Momphidae		7	1	6	
Cosmopterigidae		7			
Scythrididae		1			10
Torticidae					
Cochylinae		46			11
Tortricinae	11	32	4	15	
Olethreutinae	3	147	13	1	12
Alucitidae				1	
Pyralidae		113	9	3	13
Pterophoridae		30		3	
(Butterfly families excluded)					
Lasiocampidae	5	4	2		
Saturniidae			1		
Endromidae			1		
Drepanidae			6		
Thyatiridae	1		8		
Geometridae	41	87	151	7	14
Sphingidae			9		
Notodontidae	2		21		
Lymantridae	3	7	1		
Arctiidae		23	7		
Nolidae		4	1		
Noctuidae					
Noctuinae	3	43	4		
Hadeninae	3	20	37		15
Cucullinae	23	8	11	12	16
Acronictinae		2	14		
Amphipyrinae	37	44	6		
Heliothinae			3		
Acontiinae			4		
Chloephorinae		1	2		
Sarrothripinae				1	
Pantheinae			1		
Plusiinae		9	2		
Catocalinae	4		2		
Ophiderinae	1	4	3	1	
Hypeninae		8	3	2	
OVERALL TOTALS	147	969	541	120	
PERCENTAGE OF TOTAL	8	55	30	7	

Source: Collated from Emmet (1991a).

Migrants and continuously brooded species are not included. Data are not known for many species.

Notes: [1] – All species feed as leaf miners early in the season; [2] – All larvae feed on roots; [3] – Many details unknown; [4] – Family contains several different groups, most of 51 *Phyllonorycter* spp. are leaf miners and pupate in the mine; [5] – All are internal feeders; [6] – Many details unknown; [7] – All larvae case-bearing; [8] – Almost all of the genera *Depressaria* and *Agonopterix* overwinter as adults; [9] – Many details unknown, very varied group; [10] – Most unknown; [11] – Many larvae feed in stems, roots or seeds; [12] – Many larvae are internal feeders; [13] – Many details unknown; [14] – Diverse family, most *Eupithecia* spp. overwinter as pupae, most *Sterrhinae* as larvae; [15] – Many of the adults emerge in early spring; [16] – Many adults fly in autumn.

on decaying organic material (like so many Tineids). They can therefore certainly continue to feed in mild periods during the late autumn and early spring. Even some species that do not feed internally can feed during mild spells in the winter. For example, Archer's Dart (*Agrotis vestigialis*), which uses almost any green plant material, lives on sand dunes and can retreat under the sand surface, where it is sheltered during cold conditions.

Some species overwinter at a very early larval stage but a significant number, such as the Fox moth (*Macrothylacia rubi*), are fully fed and do not feed again in spring before pupating. The larvae of this species emerge to bask in the early spring sunshine but then spin their cocoons immediately; they obviously could move about in winter if necessary. Others, such as the Light Feathered Rustic (*Agrotis cinerea*), the Dark Brocade (*Blepharita adusta*) and many of the Tortricidae, spin their cocoons in the autumn but remain as larvae within them until the spring when they pupate. It is difficult to see the advantage here, for if the cocoons are disturbed the larvae almost invariably die, rather than being able to repair them, or move to another safer site, as might be expected.

Mention has already been made of the Sand Dart (*Agrotis ripae*), which completes its feeding in autumn and then burrows several centimetres into the sand, just above the tide line on sandy shores. In the spring, the larvae return to the surface and then immediately turn and burrow about 15 cm down, where they form a chamber and pupate. This behaviour suggests that the larvae are 'checking' on the level of the sand surface after the winter storms, to avoid their pupation site being either exposed or so deep that the adult could never struggle to the surface.

The Coleophoridae seem to be an exceptional group, in that all of the 100 or so British species overwinter as case-bearing larvae. Perhaps the cases provide particularly good protection against predators and the elements.

Overwintering pupae

Many species overwinter as pupae and this allows early adult emergence in the spring, as soon as conditions are favourable for adult feeding and flight. The *Orthosia* spp. that feed so avidly on the blossoms of 'pussy-willow' (*Salix* spp.) in early spring are the best example of this. Typically, such species then lay eggs that quickly result in larvae, which then feed in the summer period before pupating and remaining until the following spring. This is the classic annual life cycle. In fact, many moths do not emerge from their pupae until early summer, when more flowers are available and the weather is more settled; this still leaves sufficient time for development before the following winter.

Adults in winter

Some adult moths mate in the autumn and only the females survive the winter, good examples being the Brindled Ochre (*Dasypolia templi*) (erroneously reported to mate in the spring by Friedrich, 1986) and the Autumn Green Carpet (*Chloroclysta miata*). In other species both sexes survive and mating takes place in the spring; this applies to the Sword Grass (*Xylena exsoleta*) and some other members of the Cucullinae. At first sight it would seem to be advantageous for mating to take place as soon as possible after emergence in autumn but the females then have to store sperm and this may be energetically demanding. From the female perspective (speaking anthropomorphically) it seems sensible to mate as soon as a male is found, in case overwintering mortality reduces the chances of finding a mate in spring; but the male may view things differently. If he fertilises a female that fails to overwinter then this is a serious loss, whereas, if he waits to mate in the spring, he can be more sure that the chosen female will survive to produce offspring.

The Tissue moth (*Triphosa dubitata*) seems to be an exception to the patterns discussed above. Morris and Collins (1991) observed a colony of overwintering Tissue moths in an old underground building in Surrey and found that matings took place in the building from late October to late November. However, the males did not then die off and some were still seen, close to females, apparently as couples but not actually mating, until the following March. Morris and Collins did not observe matings in the spring, however, and there were always fewer males than females in the hibernation site, even in the autumn. Perhaps this species has a variable strategy. This subject is a field for further speculation and analysis; we do not yet have full information on how many species use the alternatives.

It is not clear why adult moths overwinter at all, rather than laying eggs and letting them do so, but many do move around in the winter and some even feed in mild spells. The Chestnut moth (*Conistra vaccinii*) may be found feeding on sweet plant exudates or winter blossoms at such times, as may the Satellite (*Eupsilia transversa*) (Leverton, *pers. comm.*).

QUIESCENCE OR DIAPAUSE DURING ADVERSE CONDITIONS

The adult Satellite moth that feeds in winter on mild nights has been quiescent during the cold spells. An alternative strategy is to enter a physiological state called diapause in which the organism cannot be quickly roused by local environmental changes. The metabolic rate is not merely lowered but 'switched' into this reduced state; even if the outside temperature rises and warms the diapausing larva, the basal metabolic rate remains low and food reserves are conserved. Such a state is clearly highly advantageous and most overwintering species use it. The mechanism that induces diapause is that the production of the hormones that regulate and advance development is switched off by an external cue, and is then switched on again when diapause is finished. The induction, maintenance and breaking of diapause is well summarised by Leather *et al.* (1993).

The most important environmental cue that acts to induce diapause is the length of the photo-period, although this may interact with other factors. In essence, as the season progresses and the length of daylight reduces, there comes a point when the moth responds by entering diapause. This is very simply illustrated for the parasitic wasp *Cotesia rubecula*. At 20°C and above 15.5 hours of daylight none enters diapause, whereas at 14.5 hours of daylight all do so, with varied proportions in between (Nealis, 1985). The great advantage of responding to photo-period is that it is a reliable indicator of the failing season and so the moth is certain to be in diapause in time to avoid the usual worsening weather in autumn and winter. If temperature were to be used alone there would be the risk that unseasonably warm autumn weather could lead to continued activity, immediately followed by cooler (i.e. normal) weather, which would be fatal to the unprepared larva or adult. The only price of using photo-period is that some unseasonably good weather may be 'wasted' in some years.

In practice, light levels almost always interact with temperature and this may be a simple inhibition of diapause if the temperature is above a certain level. The Codling moth (*Cydia pomonella*) shows this clearly, for if the temperature is low, around 17°C, the critical day-length that induces 50% diapause is 15 hours, whereas if the temperature is higher, around 27°C, the day-length must drop to 13.8 hours before the same proportion enters diapause (Garcia-Salazar *et al.*, 1988). This is the typical pattern and it seems to be related to latitudinal effects. It is generally cooler in the higher latitudes but day-lengths before the equinox are longer than nearer the equator. The cutworm (*Mamestra configurata*) overwinters as a pupa in Canada and, the farther north it occurs, the longer the day-length that will induce diapause, correlating well with natural differences in day-length at various latitudes (Hegdekar, 1983). Riedl and Croft (1978) found a similar relationship between latitude and day-length for the Codling moth (*C. pomonella*) in both North American and European populations.

Temperature is probably less able to act on its own but if the day-length is kept constant, an effect can be shown. For example, the European Corn-borer (*Ostrinia nubilalis*) will enter diapause in constant darkness if it is subjected to a fluctuating temperature regime in which the warm phase is 25°C and the cold phase is 15°C or less (both of 12 hours' duration) (Beck, 1982). For this species the cold phase must last 12 hours or more for the induction to occur.

Other cues that influence diapause

In the Tropics there is little difference in either day-length or temperature and so other cues must apply to tropical species that enter diapause. This can be crowding and/or food shortage, as has been demonstrated for the Indian Meal moth (*Plodia interpunctella*) and the Dried Currant moth (*Ephestia cautella*) (Bell, 1976). These species are both pests of stored food and occasionally find themselves over-crowded on the last remaining food when warehouses are being cleared, or at times of the year between crops. The agent controlling the diapause induction has been suggested by Hagstrum and Silhacek (1980) to be fouling of the food by droppings from other larvae.

For some species no cues are needed to induce diapause for it will always be entered at a particular stage in the life cycle, no matter what the immediate weather conditions. The Swallow Prominent (*Pheosia tremula*), for example, stubbornly retains a univoltine habit in Scotland. Often one species of moth may have populations in one part of the range that obey this rule, whereas other populations either do or do not enter diapause, depending on the environmental cues received. For the European Corn-borer (*O. nubilalis*) this results in some univoltine and some bivoltine populations throughout the species' range (McLeod *et al.*, 1979).

BREAKING DIAPAUSE

Once diapause is established, it will continue until another cue is received that leads to development being resumed. Usually the day-length continues to shorten after the induction of diapause, maintaining the state, but after the year turns and day-length increases once more, there will come a time at which a critical phase is reached and diapause is broken. For some species of insect a given period of time must elapse under either short days or low temperatures before diapause can be broken, even if light is made continuous under experimental conditions. Once this obligatory period has passed, lengthening days can acti-vate the insects. Deseo and Briolini (1986) (quoted by Leather *et al.*, 1993) found that once the critical latent period was passed by the Codling moth larvae (*C. pomonella*), it was an accumulation of degrees-day that acted to break diapause and so either higher than normal temperatures, or the ever-lengthening days of spring made the difference.

In autumn, the Streak (*Chesias legatella*) lays eggs, which enter diapause for the winter. This diapause is broken in spring, the larvae hatch out and begin feeding. Warm days in early spring break the diapause but, if the spring remains cool the eggs stay unhatched. By late spring, however, even a slight rise in temperature will lead to the breaking of diapause (Wall, 1974).

Overall, the typical overwintering strategy is for the cooler, shorter days of late summer or early autumn to induce diapause, followed by the milder, longer days of spring releasing it.

CHOOSING A HIBERNATION SITE

It is quite crucial for a moth to choose its overwintering site with care, particularly if this site is fixed, as it is for an egg or pupa. For an adult or larva there may be the chance to move if the first place chosen proves unsuitable, or changes, but this cannot apply to diapausing individuals, which will not rouse sufficiently to move about.

The chosen site must be protected from potential predators and from whatever degree of cold the species finds intolerable. In practice, most species retreat into sheltered crevices, in cracks or holes in trees (used by the Brindled Ochre adult (*Dasypolia tem-pli*)); in the soil (for many noctuid or sphingid pupae such as Pale-shouldered Brocade (*Lacanobia thalassina*), or the Privet Hawk (*Sphinx ligustri*)); deep in sand (for example the Sand Dart larvae (*Agrotis ripae*)); or in a shelter of spun leaves (used by the Argent and Sable (*Rheumaptera hastata*)). In many cases a cocoon of silk is made to enclose the larvae or pupae, often incorporating elements of the substrate. The Gelechiid *Teleiodes proximella* spins a cocoon amongst leaf litter on the ground surface, incorporating the dead material around it. Alder Kitten larvae (*Furcula bicuspis*) (and their close relatives) chew off bits of bark from the trunk of the larval tree to use on the surface of the silken cocoon, so that this is completely hidden on the tree trunk, until the moth emerges and the dark exit hole suddenly becomes visible.

Eggs are generally either tucked into tiny crevices or left exposed on the twigs of the foodplant. The Dark Bordered Beauty (*Epione paralellaria*) places its eggs fully exposed on the slightly roughened bark of Aspen (*Populus tremula*) and this is typical of species overwintering in this stage. However, the eggs of the Antler moth (*Cerapteryx graminis*) have a different overwintering strategy. In August, the adults scatter their eggs randomly over the ground, and they do not hatch until the following spring. It has always proved very difficult to overwinter these successfully in captivity, despite much work to try to rear this pest species, and the best result has recently been achieved by Goulson and Entwhistle (1995). They found that cool temperatures were essential, with 4°C being the best, but the main requirement was that the eggs should be underwater! They specu-late that in the wild the eggs drop to the ground surface of damp grassland or heathland and that over the wet winter months the eggs are bathed in the surface film of water.

However, even their best hatching rates barely reached 20% and so there is more to be discovered about this species.

ADULT HIBERNATION

Adult moths are rarely discovered during the winter. Members of the genera *Agonopterix* and *Depressaria* (Oecophoridae) are called 'flatbodies'; they press themselves into flat spaces under bark, split wood, thatch or into old stems of herbaceous vegetation. Some *Caloptilia* spp. overwinter in the accumulations of old twigs and leaves lodging among the short bushy twigs that emerge from burrs on the trunks of oak trees, or among 'witches broom' galls. The Tissue moth (*Triphosa dubitata*) and the Herald (*Scoliopteryx libatrix*) live in caves or old buildings that are cool and stable enough to mimic caves. Morris and Collins (1991) studied their behaviour over the winter in an old underground 'fort' in Surrey. This building has a number of rooms, which differ in their distance from the entrance. They measured the temperature in one of the lower rooms and compared it with that found outside on many days over the 1985/86 winter. The maximum variation found during the course of a night in the lower room was no more than 2°C, even on nights where the outside temperature varied by 9°C. Over the winter the temperatures ranged from around 6.5°C in November, to 2.5°C in February, to 6°C in April, when most of the moths had emerged.

The Tissue moths were always found in the lower set of rooms, which were probably cooler and more stable in temperature, but they certainly moved about to some extent, and on one occasion several deserted a room where a fire was lit! They can apparently move to a more satisfactory site if necessary and need stable conditions. The average ratio of individuals in the cooler lower to warmer upper rooms was about 30:1. The Herald moth was much less dependent on the coolest rooms, being about equally common in the upper and lower set, and avoiding only the rooms where there was an obvious draught. They also seemed to be much less active, most remaining in their chosen place throughout the mid to late winter period, after some movement in the early winter. This study shows that over-wintering adults are more mobile than was previously expected.

AVOIDING PREDATION AND OTHER OVERWINTERING LOSSES

Leather (1984) recorded up to 40% loss of pupae of the Pine Beauty (*Panolis flammea*) in winter and Varley *et al.* (1973) point out that 'winter disappearance' is the most significant loss in the life cycle of the Winter moth (*Operophtera brumata*) in Oxfordshire. Clearly, the costs of overwintering can be high in terms of direct predation or death from environmental causes and disease but the actual effects vary from year to year, and West (1936) contrasted the loss of the Pine Shoot moth (*Rhyacionia buoliana*) in Connecticut in a mild winter, at 60%, with that of a hard winter at 90%.

The losses to predation can be avoided if a moth can find a hidden retreat for the winter and this is an advantage of the habit of creeping behind bark, into soil, or amongst spun leaves. However, these strategies also help the moths avoid the problems posed by low temperatures (see below). Even at low temperatures, when metabolic rates are very low, there is still some usage of stored food. Rickards *et al.* (1987) quantified this for the tortricid

Epiblema scudderiana, which overwinters as a larva. This species is typical in that it uses glycogen as an energy store and these authors found that about 16 μmol g^{-1} (dry weight) of glycogen was used during the frosty part of the winter, and that more or less the whole store was used by spring. There is also a loss of other food types and of water. Leather (1984) notes that in a normal winter Pine Beauty (*P. flammea*) pupae lose almost half their body weight owing to desiccation. Leather *et al.* (1993) quote Deseo (1973), who lists the fecundity of the overwintering generations of some moths, compared with the summer generations, and in all cases the values are much lower. For example, the mean egg load of the tortricid *Eupoecilia ambiguella* in Hungary in the summer adults was 73, whereas the egg load of adults resulting from overwintering larvae was only 50.

COPING WITH FREEZING TEMPERATURES

Although the problem of predation in winter is severe, the most interesting consideration is how moths cope with temperatures that drop below freezing.

There are two fundamentally different strategies that moths adopt. They either accept freezing of their body contents ('freeze tolerance'), protecting the vital cell structures in some way, or they avoid freezing, despite the external temperatures, by a mixture of behavioural responses and physiological mechanisms. Leather (1995) and Bale (1993) propose a set of terms that categorise these different approaches and their terms are used here, put in quotation marks when they first appear.

TABLE 11   *Definitions of terms used to describe moths' response to cold conditions.*

Species that survive cold conditions by freezing:

'**Freeze tolerant**' – species that survive sub-zero temperatures by controlled extra-cellular freezing

Species that survive cold conditions by avoiding freezing:

'**Freeze avoiding**' – species that survive sub-zero temperatures by having a low super-cooling point and behavioural responses that keep them in temperatures above this point

'**Chill tolerant**' – species that can survive very limited exposure to temperatures that are just sub-zero

Species that cannot survive sub-zero temperatures:

'**Chill susceptible**' – species that can tolerate brief exposure to temperatures just above zero, but cannot survive even brief episodes of sub-zero temperatures

'**Opportunist survivors**' – species that can tolerate only very brief periods just below their normal operating temperatures

Source: After Bale (1993) and Leather (1995).

Freeze tolerance

Most species that are 'freeze tolerant' live in places where the winter temperatures are so low that methods of avoiding freezing are impractical. Generally, if ice crystals form inside the cells of an animal, the cells are killed and the animal dies, so freeze tolerant animals have to overcome this problem. The main mechanism for this is for insects to have especially efficient ice-nucleating agents (particles on which ice begins to form) outside the cells in the haemolymph, so that ice first forms in these extra-cellular spaces. This leads to water being drawn out of the cells, so that they shrink and the solution within them becomes concentrated and less liable to freeze. Even so the temperature at which haemolymph freezing begins is usually well below 0°C and it is said to have a supercooling point. This is caused partly by the natural effect of the body salts but usually also by the presence of an anti-freeze substance, such as glycerol. Ring (1982) notes the supercooling point of the oecophorid *Exaeretia ciniflonella*, with 8% glycerol as the anti-freeze, as −23°C. As freeze tolerant moths approach winter, they accumulate ice-nucleating agents and anti-freeze and become gradually more able to withstand low temperatures. Once they have frozen they can then be subjected to very much lower temperatures without harm, and revive fully on thawing. Most of this brief account is taken from Leather *et al.* (1993) and refers to work on beetles and aphids, but the same principles apply to moths.

Avoiding freezing in winter

The first, and sometimes only, way that 'freeze avoiding' moths survive a winter air temperature below 0°C is by choosing sites in the environment where the temperature remains above freezing point. Burrowing into the soil is a good example of this, for the temperature even 20 cm below the surface may remain permanently above 0°C in Britain and even in Russia, where the air temperature drops to −30°C, the soil may remain unfrozen below 100 cm. This effect is greatly assisted by snow cover. Turnock *et al.* (1983) found that the cutworm (*Mamestra configurata*) pupae that were in soil with no snow cover in winter in Canada mostly died, but when there was a consistent 20 cm depth of snow, survival was greater than 90%.

Snow has a similar insulating effect in other circumstances too. Hilton (1982) reports that the larvae of the tortricid *Endothenia daeckeana* only survive in good numbers in the old stems of the foodplants when they are at a level below that of the winter snows in Canada; and the same happens to the egg masses of the Gypsy moth (*Lymantria dispar*), which are laid on the trunks of trees. Leonard (1972) reports that, in the northern part of the American range of this species, the abundance of the moth is limited by the proportion of the egg batches that are below the insulating winter snow line. In Japan, Higashiura (1989) found that Gypsy moths in regions without snow laid their eggs in the canopy, whereas in snowy areas they lay them low on tree trunks, below the usual snow depth. He found that egg mortality was two to four times lower below the snow than above it.

In Britain, the Argent and Sable moth (*Rheumaptera hastata*) pupates in the spun leaves at the end of the twigs of its foodplant and survives the rather mild British winters there, (although these shelters may fall off the plants during winter), whereas in Alaska it pupates down in the leaf litter, well insulated by the deep snow. Perhaps these widely separated populations are not actually of the same species, but, if they are, this is a most interesting example of different local responses to winter conditions.

Other species make their own insulating protection by spinning shelters that effectively protect them from the lowest winter temperatures, or by inhabiting local areas that are less cold than others. In Scandinavian forests it is sometimes obvious that trees in hollows are less defoliated than those on the slopes around them, the 'green island effect', and this is because cold air tends to pond in the hollows in the winter, killing most of the overwintering eggs of the Autumnal moth (*Epirrita autumnata*), which is responsible for most of the defoliation (Tenow and Nilssen, 1990). Similar observations have been made in many other places where frost hollows are found.

Species intolerant of freezing

So far no distinction has been made between those species that are reasonably tolerant of sub-zero temperatures and those that are killed by even short exposures to them. Bale (1993) differentiates several categories here. 'Freeze avoiding' species are those that cannot survive freezing of their tissues, but which can tolerate prolonged exposure to sub-zero temperatures, as long as these are above their supercooling point. 'Chill tolerant' species can withstand some exposure to below zero conditions but not to very low temperatures, even if they have quite a low supercooling point. 'Chill susceptible' species can survive at 0–5°C but even short times below zero are fatal to them; and 'opportunistic survivors' can tolerate only very brief periods below their normal active temperatures and certainly not freezing conditions. There are obviously no specific divisions between these categories and generally the more tolerant species have a better developed set of responses to low temperatures.

Opportunistic survivors are generally restricted to tropical and sub-tropical regions, whereas gradually more resistant species are found as one progresses into higher latitudes and freeze tolerant species are found in the continental Arctic regions. Most freeze avoiders use a process of supercooling to avoid the deleterious effects of freezing. This ability usually develops gradually as winter approaches and is reduced in spring. It is achieved by decreasing the presence of particles on which ice can form (nucleating agents), most simply by emptying the gut at the onset of hibernation and by accumulating anti-freeze chemicals. Somme (1965) has shown that the small ermine moth *Yponomeuta evonymella* and the tortricid *Cydia strobilella* have an increasing concentration of the anti-freeze glycerol as autumn progresses, with a concomitant drop in the supercooling point; this process is reversed in the spring. Perhaps these changes are brought on by the onset of, and later release from, diapause.

This is a very superficial account of the basis for tolerance of sub-zero temperatures and reference should be made to Leather *et al.* (1993) for further details.

CHAPTER 5

Plants as Food for Moths

IN India there is a moth larva that sucks blood, some 'looper' caterpillars in Hawaii catch flies and in Britain at least three species prey on other larvae. In the vast majority of cases, however, plants provide the food for both adult and larval moths, although the part of the plant involved varies somewhat. More than 98% of moth larvae are herbivorous, a proportion matched among other insects only by the grasshoppers and locusts (Orthoptera) (Naumann, 1994).

Many adult moths depend on plant fluids to provide them with the fuel they need for flight and perhaps in some cases for nutrients needed to mature their eggs. The use made by adults of nectar and sappy exudations from plant wounds is discussed briefly below. However, most of this chapter is devoted to the relationship between larvae and their foodstuffs. Lepidoptera are one of only nine insect orders that are primarily herbivorous, out of the overall total of about 29 orders. Strong *et al.* (1984) believe that herbivory presents severe problems as a way of life but, once these are overcome, great opportunities are opened up. The problems are, principally, desiccation, adapting to the balance of nutrients available (both discussed below), and attachment. Moths have solved the last problem by the use of sticky silk and well adapted legs and feet with small hooks.

WHAT DO MOTHS AND THEIR LARVAE FEED ON?

Table 12 shows which food materials are eaten by the larvae of British moths (from Emmet, 1991a) and it is likely that the relative proportions are broadly similar in other parts of the world, although this information is not yet available for the tropics. Many species feed on more than one part of the plant at different times, or use more than one type of food depending on what is available. For a significant number of species the foodplant is not yet known. Furthermore, many of the macro-lepidoptera on the British list are strays, adventives or rare migrants, which have been excluded from the analysis. This means that the figures given are estimates, rather than precise numbers, and the total number of 'food preferences' (2314) does not match the total number of moths (*c.* 2490) listed. Nevertheless the broad trends are correct.

Several features in Table 12 are worthy of comment. First of all the great majority of moths feed on either the leaves or buds of vascular plants; only a small number use lichens, mosses or fungi. Other parts of the living plant are also used, especially the

TABLE 12   *The foodstuffs used by larvae of British Lepidoptera, figures given refer to numbers of species using each category.*

Larvae	L	W	R	S	Fl	Fu	Li	M	DW	Ll	N	P	T
Micro's	971	108	52	163	60	20	25	32	14	58	39	0	1542
	63%	7%	3%	11%	4%	1%	2%	2%	1%	4%	3%	–	
Macro's	606	25	31	33	42	1	23	1	0	7	0	3	772
	78%	3%	4%	4%	5%	<1%	3%	<1%	–	1%	–	<1%	
Total	1577	133	83	196	102	21	48	33	14	65	39	3	2314
	68%	6%	4%	8%	4%	1%	2%	1%	<1%	3%	2%	<1%	

Key: L = leaves and buds of vascular plants and grass stems; W = live wood and stems of herbaceous plants; R = roots; S = seeds and fruits; Fl = flowers; Fu = fungi; Li = lichens; M = mosses; DW = dead wood; Ll = leaf litter, decaying vegetable matter and stored vegetable products; N = nests of animals and animal matter; P = predators; T = total. Percentages refer to total number of species in group.

flowers and seeds (many species feed on these in sequence, as they develop), and the wood and bark (and stems of herbaceous species). Fewer moths use the roots but their number exceeds those species that do not feed on vascular plants. Dead plant material, either as wood or leaf-litter, provides food for tens of species but animal remains, which are often difficult to differentiate from plant debris in nest remains, are used by only a small group of moths.

In general the smaller micro-lepidoptera are much more varied in their diet. Perhaps their smaller size allows them to complete development in smaller packets of food, such as is provided by seeds or small corpses. Powell (1980) reviews the foodstuffs of micro-lepidoptera and notes that the earliest known families (e.g. the Micropterigidae from 135 million years ago) were associated with bryophytes. The majority of insect families originated around 50–70 million years ago, when vascular plants also appeared. The non-standard food items, such as fungi or dead wood, tend to be used by groups of taxonomically related species (Table 13): for example, the clearwings (Sesiidae) are mostly wood feeders; one group within the Tineidae are animal nest specialists; and the swifts (Hepialidae) feed on roots. Each of these foodstuffs provides a different blend of nutrients and this sometimes imposes a particular mode or rate of feeding on the species of moth that feed on them. This chapter explores these differences.

WHAT DO PLANTS PROVIDE AS FOOD FOR LARVAE OF MOTHS?

There are four main categories of nutrients that are provided by plants for the larvae of moths and these vary in relative quantity and quality between different species of plant; between different parts of each species of plant; and between different times of year. At times one or all of these may be limiting and the timing of larval feeding is often closely geared to this variation, so as to obtain sufficient of each category of nutrient.

TABLE 13   *Examples of closely related moth species which use similar foodstuffs.*

Hepialidae – roots; Nepticulidae – mostly leaf miners;

Tineidae – one group feeds on lichen, one group feeds on fungus, one group feeds in animal nests;

Gracillariidae *Phyllonorycter* spp. – 'blister' miners; Sesiidae – wood borers; Coleophoridae – many feed on seeds;

Elachistidae – mine in grass blades; Oecophoridae – some species feed on dead wood;

Gelechiidae – some species feed on mosses; Cochylinae – most feed on seeds; Tortricidae *Dichrorampha* spp. – roots;

Scoparinae – most feed on mosses; Pyralinae – some feed on leaf litter and some on stored vegetable material;

Geometridae *Perizoma* spp. – seeds; *Eupithecia* spp. – many feed on flowers;

Lithosiinae – lichens; Noctuidae *Hadena* spp. – seeds; Amphipyrinae – some species feed in grass stems.

Water

The Drinker moth larva (*Philudoria potatoria*) is reputed to drink from droplets of dew, behaviour that may also apply to a small number of other species. However, it certainly does not apply to most. The force of gravity has little effect on very small animals, including moth larvae. If they fall from a tree, even if they do not spin the usual silk thread, so as to be able to climb back to their food, their fall to the ground will be inconvenient but will not result in injury. However, if a small larva touches a drop of water, the surface tension will be sufficiently strong to trap and ultimately drown it. Many larvae have a coat of hairs, which may help to shed rain drops that fall on to them but most have to hide from rain to avoid being trapped. Presumably, the Drinker moth larva is just big enough to resist the effect. It is well known by people who rear larvae that condensation on the sides of the rearing jars risks drowning the larvae and, if a gentle spray is needed to revitalise the foodplant, the size of the droplets must be very small. A few larvae thrive only when given a frequent fine spray (perhaps they too are 'dew drinkers') but the great majority avoid liquid water and so have to obtain their ration directly from the plants on which they feed. The problem of desiccation applies to larvae living on the surface of leaves, where evaporation is high and the humidity of the air low. The use of shelters made by spinning rolls or bunches of leaves helps to provide a humid environment and possibly the tendency of larvae to feed at night is as much to do with avoiding dry air as with avoiding predators (Carter *et al.*, 1988).

In most circumstances it is possible for larvae to obtain their water from plants, for leaves typically contain 70–90% water by weight and so there is in effect an excess. Larvae that feed wholly on leaves in non-droughted conditions probably get all they need without any restriction. However, the amount of water present in leaves varies considerably. Some plants, typically those with flimsy pale green leaves, always have a higher water content than do those with rigid, dark leaves but all leaves are susceptible to dry weather and their water content in serious droughts may drop from 80% to 40% (see Table 14). In such circumstances there is too little water left to supply the larvae and they too will suffer, either stopping feeding until the leaves rehydrate or dying with them. Scriber (1977) observed that the growth and metabolic efficiency of the Robin moth (*Hyalophora cecropia*) larvae was lowered when fed on leaves of the Black Cherry (*Prunus serotina*) that were short of water. Wilting in this way may be a daily phenomenon, with turgid leaves during the cooler night time and wilted leaves in the hotter day, so that the larvae may have to wait until night to feed. However, in a prolonged drought there is an insuperable problem. In Britain during 1975 and 1976, there was a very serious drought and it was observed that the foodplants of many moths were less abundant, less well grown and frequently wilted. Some moths also became very scarce in 1976 and this was ascribed to poor availability of their foodplants; however, it may also have been due to direct mortality on wilted food. The 'Talisker' burnet (*Zygaena lonicerae jocelynae*), which lives on the undercliff on the coast of the island of Skye, feeds on Meadow Vetchling (*Lathyrus pratensis*) but, in the very dry spring of 1993, the larvae were observed to switch to the more drought resistant Bird's-foot Trefoil (*Lotus corniculatus*) (Bourn, *pers. comm.*).

There is also a trend for spring and early summer leaves to contain more water than those later in the summer but this variation is paralleled by so many other changes in leaf chemistry that it cannot be viewed alone. Consequently, the seasonal trend in larval abundance (discussed below) has to be considered in a wider context than merely that of water availability. Furthermore, when water is scarce in a plant the relative nitrogen levels may be higher and it has been suggested that this will favour herbivores. The 'stress-outbreak' hypothesis suggests that if plants are stressed by mild drought then herbivores may grow better and produce exceptionally high population levels. There is little evidence for this for moth larvae, however.

Carbohydrate

Carbohydrates are the products of photosynthesis and therefore the green parts of plants and their storage organs will tend to contain a wealth of such material. Carbohydrate forms an important component of the diet of moth larvae but is rarely limiting, except for those species which do not feed on the plant parts noted above.

Nitrogen

It is quite a different matter with nitrogen, however, for typically an animal contains much more nitrogen, mostly in the form of protein, than do plants (Table 14). It must therefore process large volumes of plant material to gain sufficient nitrogen. Different parts of the plant may contain more or less nitrogen but in general larvae take in an excess of water and carbohydrate to obtain sufficient nitrogen. This is a similar situation to that faced by aphids, which suck the phloem sap of plants and excrete a large volume of excess water and carbohydrate as the sticky and sweet 'honey-dew'. Moth larvae, although they face a similar problem, do not secrete a similar liquid, for most do not drink plant sap but use a less liquid diet.

There is an excellent butterfly example which illustrates the importance of nitrogen. Myers (1985) showed that female Small White butterflies (*Pieris rapae*) lay most of their eggs on individual foodplants that are high in nitrogen. Then Loader and Damman (1991) found that *P. rapae* larvae also grow faster on leaves with a high content of nitrogen and that, as a result of longer residence times on poor leaves, predation and parasitism of larvae was greater on them.

Essential amino-acids and trace minerals

Most nitrogen in plants and animals is in the form of structural and other proteins but some is contained in free amino-acids, some of which cannot be synthesised by larvae. In other cases trace minerals are in very short supply in leaves and may then become important to the larvae. Plants can use such precious compounds as rewards to essential insect visitors, such as pollinators, and it is now known that nectar frequently contains minerals and amino-acids, as well as water and sugar.

CHOOSING WHICH PART OF A PLANT TO EAT

As is shown in Table 14, different parts of a plant contain very different proportions of each of the substances listed above. Consequently, larvae that feed specifically on various parts must adopt appropriate strategies.

TABLE 14   *Parts of plants and the nutrients that they provide for moths.*

Plant part	% Dry weight nitrogen[1]	% Dry weight carbohydrate	% Wet weight water
Leaves	<1–5	5-17	(40)[2]–90
Tree trunks	<1	?[3]	20–30
Phloem sap	<0.6	20	70–80
Seeds	1–10	Low (no store) High (store)[4]	30–50
Pollen	Up to 50	Very low	30–70
Nectar	<3 + AA[5]	>30	50–80

Notes:
[1] Nitrogen varies greatly through the season. It is difficult to measure the amount available for digestion, these are generalised figures.
[2] Droughted leaves may have very low water levels.
[3] Tree trunks may have high levels of structural carbohydrate which is unavailable for digestion.
[4] Some seeds have stores of carbohydrate associated with the embryo, others have very little.
[5] Nectar may contain significant quantities of amino-acids, such as methionine, which are essential for insects.

Leaves

Leaves are generally rich in water and carbohydrates, and low in nitrogen in its different forms. Large volumes of leaf must be eaten to obtain sufficient nitrogen, but as there are large volumes of leaf on a tree, there is often no apparent shortage. A quick glance outside in the summer shows an abundance of green tissue and apparently little likelihood of shortage or competition between those larvae that feed on it. However, the quality of the green tissue varies dramatically and only a small proportion may be really palatable. First of all there may be a problem of wilting, which may be more severe in some plants than in others or in some leaves than in others. Lower, semi-shaded leaves may not become so hot and wilted as those in full sun on the same plant and may remain more palatable, but they may have a lower photosynthetic rate and may not contain so much of the other nutrients.

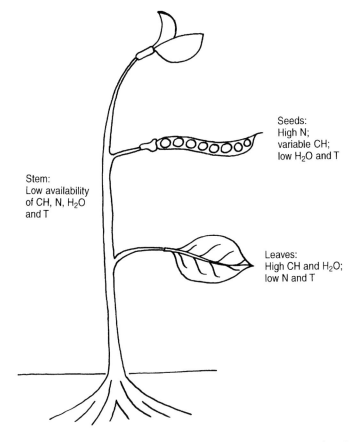

FIG 27   *A stylised diagram of a plant, showing the food resources it provides. CH, carbohydrates; N, proteins; H₂O, water; T, trace elements. As explained in the text, the relative amounts of all food resources may vary through the season.*

Many larvae of the Tortricidae spin tubes, cones or shelters among leaves, within which to feed and, as well as potential advantages in avoiding parasites or predators, and in sustaining humidity, the leaves may remain more turgid than those which are not so spun.

Soumela *et al.* (1995) observed the growth rate and eventual success rate of Autumnal moth (*Epirrita autumnata*) larvae on Downy Birch (*Betula pubescens*) and found that some leaves on each tree produced better results. Those leaves on the north side of the tree, the upper leaves, the smallest leaves and the innermost leaves resulted in faster growth than the others, although the factors involved have not been identified.

Later in the summer less water may be available in the leaves but there are also other seasonal changes. Figure 30 shows that, as the season progresses, there is frequently distinctly less nitrogen present in leaves, posing a serious problem. The lower availability of nitrogen may well be much more important than the reduction in water but there are other factors to consider. Plant defences also build up as the early season passes and so do the structural materials that keep the leaf arrayed correctly in the sun but also act to make the leaf tougher and less digestible (Feeny, 1970)(see Chapter 6). There is no way of distinguishing which of these factors is most important in limiting the use made of the leaf by larvae, for it is likely that all combine. The result is that many leaves are less suitable as food than their colour suggests and much of the general greenness of the countryside may not really be available to moth larvae. The younger leaves are usually the most nutritious; when Oak trees (*Quercus* spp.) produce their flush of new leaves in spring, these are competed for by an abundance of larvae. Subsequently, there are no new leaves and correspondingly fewer larvae are present. (However, in July the Oak grows by producing new extended shoots, with new leaves, called the 'Lammas' growth after the old name for that season. The new leaves can also be eaten.) Niemala and Haukioja (1982) found that trees which continue to produce leaves all summer, like poplars and aspens (*Populus* spp.), also have high numbers of larvae present throughout the summer.

Stems and trunks

The stems and trunks of plants are structural elements that are usually not photosynthetic. The trunks of trees are made up mainly of dead cells whose lignified cell walls provide support. Nearer the outside there are transport cells that take water up to the leaves (xylem cells) and bring the products of photosynthesis down to the roots (phloem cells) but these make up a very small part of the mass of a large tree trunk. Although the stems of herbaceous plants are much less woody and may have a photosynthetic outer layer, they are less nutritious than leaves.

At first sight it is difficult to see why a moth larva should feed in a tree trunk. Very large volumes of wood have to be eaten to provide sufficient food for the larvae and the rate of digestion is low. Larvae have to spend long periods of time feeding on wood, typically up to four years for the Goat moth (*Cossus cossus*), three for the Leopard moth (*Zeuzera pyrina*), and even three years for the smaller Welsh Clearwing (*Synanthedon scoliaeformis*), which feeds in birch trunks. Such a long larval life would be untenable for a free-living larva, for this would expose it to an extreme risk of predation or parasitism, but one advantage of being inside a tree trunk is that such risks are reduced. Woodpeckers are not common and most opportunistic predators and parasites cannot get at the larvae. The larvae can also remain active over the winter, continuing to feed very slowly during the milder periods.

Another advantage of feeding inside tree trunks is that there is very little competition for the resource, although a range of beetle species may also chew wood. As shown in Table 12, few moth larvae feed in wood.

The most nutritious part of the tree-trunk is the outer layer of wood proper, where the transport cells are found, and the inner layer of bark. This part of the trunk hosts most wood feeding moth species, especially the smaller ones, but a wide range of beetles choose the same part, so that competition is greater there. The micro-moth *Argyresthia glaucinella* feeds under the bark of oaks and the characteristic piles of reddish-brown frass in the crevices of the bark are a sign of its presence. A few species of the Nepticulidae (which are almost invariably leaf miners), feed under the bark of young branches of trees. For example, *Ectodemia atrifrontella* feeds on Oak, and the long galleries show as raised tracks on the bark.

Flowers

The great advantage of using flowers and seeds as a food resource is that they contain much higher levels of nitrogen than do any other parts of the plant. Nitrogen is richest in the pollen and in the developing ovule and the seeds. Clearly, this makes these plant parts very attractive to herbivores but there are some limitations that restrict the numbers of species using them. Firstly, flowers and seeds are only a very small part of the bulk of a plant and so there is a limit to the size of herbivore that can use them; secondly, they are present for only a very brief period during the season. The need that many plants have to advertise their flowers to pollinators means that they are not difficult to locate, although the seed capsules are less conspicuous.

These limitations mean that a typical herbivore using flowers must be small; very fast developing during the short flowering season (which is possible owing to the relatively rich diet); and with a precise timing to match that of the flowers. Moving from flower to flower will allow more material to be eaten and so flowers held in groups, especially if they develop sequentially, will be particularly useful to herbivores. Some examples will help clarify these features.

'Pug' moths (*Eupithecia* spp.) are small members of the Geometridae, many of which feed on flowers and developing seeds. The Foxglove Pug (*E. pulchellata*) lays its eggs on the flower buds of Foxglove (*Digitalis purpurea*) and the emerging larvae burrow into the developing ovules. When slightly larger they sit inside the tubular flower, feeding on the ovules, and they protect their position by spinning up the lip of the flower, so closing the tube. Foxglove flowers develop in sequence, so the larvae bore out of a flower, once they have finished eating it, and make their way into a younger one. The exit hole and spun lip are certain signs that larvae have been there. The moths are quite small and the larvae can achieve their full size in 2–3 weeks, fitting their growth into the flowering season of the plant. Despite their small size and rapid growth, however, they cannot achieve a second generation in one season because the Foxglove has only one flowering period. Those pug moths which do have two broods, and very few of them do in Britain, have to use a different species of flower in which to develop. The White-spotted Pug (*E. tripunctaria*) is said to use Elder blossom (*Sambucus nigra*) in early summer and various Umbelliferae, especially Angelica (*Angelica sylvestris*), in late summer.

Larvae of larger moths have to be able to move freely to find new flowers and there are very few that use this strategy. The Broad-barred White (*Hecatera bicolorata*), a small

Noctuid, feeds on the flowers of various Compositae. Typically, such flowers are large, for they are made up of a collection of florets. This helps the moth larvae, but even so they must move on to new flowers frequently, if they are to find enough food.

Seeds

Seeds vary in food quality depending on their stage of development. While still on the plant they may contain relatively large amounts of water, as well as high nitrogen levels, but during ripening the quantity of water is reduced. For seeds to lie dormant successfully they have to reduce their metabolism to imperceptibly low levels and this is facilitated by becoming very dry. Therefore, ripe seeds may be a very demanding resource for larvae, compared to those that are still moist and developing. Another reason why it may be easier to feed on developing seeds is that they are often held together in quite large numbers on the plant. Once ripe, they are dispersed widely in the environment where they are difficult to find and insufficient on their own to feed a larva. Consequently, most seed feeding moth larvae live on developing seeds on the parent plant.

The seeds of Sallow bushes (*Salix* spp.) are held in the familiar fluffy 'pussy willows' that are seen in the spring. The flowers of Sallows appear before the leaves and are very attractive to both diurnal and nocturnal insects, including almost all of the Geometridae and

A caterpillar feeding on the ripening seeds of a campion plant.

Noctuidae that are active as adults in the spring. 'Sallowing', as a technique for catching moths, is described in Chapter 9. The Slender Pug (*Eupithecia tenuiata*) does not in fact feed at the flowers for the adults appear in early summer but the females lay their eggs on the new shoots close to what will become the flowers. Most of the year is spent as an egg but the larvae hatch just as the seeds are developing the following spring and feed inside the groups of seeds, growing fast and emerging to pupate in the soil after about two weeks. Infested flowers seem to fall from the tree before the seeds are ripe and so much of the larval feeding is carried out while the old flower is on the ground. If newly fallen flowers are collected and laid over a layer of peat in a tray, the larvae will pupate there and in due course the adults will emerge.

Other larvae will also be seen in the trays of Sallow flowers; noctuids such as the Pink-barred Sallow (*Xanthia togata*) lay their eggs on the twigs the previous autumn, the larvae hatch and begin to feed on the seeds but then use up this food and emerge from the old flowers to feed on the leaves of herbaceous plants on the ground. This mixed diet obviously provides many advantages and there are several related species that adopt a similar strategy.

Only a few Noctuidae species are found feeding wholly on seeds but the genus *Hadena* specialises on the seeds of the *Silene* genus and its close relatives within the plant family Caryophyllaceae – the campions and catch-flies. In Britain, nine moth species share out the plant species between them; they are listed in Table 15.

It is clear that some of the moth species are specialists on one plant, which they do not have to share with other moths. The Lychnis (*H. bicruris*) is the only moth that uses the red flowered *S. dioica*, apart from some polyphagous species. Other plants are host to a range of species but more subtle distinctions also apply; for example, the inland colonies of *S. vulgaris* tend to be host mainly to the Tawny Shears (*H. perplexa*).

In all cases, except Barrett's Marbled Coronet (*H. luteago*), the larvae feed within the swollen seed capsules of the plants, hiding within them when small enough to do so but only partly hidden when more fully grown. They move readily to new seed pods and the plants' colonial habits help this. On many occasions it is difficult to find uneaten seed pods in a colony of the plants, except on isolated plants or those that have been either atypically early or late in flowering. The moths start feeding when the seeds are still green and unripe but by the time that they are fully grown the seeds are often black and hard and must contain very little water.

CHOOSING WHICH SPECIES OF PLANT TO EAT

Some moths are polyphagous, that is they feed on a wide variety of foodplants. The Winter moth (*Operophtera brumata*), for example, will feed on almost any species of deciduous tree and recently has also adopted Sitka Spruce (*Picea sitchensis*) and Heather (*Calluna vulgaris*) as part of its range of foodplants. Others are either completely oligophagous, (having a single foodplant) or are restricted to a small number of closely related species. For example, the Diamond Back (*Plutella xylostella*) will use a range of relatives of *Brassica*. As there is something of a gradation between these two positions, it is difficult to provide precise figures for the relative numbers that are polyphagous or oligophagous. In general, however, truly polyphagous species are not very common. Emmet (1988) lists about 100 species of micro-lepidoptera out of the British total of around 1500 as being definitely polyphagous, with

TABLE 15 *Related plants from the Caryophyllaceae and the seed feeding moths that feed upon them.*

Plant species	Moth species	Comments on moths
Silene nutans	*Hadena albimacula*	S coast only
	H. perplexa	Widespread in S
S. otites	*H. irregularis*	Breck only – extinct
S. dioica	*H. bicruris*	Very widespread and common
S. alba	*H. perplexa*	Widespread in S
	H. confusa	Widespread, esp. on coast
Lychnis flos-cuculi	*H. rivularis*	Widespread
Dianthus barbatus	*H.compta*	Moth a colonist
	H. bicruris	Plant introduced
S. vulgaris (= *inflata*)	*H. confusa*	Widespread, esp. on coast
	H. luteago	SW coast only; in stems and roots not seeds
	H. caesia	NW coast only, seeds then leaves
	H. perplexa	Widespread in S
	(*H. compta*	Moth a colonist)
S. maritima	*H. perplexa*	Widespread in S
	H. luteago	SW coast only; in stems and roots not seeds
	H. confusa	Widespread, esp. on coast
	H. caesia	NW coast only, seeds then leaves
	H. rivularis	Widespread and common

the rest generally being restricted to groups of related plants. Clearly, there must be some advantage to having a limited range of foodplants, to counteract the obvious advantage of being able to use any plant that presents itself.

OLIGOPHAGY – FEEDING ON ONLY A SMALL NUMBER OF PLANT SPECIES

If a species of moth uses only one or few foodplants, it has to find them among the mass of other plants and its abundance and distribution are limited by those of the foodplant. Some moths are indeed restricted by the range of their foodplants; for example, the pyralid *Mecyna asinalis* is found only in southern England, matching the range of the Wild Madder (*Rubia peregrina*) on which its larvae feed. There are almost no moths (or other herbivores) that specialise on really rare and highly localised foodplants, presumably because this would be too restricting and even Britain's rarest moths are almost all associated with common plants. For example, the Welsh Clearwing (*Synanthedon scoliaeformis*) bores into the trunks of birch trees and yet the moth is apparently restricted to four sites in Britain.

The compensating advantage of feeding on only one or a few related plants is that the physiology and the phenology of the moth may be adapted closely to that of the foodplant. In this way the larvae can emerge at the correct time, move to the appropriate part of the plant, digest the particular chemical features of the plant and generally make an efficient job of utilising it. This will include the important task of overcoming the plant defences (see Chapter 6).

POLYPHAGY – GENERALIST FEEDERS

Conversely, a polyphagous moth will have to invest in a wide range of digestive capabilities to cope with the varied balance of chemicals in its food. It may emerge at a time that is not ideally suited to using the most nutritious part of each particular plant, it will have to be able to handle a great number of defensive chemicals and generally it will make an inefficient job of using the foodplant. If an oligophagous and a polyphagous species are feeding on the same foodplant at the same time one can predict that the oligophagous species should 'win' the competition for resources, because of its finer adaptation to that plant, which will allow it to feed faster, or perhaps to avoid the adverse effects of defensive chemicals.

The polyphagous species will have the great advantage of being able to find a usable foodplant in most areas and conditions. Even if such a moth strays well beyond its usual habitat it may be able to breed successfully and even if a preferred plant should become rare for some unexpected reason an alternative may be accessible. Occasionally, larvae become abundant and defoliate their foodplants; for example, 'small ermine' moths *Yponomeuta evonymella* may completely strip Bird Cherry trees (*Prunus padus*) and then find themselves with no more food, whereas the Scarce Umber (*Agriopis aurantiaria*), which sometimes defoliates birch, can move to feed on whatever else is nearby. If environmental changes take place, rapidly altering the relative abundance and/or the distribution of plants, this may have a greater effect on specialised larvae than on generalists. It can be predicted that in rather stable periods (either at the scale of a series of years or of evolutionary time scales) oligophagous species should have the opportunity to score over their polyphagous competitors, whereas the reverse should be true in changeable periods.

If this is so, our own effects on the world's flora, producing rapid and dramatic changes, should lead to a greater decline in oligophagous than polyphagous herbivores. Time will tell if this is true, meanwhile it may also be predicted that the rarest and most localised species should be more likely to be oligophagous and the commoner and most widespread should be polyphagous. Defining a precise distinction between the two types of feeding makes it difficult to refute or support this prediction but of the 78 species of moth that are listed as the rarest in Britain (as judged by inclusion in the top three categories in the Red Data Book – see Chapter 10) 11 may be said to be definitely polyphagous and another 11 either intermediate or unknown in this respect. This proportion is not very different from the overall ratio for all of Britain's moths and it seems therefore that rare moths are not necessarily more likely to be oligophagous.

Futuyama (1976) suggests that stable food resources, like trees, should host more oligophagous herbivores, whereas unstable food resources, like weeds, should be used by polyphagous species. However, he found that the reverse seems to be true, for reasons which are not clear. Gaston *et al.* (1992) found that in general internal feeders, which presumably need to be closely adapted to their mode of feeding and to the precise nature of their foodplant, are more commonly oligophagous than external feeders.

WHY DO CERTAIN SPECIES OF PLANT SUPPORT MORE THAN THEIR SHARE OF MOTH HERBIVORES FEEDING ON THEM?

Some plants have virtually no moth larvae that feed on them, whereas others have many. In some cases the explanation for this is simple and rather trivial. Some plants are known to contain large quantities of toxic chemicals, such as the Deadly Nightshade (*Atropa belladonna*), with which only one species of moth, *Acrolepia autumnitella*, is associated in Britain and, although it is not certain that any chemical that is toxic to us will necessarily be toxic to moths, it is probable that the presence of the toxins protects the plant. Such simple explanations do not apply to many plants, however, and Southwood (1961) opened the more general debate on this subject with what is now a classic study on why certain trees have more herbivore species associated with them than others.

Which trees host most moths?

Southwood (1961) collated the data that then existed on the species of moth herbivore feeding on British trees and asked why it was that some trees were eaten by so many species. He hypothesised that trees that had been long established in Britain, more or less since the ice had retreated following the last Ice-age, and were widespread and common, would be expected to have more herbivore species than those that were recent colonists and/or were scarce and localised. He found it difficult to find a measure that summarised these criteria but settled on the number of sub-fossil remains of each of the trees that were known in Britain, believing that more remains would be found for common, long-standing, native species. He then plotted the number of sub-fossil remains of each tree species against the number of associated herbivores and found the clear positive relationship shown in Figure 28. This relationship is easy to rationalise. Length of residence gives time for herbivores to find and adapt to using a tree and commoner trees will be a more easily usable resource. Southwood found that Oak (*Quercus* spp.) had the most herbivores and yet the leaves of Oak are rich in tannin, which is thought to be a defensive chemical (see Chapter 6). If it is, then it has been overcome by a wide range of herbivore species!

Since 1961, many other authors have taken Southwood's analysis further, but before following these studies it is important to see whether moths show the same patterns of tree use

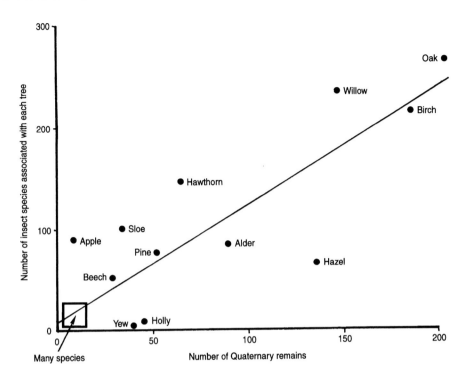

FIG 28   *Southwood's 'classic' graph of 1961, relating the number of insect species associated with various British trees to the number of Quaternary remains of those species. (Source: simplified from Southwood, 1961, with permission from Blackwells Scientific)*

as do other types of herbivore. Table 16 lists many of the trees found in Britain and enumerates their moth herbivores. Data for this have been taken from Emmet (1988) and (1991a) but it is very difficult to produce accurate figures. First of all, as Owen (1987b) and Fielding and Coulson (1995) make clear, the literature is often wrong or incomplete in the lists of moth foodplants. Emmet has checked information carefully but had to rely on published sources and so could not claim complete accuracy. Secondly, larvae may occasionally turn up on the 'wrong' foodplant, for reasons of chance or exceptional local shortage, and this may be reported but be misleading. Thirdly, it is difficult to place species in the list if they feed mainly on one plant species, sometimes on a second, and only occasionally on a third. Despite these problems, the general pattern revealed by this list is certainly reliable.

The data in Table 16 reflect the pattern shown for all herbivores and would fit nicely on to Southwood's graph. Although polyphagous moth species outnumber all others, Oak, Birch and Sallow dominate the list of trees. They are all abundant, widespread, native species, which have exceptionally large numbers of herbivores feeding on them. Fewest moth species feed on Yew and Holly, both of which are tough-leaved and Yew contains powerful toxins.

TABLE 16   *The number of moth species feeding on different tree species in Britain.*

	No. of moths	Status of plant
Native deciduous species		
Oak *Quercus* spp.	119	Common, widespread
Beech *Fagus sylvatica*	21	Common in south
Hornbeam *Carpinus betulus*	24	Local in south
Hazel *Corylus avellana*	35	Common, understorey
Sallows *Salix* spp.	108	Common, widespread
Black poplar *Populus nigra*	26	Very rare, local
Aspen *Populus tremula*	46	Local, widespread
Birch *Betula* spp.	121	Common, widespread
Alder *Alnus glutinosa*	42	Local, widespread
Elm *Ulmus* spp.	29	Local, widespread
Ash *Fraxinus excelsior*	16	Common, widespread
Lime *Tilia* spp.	17	Local, southern
Field maple *Acer campestris*	20	Local, southern
Hawthorn *Crataegus* spp.	74	Common, widespread
Wild apple *Malus sylvestris*	62	Scarce, southern
Rowan *Sorbus aucupariae*	23	Local, widespread
Non-native deciduous species		
Sycamore *Acer pseudoplatanus*	16	Common, widespread
Sweet chestnut *Castanea sativa*	10	Local, southern
Other native species		
Holly *Ilex aquifolium*	3	Local, widespread
Yew *Taxus baccata*	1	Scarce, widespread
Juniper *Juniperus communis*	17	Local, widespread
Scots pine *Pinus sylvestris*	34	Local, widespread
Other non-native species		
All pine, including *P. sylvestris*	54	Common, widespread
Larch *Larix* spp.	14	Common, widespread
Firs *Abies* spp.	18	Common, widespread
All spruce *Picea* spp.	39	Common, widespread
Sitka spruce *Picea sitchensis*	14	Common, widespread
Polyphagous species of moth	126	

Source: Data from Emmet (1988) and (1991a).

Do native trees host more moth species than introduced trees?

There is an expectation that native species should have more herbivores than non-natives and this is broadly correct. However, the difference is by no means as marked as might be expected and there are exceptions to the rule.

Sweet Chestnut, which is locally common in southern England but is not native, has only 10 moths found on it, fewer than any but the heavily defended Holly and Yew. Sycamore, a non-native that is generally reviled by conservationists for its invasive tendencies, has only 16 and is also near the bottom of the scale, despite being very common and widespread throughout Britain and having been here for hundreds of years. Nevertheless, Ash, an ecological equivalent of Sycamore and an undoubted native, also has only 16; Lime (all species) only 17; and Field Maple, Britain's closest relative of Sycamore, only 20. These figures are barely different. It might be claimed that Field Maple includes a number of specialised oligophagous moth species, such as the Maple Pug (*Eupithecia inturbata*), whereas the Sycamore generally only hosts common polyphagous species, but Sycamore also has its own specialists, such as the 'blister-miner' *Phyllonorycter geniculella*, which are also invaders. Several native species, as well as those already mentioned, have a sparse fauna, including Beech (21), Rowan (23) and Hornbeam (24), despite being common and well dispersed. It is especially interesting and unexpected that closely related species, like Oak and Beech, can nevertheless be found at the upper and lower end of the scale in terms of numbers of moth herbivores.

The native conifer Scots Pine has 34 associated species, broadly similar to many native deciduous species, but it does not act as host to so many polyphagous species and so its overall fauna is lower than most deciduous species. Juniper has only 17 species feeding on it, but is more like a bush than a tree, and the non-native conifers have similar numbers. Sitka Spruce has 14 species recorded from it, putting it into the low end of the normal range.

OTHER FACTORS THAT INFLUENCE THE CHOICE OF HOSTPLANT – 'APPARENCY'

It was clear from Southwood's data that some extra factors had to be considered if full sense was to be made of the patterns he observed. Two examples illustrate this. Apple is quite widely spread but is very sparse and it has many more associated herbivores than might be

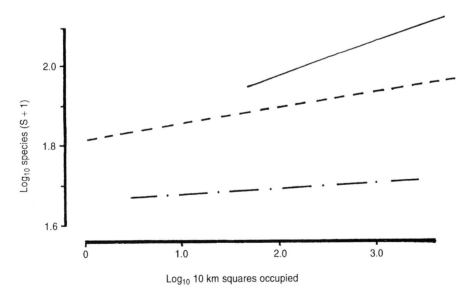

FIG 29   *The relationship between plant range (log$_{10}$ 10 km squares occupied) and the number of macro-lepidoptera associated with plants of the family Rosaceae. —— trees; – – – shrubs; – · – · – herbs. (Source: simplified from Leather, 1990)*

expected. Conversely, the very common and widespread Hazel has rather fewer than it should have. Southwood suggested that Hazel is found only in the understorey and is hidden from herbivores, when compared with larger forest trees. By contrast, Apple occurs either on its own or on the edge of scattered woodland and so will be much more obvious to herbivores searching for a suitable foodplant. He introduced the idea that some plants are more 'apparent' to herbivores than others.

Many other workers, including Lawton and Schroder (1977), Kennedy and Southwood (1984) and Lawton (1986) have followed up Southwood's original ideas. They have refined his data on the herbivores on each foodplant, trying to include more insect groups, more certain feeding associations, more different feeding niches (such as wood borers as well as leaf chewers); and they have extended the types of plant to include not just trees but also herbs, shrubs and a wide range of others. They have also examined other plant characteristics, such as the complexity of plant architecture.

Leather (1990) provides a good example of a more complete analysis of the number of herbivores associated with different plants, in this case members of the Rosaceae. He found that trees tended to harbour more herbivore species than did shrubs, with fewest of all on herbs and that within each group there was an increase with wider geographical range and with greater plant complexity (Figure 29). High apparency has led to high herbivore numbers.

Apparency is a combination of various factors and includes:

(a) length of residence in an area – native species have been around the longest and there has been more time for moths to find them;
(b) extent of distribution – widespread plants will be available to northern species of moths, as well as southern ones; will be found wherever a moth should stray; and so are highly apparent;
(c) abundance – common plants will be easier to find and will support a larger number of herbivores;
(d) plants found in large clumps (such as forests) – will be easier to locate than scattered plants;
(e) size – large species, such as Birch or Oak, will be easier to find and will support more larvae, than small plants like Primrose (*Primula vulgaris*);
(f) 'architecture' – a complex plant, with many different structures and parts, such as a large tree, will have many more 'niches' available than a simple plant like a grass;
(g) length of life – a perennial plant will be present not only for the whole life of a moth larva but will be present again, in a predictable place, for succeeding generations;
(h) predictability – a weed species of plant, which will disperse widely between generations and whose next site is not predictable, will be difficult to use as a foodplant, because it will be difficult to find.

Overall, large, abundant, widespread perennials, that tend to live in large groups (like Birch) have many moth herbivores, whereas rare and local annual herbs have very few, if any.

If this is true, the large perennial plant, which is more prone to attack from herbivores, should have more need of effective defences than the small annual. Scriber and Feeny (1979), who found that larvae tend to grow faster on herbs than trees, ascribe this to the higher levels of defensive chemicals in trees, which tend to reduce larval growth rates.

FINDING A FOODPLANT

It is important for a female moth to locate the correct foodplant as efficiently as possible and each species has a behaviour pattern that helps lead to this end. In general, moths follow a search pattern, until they find a plant that has the right long-distance characteristics. They orientate to this and land on it, provided that the nearer cues remain favourable and then they evaluate its surface before finally accepting or rejecting it as the right place on which to lay an egg (Renwick and Chew, 1994).

At long range, shape and colour are undoubtedly the most important cues. Plants must be the right shade and have leaves of the right general shape before they will be approached. This can apply even for night-flying species; for example, the Cotton Bollworm (*Heliothis zea*) has been shown to approach yellow leaves much more readily than other colours. However, there is also evidence that some odours act at long distance to attract moths to fly towards a plant. The female Leek moth (*Acrolepiopsis assectella*) has been shown to fly towards the sulphur-containing compounds present in leek leaves and the Cabbage Looper moth (*Trichoplusia ni*) orientates towards volatile chemicals released by soybeans. Many of these studies have been carried out in wind tunnels, sometimes with 'y-tubes', where a choice has to be made between channels containing different odours. In the Navel Orangeworm (*Amyelois transitella*) it was found that only gravid females chose to fly upwind towards almond oil, the smell of their host plant, and for some species, such as the Tobacco Budworm (*Heliothis virescens*), it has been shown that the odour of a susceptible strain of the host plant will elicit a positive response, whereas the odour of a resistant strain will not. Injured foodplants of the European Corn-borer (*Ostrinia nubilalis*) produce volatile chemicals that actually repel the moths.

Once a female moth lands on a plant it begins to evaluate it. Red Underwings (*Catocala* spp.) prefer hairy-leafed plants, perhaps because they can grip such leaves more easily than smooth ones, but the Maize Borer (*Chilo partellis*) is deterred by some maize cultivars, because they are too hairy. The chemical nature of different leaves is detected by sense organs that may be on the front tarsi, or the proboscis, or the ovipositor of moths, with different species having a different set of such sense organs. Spruce Budworms (*Choristoneura fumiferana*) test the waxy layer on the needles of their fir trees with their proboscis, whereas the Potato Tuber moth (*Phthorimaea operculella*) drags its ovipositor along to test the smell of its foodplants.

Specific chemicals lead to the onset of egg-laying. The Diamond Back (*Plutella xylostella*) female is stimulated to lay by sinigrin, which contributes to the characteristically sour smell of cabbage leaves, and *H. virescens* is attracted by two triterpenes from tobacco leaves.

If there are already eggs or larvae on a plant, the female may not lay and the African Cotton Leafworm (*Spodoptera littoralis*) is deterred by the droppings of larvae already present (examples as reviewed by Thompson and Pellmyr, 1991 and Renwick and Chew, 1994).

It is no surprise that most of these examples are taken from pest species, for scientists have discovered them while searching for the means to deter the pests from laying on valuable crops or for chemical lures to lead the moths to traps.

CHANGING TO NEW FOODPLANTS

The most obvious change of foodplant occurs when a plant invades a new area, or is planted there. In Britain there have been many examples of this but the most extensive involves the large-scale planting of exotic trees for forestry or as amenity trees in gardens. The Sitka Spruce (*Picea sitchensis*) was unknown in Britain until relatively recently but now covers huge areas, especially in northern England and Scotland. The same applies to greater or lesser degrees to species of Larch (*Larix* spp.), Fir (*Abies* spp.), Southern Beech (*Nothofagus* spp.) and non-native Pine (*Pinus* spp.). This last illustrates the fact that the newcomers may either be rather unrelated to native trees or may be congeneric with them. It would be expected that the closely related newcomers would find moths adapting to them more readily than unrelated ones.

The moths that come to use newly introduced plants fall into several types. There are those that invade with the new species or disperse to find them and settle in Britain. A good example is the cone-forming *Caloptilia rufipennella* that has invaded Britain from the Continent recently and feeds on Sycamore. Such moths have not changed their foodplant but have followed it to new locations. The second type of moth that uses newly available foodplants is the polyphagous species that has already shown its ability to feed on almost any plant. Almost all deciduous trees, of whatever species, may be used by the Mottled Beauty (*Alcis repandata*) (although even this species might show some specialisation if it were to be better studied. Harper (*pers. comm.*) believes it prefers Honeysuckle (*Lonicera periclymenum*) in the spring). Winter (1974) records many polyphagous species that have recently been found feeding on exotic conifers and Hatcher (1991) found that many moths that usually feed on broad-leaved trees have taken to conifers in Bernwood Forest, Oxfordshire. He did find, however, that there was also a strong taxonomic influence, with new hostplants tending to be related to the previous ones.

The last and most interesting moths are those that usually show some specialisation but which make a change, often to a related tree. The Southern Beech shows affinities in leaf chemistry and structure, as well as in its taxonomic position, to other Fagaceae in Britain, notably to Beech but also to Oak. Welch (pers. comm.) suggests that this affinity is the reason why Southern Beech has been accumulating moth herbivores in Britain reasonably quickly, compared with less related invaders, even though its natural range in New Zealand, Australia and South America is so far away that none of its normal fauna can reach it. In Aberdeen botanic gardens, where a few Southern Beech have been planted within the last 50 years, they act as host to a small but definite range of moths, including the leaf miner *Phyllonorycter messaniella*, which usually uses native Oak and Beech. It would be useful to compare the numbers of herbivores now found on a variety of different invading plants. However, the fact that each of these plants occurs in widely different abundance and range and has been here for different periods, makes such as comparison too multi-factorial to be useful. The Gingko (*Gingko biloba*) and the Dawn Redwood (*Metasequoia glyptostroboides*) have no associated moths, but both are rare and scattered and the Redwood is a recent arrival. How are they to be compared with the European Larch (*Larix europea*), which is abundant, universal and a long-standing resident?

THE WINTER MOTH AND ITS NEW FOODPLANTS

Occasionally a foodplant shift is sufficiently radical or potentially damaging to be worthy of further study. The Winter moth (*Operophtera brumata*) has recently been found feeding on Sitka Spruce and on Ling (*Calluna vulgaris*), neither of which has been previously recorded. Sitka Spruce apparently provides a 'poor quality' diet, compared with Oak (a usual foodplant) but the larvae complete their growth on it and the habit is now established (Watt and McFarlane 1988). Spruce also holds an advantage for the moth, because the newly hatched larvae must find food quickly; on Oak, disaster may strike if they hatch before the buds are sufficiently open in the spring. The loose terminal shoots of the spruce are always available so timing of the hatch is not critical on this tree.

Heather defoliated by Winter moths was first noticed on the island of Orkney but has been studied principally on the Scottish mainland, where outbreaks have occurred in isolated places since 1980. At first it was thought that the Heather was only being used after Blaeberry (*Vaccinium myrtillus*), a preferred foodplant, had become used up in a site (Kerslake *et al.*, 1996). However, some Heather outbreak areas have no Blaeberry and so Heather must be a primary foodplant. Larvae do not grow so well on Heather as on more usual hostplants but they do survive and the moths persist in the outbreak areas, even in years when the ground is snow covered in the season of adult emergence. No-one yet knows how the moth has effected the change – perhaps a genetic mutation has provided the digestive capability to handle the tough and nutrient-poor Heather leaves.

CHANGING A FOODPLANT MAY ALLOW A CHANGE OF RANGE

Bretherton *et al.* (1983) and Burton (1991) document the changes of foodplant of Blair's Shoulder-knot (*Lithophane leauteri*), which was first recorded in Britain in 1951 and is still spreading north. In southern France the species originally used Juniper (*Juniperus communis*) and Common Cypress (*Cupressus sempervirens*) but in Normandy and Britain it has adopted Monterey Cypress (*C. macrocarpa*), which is widely planted as an ornamental tree, and also the more frost-hardy Lawson's Cypress (*Chamaecyparis lawsonia*) and the abundant Leyland Cypress (*Cupressocyparis leylandii*). With these new foodplants the moth will be able to spread to its climatic limits in Britain.

Rosebay willowherb (*Epilobium angustifolia*) is not an exotic plant but it has changed in the last 100 years from being a localised to an abundant and widespread species. This has allowed many more herbivores to use it as a foodplant, among them *Scythris inspersella*, which may have invaded from the continent, and the Large Elephant Hawk moth (*Deilephila elpenor*), which has always been recorded from other *Epilobium* species but which now seems to be almost wholly associated with Rosebay Willowherb.

The Mullein moth (*Cucullia verbasci*) has taken to the introduced, perennial and abundant garden shrub *Buddleia*, which has allowed it to sustain more stable populations than when restricted to the transient biennial Mullein (*Verbascum thapsus*) (Owen, 1984). So far, however, this has not led to an extended range.

FEEDING STRATEGIES

Eggs laid singly or in groups

The life of a female moth is a hazardous one and she will benefit from laying her eggs as fast as she can, before a predator or a spell of unfavourable weather kills her. Her newly hatched larvae depend on her having positioned the eggs in as favourable a place as possible, for they do not usually have the capability of moving to a new and better site themselves. The quickest way to lay all the eggs would be to deposit them in a large batch, but the best positioning may require the female to lay each separately, scattering them over the available foodplants, so as to avoid competition between the offspring.

If a moth is to lay in a batch then certain conditions have to apply. Either the foodplant resource must be concentrated, so that no shortage will happen, or the larvae must be able to disperse themselves. Trees provide a substantial resource all in one place and so the Gypsy moth (*Lymantria dispar*) (for example) can afford to lay batches of eggs on the trunks of the forest trees that it uses for food. The Emperor moth (*Pavonia pavonia*) also lays batches of eggs, but rather smaller ones of around 15 eggs, on Ling (*Calluna vulgaris*) on moors. In this case each heather plant is quite small but characteristically occurs among a host of others, so that the larvae are surrounded by food. Emperor moth larvae begin feeding close together beside their old egg site but they then gradually disperse, becoming solitary by their last instars.

If the food resource is not great, the larvae first have to disperse from their egg batch site. Vapourer moths (*Orgyia antiqua*) have wingless females that lay their eggs in one batch on the old cocoon and the first thing the newly hatched larvae do is to spin a very fine thread of silk, which acts as a parachute and carries them off until the silk tangles around a new twig.

Batches of eggs represent a large cache of food for a potential predator and a possible great loss for the moth. Therefore, they have to be well protected, as do the larvae that hatch from them. The Brown-tail (*Euproctis chrysorrhoea*) has larvae with very irritant hairs. The larvae can live in groups in a silken web, protected by the hairs. The Brown-tail's eggs are also covered with hairs, which the female puts there from her very large anal tuft, and the pupae are also protected by the larval hairs, which remain attached to the old skin on the outside of the pupa. Cinnabar moth (*Tyria jacobaea*) larvae are toxic and warningly coloured in black and orange. They congregate on their foodplants, close to the bright yellow egg batches. The foodplant is Ragwort (*Senecio jacobaea*), which often grows in clumps, presumably the feature that allows the larvae to be grouped, but the strategy is not always successful in this species, because sometimes the larvae do run short of food.

Most moths lay their eggs singly, placing them in the most advantageous positions, avoiding the chance of competition with other larvae of the same brood and reducing the chance of predators finding the solitary larva. The trade-off is that the females have to use time and energy dispersing the eggs but even wingless females crawl about doing so (for example the Pale Brindled Beauty (*Apocheima pilosaria*)), so the advantages must be worthwhile. It would be advantageous if females could detect the presence of existing eggs, so that they could avoid placing one of their own close to them. This occurs at least in the European Grapevine moth (*Lobesia botrana*) and the European Corn-borer (*Ostrinia nubilalis*), both of which leave egg-laying deterrent pheromones on eggs as they are laid

(Renwick and Chew, 1994). Such pheromones are detected by other females while searching for egg-laying sites. The ability to detect eggs visually in heliconid butterflies is taken advantage of by their foodplants *Passiflora* spp., some of which mimic eggs by producing small yellow spheres on their leaves, so deterring true egg-laying by the butterflies.

Food competition and cannibalism

When food is in short supply conspecific larvae may well meet on the foodplant. In most circumstances there is no real interaction except the sort of shaking movement that larvae use to detach any other insect that touches them. However, some species are cannibalistic or predatory and attack the intruder. Species like the Dunbar (*Cosmia trapezina*) can be reared on a purely vegetarian diet, but they routinely feed on other larvae, including smaller examples of their own species, if they can find them. The Satellite (*Eupsilia transversa*) has the same habit. It provides a high protein diet and the larvae grow faster and achieve a higher pupal weight if they can find other larvae to feed on.

The Silky Wainscot (*Chilodes maritima*) takes the predatory habit further, for it depends wholly on a diet of other insects, finding these inside the stems of Common Reeds (*Phragmites australis*) (Bretherton *et al.*, 1983). A number of fairly closely related moths have larvae that feed inside reed stems, but on vegetable material, and it may be surmised that the Silky Wainscot's ancestors did the same. Perhaps other species are partly predatory but it seems odd for an obligate carnivore to be restricted to the stems of one plant.

Timing of feeding

The time during a season that larvae feed may be closely controlled to take advantage of the very best conditions. The classic examples are the moth herbivores of Oak. It has long been known that there are myriads of larvae found on Oak leaves in spring and early summer but many fewer later. Many factors contribute to this situation.

Feeny (1970) measured the quality of the Oak leaves at different seasons and found that several factors change during the season. Some of these are shown in Figure 30 where it is clear that the nitrogen and water content are at their highest early in the season and decline significantly thereafter. The structural protein, tannin, thought to be both a stiffening for the leaves and a feeding deterrent (see Chapter 6), is low in concentration as the leaves expand in the spring but then increases quickly and steadily later. Feeny suggested that the glut of larvae, which are mainly of only a few species including the Winter moth (*Operophtera brumata*), the Northern Winter (*O. fagata*), the Mottled Umber (*Erannis defoliaria*), the Scarce Umber (*Agriopis aurantiaria*) and the Green Oak-roller (*Tortrix viridana*), are present in the spring to take advantage of the higher quality food and to avoid the high tannin levels.

Other workers have surmised that the high density of larvae overwhelms the bird predators, whose own density has to be set to the lower levels of food available at other times, and it is possible to show that the maximum numbers of larvae that can be eaten by the birds is well below the numbers of larvae present at peak time. Even so, the birds benefit from the easy availability of food and time their own broods of chicks to coincide.

The clear disadvantage to the larvae is that they may become so numerous as to disturb one another constantly, or to eat all the food. Certainly, Oaks do become defoliated in

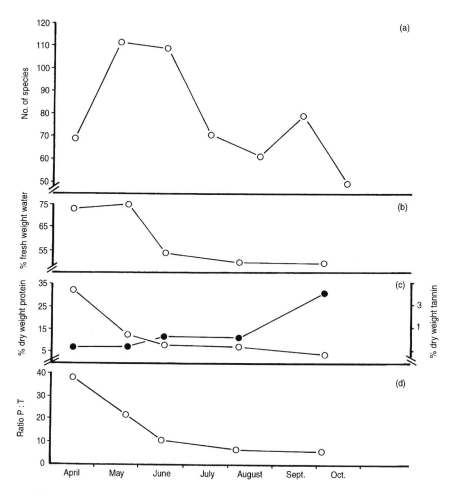

FIG 30 *Seasonal changes in oak and its moth herbivores. (a) Changes in the numbers of species of Lepidoptera feeding on Oak in Britain through the season; (b) percentage fresh weight of water in leaves; (c) (○) percentage dry weight of protein in leaves; (●) percentage dry weight of tannin in leaves; (d) ratio of protein to tannin in leaves (Source: Feeny, 1970, with permission from Blackwells Scientific)*

some years in Britain. At such times the larvae may descend from the trees and feed on low plants but it is not known whether this allows successful development.

Winter moths make loosely spun shelters and can easily re-make these, even if the shelters are eaten by other larvae. This appears to cause no disturbance to the larvae. Green Oak-rollers also make tubes, but they are much more affected if these are eaten, having to devote precious time to renewing them and failing if they are constantly disturbed. This represents 'asymmetric competition', with Winter moths unaffected and Green Oak-rollers at a disadvantage.

LEAF MINERS AND THEIR MODE OF FEEDING

Most leaf miners are intolerant of disturbance and blister miners of the genus *Phyllonorycter* cannot repair their mines if they are accidentally damaged by externally feeding larvae. Most blister miners on Oak make their mines in late summer but West (1985) has shown that if you induce *Phyllonorycter* species to produce early mines, i.e. in spring at the time of high food quality, and you protect them from interference from other larvae, they grow faster than usual and produce larger moths. They obviously benefit from spring foliage but

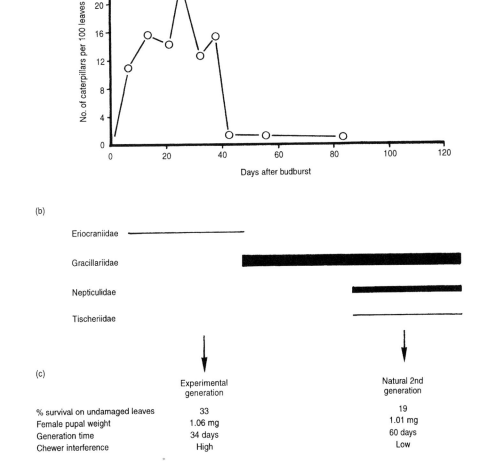

FIG 31   *The influence of leaf quality and free living caterpillar interference on leaf miners on Oak. (a) Numbers of caterpillars on leaves; (b) proportionate abundance of four groups of leaf miners at different seasons; (c) features of experimental and natural* Phyllonorycter *spp. miners. (Source: West, 1985, with permission from Blackwells Scientific)*

do not usually feed on it. If the early mines are not artificially protected, most are damaged and the mortality rate is so high that the population could not be sustained. It seems clear that *Phyllonorycter* have to feed later to avoid mortality and therefore have to put up with poor quality food. *Eriocrania* spp. also produce blister mines but they feed in the spring, just when the glut of external feeders are present. However, they feed up very quickly, are capable of repairing minor damage to their mines and also it seems that other larvae avoid them. Perhaps their mines are distasteful to other larvae, or perhaps they choose to feed on the poorest quality spring leaves, i.e. those generally avoided by the other larvae. This is not yet fully studied but Hartley and Lawton (1987) have shown that external feeders do avoid *Eriocrania*-mined leaves.

Those few larvae that do feed on Oak later in the season have to make do with poorer quality food (Hunter, 1987b). *Diurnea fagella* larvae feed from June to October, growing very much more slowly than spring feeding larvae of equivalent size. This extended feeding period renders them more liable to predation and parasitism than usual but they do not seem to have any extra mechanism for deterring predators. They

Birch leaves showing the characteristic 'cut-outs' made by caterpillars of Incurvaria pectinea.

have strangely inflated front feet, however, with which they can vibrate the spun leaves within which they feed and Hunter (1987a) has speculated that this action may deter insect predators or parasites.

SPECIALISED FEEDING HABITS

Some moth larvae show highly specialised behaviour when feeding and almost every possible organic source can be used by one species or another. Often feeding is possible only at night, when predators are less able to find the larvae, which have to hide during the day. Many of the Geometridae resemble twigs and many Noctuidae are camouflaged against leaves or spend the day in the upper layer of the soil. The Merveille-du-jour (*Dichonia aprilina*) larvae crawl down to sit camouflaged against the oak trunks by day and the Sand Dart (*Agrotis ripae*) crawls off its foodplant at the upper strand line and burrows in the sand.

Sap-feeding leaf miners

Many larvae from the families Gracillariidae and Phyllocnistidae show a very unusual and specialised form of feeding associated with their leaf mining habit. The larvae bore out of their eggs and into the leaf and begin feeding on the epidermal cells. As these are just under the surface of the leaf and the mine is very thin, the larvae are highly flattened, particularly on the head, which has a long, tapering and flat lateral aspect, instead of being rounded, like that of most larvae. The jaws are highly modified and the mandibles are semi-circular, with a sharp outer edge which is set facing forward. They cut into the epidermal cells by oscillating the mandibles from side to side, instead of chewing, and the larvae then suck up the sap that is released. The 'upper lip' or labrum stretches out above the mandibles, perhaps to help prevent the outer leaf layer from being ruptured (Emmet *et al.*, 1985).

Most of the genera within the Gracillariidae (for example *Caloptilia*) have two sap-feeding instars; at the end of this time the larvae are inside a thin blotch. They then change to a parenchyma-chewing form, in which the head becomes rounded and the mandibles point obliquely downwards and become adapted for chewing. They eat the cells beneath their blotch but this is insufficient for them and they then come out of the mine and feed within leaf rolls or folds. The members of the genus *Phyllonorycter*, however, suck sap for three instars and by the end of this time have excavated a mine which is so large that the parenchyma beneath it is adequate for the remainder of the life of the larva. The cell-eating phase can be spent entirely within the mine and pupation also takes place there. The larvae spin fine silk threads across the thin outer leaf surface to strengthen it and this pulls the mine into a puckered blister. Only very minor leaf repair is possible by *Phyllonorycter* larvae and normally if their mine is ruptured they cannot survive. Larvae of members of the family Phyllocnistidae remain sap suckers throughout their feeding period, developing spinnerets only in a final non-feeding instar which prepares the cocoon, and this stage hardly resembles a lepidopteran at all (Emmet, 1985). In all these species, where there is the extra change from sap to cell feeding, the whole process is termed hypermetamorphosis.

MOTHS THAT DO NOT FEED ON PLANTS

Lepidoptera are such inveterate plant feeders that it is unusual to find that some feed on feathers, hide and a variety of other foodstuffs. They are not necessarily more recent or specialised in an evolutionary sense, but are mainly found in one family, the Tineidae. It seems likely that the route to non-plant feeding was via that of feeding on decaying plant tissues. Some tineids are pests of stored vegetable products, as well as some being inhabitants of bird's nests or corpses.

CHAPTER 6

Plant Defence against Larvae

W HEN moth larvae feed on plants we assume that the plants will be damaged and that there will be strong selection pressure in favour of individual plants with some sort of defence against the larvae. This defence need not be active; it may just be that plants which are less palatable host fewer larvae.

DO MOTHS DAMAGE THEIR FOODPLANTS?

It seems obvious that larvae will damage their foodplants and for herbaceous species this needs no further study. The Ragwort plant (*Senecio jacobaea*) that is fully defoliated by Cinnabar moth (*Tyria jacobaeae*) larvae does less well than its uneaten neighbours, producing no seeds or having to re-grow its leaves and flowers so late in the season that they do not succeed (Crawley and Nachapong, 1984). The invasive cactus *Opuntia* spp. is also dramatically reduced by its biological control agent, the moth *Cactoblastis cactorum* (Strong *et al.*, 1984).

It is less easy to measure the effect on long-lived trees but Crawley (1985) found that oak trees that suffered 8–12% leaf-loss produced 25–30% fewer acorns, than trees that were protected from insect herbivores over a four-year period. It has also been shown in America that, whereas complete defoliation of oaks by Gypsy moth larvae (*Lymantria dispar*) in one year causes no extra mortality, if this is repeated for three consecutive years, up to 80% of the trees may die (Stephens, 1971). Bird Cherry trees (*Prunus padus*) are frequently defoliated by the colonial larvae of a species of 'small ermine' moth *Yponomeuta evonymella*, which live in conspicuous silk webs. Sometimes trees are defoliated for several years in a row and, although they may produce a small crop of replacement leaves late in the summer, it is difficult to believe that they are not seriously disadvantaged. Nevertheless, the trees do not often die and most survive to produce cherries in later years. Myers (1981) found that Western Tent moth (*Malacosoma californicum pluviale*) larvae frequently defoliate the rose bushes on which they feed, without eating the flowers and seeds, and this led to a 10-fold reduction in seed production in her study.

In some cases, plants can compensate for damage, growing extra leaves or concentrating resources into undamaged parts of the plant. Hendrix (1979) showed that when larvae of the oecophorid moth *Depressaria pastinacella* ate out the terminal flower buds of the Wild Parsnip (*Pastinaca sativa*), the secondary, lateral buds survived and the tertiary buds, which on an undamaged plant are often aborted, produced sufficient seeds to compensate for the loss of the terminal buds. In grasses, rapid leaf growth often follows grazing, although this may be at the expense of root growth.

If plants are to deter larvae, they must either be less palatable or less apparent than other plants, or they must have a defense, such as: physical features like spines; toxic or distasteful chemicals; or an ecological strategy.

PHYSICAL DEFENCE

Many plants, such as roses (*Rosa* spp.) or Acacia trees (*Acacia* spp.), have very obvious spines, but these are so large and widely spaced that they are clearly designed to deter larger herbivores rather than moth larvae and anything that can be called a spine is probably of no relevance to moths. However, stiff hairs may well have the same function and even a felt of fine hairs may prevent larvae from reaching the leaf surface or from moving easily across it. (Hairs may also have other functions, including the reduction of water loss from leaves, which may be their primary use in some plant species.)

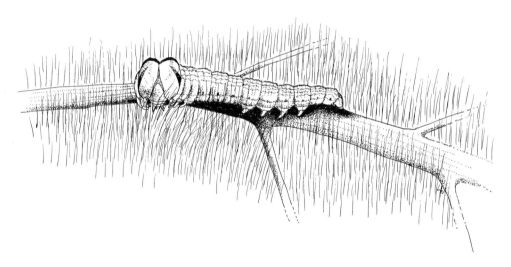

Hairs on a leaf pose a problem for a newly emerged caterpillar.

Tropical plants of the genus *Solanum*, tomatoes and potatoes as well as nightshades, may have a mat of hairs on their leaves and this certainly prevents ordinary larvae from holding securely on to them. In other cases the trichomes may be hooked, catching or impaling larvae, or may be glandular, releasing toxins when damaged (Levin, 1973). However, some Lepidoptera have special ways of overcoming this defence. Ithomiid butterflies spin a silk platform on to the top of the leaves and then feed on the edge of the leaf, so avoiding the hairs; whereas *Pardasena* sp. larvae (Noctuidae) mow off the hairs, producing a roll of discards, before feeding on the denuded strip and then repeating the process (Hulley, 1988). There is also a sphingid species, which feeds on a spurge (*Euphorbia* sp.) preferentially eating the hairs themselves and so avoiding the milky fluid that oozes from cut spurge leaves, which is the main defence of that plant genus. Dussourd and Eisner (1987) found that a Muslin moth (*Cycnia tenera*), which feeds on another latex producing plant, a milkweed (*Asclepias* sp.), avoids the latex by cutting a groove across the veins of a leaf and then feeding on the isolated part of the leaf beyond the groove.

Thick cuticle

Holly trees (*Ilex aquifolium*) have glossy, thick leaves, most of them with spines, especially those low on the tree. The spines seem to deter only larger herbivores but the glossiness of the leaves may well make them very difficult for moth larvae to cling on to and the thick cuticle may make an effective barrier to the mandibles of small larvae. All larvae have to start tiny and it may be at this stage that the thickness of the cuticle will be of prime concern. Many young larvae feed in a different way from when they are older and a common difference is that at first only one surface of the leaf is attacked, leading to the development of translucent 'windows' (the feeding is called fenestration). Later the whole leaf blade is removed by the larger larvae.

Holly is eaten by very few larvae and even these avoid the fully developed leaves. Almost no polyphagous species can handle it and those that do are specialists. The Double-striped Pug (*Gymnoscelis rufifasiata*) and the Yellow-barred Brindle (*Acacis viretata*) feed primarily on the flowers, as does the Holly Blue butterfly (*Celastrina argiolus*). However, the last species continues to use the developing seeds on the female trees, a strategy that is not open to it on male trees. In this case, the larvae switch to feeding on the young expanding leaves, which are also the food of the only moth to be completely dependent on Holly. This is the tortricid *Rhopobota naevana*, which ties the young leaves into a loose spinning within which to feed. All of these species avoid the mature leaves and the Holly suffers little insect damage, except by a fly *Phytomyza ilicis*, which mines the leaves and is very abundant and widespread. Mining also avoids the tough outer cuticle, except at the entrance site. It seems that a really thick and tough cuticle makes an effective defence and yet it is found on very few plants. Perhaps its production is very costly in resources, or the thick outer layer makes photosynthesis less effective. It could be claimed that many plants, especially trees, do thicken their leaves to some extent, and the discussion below about tannins in oak takes this topic further.

Varied leaf shapes and trembling leaves

The most effective shape for a leaf should be that which offers as large a surface area to the sun as possible, within the constraints of the need to keep it rigid and correctly aligned. In very windy or wet places there will also be the need to shed water quickly and to avoid physical damage. Even so, a simple circular or ovoid form would seem to be logical and yet tree leaves vary greatly in form. It benefits a plant if its flowers are readily differentiated from those of other species, so that pollinators are attracted efficiently, but there does not seem to be an obvious reason why tree leaves should need to be easily recognisable. This has led to much speculation as to why there is so much difference between plant species in this respect and even between leaves on the same individual plant.

A possible explanation is that non-standard shaped leaves are not so easily recognised by herbivores as normal leaves, so that such leaves suffer less damage. Evidence for this is shown in *Passiflora* vines, which are hosts for *Heliconius* butterflies. These vines show a wide range of leaf shape both between species and between populations of the same species, making it very difficult to recognise individual species and even whether a given vine is actually a *Passiflora*. For butterflies or moths which use vision to locate their host plants this must be a distinct disadvantage, benefiting the unrecognised plant. On these vines, as well as on many other plants, the leaves near the flowering and seeding shoots are very different from those on the main body of the plant. This may again benefit the plant, for moths may not recognise the flowering shoots as being part of the foodplant and so lay their eggs away from these vulnerable parts.

Further on it is suggested that leaves that have been damaged tend to have higher levels of defensive chemicals than those which are intact. Hence it would be advantageous for moths to choose to lay their eggs on undamaged leaves, so as to avoid these chemicals; Faeth (1985) found that females of some leaf-mining species do avoid damaged leaves for egg-laying. If a leaf has a shape that suggests that pieces have been cut out, such as the deeply scalloped edges of some maples (*Acer* spp.) or oaks (*Quercus* spp.), this might deter the rate of attack by potential herbivores. There is some experimental evidence to show that this is so and that moths lay less on such leaves.

Highly dissected leaves and those with scalloped and spiky edges are said to be much more difficult for a larva to hold on to than an even-edged leaf, but there does not seem to be any real evidence that this is so. There are comparatively few plants with very divided

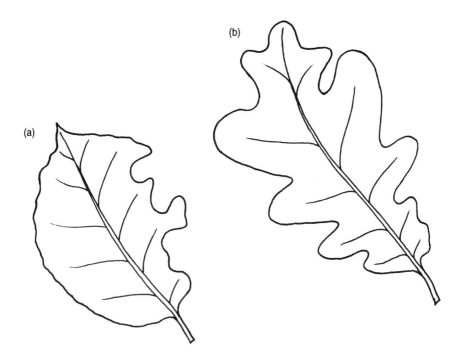

FIG 32   *A leaf eaten by a caterpillar (a) and a naturally scalloped Oak leaf (b).*

leaves, presumably because the shape reduces photosynthetic efficiency greatly, and therefore the fact that such plants seem to have rather few moths associated with them does not mean much. There is scope for a detailed comparison of closely related plants that differ greatly in leaf shape, if such could be found.

A further advantage of a non-standard leaf could be that such leaves tend to wave about more in the breeze, so making it more difficult for egg-laying moths to land, and/or for larvae to retain their hold. For example the Aspen (*Populus tremula*) has a rather ovate shaped leaf but has a flattened petiole section near to the leaf. This allows the petiole to bend easily and the leaf trembles violently in even a gentle breeze. From a distance the leaves can be seen to be in strong motion and they make an obvious clattering noise. However, Aspen has 46 moth herbivores, slightly higher than would be expected (see Chapter 5), given that the tree is rather localised, even if widespread, in Britain.

CHEMICAL DEFENCE

Secondary compounds in plants

It has long been known that plants contain quite high concentrations of chemicals, such as alkaloids or terpenes, that do not seem to be of immediate metabolic use, although they usually derive from normal metabolic pathways. These substances are called 'secondary plant compounds'. It has been suggested that they are formed and stored as inactive waste products – i.e. they are a way of removing potentially toxic waste products from the functioning chemical pool of the plant. However, they are placed in specific sites that seem unlikely waste stores, and are very actively and quickly recirculated, so it is now generally agreed that they have a role in deterring herbivores. (Some of these compounds, like nicotine or the active elements in spices, are used by ourselves.) Of course, it may be that chemicals that were once waste now serve a definite purpose in defence against herbivores.

Such defensive chemicals may be expensive to produce, unless they are genuinely only waste products. Also, only the minimum should be used and they should be placed in the most vulnerable part of the plant, at times when herbivory levels are highest. Certainly these compounds are most abundant at the surface of the plant, which herbivores must attack, and in young shoots, seeds and other especially vulnerable areas. They also seem to be most used by plants that are very likely to be attacked, namely the most apparent plants (see Chapter 5). However, there is not a very good match between apparency and the use of chemical defence, so an extra factor has recently been suggested. This is that plants that can grow quickly and readily replace material lost to herbivores will generally need less defence (Coley, 1980). If these chemicals are expensive to produce, it would also be expected that they would only be manufactured once the plant has been attacked and it is sure that defence is needed. To some extent this is true and the topic of induced defence is discussed further below.

Qualitative chemical defence

There are two rather different types of defensive chemicals. The first are called 'qualitative' defences and are very toxic, even at low concentrations. An example is the use of cyanides by various vetches and clovers. In this case the plants store the precursors of cyanide, a series of glycosides, often only in the young shoots or seeds. If the leaves are attacked enzymes are released, which act on the glycosides to synthesize cyanides, which are then toxic to some herbivores. However, some moths, notably the burnet moths (Zygaenidae), are able to detoxify cyanide and so they can feed unhindered on plants which are otherwise avoided. There is little real evidence that cyanogenic clovers are avoided by moth larvae but rather more that they are not fed on as much as would be expected by slugs!

Coley (1980) predicts that qualitative defence should be more abundant in fast-growing and unapparent plants, and this seems to be broadly correct.

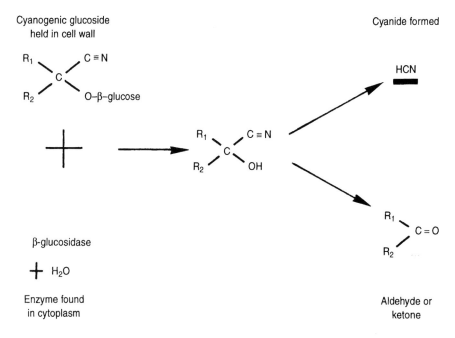

FIG 33   *The production of cyanide when a cyano-genic plant, in this case Sorghum* (Sorghum bicolor), *is attacked by a moth larva. In the undamaged plant, the precursor and the enzyme are held in separate parts of the cell; they are brought into contact when the cells are broken.*

Quantitative chemical defence

The second type of chemical defence involves 'quantitative' chemical defences, in which the effect depends partly on the amount of the chemical that is present. The most familiar examples of this type of chemical are tannins, which are present in many trees like Oak (*Quercus* sp.) and Beech (*Fagus* sp.). In some cases, these chemicals may make up to 60% of the weight of the leaves, often concentrated in the outer layers and they provide the tough-ness that is so obvious in old oak leaves. As noted in Chapter 5, the level of tannin in the leaves of oak rise quickly throughout the season. The young, tender and expanding leaves have low levels but by mid-summer the leaves are fully hardened and have high levels of tannin. The effectiveness of the defence that they provide increases as the levels build up, so that the young leaves are the least defended and this corresponds with the time of main attack by larvae.

Feeny (1970) investigated the causes of the spring feeding boom on oaks by caterpillars and he showed very clearly that larvae of the Winter moth (*Operophtera brumata*) fed on young leaves achieve a much higher peak weight than those fed on 'old' (actually just June) leaves (see Table 17). In fact no adult moths arose from the smaller larvae. However, he also investigated whether the effect was caused by a toxin or merely by the greater toughness of the June leaves, by providing ground-up old and young leaves as food; neither food was quite so good as unground young leaves but old ground leaves were as good as young ground leaves, suggesting that it is the structural, rather than the chemical, effect of tannin that is important. He suspected that later in the summer, when nitrogen levels have declined, even ground leaves would not prove to be usable by Winter moth larvae. Nevertheless, Feeny (1968) also showed that adding even as little as 1% tannin to larval diets can reduce growth rates, by reducing the digestibility of protein, rather than by a strictly toxic effect.

TABLE 17   *The ultimate weight of Winter moth larvae fed on different aged oak leaves.*

Type of leaf	Final weight achieved by Winter moth larvae (mg)
Normal young leaves (collected in May)	45
Normal older leaves (collected in June)	18
Ground young leaves	35
Ground older leaves	37

Source: Simplified from Feeny (1968), with permission from Elsevier Press.

There are other examples of moth larvae that do better on early leaves, such as the various Cucullinae observed by Schweitzer (1979) and the many different herbivores of birch studied by Fowler and Lawton (1985). They offered young and old leaves and found that growth and survival was universally better on the young leaves. Damman (1987) also found that the pyralid *Omphalocera munroei* did better on young leaves of its foodplant but despite this it always feeds late in the season in the wild. He found that the reason for this was that it lives in groups of around 20 individuals, within a 'tent' of leaves, and these tents can only be made using tough older leaves – younger ones tear apart!

CAN MOTHS DETOXIFY PLANT CHEMICALS?

Many, perhaps most, plants have secondary chemicals that have been implicated in defence against larvae but each plant has a distinct set of moth species that feed on it and so it is clear that these species have developed the ability to detoxify or digest the chemicals that deter others. Even the most toxic plants (when toxicity is measured in our human terms) may support moth larvae. For example, the Deadly Nightshade (*Atropa belladonna*), which uses the alkaloid atropine as its poison, is host to the micro *Acrolepia autumnitella* – its only moth herbivore, although it is also attacked by slugs. Hemlock Water-dropwort (*Oenanthe crocata*), which has a poisonous resin, is the foodplant of *Depressaria daucella* and the infamous Hemlock (*Conium maculatum*) hosts *Agonopterix alstromeriana*.

It has been suggested that as plants developed defensive chemicals in response to the selective pressure of herbivory, so insects developed the capability to detoxify these chemicals. This evolutionary arms race is quoted as an example of co-evolution but it is difficult to prove this, because all we see now is the result of past evolutionary events, rather than the process in action.

ECOLOGICAL DEFENCE

Timing of leaf burst

Individual oak trees vary greatly in the timing of bud-burst in the spring. Some are invariably later than others, which seems odd, because being late producing leaves must 'waste' part of the growing season. However, it is noticeable that in some years the later-leaved trees suffer much less feeding damage by moth larvae than do the normal or early trees (Crawley, 1985). Perhaps their compensation for missing some of the season is reduced damage, although they may also avoid damage from a late frost.

From the point of view of the moth larva the timing of bud burst is critical. The survival of Winter moth larvae that hatch before the oak buds have opened is measured only in hours and in fact they rapidly disperse if they hatch before young leaves are available. This they do by spinning very fine silk threads, which act as parachutes, and when these entangle with other branches the larvae crawl up the silk to search for food. Winter moths are polyphagous, so that this strategy can work – they can feed on almost any tree or bush. However, the Green Oak-roller *Tortrix viridana* is oligophagous on oak and it would die if it dispersed to a different species of tree (Hunter and Willmer, 1989). Perhaps because of this it does not disperse away from closed buds but is capable of surviving for longer than Winter moths, while it waits for the leaves to appear. Its survival as an unfed newly hatched larva is measured in days not hours.

Baltensweilor *et al.* (1977) have shown that if Larch (*Larix* sp.) is defoliated by *Zeiraphera diniana*, in succeeding years there is a reduced survival and growth of *Z. diniana* on the trees in question. Although this is partly due to induced defence (see below) it is also because the damaged larch produce their leaves later in the season and the larvae tend to starve in the spring.

Timing of seed production

There is little that a plant can do to protect developing seeds, except by using chemical defence, but this phase is usually brief and the seeds are often dispersed very quickly once they are ripe. It is rather rare to find large packets of ripe seeds still on their parent plant,

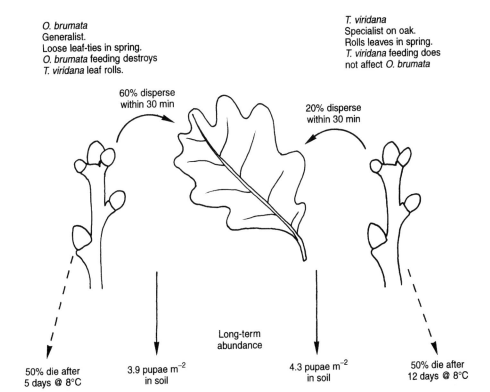

O. brumata
Generalist.
Loose leaf-ties in spring.
O. brumata feeding destroys
T. viridana leaf rolls.

T. viridana
Specialist on oak.
Rolls leaves in spring.
T. viridana feeding does
not affect O. brumata

60% disperse
within 30 min

20% disperse
within 30 min

Long-term
abundance

50% die after
5 days @ 8°C

3.9 pupae m^{-2}
in soil

4.3 pupae m^{-2}
in soil

50% die after
12 days @ 8°C

FIG 34   *Long-term abundance levels, dispersion rates from unopened birds, and star-vation rates on unopened buds of Winter moths* (Operophthera brumata) *and Green Oak Leaf-rollers* (Tortrix viridana) *on Oak. (Source: Hunter, 1990, with permission from Blackwell Scientific)*

although the very conspicuous tassels of Ash keys (*Fraxinus excelsior*) in early winter are an exception. Most seed feeding moths have larvae that feed-up quickly on the developing seeds on the plant, e.g. *Hadena* and *Eupithecia* spp. mentioned in Chapter 5.

Unpredictable plant occurrence

Plants that are unpredictable in their time and place of occurrence are obviously not very apparent to herbivores. The best examples of such plants are weed species, for these specialise in dispersing effectively to find newly cleared ground, where they can flourish without the competition of other established plants. Weeds are also usually small and develop very quickly before other plants grow to smother them. Such features also make them unsuitable as regular food for moth larvae. However, because they are so unapparent, it can be predicted that they will use few chemical defences and so may be palatable to a range of polyphagous moth larvae. It seems likely that they should be host to almost any polyphage that finds them, but that they should have few regular specialist herbivores.

The classic arable weeds, such as Poppies (*Papaver* spp.) or Scarlet Pimpernel (*Anagalis arvensis*), have no specialist moths in Britain. Nor does the typical weed, Shepherd's Purse (*Capsella bursa-palustris*), which appears like magic on newly disturbed ground, flourishes very briefly as a very small plant, and then sets seed and dies. The very common but small and opportunistic common Groundsel (*Senecio vulgaris*) is listed by Emmet (1991a) as having only one moth restricted to it and that is a migrant, namely the Gem (*Orthonama obstipata*), which is said to feed on Groundsel in captivity. By contrast, its larger, biennial relative Ragwort (*S. jacobaea*), which contains abundant, poisonous alkaloids, is listed as hosting nine species. One agricultural weed, Knotweed or Redshank (*Polygonum persicaria*), which has very few specialist moth herbivores of its own, is very well known by moth breeders as a plant that will be accepted by virtually every polyphagous moth larva – the ultimate undefended plant.

The encouragement of predators of herbivores

Many predators actively search plants for moth larvae and a plant that could recruit more predators could do well. Lawton (in Strong, Lawton and Southwood, 1984) reports on active predation by ants on larvae of the Indian Meal moth (*Plodia interpunctella*) placed experimentally on Bracken (*Pteridium aquilinum*) fronds (not one of their foodplants), so that most were removed in a few hours (although the natural herbivores of Bracken seemed to be able to avoid the ants). The ants could have been on the Bracken merely to search for prey but Bracken is one of many plants that have extra-floral nectaries, small but conspicuous glands that secrete a fluid similar to nectar, which attracted the ants to feed. Consequently, more ants were present than there would have been had the plant not encouraged them and predation of larvae was greater. The plant obviously benefits from this, so perhaps the extra-floral nectaries are there partly to attract these predatory ants.

Predators of herbivores search more on damaged leaves

Moth larvae are an important source of food for many species of bird, which often search trees assiduously for larvae. Sometimes the larvae are obvious and easily collected but, like the oak feeding caterpillars in the spring, their numbers may overwhelm the ability of the birds to collect them. At other times, they may be harder to find, so that the birds have to use any clues available. One such clue is the damage that is caused to the leaf by the larva. Heinrich and Collins (1983) have shown that chickadees quickly learn to search for insect larvae near leaves that are damaged. The lepidopterist often uses the same clues but it soon becomes clear that most larvae very quickly move on from the site of their feeding site, putting distance between them and the incriminating evidence. By contrast, larvae of the Tomato Sphinx (= Tobacco Hornworm, *Manduca sexta*) chew through the petiole of the leaf that they have just been eating, so that the obviously damaged leaf falls to the ground and they are not given away by it (Heinrich, 1971).

Birds use vision to recognise damaged leaves and perhaps the naturally ragged shape of some leaves may be mimicking damage to attract potential predators. However, there is no satisfactory evidence for this. Nevertheless, volatile chemicals may be released from the broken edges of leaves and Bruin *et al.* (1995) report that the parasitoids of the Small Mottled Willow (*Spodoptera exigua*) are attracted by these chemicals. Faeth (1990) also found that

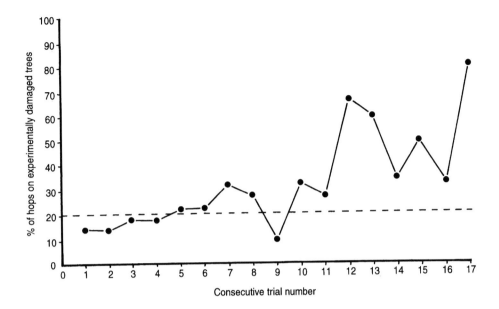

FIG 35   *The frequency of hops by a chickadee on trees with experimentally damaged leaves and hidden mealworms, as a function of total hops on all trees. The horizontal dashed line represents the frequency of hops expected if all trees were searched at random. (Source: Heinrich and Collins, 1983)*

the predators and parasitoids of *Cameraria* spp. (Gracillariidae – leaf miners) tend to search damaged leaves.

PLANT RESPONSES TO FEEDING DAMAGE – INDUCED DEFENCE

Induced production of defensive chemicals

In the 1970s, Haukioja and Niemala (1977) noticed that larvae of the Autumnal moth (*Epirrita autumnata*) grew more slowly when fed leaves that had previously been damaged. Many other researchers have since found similar situations. For example, Leather *et al.* (1987) showed that Pine Beauty moth (*Panolis flammea*) females laid fewer eggs on Lodgepole Pine (*Pinus contorta*) saplings that had been defoliated previously and that resulting larvae grew more slowly than on undamaged saplings; Bergelson *et al.* (1986) observed that the case-bearing larvae of *Coleophora serratella* moved away from leaves that were pierced experimentally. The effect was often seen within hours of the damage, but could last for up to three further years (Haukioja, 1980; Haukioja *et al.*, 1985). The obvious explanation was that the feeding damage was inducing an increase in 'defensive' chemicals, such as tannins, but there was much controversy about whether these were truly defensive or whether the feeding deterrence was a by-product of chemicals associated with wound healing (Edwards and Wratten, 1985). The greatest concentration was found in the damaged leaves but even nearby leaves, which might be the next target for the feeding larvae, showed increased defensive levels.

One ingenious way that larvae can avoid this decline in leaf quality is to make a roll of leaves around an opening bud. Sagers (1992) studied rolls made by pyralid and ctenuchid moths on a Panamanian shrub and found that the leaves which emerged within the shaded bud remained softer and with lower tannin levels than usual, without any decline in nitrogen or water content. Loeffler (1996) studied the gelechid *Dichomeris leuconotella*, whose larvae spin shelters on Goldenrod (*Solidago rugosa*) in America. She frequently disturbed the larvae, so that they had to spin new shelters, to see whether this were a physiologically costly process, predicting that disturbed larvae would grow more slowly. In fact, they grew more quickly than larvae that stayed in one shelter and the explanation was that the leaf quality in old shelters declined, whereas the new shelters of disturbed larvae were made

A leaf-roll made by a 'micro' caterpillar on oak.

among young leaves, which provided high quality food. The question 'why don't all larvae spin new shelters frequently?' is answered by the observation that disturbed larvae tended to fall from the plant while prospecting for new leaves. They are probably also more liable to predation at that time.

(An interesting sidelight is that Danell and Huss-Danell (1985) found that moose grazing on birch actually led to an increase in caterpillar damage in subsequent years. In this case the moose were removing not just parts of the leaves but the buds and twigs as well.)

TALKING TREES?

An even more controversial topic was raised by Baldwin and Schultz (1983) and Rhoades (1983), who claimed that trees *near* those being damaged by caterpillars (but unconnected to them) would respond by increasing the concentrations of defensive chemicals in their own leaves – this was referred to as 'talking trees'. These findings were strongly disputed by many authors, such as Fowler and Lawton (1985), who were unconvinced by the experiments that had been done and by the interpretation of the findings.

Bruin *et al.* (1995) have reviewed all the evidence so far and conclude that chemicals do increase in a plant following insect grazing, and that this does deter further feeding, but there is still the possibility that the chemicals are merely associated with damage repair. They also conclude that there is excellent evidence that some of these chemicals are volatile and diffuse away from the plant, so that they may be detected by nearby plants, which can then respond by increasing their own chemicals. These plants are 'listening', even if the damaged plants are not deliberately 'talking'.

Presumably it is costly to manufacture chemical defence and so plants save on these costs by only producing them in quantity in times of need – that is once a herbivore has begun to eat their leaves. Recently, one of the mechanisms for this process has become clearer. Baldwin (1995) studied Tobacco plants, which use nicotine as their defensive agent. If the leaf of a wild Tobacco plant (*Nicotiana sylvestris*) is attacked by insect larvae, a messenger chemical called jasmonic acid is produced within five minutes. This acts like a hormone, taking a message to the plant roots over the next two hours. The plant response is to increase the manufacture of nicotine, so that by five hours after the initial attack a dramatic increase has appeared in the leaves. This rate of response would be sufficient to prevent the larvae from feeding very extensively on the plant and in an American Tobacco species (*N. attenuata*) the levels of nicotine reach 120 mg g^{-1} of leaf weight – a much higher concentration than is found in cigarettes.

Baldwin has also shown that a plant can 'remember' insect attacks, so that it can respond faster to subsequent incidents. In this way the defences act rather like the vertebrate immune system. If plants are repeatedly dosed with jasmonic acid, at intervals of a few days, they respond much faster to the later doses, not increasing their eventual concentration of nicotine but mobilising it faster (Farmer *et al.*, 1992). Presumably the first attack by a larva is likely to be followed by others, for example if eggs hatch soon after one another from batches; so it makes sense for a plant to prepare for a quick response after the first feeding.

HOW DO MOTHS RESPOND TO PLANT DEFENCE?

Detoxifying chemical defence

Even plants that have few defensive chemicals will contain a wide range of substances requiring digestion, so that their herbivores must have a suitable array of enzymes. Plants are very varied in their composition, and tend to have rather specific herbivores associated with them (see Chapter 5), whereas animal protein is rather lacking in variety, so that carnivores tend to be able to digest almost any flesh that they can catch.

If a herbivore is to succeed in feeding on a defended plant, however, it must either metabolise toxic chemicals, or store them in a position where they will not be metabolically active. The general term for the main class of enzymes that detoxify defensive chemicals is 'mixed function oxidases', or MFOs, and these include a wide range of enzymes that tend to convert fat-soluble chemicals into water-soluble ones, that can then be disposed of by the usual excretory system of the moth. The centres of activity of these enzymes in insects are in the gut and malphigian tubules. Brattsten *et al.* (1977) have shown that Southern Armyworm larvae (*Spodoptera eridania*) show much higher MFO activity when feeding on unnatural foodplants, compared with their usual diet of lima beans. On a different scale, Krieger *et al.* (1971) have examined the enzyme activity of many larvae that are either oligophagous or polyphagous and have shown that the polyphagous species have a higher detoxifying ability than the oligophagous species, presumably because they are likely to come into contact with a much wider range of plant compounds. Rothschild *et al.* (1979) found that the Tobacco Hornworm larva (*Manduca sexta*) excretes the nicotine that is present in its foodplant, whereas it stores atropine if it feeds on Deadly Nightshade.

Moths that use plant chemicals as their own defence

Many moths that feed on plants containing defensive chemicals have the ability to take in and store these chemicals and then employ them to their own advantage. However, this does not always happen and is more complicated than might be expected.

Most of the burnet moths Zygaenidae feed on clovers and vetches that use cyanide as their defence. This chemical is not very stable and is also very toxic, so that in the plants glycosides, the precursors of cyanide, are stored and cyanide is formed only when the plant cells are ruptured and enzymes act to convert the glycosides. The burnet moths do not use the cyanide themselves but can synthesise their own, which is probably their most potent weapon against predators. However, they also contain several other poisonous chemicals, at least one group of which, the pyrazines, they sequester from their foodplants.

Caterpillars of the Eastern Tent moth (*Malacosma americanum*) feed on Black Cherry (*Prunus serotina*) leaves and have been observed deterring ant predators by regurgitating a noxious fluid (Peterson *et al.*, 1987). The leaves vary in the amount of cyanide they produce and it was found that caterpillars feeding on more toxic leaves also produce fluid which is more effective against ants. However, although the fluid contains some cyanide, it also contains much benzaldehyde and it is this which is active against the ants. The benzaldehyde is produced by the plant as a by-product of cyanogenesis and this is sequestered by the caterpillars as their own defence.

Many examples exist of other moths that sequester chemicals; they are listed by

Plate 1 MOTHS THAT REST ON BARK

Hydriomena furcata, **the July Highflyer** *(right)*. An abundant and highly variable species, the July Highflyer nearly always rests on bark. Despite its camouflage, Rothschild (1985) believes it is also mildly distasteful.

Brachionycha nubeculosa, **the Rannoch Sprawler** *(left)*. Confined in Britain to certain old birch woods in the Scottish Highlands, this moth is wonderfully cryptic when resting on the gnarled trunks in spring.

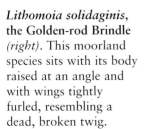

Lithomoia solidaginis, **the Golden-rod Brindle** *(right)*. This moorland species sits with its body raised at an angle and with wings tightly furled, resembling a dead, broken twig.

Plate 2 MOTHS THAT REST ON FOLIAGE

Thalera fimbrialis , the **Sussex Emerald** *(above)*. This rare species is a colonist, currently found only at Dungeness, Kent. As with all 'emerald' moths, the green pigment is very unstable and soon fades.

Atethmia centrago, the **Centre-barred Sallow** *(right)*. Many autumnal moths are orange, yellow or russet-brown, to match the bright colours of the changing and fallen leaves.

Drepana lacertinaria, the **Scalloped Hook-tip** *(right)*. Dead leaves are frequent at any time of year. The colour, size, wing shape and resting posture of this hook-tip, photographed in May, all contributed to its resemblance to a curled, dead birch leaf.

Plate 3 MOTHS THAT REST ON ROCKS

Entephria caesiata, the **Grey Mountain Carpet** *(right)*. Grey, northern and western rocks are the resting place of this characteristic species. In spite of such excellent camouflage, it is unusually active, and flies away rapidly if disturbed.

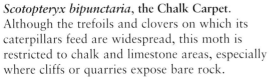

Scotopteryx bipunctaria, the **Chalk Carpet.** Although the trefoils and clovers on which its caterpillars feed are widespread, this moth is restricted to chalk and limestone areas, especially where cliffs or quarries expose bare rock.

Acronicta euphorbiae myricae, the **Sweet Gale Moth.** Many species which sit on rocks share a similar grey mottled appearance.

Plate 4 MOTHS THAT RESEMBLE SPECIFIC PLANTS

Anarta myrtilli, the Beautiful Yellow Underwing *(left)*. The twigs, buds and old flowers of Ling heather (*Calluna vulgaris*) are tinged with pink, matched by the wing colour and intricate pattern of this day-flying moth.

Archanara dissoluta, the Brown-veined Wainscot. This species, like many of its relatives, inhabits reed beds (*Phragmites australis*). All share the bleached brown colour of old reed stems.

Panolis flammea, the Pine Beauty. When sitting head-down at the tip of a twig, this moth resembles the spring buds of its foodplant, pine (*Pinus*). Its specialised resting behaviour has only recently been recognised, even though the moth is an abundant pest in some forestry plantations.

Plate 5 WARNINGLY COLOURED MOTHS

Abraxas grossulariata, the Magpie Moth *(right)*. The larvae, pupae and adults of this species are all distasteful and conspicuously marked with yellow and black. The pupa is enclosed in a flimsy cocoon through which its colours show and the moth itself rests in full view on the upper surface of leaves.

Euproctis similis, the **Yellow-tail**. Irritant hairs from the cast larval skin are gathered by the female moth into her tail tuft during emergence from the cocoon. They are then used to cover and protect the egg batches. The yellow tail is also revealed in a threat display when the moth is disturbed, as shown here.

Zygaena lonicerae, the **Narrow-bordered Five-spot Burnet Moth**. This species is typical of most burnet moths, where the red spots on a glossy, dark ground advertise the presence of cyanide and other toxins. Burnets are conspicuous day-flying species that rest fully exposed.

Plate 6 MOTHS THAT MIMIC OTHER INSECTS

Sesia bembeciformis, the Lunar Hornet Clearwing *(left)*. Resembling a large wasp or hornet in every respect apart from the sting, these day-flying moths emerge from the larval borings in the trunks of sallows (*Salix*) in early morning. Once their wings are dry they quickly fly up into the tree tops.

Synanthedon tipuliformis, the Currant Clearwing *(right)*. This species was once a pest of currants but is now scarce. It mimics solitary wasps, both when sunning itself and in its style of flight.

Acherontia atropos, the Death's Head Hawk *(left)*. The yellow body stripes and hind-wings are warning colours but the 'skull' mark may actually resemble an exaggerated head of a queen honey-bee. The moth raids bee-hives for honey and it has been suggested that the guard bees may be pacified by the thorax pattern and the squeaking that the moth can produce.

Plate 7
WHITE AND FEATHER-LIKE MOTHS

Lomographa bimaculata, the White-pinion Spotted *(right)*. Perhaps this species is adapted to blend into dappled light and shade, or to match the blossoms of its foodplants, hawthorn and cherry.

Amblyptilia punctidactyla, a 'plume' moth *(left)*. 'Plume' moths are named for their supposed resemblance to feathers. They do not look like other moths and so may not be recognised as such by potential predators. In spite of its fragile appearance, this species hibernates as an adult.

Cilix glaucata, the Chinese Character *(right)*. Bird droppings are unpalatable and moths from many families avoid predators by resembling them. The Chinese Character copies the faecal sac of a nestling bird, still apparently glistening and wet.

Plate 8 CATERPILLARS OF VARIOUS COLOURS AND SHAPES

Mormo maura, **the Old Lady.**
This is typical of many caterpillars which feed at night and hide by day. Their sombre colours merge with debris amongst soil or under bark.

Crocallis elinguaria, **the Scalloped Oak.**
A typical 'stick' caterpillar, which closely matches a twig of its foodplant. It must remain absolutely motionless by day if its camouflage is to work.

Xylena exsoleta, **the Sword-grass.**
The bright colours of this species do not necessarily make it conspicuous but act to break up its shape (disruptive colouration), amongst varied vegetation.

Deilephila elpenor, **the Elephant Hawk.**
In some species the caterpillars have different colour forms. Here the grey-brown form is more usual, a fanciful resemblance to an elephant's trunk giving the species its common name. However, to a small predator, the 'eye' marks may suggest a snake, best left alone!

Plate 9 EGGS AND CATERPILLARS

Orgyia antiqua, the Vapourer *(above left)*. The egg batch of this species is laid by the wingless female on her cocoon. Here the caterpillars are just hatching and some partially-eaten egg shells are visible.

O. antiqua, the Vapourer. *(above right)*. This is a 'classic' hairy caterpillar, whose prominent tufts of barbed hairs make it unpalatable; the bright colours convey a warning.

Acronicta leporina, the Miller moth *(left)*. These young caterpillars are feeding on the underside of a birch leaf, creating translucent patches called 'fenestrations'. The dark spots on the caterpillars break up their shape, so that they are inconspicuous on the partially eaten leaves.

A. leporina, the Miller moth *(right)*. To a predator these older caterpillars of the Miller moth may look like a feather, or perhaps a spider's web – at least they do not look like caterpillars!

Plate 10
CATERPILLARS, PUPAE
AND PARASITES

Euproctis chrysorrhoea, the
Brown-tail *(left)*. Caterpillars
of this species have seriously
irritant hairs and at times
are a public health hazard
in coastal, south-east
England. They live colonially,
emphasising their warning
message, and rest fully
exposed on a nest of silk.

Leucoma salicis, the White Satin
(right). This caterpillar is warningly coloured and has obvious
irritant hairs. Cuckoos are
undeterred and feed avidly on
them, as they do on other hairy
caterpillars, and parasites can
also lay eggs in them successfully.

L. salicis, the White Satin
(below). Most pupae are
vulnerable and are well hidden
but this species is hairy and so
presumably distasteful. Its obvious colours show through the
loose weave of the cocoon
(partly opened here).

Lycia zonaria, the Belted Beauty *(right)*.
Seven parasitic larvae of a microgasterine wasp have
recently emerged from this caterpillar and have spun
their cocoons on its back.

Plate 11
EMERGING AND MATING MOTHS

Lasiocampa quercus callunae, the Northern Eggar *(above left)*. The freshly-emerged male is in the last stages of drying its newly-expanded wings. Virtually all moths adopt this wing-drying position. Note the strongly pectinated (feathery) antennae.

Epione paralellaria, the Dark Bordered Beauty *(above right)*. The paler female is 'calling', releasing an attractive pheromone from glands on the extended tip of her abdomen. This species is sexually dimorphic, and the darker male has just arrived to begin courtship.

L. quercus callunae, the Northern Eggar *(left)*. This is another sexually dimorphic species. The female is larger and paler. It is one of a group of moths which mate face-to-face, rather than end-to-end, as do most others.

Plate 12 SEXUAL DIMORPHISM AND MELANISM

Diaphora mendica, **the Muslin moth** *(below)*.
In this species the white female is day-flying, whereas the dark male flies at night. Both sexes display 'warning' orange legs when disturbed.

Operophtera fagata, **the Northern Winter moth** *(top right)*. This species is typical of many which emerge in late autumn and winter and has flightless females with dramatically reduced wings.

Apocheima pilosaria, **the Pale Brindled Beauty** *(above)*. Like many of its relatives this species has a melanic form which is commonest in polluted urban areas but is scarce in the cleaner countryside. These are males, the females are wingless.

Plate 13 VARIABLE AND DISPUTED SPECIES

Orthosia incerta, the Clouded Drab *(above)*. The Clouded Drab hides by day amongst low vegetation, leaf-litter and other debris. Perhaps because it has no particular resting site, it is exceptionally variable throughout its range

Aporophyla lutulenta, the Deep-brown Dart (Sussex). This is the typical, southern 'race' of this species, which is rather dull and con-stant.

A. lueneburgensis, the Northern Deep-brown Dart (N E Scotland). Some regard this as a northern 'race' of *A. lutulenta*, others as a separate species. It is grey or black, rather than brown, and is frequently paler and more variegated.

Plate 14
MOTHS AT 'SUGAR'
AND VARIABLE SPECIES

Moths at sugar *(left)*. Sugar is notoriously unpredictable, attracting many moths on some nights but few or none on others. These are mainly *Xanthia togata*, the Pink-barred Sallow.

S. lubricipeda, the White Ermine (NE Scotland) *(left below)*. In Ireland and Scotland the ground colour is often suffused with buff or brown and the spots may be streaked or confluent. This example is darker than average.

Spilosoma lubricipeda, **the White Ermine** (Sussex) *(below)*. In southern Britain this species is generally milky-white and rather invariable in its colour and the extent of its black spotting.

Plate 15 MIGRANT MOTHS

Heliothis armigera, **the Scarce Bordered Straw** *(left)*. This is an agricultural pest in Mediterranean and sub-tropical areas, but fortunately is only a scarce migrant or importation to Britain. This specimen was bred from a caterpillar found in mange-tout peas from Zambia.

Rhodometra sacraria, **the Vestal** *(top right)*. Originating in the Mediterranean, this delicate species visits southern England in most years. During hot summers it sometimes breeds in stubble fields but cannot survive British winters.

Catocala fraxini, **the Clifden Nonpareil or Blue Underwing** *(above)*. This spectacular migrant occasionally reaches Britain from the east in early autumn. Its cryptic forewings hide the bright 'flash colouration' of the hindwings, when at rest.

Plate 16 COLONISTS AND RARE SPECIES

Lithophane leautieri, Blair's Shoulder-knot *(right)*. First recorded in Britain only in 1951, this moth has now become firmly established over much of the south, where its caterpillars feed on garden cypresses.

Hadena albimacula, the White Spot *(below left)*. This species is found only on the south coast of England, perhaps restricted by climatic factors. It is further confined to a handful of sites by its dependence on a single foodplant, Nottingham Catchfly (*Silene nutans*), which itself is very local.

Zygaena viciae, the New Forest Burnet moth *(below right)*. This species is now restricted to a single coastal location in western Scotland, having become extinct in the New Forest in 1927. It has critically low population numbers and is the subject of a conservation scheme.

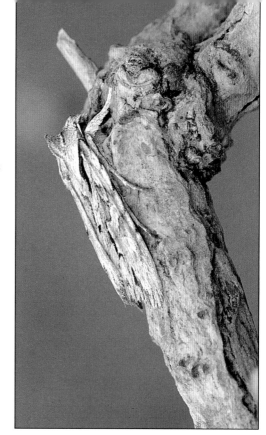

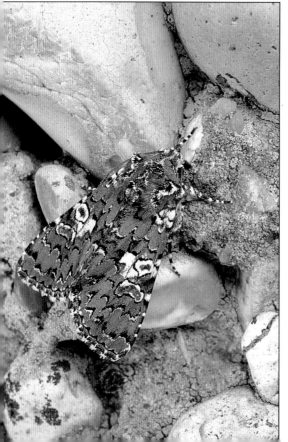

TABLE 18   *Defensive chemicals used by moths.*

Moth species	Chemicals involved
	Chemicals sequestered from foodplants
Zygaena filipendula	Pyrazine
Arctia caja	Cardiac glycoside (from *Digitalis*) Alkaloid (from *Senecio*) Pyrazine
Spilosoma lubricipeda	Alkaloid (from *Senecio*)
Callimorpha dominula	Alkaloid (from *Symphytum*)
Tyria jacobaea	Alkaloid (from *Senecio*) Pyrazine
	Chemicals synthesised by moths
Zygaena filipendula	HCN Zygenine (protein) Acetylcholine
Abraxas grossulariata	Histamine
Euproctis chrysorrhoea	Histamine
Arctia caja	Acrylylcholine Choline esters Histamine Cajin (protein)
Spilosoma lubricipeda	Acetylcholine Histamine
Tyria jacobaea	Acetylcholine Histamine

Source: Simplified from Rothschild (1985).

Rothschild (1985). They include the Spurge Hawk moth (*Hyles euphorbiae*), which obtains diterpenes and other substances from its foodplants, which are spurges (*Euphorbia* spp.). Many Arctiidae (tiger and ermine moths) are poisonous and use pyrazine alkaloids from their plants. The Scarlet Tiger (*Callimorpha dominula*) obtains these from Comfrey (*Symphytum* sp.), and the White Ermine (*Spilosoma lubricipeda*), uses the same chemicals.

Leaf mining as a way of avoiding plant defence

Quite large numbers of moth larvae are leaf miners, that is they feed between the surface of leaves. Among the advantages of this way of life is that the larvae avoid plant defences, which are often localised in the leaf cuticle. However, there is also the overwhelming disadvantage that the size of the moth species is severely limited – only a relatively tiny larva can fit inside a leaf. All members of the Nepticulidae, almost all of which are leaf miners, are tiny and include the smallest moths of all. The leaf mining genus *Phyllonorycter* is also made up of small moths, whereas the related but larger *Caloptilia* species mine only in their early instars.

The eggs of leaf miners (for instance those of the Nepticulidae) are often laid on the leaf surface and at hatching the larvae bore into the leaf. At this stage they face the tough cuticle of the plant, which may be a real barrier to success. However, it seems to be rare for miners to fail during this invasion. In some other groups of miners (for example the Eriocraniidae) the female cuts a slit in the surface of the leaf or bud, into which she lays her egg, so removing the need for the emerging larva to cut its own entrance (Heath, 1976). Once inside the larvae can feed on the plant sap or the parenchyma, sometimes restricting themselves to the pallisade layer, but in other species removing all of the inner leaf tissue, always without having continually to chew through the cuticle. This is a strong contrast to the free-living larvae that must constantly cut through the cuticle to obtain food. Plants often place their defensive chemicals specifically in the outer layers, where they will deter feeding and act as structural elements. Leaf miners avoid them.

Other advantages for leaf-mining larvae are that they have a humid environment; a degree of protection from predators and parasites; and they can therefore feed more or less continuously. They are totally dependent on their leaf, of course, and, if it is eaten or otherwise damaged, they too are lost. A few species have the ability to change leaves but the great majority cannot do so and cannot even repair minor damage. Some, like the Tischeridae, cut a small slit to the exterior, through which they evacuate their frass, but most retain this within the mine, often laying it out in characteristic patterns.

'GREEN ISLANDS' AND MINING LARVAE

Certain species of leaf miner, such as *Ectodemia argyropeza*, which feeds on Aspen (*Populus tremula*), or *Stigmella tityrella* on Beech (*Fagus sylvatica*), form what are known as 'green islands'. These are patches of leaf surrounding or distal to the mine that remain green, even after the rest of the leaf has turned brown in the autumnal senescence. They can be very conspicuous, especially among a pile of fallen leaves, and the larvae often continue to feed after the leaves have fallen from the tree. This carries obvious advantages. The season is prolonged for these larvae, allowing them time to fit in a second generation more easily and perhaps to feed at a time when there are fewer competitors. This can be very important to the larvae, for mined leaves sometimes fall from the plant early, a significant cause of mortality among some species of miners (Preszler and Price, 1993). However, the green islands are very visible to potential predators or parasites, although it is not known whether they are actually eaten or parasitised more freely because of this.

Very early authors noticed these green islands and speculated on their cause, noting that they can also be associated with some galls and plant infections. Wood (1894) suggested that the larvae may secrete a chemical that sustains the photosynthetic ability of the leaf but he was unable to suggest what this chemical might be. Tragardhs (1913) wondered whether the larvae severed the vascular bundles proximal to the island, so preventing the plant from initiating the process of ageing, but Townsend (1985), among others, has shown that the vascular bundles need not be cut in this way. Hering (1951), in his classic account of leaf mining, suggested that some product of larval metabolism, perhaps a nitrogenous chemical in the frass, or even merely the respired CO_2, may act to provide nutrients to the leaf, keeping it actively photosynthesing.

A change in emphasis followed the discovery in the 1950s of substances called cytokinins, which have been found to promote cell division and delay senescence, even in excised leaves (Mothes *et al.*, 1961). Cytokinin was found by Engelbrecht *et al.* (1969) to be present in raised levels in the green tissue surrounding the larvae of two nepticulid species, as well as inside the larvae, with the highest concentrations in their labial glands. The frass also contains cytokinin but only in similar quantities to that found in the leaf tissue and by 1971 Engelbrecht had speculated that the larvae secrete the substance from their labial glands; that this is taken up by the leaf tissue with the result that it remains green; that this tissue is then eaten by the larvae and the cytokinin is passed undigested with the frass. Even if this is not the precise mechanism, it is probable that it is broadly correct.

Hering (1951) noticed that the frass is often placed close to the vascular bundles in the leaf and, as noted above, he speculated that it may have been something within frass that was most important. However, a nepticulid called *Ectoedemia subbimaculella* provides evidence that this is unlikely, for it has a slit through which its frass is ejected from the mine but it also forms green islands. This helps support the theory that it is the labial gland that is most important in the secretion of the cytokinin.

It is frequently suggested that the interplay of herbivores and plant defence is an example of co-evolution, an evolutionary 'arms race'. This may not be strictly true but it is obvious that plants are not passive victims of herbivores but carry subtle and powerful defence, which acts to deter feeding and keep the world green!

CHAPTER 7

The Mating Behaviour of Moths and the Use of Pheromones in the Control of Moth Pests

FINDING A MATE

Pheromones and behaviour – an introduction

'Candle in hand we proceeded thither [to the room where the female moth was trapped], and what we beheld was something never to be forgotten. With a soft flick-flack the big moths were circling about the wire-screen prison, alighting on it, leaving it, flying up to the ceiling, and then flying down. They came with a rush toward the candle, extinguished the flame with a stroke of their wings, alighted on our shoulders, clung to our clothing, and lightly brushed against our faces. . . .' (Fabre, 1937)

The wonderful sight that Fabre was describing so eloquently was that of male Giant Peacock moths (*Saturnia pyri*) attracted to a virgin female that was 'calling' them with her scent. Most breeders of moths will have seen something similar, although probably not on so grand a scale, and it is true that for almost all moths the business of finding a mate is accomplished using such chemical messengers. Chemicals released by one individual into the environment, where they serve as messages to others of the same species, are called 'pheromones'. Discussion of them forms a large part of this chapter.

As well as the sex pheromones, which are discussed in detail below, insect pheromones have several other purposes. 'Aggregation' pheromones have not been found in moths but cause many other insects to group together for various reasons. 'Alarm' pheromones, which stimulate escape or defensive behaviour, have also not been found in moths. Nor, of course, have the various different chemicals used to regulate social behaviour in Hymenoptera and Isoptera. However, some moth species do use 'trail' pheromones, which act by marking a route and are used by some larvae to help them move around in organised groups to new food resources. There are also 'spacing' or 'dispersion' pheromones which elicit behaviour that results in individuals moving farther apart, a good example being the messages left on eggs that deter other females from laying their own eggs nearby. 'Recognition' pheromones identify their releasers, often giving information on species, sex, readiness to mate or other physiological features.

A male Emperor moth (Pavonia pavonia) *arriving at a 'calling' female.*

This makes an impressive array of functions and it is not an exaggeration to say that most intra-specific communication in moths is carried out by the use of pheromones.

Vision is certainly important in some ways, particularly for day-flying species, and many butterflies and day-flying moths are sexually dimorphic in their colours and patterns. Male Orange-tip butterflies (*Anthocharis cardamines*) have a very conspicuous orange blob on their wing, which advertises their sex. A very interesting example amongst the moths is that of the Ghost Swift moth (*Hepialus humuli*). The male is pure white and has a characteristic hovering flight at dusk, when it seems to be swaying on the end of an invisible pendulum and its colour makes it look a little like a ghost. Males often group together and the females locate them visually, flying rapidly up to one and almost knocking it to the ground in their attempt to mate, rather in the way that female grouse select males displaying on a lek (Turner, 1988). In Shetland, where even the darkest part of the June night is barely as dark as dusk elsewhere, the males are almost as orangey-brown as the females and the conventional but untested explanation for this is that the males cannot afford to be too conspicuous in the lighter conditions, for fear of attracting predators.

Mate finding in moths – the problem

Moths are very small organisms in a very large environment and so for most species it is important that the males find the females effectively and quickly. Speed is essential because there is the ever-present threat of predation or death owing to unfavourable weather conditions, and it is imperative that the female lays her eggs as expeditiously as possible. Perhaps there are some species that are never far from a potential mate, because they live in closely defined colonies and emerge close to other individuals. Species that use small marshes, like the Silver Hook (*Eustrotia uncula*) in western coastal Scotland, are found in aggregations but even these must have mate location abilities. The highly colonial burnet moths (*Zygaena* spp.), which often abound in small sunny hollows, use a female scent which is so effective that males may often be found clustering around the cocoon from which a female is about to emerge, so that she may mate before even beginning to expand her wings.

The majority of moth species do not live in tight colonies and so may have a harder task in locating a mate. The use of vision requires that at least one of the sexes becomes obvious, a dangerous situation, and one that will not work very easily at night, when most moths are active. Sound is used very effectively by grasshoppers, crickets and Death Watch beetles but has never been found in use by moths. The only real alternative is the use of scents, of which moths have become masters. A scent may be released without the sender being visually obvious; it may act over many tens of metres; the message is persistent and may contain very precise and complicated information; and it is dependent only on there being at least a gentle breeze.

Although it is possible for predators to have evolved to use moth pheromone mimics to attract or detect moths as prey, this does not seem to have occurred often. However, some 'bolas spiders' (*Mastophora* spp.) do use pheromones to attract moths to their sticky lure (Yeargan and Quate, 1996).

Males emerge first

It is usual for male moths to emerge before females. This has been noted many times, usually anecdotally but sometimes in closely controlled studies. Bourn (1995) records that male Transparent Burnets (*Zygaena purpuralis*) and 'Talisker' Burnets (*Z. lonicerae jocelynae*) appear on average four to six days before the females. The usual explanation for this is that it allows the females to mate as soon as possible after emergence from the pupa, so that they may make full use of their adult lifespan for egg-laying. Amateur moth enthusiasts know that it is rare to catch a female moth in the wild that is not already mated, regardless of her wing condition (unless she is a migrant). Clearly it would be disadvantageous for males to emerge too early for they would then be likely to die or be killed before they had a chance to mate. Conversely, a male that emerged after the females would tend to find that most potential mates had already mated and would not mate again.

It used to be thought that most female moths mate only once and this is still considered

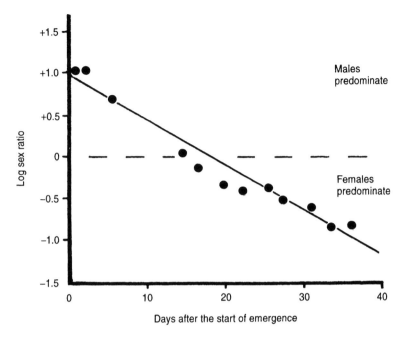

FIG 36   *The changing sex ratio of a population of the Narrow-bordered Five-spot burnet moth* (Zygaena lonicerae) *on Skye, Scotland in 1992. Males predominated until the 18th day after emergence started and females predominated thereafter. (Line fitted by regression:* y = -0.055 + 1.069; r² = 0.945). *(Source: Bourn, 1995)*

to be the general rule but there are some examples of second matings, as in some *Zygaena* spp. (Tremewan, 1985). Bretherton, Goater and Lorimer (in Heath and Emmet, 1983) suggest that the Dotted Chestnut (*Conistra rubiginea*), which overwinters as an adult, needs to mate twice, their evidence apparently being that many females caught in the spring lay infertile eggs. However, a few males also overwinter and perhaps the infertility merely reflects the fact that they have not yet mated. Nevertheless, a late male will usually find few available mates and so will be at a selective disadvantage. On balance, selection has favoured a short male lead time and so when a female emerges she will almost inevitably find mates in wait for her. Even in species where the female needs some days in which to feed before her eggs mature and are laid, she will usually mate as soon as possible after emergence.

FEMALE PHEROMONES – THEIR CHEMISTRY AND PRODUCTION

It is the general rule that the female moths release the pheromone that attracts the male from a distance, although both sexes may produce pheromones that act over short range during courtship once they are close together. Females are heavier bodied and so they are less likely to use energy in flight to find a male. However, a few species, such as the Wax moth (*Galleria mellonella*) and the Lesser Wax moth (*Achroia grisella*) have male pheromones that act to aggregate females to them (Shorey, 1976). These scents are detected primarily by sense organs on the antennae. Most female moths have simple antennae, whereas it is common for males to have varying degrees of side-branching on theirs, increasing the effective surface area on which the sense organs are located.

Many mate attraction pheromones in female moths have been extracted and characterised since 1960, when the first was isolated from the Silk moth (*Bombyx mori*). Some are alcohols, some acetate esters and some aldehydes; a small selection is listed in Table 19. These pheromones are remarkably similar in their general structure, usually being unbranched carbon chains of 10–18 atoms, with one or two unsaturated points and a functional endgroup. In most cases the actual pheromone is a mixture of two or more of these chemicals, in a precise combination that is highly host specific. David and Birch (1989) provide some examples of such mixtures, culled from other studies, showing how closely related species of moth may be prevented from interbreeding by the ratios of chemicals that they produce. The Fruit Tree Leaf-roller (*Archips argyrospilus*) uses a blend ratio of 60:40:4:200 of (Z)-9, (E)-11-tetradecenyl acetate, (Z)-9-tetradecenyl acetate and dodecanyl acetate, whereas the very similar species *A. mortuanus* uses a ratio of 90:10:1:200. For the Red-banded Leaf-roller (*Argyrotaenia velutinana*) there is a critical ratio of (Z)-9 to

TABLE 19   *Examples of the types of sex pheromones used by moths (from references in text).*

Species of moth	Type(s) of sex pheromones used
Spodoptera littoralis African Cotton Worm	(Z)-9,(E)-12-tetradecadienyl acetate
Panolis flammea Pine Beauty	(Z)-9-tetradecenyl acetate (Z)-11-tetradecenyl acetate (Z)-11-hexadecenyl acetate
Trichoplusia ni Cabbage looper	(Z)-7-dodecenyl acetate
Lymantria dispar Gypsy	(Z)-7,8-epoxy-2 methyloctadecane
Plodia interpunctella Indian Meal moth	(Z)-9,(E)-12-tetradecadienyl acetate
Cydia pomonella Codling moth	(E)-8,(E)-10-dodecadienol dodecanol tetradecanol
Archips argyrospilus Fruit Tree Leaf-roller	(Z)-9,(E)-11-tetradecenyl acetate (Z)-9-tetradecenyl acetate dodecenyl acetate
Pectinophora gossypiella Pink Bollworm	(Z)-7,(Z)-11-hexadecadienyl acetate (Z)-7,(E)-11-hexadecadienyl acetate

(E)-11-tridecenyl acetate necessary to produce the aggregation of the males, while the third component of the pheromone, dodecanyl acetate, seems to induce wing fanning by the male, a behaviour used in courtship.

Many species have more than one chemical in the pheromone that they release, although the Larch Case-bearer (*Coleophora laricella*), for example, seems to have just a single one. Obviously it is possible to transmit more complex messages if several different chemicals are involved but, as discussed below, even one chemical can produce different behavioural responses, when it is present at different concentrations.

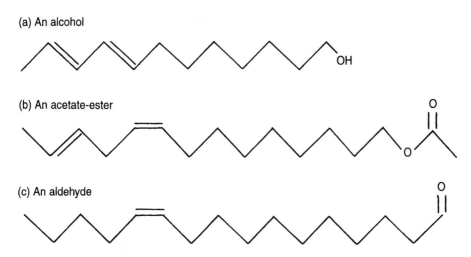

(a) An alcohol

(b) An acetate-ester

(c) An aldehyde

FIG 37   *The structure of three sex pheromones. (a) trans-8, trans-10-docecadienol (an alcohol from the Codling moth,* Cydia pomonella*); (b) cis-9, trans-12 tetradecadienyl acetate (an acetate ester from the Mediterranean Brocade,* Spodoptera littoralis*); (c) cis-11 hexadecanol (an aldehyde from the Cotton Bollworm,* Heliothis zea*). (Source: Shorey, 1976)*

Calling females

The female pheromone is released from glands on the last abdominal segment and these are extruded when the female is 'calling'. Generally, the moth will take up position in a reasonably open position, where the breeze can disperse the pheromone, allow her abdomen to droop and then evert the glands. She is in control of the release and chooses when and where to carry this out. Most species have a characteristic time when this is done and the female will also choose appropriate weather conditions. The effectiveness of the system depends very much on the scent being dispersed in an organised plume and if there is too much or too little turbulence, then the message is not effective. Whereas most species are nocturnal and call at various times from dusk onwards, day-flying species call then. The Emperor moth (*Pavonia pavonia*) calls in the mid to late afternoon but the Northern Eggar (*Lasiocampa quercus callunae*) does so from mid-morning to early afternoon (Leverton, *pers. comm.*). The males of the Kentish Glory (*Endromis versicolora*) fly from mid-morning to early afternoon and then again after dusk; possibly the females also call at both those times. In these day-flying species, the wandering flight patterns of the males that have not found a scent, and then the progress that they make when following pheromone trails, can sometimes be easily seen on their open moorland habitat.

Various factors influence the precise way in which females release their pheromones. Older females, which may have less pheromone left for use, and so may produce less potent scent plumes, often begin calling earlier in the night than their younger conspecifics, perhaps because this allows them to attract males before there is a plethora of trails available (McNeil, 1991). This is not always the case, however, for the older Cabbage Looper (*Trichoplusia ni*) females release pheromone at a higher rate (up to 10^{11} mol s^{-1}) than do young ones but for shorter periods. Bjostad *et al.* (1984) noticed that the rate of release by this species decreases as the calling period proceeds; however, no-one knows whether this results in declining attractiveness. In some species, the females will only call when in the presence of the correct foodplant odour. The Sunflower moth (*Homoeosoma electellum*) called for longer when in the presence of sunflower pollen and began calling at a younger age than specimens not exposed to the pollen (McNeil and Delisle, 1989).

Hendrikse and Vos-Bunnemeyer (1987) found that the females of 'small ermines' *Yponomeuta* spp. show increased release of sex pheromone when in the presence of the odour of their host plant, and that they were more attractive to the males when close to the plants.

Weather conditions also affect the time of calling. There is an optimum windspeed, for *T. ni* below 4 m s^{-1} and above still conditions (Kaae and Shorey, 1972), but this species also fans its wings when calling, presumably to help disperse the scent. Surprisingly little is known about the actual effects of windspeeds on the success of pheromone attraction in reality, beyond the observation that it does not work when winds are strong and gusty. If the night is cool, calling may begin earlier in many species but the response is very variable and also depends on light levels, so that it is not possible to produce a clear and unified account of the effect of temperature (McNeil, 1991).

Aerial trails and the behaviour of males

Pheromones do not diffuse readily through still air, for they are large molecules. Moths depend on them being dispersed as a plume and much work has been carried out to investigate the shape of such plumes and how male moths respond to them.

As the pheromone is released into the breeze the molecules stream out as does smoke from a fire, but with the added complication that the pheromone is produced in a series of pulses. Variations in windspeed and direction, plus turbulence caused by ground roughness (including trees and local topography), mean that the plume of scent is very rarely a smooth and uniform stream but becomes erratic and wandering as distance increases over the countryside. In general, the concentration of the chemicals is greatest close to the calling moth and also in the centre line of the plume but the fluctuations mean that there are many areas of abnormally high and low concentration. The old idea that a male moth can fly steadily up an organised odour gradient has to be revised!

Murlis *et al.* (1992) review the attempts that have been made to describe the behaviour of plumes, using mathematical models from meteorology, but these have not so far met with great success and our understanding of how male moths respond to pheromone plumes is still rather basic. The best strategy for a male moth that is searching for a mate is to fly roughly across the wind – this will maximise his chances of flying into an odour trail. He should then turn and fly upwind and it seems that moths can detect the movement of the ground under them to ensure that they are doing so. They must avoid side-slip over the ground if they are to make proper progress upwind (David and Birch, 1989). Even so, the fact that the plumes are irregular and wandering means that they will soon fly out of them, unless they can detect when they are nearing the edge and turn back. Ford (1955) thought that male moths could detect the lowering of the concentration near the edge of the plume by comparing the concentration being detected on each antenna; however, this is now known to be too simplistic – it would not work in a complex and irregular plume. Instead the moths seem to show a zigzagging upwind flight when in the plume, probably with a greater frequency of turn when the pheromone concentration is high, and with reversion to wide crosswind flights and turns if they fly out of the trail. This 'correction' takes place in well under a second. The resultant track of an odour-following male is a series of upwind dashes, punctuated by wide diversions to regain the trail (David *et al.*, 1983), as shown in Figure 38.

10 m

FIG 38　*The tracks of male Gypsy moths* (Lymantria dispar) *approaching female pheromone lures. The arrows record the wind direction and the circles the position of the lures. The thick lines show the tracks of males when in the odour plumes and the thin lines their tracks when not in the odour plumes. (Source: David and Birch, 1989)*

As the female is approached, the concentration in the odour plume increases and it is a common feature of the chemicals used that, whereas at low concentrations they initiate flight in males, at higher concentrations they stimulate landing and the start of courtship. This may occur a few centimetres from the calling female and the males either crawl about at random apparently searching for the female, or they have already seen her from that distance and so can move directly towards her (Murlis *et al.*, 1992).

Distances travelled and concentrations detected

It can be shown that male moths can detect almost imperceptibly small numbers of molecules of the sex pheromones. Laboratory studies with antennal nerve cells connected to amplifiers have shown that even a few individual molecules blown over the cells will initiate nerve 'firing'. It is quite another matter to discover the distances and concentrations involved in the actual attraction of moths in the field. Although it may be possible to show that pheromones could be detected over a kilometre away, it is likely that in practice distances are usually only some tens of metres, with a few anecdotal observations of moths apparently flying determinately over 100 m to a calling female. Allan (1937) watched a male Kentish Glory (*Endromis versicolora*) take off from a bush and fly direct to a newly calling female over a distance of 380 'paces' (?around 300 m). In the context of the problem of a male moth finding a willing female (for species that are not widely migratory and have defined habitat boundaries), such distances are surely more than effective. An analogy is with the 10–20 m effective radius of a light trap (see Chapter 3), which even so may catch hundreds or thousands of moths in a night. A pheromone that can act over 100 m is a very effective location system.

COURTSHIP AND MATING

Close range scents

Once a male has located a receptive female (and if a female is calling this indicates that she is ready to mate), he has to signal to her that he is a suitable and willing partner, so that mating may actually take place. It is likely that female moths exercise some choice in the matter of whether a male is suitable; Gullan and Cranston (1995) report that there is evidence that some female moths show a preference for large suitors and it is a common observation of moth breeders that a calling female may ignore apparently satisfactory males and then mate with one that differs in no obvious way. In most cases, however, the male that arrives at the female is accepted and courtship proceeds.

Male scents

The behaviour that males exhibit is probably normally initiated in response to the female pheromone. Once this chemical is detected at high concentration, the male settles and approaches the female. If the behaviour of the Cabbage Looper (*Trichoplusia ni*) is typical, as described by Shorey (1976), the next step is for the male to contact the female, by which time her pheromone concentration will be very strong. He then produces a pheromone of his own, which acts to inhibit the movement of the female (as well as identifying its producer). The release of this chemical has rarely been observed but, in the few cases where it has, the males may have eversible brushes, which act to disperse the scent. Perhaps the arrestment of female movement is followed by, or accompanied by, a release of mating inhibition in the female, for copulation often follows with no obvious extra preamble. Consequently, courtship in moths can be very simple and quick, and the males may be very unselective and mechanistic; Shorey (1979) noted that *T. ni* males will carry out all their courtship behaviour, including an attempt at copulation, even when the only stimulus is a spot of female pheromone on a tissue.

The actual pheromones produced by male moths have not been fully identified but in the case of the Queen butterfly (*Danaus gilippus*) it is a molecule called 2,3-dihydro-7-methyl-H-pyrrolizin-l-one that acts to arrest the flight of the female, so that she lands and mating can take place (Brower and Jones, 1965). In this case it is certain that the chemical is dispersed from eversible brushes at the tip of the abdomen.

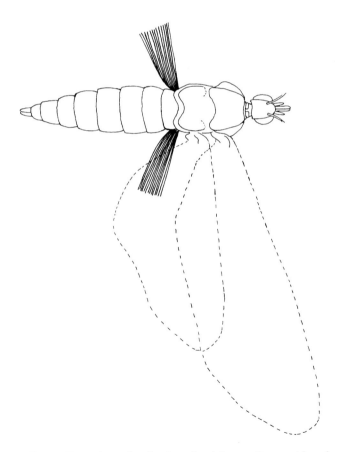

FIG 39   *Everted scent brushes from the abdomen of a noctuid moth.*

However, not all male moths seem to have eversible brushes and so perhaps there are other less obvious glands as well, which may be associated with the release of the male pheromone. Birch (1979) has reviewed the known occurrence of eversible structures, which range in position and anatomy, from brushes made up of several to many hairs, located on the legs, or the front or rear of the abdomen, to eversible sacs, called coremata, often near the end of the abdomen. These sacs are inflated by air pressure from within the adjacent tracheae. Most often the coremata and brushes are held in pockets which seem to have glandular tissue on their walls. Birch believes that these chemical dispersers have evolved independently many times but that their functions may be generally similar. Evidence for this function is very thin and defensive chemicals may be released from them by some species, such as the Death's Head Hawk moth (*Acherontia atropos*) or the Elephant Hawk (*Deilephila elpenor*). In the few cases where they have been observed in action, however, they accompany courtship. Carde *et al.* (1975) noted that mating in the Oriental Fruit moth (*Cydia molesta*) follows eversion of hair pencils; Shorey (1976) found the same with *T. ni*; and Grant and Brady (1975) showed that female Indian Meal moths (*Plodia interpunctella*) become stationary and adopt a mating posture when males liberate scent from brushes at the base of their wings.

Many intriguing questions remain unanswered, such as why the White Ermine (*Spilosoma lubricipeda*) has prominent coremata, (although it has never been observed to use them), whereas its immediate relative the Buff Ermine (*S. lutea*) has none? If they are needed by one species how does the other cope without them?

Competition for mates

If potential mates are scarce, moths may be expected to mate quickly with the first compatible mate that appears. This strategy does not allow for differential selection of 'high quality' partners, and yet their selection may result in offspring being more capable of survival and reproduction. 'High quality' may merely mean being a large moth, for example, for a larger female may produce a larger batch of eggs, or it may mean being a physiologically superior moth, in some way, which may confer a different advantage. Mammals devote much time and effort to selecting an optimal mate but it has only recently been realised that insects may also be selective.

Males may mate more than once and so it can be postulated that they will be less selective than the females. Even if the female that they approach and begin to court is less than perfect they may well have other mates in future and the chances are that some at least will be of superior quality. Of course, no-one knows how often males do mate in natural conditions and it is only breeding cage experiments that show us that they do mate more than once. Bourn (*pers. comm.*) has observed marked, wild male burnet moths (Zygaenidae) mating with more than one female.

Female Burnet moths may also mate more than once (Tremewan, 1985) and this may well apply to many other species, although most will lay their full egg load, with complete fertility, after one mating in captivity. In species where females usually mate once, it should be important to a female to select a high quality male with which to mate. It was noted above that calling females may frequently not mate with the first arrival but may choose a mate that appears to us to be indistinguishable in quality, except perhaps in size. The cues that females use to choose a suitable mate are almost completely unknown and yet this topic lends itself to experimental analysis by the presentation of different 'conditions' of males to virgin females. Leverton (1991) describes a situation where a female Large Yellow Underwing (*Noctua pronuba*) was being courted unsuccessfully by a 'clumsy' male, when a new male arrived and mated immediately. Whether the successful male was just more experienced, as Leverton suggests, is quite unknown!

In most cases, when a female has mated she immediately begins to lay eggs. In one example a female Muslin Footman (*Nudaria mundana*) was mated while still drying her wings on her cocoon and then laid an egg batch on the cocoon the same morning. In some other cases the female feeds for a while before her eggs are mature; female hawk moths (Sphingidae) feed in this way before mating (Friedrich, 1986). Although it may be usual for the female not to mate more than once, there are many species that do so if males present themselves and, where this is a possibility, it leads to a problem for the original mate. He will lose out if his sperm are replaced by the sperm of a later rival. This can happen because moth sperm are deposited in packets, called spermatophores, and the eggs are only fertilised as they pass down the oviduct on the way to being laid. Spermatophores are placed in a special chamber called a spermatheca within the female and they persist even after their sperm have been used up. Knowledge that female moths may mate more than once has come from the finding of two or more spermatophore remnants in the spermathecae of wild caught females (although it is possible that in some cases a male may have transferred more than one).

Male mate guarding

It will benefit a male to ensure that only his sperm are used to fertilise the female's eggs and in many species of insect intricate mechanisms and behaviour patterns help to ensure this. Some male damselflies (Odonata; Zygoptera), for example, remain attached to the female, or fly directly over her during egg laying, so that rival males cannot get access to her (Conrad and Pritchard, 1990). They may also have scoop-shaped ends to their intromittent organs, designed to winkle out the spermatophores of earlier rivals from the spermathecae of the females, so that their own can replace them. Male moths do not seem to use similar mate guarding or sperm removal techniques but they do have some mechanisms to help ensure their paternity. Firstly, their sperm packet may merely be placed on top of that of the earlier mate, so that their sperm are nearer the entrance of the sperm duct. Secondly, they may prolong mating, so that they occupy the female for hours, until either she is no longer attractive to other males (perhaps her pheromone has evaporated) and/or her eggs have matured and she is ready to lay them, instead of mating again. Leverton (*pers. comm.*) has noted mating prolonged into many hours for the following species: burnet moths Zygaenidae; Puss moth (*Cerura vinula*); Buff-tip (*Phalera bucephala*); Garden Tiger (*Arctia caja*); White Ermine (*Spilosoma lubricipeda*); Poplar Hawk (*Laothoe populi*); and Sword Grass (*Xylena exsoleta*).

There are clear problems with mate guarding. The male is occupied and cannot be searching for and mating with other females. Furthermore, both sexes are very vulnerable during copulation, for they are clumsy and cannot fly well; consequently prolonged mating may be possible only for large, well protected species (like the burnets or tigers) or for very cryptic species (like the Sword Grass). Even so there are equally large and protectively coloured species, like the Emperor (*Pavonia pavonia*), that remain in copula for only 20–30 minutes. This is the time period that is necessary for basic spermatophore transfer and many species mate for this length of time. Only a minority of moths used prolonged copulation as a mate guarding strategy but an unknown number use sperm packing.

PEST CONTROL USING PHEROMONES

The use of attractant pheromones

So many environmental problems attend the use of insecticides and so many insect species have become resistant to them, that alternatives are urgently needed. Various natural enemies are being tried in biological control trials, including viruses and bacteria. Alternatively, resistant crops are being bred and crop husbandry techniques are being modified to make crops less susceptible. A recent and very promising plan is to make use of pheromones to attract moths to killing baits or traps, or to confuse mating systems, so that natural populations do not reproduce effectively.

In the 1940s in the USA, the abdominal tips of female Gypsy moths (*Lymantria dispar*) were collected and a rough extract made from them to see if this would attract male moths to traps. This attempt was not successful and further serious attempts were then delayed until after the first synthesis of sex pheromones in 1960 (Jutsum and Gordon, 1989). Even then the early schemes were not very hopeful, largely because unrealistically ambitious goals were set on the basis of inadequate scientific knowledge. At the start too little was known about the composition of the pheromones for the species concerned, or about their mating systems. As a result, the baits were ineffective at attracting males, or acted over too small a section of a wide-ranging population, or were used at inappropriate times during the night, or did not span the full emergence period (McNeil, 1991). More recently better researched schemes, often combined in integrated programmes, have achieved much more effective results. Recently particular attention has focused on the ways in which the pheromones are released, so that they mimic more closely the natural conditions.

Recently, pheromones have been used in three main ways: to attract males which are then counted, so that early warning is provided when populations are approaching pest numbers; to attract males to killing traps; to disrupt the normal wild mating systems by swamping the area concerned with artificial pheromone. In practice all of these functions may be combined but the best results are when a scheme is carefully designed to achieve a clearly defined objective.

Disrupting mating patterns

Carde and Minks (1995) set out the theoretical background to the use of pheromones to disrupt mating in moths. The modes of action may be one or more of the following, all of which would result in a reduction of wild matings.

(a) The release of synthetic pheromone might stimulate the males over a period, habituating them and raising the concentration of chemical needed to produce a reaction. When a wild female produced her own pheromone, the males would be less likely to respond.
(b) If a very high concentration were used, it might be sufficient to induce the males to land, rather than fly upwind, as happens when the males come close to a calling female.
(c) If the pheromone is released continuously or at an unlikely time, it may confuse the normal male response.

(d) A general presence of pheromone in the air may either swamp the females' pheromone, so that their trails are not followed, or confuse the plume structure that is necessary if a male is to locate a female by organised upwind flight.

(e) If many release points are used, the males may waste time visiting these sterile sources, rather than finding females. This would hinder mating even if killing traps were not used. (In many cases the pheromone source has a sticky or poisonous surface which acts to kill the male when it arrives.)

(f) If the balance of chemicals in the artificial pheromone is unnatural, this may produce a mixture that confuses the males. Alternatively, the blend may be super-attractive, so that the males visit the lures rather than the females.

Several of these effects may operate at once.

EXAMPLES OF MOTH CONTROL PROGRAMMES USING PHEROMONES

The following examples of control schemes based on the use of pheromones illustrate both the advantages and the shortcomings of the system. Fortunately, success is becoming more assured as experience is gained, and pheromones are likely to play an ever larger part in the control of moth pests.

TABLE 20   *Examples of pheromonal control and monitoring attempts for moth pests (from references in text).*

Date of trials	Details of trials
1940s	Use of crude extract from Gypsy moth *Lymantria dispar* to attract to traps
1950s–1960s	Crude extract from *L. dispar* used to monitor moth in central Europe
1960	First individual pheromone identified from Silk moth *Bombyx mori*

Pink Bollworm *Pectinophora gossypiella*

1978	First hollow fibre tests in USA
1981–86	Extensive field trials in USA
1981	First full-scale trials in Egypt
1984	Commercial availability in Egypt
1990–93	Good success with twisted rope schemes in USA

Codling moth *Cydia pomonella*

1973	First trials of mating disruption
1986	Trials of twisted rope dispensers in USA
1987–90	Unsuccessful commercial use in Switzerland
1988–91	Successful trials in Austria
1990–93	Commercial use in Austria
1991	Commercial use begun in USA

Controlling the Codling moth

The Codling moth (*Cydia pomonella*) has become a serious pest of apples and other rosa-ceous fruits throughout the world, for it has been able to adapt to many climates. The lar-vae bore into the fruits, and although only a small part of the flesh may be eaten, even minor damage causes the fruit to become unsaleable. As a result, population levels of the moth have to be kept very low in commercial situations (Bradley, Tremewan and Smith, 1979). If even 2–3% of the fruit is infested then the entire crop is unsaleable in a commer-cial market. The moth itself has become immune to chemical insecticides in places and in many areas the use of wide-spectrum formulations has eliminated natural predators and parasites, so that infestation levels have risen. Such a situation is clearly ripe for the intro-duction of pheromone controls.

In 1971 Roelefs *et al.* characterised the female pheromone, although some extra minor components have been found since, and there have been many attempts at control. Some have succeeded but others have failed. Charmillot (in Ridgway *et al.*, 1990) has suggested that for a scheme to succeed it is necessary that the treated orchards should be: isolated by at least 100 m, to prevent immediate re-invasion; large enough to act as a population unit, that is 3 ha or over; have an initial infestation level that is below 2–3 diapausing larvae per tree, (for the treatment cannot handle a major outbreak that has started but can prevent one from occurring); provided with a buffer zone of traps around the edge. Furthermore, a sequence of pheromone release periods must be used in latitudes where the moth has more than one generation each year.

Variations have been tried in the exact formulation of pheromone and the concentra-tions used, the timing of release, and the type and density of dispensers used. Recent com-mercially registered formulations in the USA use two seasonal applications of a mixture of 10:5:1 (E,E)-8,10-dodecadien-1-ol, dodecanol, tetradecanol, dispensed using 20 cm long, hollow, polyethylene strips twisted into 'ropes' and set at 1000 per hectare, and using this method 4000 ha were treated in 1993 (Carde and Minks, 1995). In general, apple infesta-tion levels well below 1% have been achieved. However, control is poor in cool conditions, probably because the rate of release is too low from the ropes.

In gardens, triangular sticky traps are used with pheromones (called 'Delta' traps). A much higher rate of infestation is acceptable in gardens, because fruit for the table is sorted by hand, but even so the success of these traps is very questionable in places where control is practised in only a few gardens amongst many!

The Pink Bollworm and other pests

The Pink Bollworm (*Pectinophora gossypiella*) is a pan-tropical pest of cotton that is very dif-ficult to control by conventional means, because its larvae feed within the flowers and bolls of cotton, where it is not easily affected by pesticides. It has been subject to major pheromone control programmes, as summarised by Campion *et al.* (1989). The pheromone produced by the pink bollworm females is rather simple, with only two com-ponents (Z,Z)- and (Z,E)-7,11 hexadecadienyl acetate in equal proportions and both these are relatively stable and so can be dispensed quite easily. Used in hollow fibre systems, this formulation was the first to be registered for agricultural use in the USA in 1978; similar methods have subsequently been used in Egypt and Pakistan.

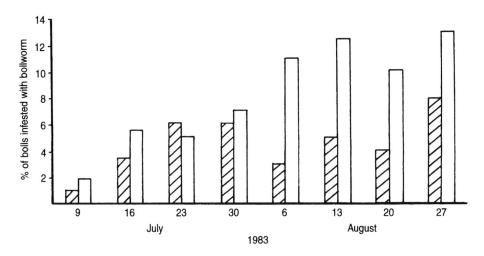

FIG 40   *The comparative success of micro-encapsulated pheromone* ▨ *and conventional insecticide* ☐ *control schemes for the Pink Bollworm* (Pectinophora gossypiella) *in a 25-ha area of cotton in Egypt in 1983.* (*Source: Campion* et al., *1989*)

In some of these instances there has been considerable success, most notably in Arizona in 1990–93 (Carde and Minks, 1995). There, 11 000 ha were treated in an area which initially had a boll infestation level of around 23%, even after the use of conventional insecticides. Following the use of pheromones this decreased to 10% in 1990, 1.4% in 1991 and none at all in 1993. Although there have been similar results elsewhere, there have also been instances where populations have suddenly increased again and so the use of pheromones for this species has not been wholly satisfactory.

The Western Pine-shoot Borer (*Eucosma sonomana*) attacks the leading shoots of Ponderosa pine, which leads to multiple shoot formation and so loss of value. The pheromone control of this species has resulted in a reduction of between 67 and 88% in the number of shoots damaged in experiments using different dispensation methods (data from Daterman, quoted by Speight and Wainhouse, 1989), and large scale trials have been promising. As a cautionary tale, however, mass pheromone trapping of Gypsy moths (*Lymantria dispar*) in the USA has not been very successful, so far, but it has been realised that the chemical being used is not the most attractive portion of the moth pheromone mixture and so the trials will have to be repeated. Very careful chemical separation and screening schemes are needed before success is likely.

MONITORING POPULATIONS OF PEST SPECIES

A very important aspect of the use of pheromones is to monitor the numbers of individuals present, so that control measures are used only when outbreak levels are developing. This allows control to be targeted carefully and employed only when necessary, saving huge expenditure, greatly reducing the amount of pesticide used (with all the environmental benefits that this implies), and increasing the chances of successful control. Wall (1989) sets out very fully and clearly both the benefits that accrue and also the limitations of the method. Pheromone traps can be used to define the geographical extent of a species, confirming where and when it is absent and providing evidence of when it has migrated into an area, so that control may be needed in the near future. The highly mobile African Cotton Leaf-worm (*Spodoptera littoralis*) is a pest that varies in its numbers from place to place and time to time and so therefore control is only occasionally needed. Pheromone traps provide the data that allow this control to be activated.

Timing of treatment of the Pea moth (*Cydia nigricana*) and the Codling moth (*C. pomonella*) is set by the use of pheromone traps, which identify the start of the adult flight period. The rate of build up of the catches indicates whether there is likely to be a problem worth controlling in that year. Similarly, pheromone catches are used to indicate whether control measures have been successful in reducing the population of the pest, with the implications that this has for future seasons.

Further advantages are that the traps are cheap, need no power source (unlike light traps) and trap specimens at population levels way below those detected by conventional traps. They are also highly selective, with the twin advantages that there is no taxonomic knowledge needed in sorting the catches and there is no loss of non-target species. Their cheapness means that they can be set over wide areas and so provide a wealth of data.

Monitoring Pine Beauty moth numbers

If these traps are to be useful they must be known to be sensitive and accurate, and so some comparisons have been made with conventional monitoring methods. Speight and Wainhouse (1989) have collated data on the numbers of male Pine Beauty moths (*Panolis flammea*) caught in pheromone traps in various trials in Europe, compared with numbers of pupae collected from the soil, which is the standard way of assessing population levels. Table 21 shows these data and there is a good relationship between the two sets of results. Furthermore, these results show that the pheromone traps detect the presence of the moths at densities below the threshold of detection in pupal counting. Either the traps are catching immigrating males, or they catch at moth densities too low for other methods to succeed.

TABLE 21   *The numbers of Pine Beauty moths (*Panolis flammea) *caught in pheromone traps and detected as pupae in soil at each of six sites.*

Location	Pupal density m^{-2}	No. of males per trap
Eastern Scotland	10.8	80.1
Northern Scotland	7.2	92.8
Poland	0.7	13.7
Germany (Bayern)	0.2	3.5
Germany (Niedersachsen)	0.0	1.1
Austria	0.0	0.2

Source: Data from Speight and Wainhouse (1989).

Monitoring numbers of other species

Numerous studies have shown that the efficiency of pheromone traps declines when the population levels are high, perhaps because their effectiveness is being diluted by the presence of many pheromone-liberating females. Croft *et al.* (1986) used caged virgin females of the leaf-roller *Argyrotaenia citrana* to provide competition to pheromone traps and found that the traps were adversely affected by high densities of females. Elkington and Carde (1984) also observed reductions in the catches of Gypsy moths (*Lymantria dispar*), when they added 200 bred females to the experimental site that they were using. Hartstack and Witz (1981) worked with Tobacco Budworms (*Heliothis virescens*) and found that in the early part of the season, when population levels were low, their traps were effective for estimating population densities, but that at high levels, in the full season, they were swamped by the wild females.

The 'feathered' antennae of a male moth.

These studies suggest that it is difficult to make precise population estimates using pheromone traps, at least when populations are high, and so the numbers caught must be interpreted carefully. It is probably safe to use pheromone traps to detect the start of emergence, the onset of immigration, or a low threshold for damage control; but it is often difficult to monitor higher levels accurately. Wall (1989) provides an example of how these threshold catches are applied to catches of the Codling moth (*Cydia pomonella*). In England a catch of five moths per trap per week is used to indicate the need to spray to control larvae after 140 day-degrees, with a further spray after another 100 day-degrees. (Degree-days represent the time for larval development, which will vary depending on the temperatures experienced.) In Switzerland, pheromone traps are used in conjunction with winter sticky bands on tree trunks, which catch overwintering larvae. Pheromone traps are set at the start of May and the catch collected after 250 day-degrees. At this point a total of fewer than 20 moths per trap indicates that no control is needed; 20–50 moths indicates one spray will suffice; whereas more than 50 suggests that two sprays may be needed. However, these numbers are double-checked against the previous winter's larval catches. Such detail demands standardisation in trap design and chemical formulation but this is rarely achieved.

Pheromones are still thought to offer an excellent chance to improve the control of moth pests in an environmentally acceptable way but there is the realisation that control programmes need to be very carefully prepared. In particular, the biology of each moth needs to be well known, so that the control schemes can be targeted precisely. The early promise of pheromones has only occasionally been achieved.

CHAPTER 8

Moth Predators and Population Dynamics

WHAT CAUSES MORTALITY IN MOTHS?

UNTIL the 1970s most studies into the causes of death in moths concentrated on predation, which was thought to be the most important cause, but now there is a realisation that other things, such as disease, parasitism or bad weather, may be equally important.

Starvation

Female moths generally choose the place where they lay their eggs with some care, so that there will be sufficient suitable food available for their larvae, but on occasions this supply fails and the larvae go short. This may be as a result of: competition from another herbivore, often another larva of the same species; drought or disease affecting the foodplant; a badly chosen egg-site on a small plant.

The most obvious time when excessive competition affects moth larvae is when the populations have risen to plague levels and complete defoliation of the foodplants occurs. When Bird Cherry (*Prunus padus*) trees become defoliated by larvae of the 'small ermine' *Yponomeuta evonymella* there are usually adjacent trees on to which the broods can transfer, for this tree grows in groups. However, every so often the numbers of larvae are so large that all the trees are stripped and in these cases the larvae do move on and use the leaves of adjacent trees. Very few other moths, even amongst the polyphagous species, use bird cherry and so perhaps the moths avoid competition by specialising on it.

Where Cinnabar moths (*Tyria jacobaea*) are abundant, as they often are on coastal sand dunes, they frequently eat their Ragwort (*Senecio jacobaea*) foodplants down to bare stalks and then have to crawl off across the sand to try to find uneaten plants. If nearby plants have also been eaten then starvation results, for this species cannot feed on other foodplants. The population then crashes temporarily and has to recover from a low ebb, or the location has to be recolonised from elsewhere. Van der Meijden (1979) found a frequent shift in location of this moth, between foodplant patches, with local extinctions a regular feature. Myers and Campbell (1976) demonstrated that the female moths adjust the size and dispersion of their egg batches, depending on the abundance of the ragwort plants in each location.

Occasionally larvae are found feeding on tiny isolated plants that will obviously be too small to sustain all their growth. On occasions this applies to Herald moth larvae (*Scoliopterix libatrix*), which are sometimes found on seedling sallows with no more than 10 leaves. Presumably these larvae are doomed to starve, unless there are other larger sallows immediately adjacent. Leverton (*pers. comm.*) reports finding dwarf specimens of the Brindled Ochre (*Dasypolia templi*) and he assumes that these result from larvae that had to make do with small plants of Hogweed (*Heracleum sphondylium*), within the stems of which the larvae feed.

There is better evidence of the adverse results of hatching before food is available in the spring. Winter moths (*Operophtera brumata*) lay eggs on oak and other deciduous trees. The eggs hatch just as the buds of the trees are bursting in the spring and it sometimes happens that they hatch too soon. Such larvae spin fine silk 'parachutes' and balloon off if their natal tree has no leaves available (Hunter, 1990). The Green Oak Leaf-roller (*Tortrix viridana*) is restricted to oak, so dispersal would be a more risky strategy. It has been found that larvae of this species tend to remain on their leafless oak tree and wait for the bud burst. They are much more resistant to starvation. Hunter found that whereas 50% of Winter moth larvae die after five days of starvation (at 8°C), it takes 12 days of starvation before 50% of the Green Oak Leaf-roller larvae die. There is a realistic chance that the oaks will leaf-up in this time. He also found that 60% of Winter moth larvae tend to disperse within the first hours after hatching, when no food is available, but that only 20% of Green Oak Leaf-rollers do so. If there are strong winds in spring, Green Oak Leaf-rollers may be dislodged from the oaks and they then starve on the forest floor.

Despite these examples, starvation is probably a rather infrequent cause of death in moth larvae, in temperate localities at least, and is greatly outweighed in normal circumstances by other causes of mortality.

Disease

Except in the context of finding novel control methods for pests, the diseases of moths have been neglected. Adult diseases are almost unknown but larvae, and to a lesser extent eggs and pupae, suffer from a wide range of contagious and infectious diseases. They are very noticeable in the breeding cages of lepidopterists (who inevitably crowd larvae, keep them under-ventilated and provide substandard food), but they are also important in the field, perhaps most often when larvae are in plague proportions. *Bacillus thuringiensis*, a bacterium originally isolated from the Meal moth (*Ephestia kuhniella*), is now the subject of intense research, to improve its use as a biological control agent for a wide range of insect pests. Clayton and Wolfe (1993) review the topic of self-medication by animals and report work by Krischik *et al.*, which shows that Tobacco Hornworm larvae (*Manduca sexta*) derive some resistance to *Bacillus thuringiensis* from nicotine, which they obtain by eating tobacco plant leaves.

Larvae infected with different types of disease-causing agents tend to have characteristic symptoms. Bacteria cause a flaccid appearance, with an evil smelling discharge from mouth and anus and liquefied body contents. Viruses also cause the larvae to become floppy, so that they hang down by their legs after death, but they do not generally smell. Some viruses also cause a characteristic iridescent sheen on the larvae. Fungi leave the larvae covered with a fine felt of hyphae and sometimes with fruiting bodies but they often cause the body to become hard and distended as the hyphae pack the body cavity. Protozoans may cause small discoloured areas and irregular growth but these symptoms may be shared with parasitised larvae.

In all cases, the diseases are easily transmitted by infected faeces or vomit, or by contact with the diseased or dead larva itself. Apparently healthy larvae may shed infective agents on to the foliage long before they succumb. Viruses may also be transferred from generation to generation by passage in the egg. Parasitic and predatory insects can also take an infection from one area to another, for bacteria and viruses can survive on or in the mouthparts or ovipositors of these creatures. Some bacillae will also survive passage through the gut of predatory birds, so being spread by their droppings. Finally, some spores are known to be windborne and so larvae may become infected even if far from others.

Do diseases affect moth populations?

Rivers (1976) gives an excellent general account of the various types of disease that inflict moths. There have been few studies of the role of disease in the population dynamics of moths and it is sometimes assumed that disease is not of great importance, compared with other factors. However, Werner (1977) believed that larval disease (and pupal parasitism) acted to reduce an Argent and Sable (*Rheumaptera hastata*) outbreak in Alaska. Other examples are provided by old accounts of pests that were exterminated, at least in local areas, by disease. For example, Rivers quotes a case where the Diamond Back moth (*Plutella xylostella*) was controlled naturally in South Africa by the well known fungus *Entomophthora*; perhaps future workers should pay the topic further attention.

Inclement weather

If a larva experiences cold weather, it will grow less quickly but it may not be killed. However, slow growth may lead ultimately to failure, because the larva may not complete its growth within the season, or its prolonged larval life may lead to increased chance of predation while in this vulnerable stage. Pollard (1979) showed that slow development of White Admiral butterfly (*Ladoga camilla*) larvae and pupae during cool spring and early summer weather led to increased mortality rates from bird predation. Barbour and Young (1993) found that larvae of the Kentish Glory moth (*Endromis versicolora*) were dislodged and lost from their birch host trees during windy weather. In very wet weather, larvae in leaf-shelters sometimes drown and this even happens to some leaf miners, such as *Eriocrania* spp., if water can penetrate into their mines.

Adult moths are also affected, as they will be unable to fly or carry out their normal activities in cold weather. This may lead to death before mating or egg-laying has occurred. Weather may also be too wet, too dry, too hot, too windy or a range of other extreme conditions. Although this problem is very difficult to quantify and will act randomly on different generations or in different places, there is some indirect evidence of its importance. The 'lie-over' of larvae and pupae, described in Chapter 4, is an adaptation for avoiding seasons with atypically poor weather.

PARASITES AS A CAUSE OF MORTALITY

In contrast to disease agents or inclement weather, parasites have received more attention from lepidopterists, but much of the information about them is still incomplete or inaccurate. Even so, there is no doubt that parasites are one of the main causes of death in moth larvae. Almost all the species of parasite are of the type known more properly as parasitoids, for each individual parasite kills the host, rather than merely feeding from it but leaving it alive. The species of parasite typically does not infest all the host population, so that overall the host survives.

All stages of moths except adults may be parasitised and almost all parasites are either wasps, of various families, or flies of the family Tachinidae. Some are sufficiently small to fit their entire feeding within a lepidopteran egg. Many are larger, however, and need a larva or pupa in which to develop. Most are highly specific in their egg laying behaviour, for example the wasp *Pteromalus puparum* attacks only soft freshly formed pupae (Shaw and Askew, 1976). Most parasites are solitary but a small number occur in groups within a moth larva, occasionally all developing from one egg, following asexual reproduction. Some species have only been found as females, but most have both sexes; in the wasps the females are diploid and result from fertilised eggs, whereas the males are haploid, from unfertilised eggs.

The appearance of the parasite cocoons, or the mummified remains of the larvae, within which the parasite pupae are found, are often very characteristic in appearance. Shaw and Askew (1976) provide excellent pictures of many of them. Occasionally, parasitised larvae also have an obvious sign of the parasite's presence, usually a discoloration or spot, or a swelling or mis-shapen segment. However, the most frequent sign of parasitism is often delayed growth or an abnormal sluggishness or altered behaviour pattern.

Types of parasites

Some parasites of moth larvae feed from the outside of their hosts – ectoparasitoids, whereas some feed internally – endoparasitoids. A further major subdivision is between those that kill or paralyse their hosts at or near the time that the parasite egg is laid, called idiobionts; and those that leave their hosts alive and feed within them as the larvae develop, called koinobionts, only killing the host larva once the parasite is fully fed. In general, the koinobionts are internal feeders, with rather high specialisation, whereas the idiobionts are more generalised in their requirements. Few parasitoids are strictly host specific but many show a broad association with a taxonomically related group of hosts, or a form of ecological specificity, which is of great interest. Some species parasitise the primary parasites and these are called hyper-parasites.

Defences against parasites

Larvae may show quite well developed anti-parasite devices, such as long hairs, or the fiercely waved threads on the last abdominal segment of the Puss moth larva (*Cerura vinula*). A very common response to the presence of a female parasite is a violent wriggling or dropping off the foodplant on a silk life-line to displace the parasite. Even after the female has laid her egg it may be that the parasite will fail, for sometimes an external egg is shed at moulting or an internal egg is encapsulated, although this happens most often when an egg is laid in a host that is not usually used by that parasite species. Exceptionally, English-Loeb *et al.* (1990) found an example of an arctiid moth that sometimes survives successful parasitism by a tachinid fly and they also noted two other examples quoted in the literature. In this case there was no reduction in fecundity in the female moths that had been parasitised as a larva, even when up to three fly larvae had emerged from the caterpillar. The mechanism of the survival is not known.

The host ranges of parasites

Unfortunately it is seldom possible to have full knowledge of the host range of a parasitoid. Shaw (1994) sets out the many reasons for this. It is easy to study the range of parasites from one host, by making careful collections of larvae of this host, but even this can be more difficult than it might appear. Askew and Shaw (1986) report the case of the larva of the White Satin moth (*Leucoma salicis*), collected by Shaw from sandhills in Lancashire. Larvae found feeding on Creeping Sallow (*Salix repens*) were parasitised almost exclusively by a wasp called *Aleiodes pallidator*, whereas larvae found on nearby poplar trees (*Populus* sp.) hosted both *A. pallidator* and another species *Cotesia melanoscelus*, which was much commoner. The precise location of larvae can alter their parasitism but the precise time of collection can also be important. When the same authors collected Square-spot Rustic larvae (*Xestia xanthographa*) on 2 March 1979 they found a 33% parasitism rate, caused by eight species of parasite, whereas their samples on 12 May 1979 yielded only one (different) species of parasite that infested 11% of the larvae.

Another interesting difference can be found between parasites at different altitudes. Randall (1982) recorded the parasites of the case-bearing moth larva *Coleophora alticolella* and found seven species at near sea level, one species at 395 m and none at all above that level. Clearly the parasites are less adaptable than the moth in their response to altitude. This moth has recently been recorded at increasing altitudes, an observation that has been tentatively ascribed to the effects of climatic warming, but no-one has studied the parasites to see if they are changing their own altitudinal limits.

Shaw (1994) has listed the problems of ensuring that a reliable host range has been obtained for a parasite as follows:

(a) Most published data are of questionable taxonomic validity, for parasites are poorly known in this respect.
(b) Even host species are sometimes misidentified.
(c) Primary and hyper-parasites may be confused.
(d) Most data come from studies of a single host species and so, by definition, no attempt has been made to sample all possible parasite hosts.
(e) Hosts may have been collected only from one part of the habitat, or one foodplant, or at one time, so biasing the results.
(f) Occasional host records may be given the same weight as usual hosts, so unbalancing the true host range.
(g) Often less care has been given to ensuring that the parasite data are full and reliable than has been taken for the host.

The result has been that the published literature on parasite host ranges is rather incomplete and unreliable. Shaw (1994) gives an excellent example of this. He has analysed the published and real host range of a common species called *Aleiodes alternator*, which is restricted ecologically to hairy larvae of the families Arctiidae, Lymantriidae and Lasiocampidae, when these are feeding on low vegetation. The literature incorrectly lists other hosts, from hairless larvae of Noctuidae (probably due to taxonomic confusion between very similar parasites), hairy larvae of Noctuidae (probably due to misidentification of the hairy mummified larval remains), and Tortricidae (possibly because the collections of the tortricid foodplants included cocoons of the parasites). More detailed examination of this species of parasite reveals that it has two forms, which differ in the time of the year at which they attack their hosts, and it is possible that the forms represent incipient species.

TABLE 22 *Published true and mistaken hosts of the parasitic wasp* Aleiodes alternator.

True hosts		
Hairy larvae on low vegetation	Lymantridae	e.g. *Orgyia antiqua* *Dasychira pudibunda*
	Lasiocampidae	e.g. *Lasiocampa quercus* *Macrothylacia rubi* *Philudoria potatoria*
	Arctiidae	e.g. *Arctia caja* *Spilosoma lubricipeda*
Mistaken hosts		
Noctuidae	Misidentification of parasites	
	Misidentification of hairy larvae as Noctuidae	
Tortricidae	Parasite pupae amongst leaves being used by tortricid larvae	

Source: Simplified from Shaw (1994), with permission from Oxford University Press.

Some parasites show 'ecological' specificity

Askew (1994) examined the ecological specificity of parasites of leaf miners of the gracillariid genus *Phyllonorycter*. These feed for relatively long periods in their leaves and also pupate therein, so that they are readily found by parasites (or are 'apparent' to them, in the sense used in Chapter 5), whereas Nepticulidae feed for only very brief periods and then leave the mine, so that they are difficult to find or less apparent. In general, the Nepticulidae have specialised parasites, especially when their foodplants are the less apparent herbs, rather than more apparent trees. In contrast, the *Phyllonorycter* spp. tend to have parasites with broad ecological specificity.

The most specific of the parasite groups that feed on *Phyllonorycter* spp. are those in the wasp genus *Achrysocharoides*. These tend to have a specificity to one or a range of tree species but to feed on all the *Phyllonorycter* spp. on such trees. For example, the following associations have been found:

Parasite species	Associated tree species
Achrysocharoides acerianus	*Acer* spp.
A. atys	Almost all rosaceous trees
A. butus, A. latreillei	*Quercus* spp.
A. carpini	*Carpinus betulus*
A. niveipes	*Betula* spp.

Apart from the above, most other parasites of *Phyllonorycter* spp. are much less specific and their host ranges include many other leaf miners that are found on the same trees. For example, *Pnigalio pectinicornis* (an extreme generalist) has been reliably recorded from the following genera of moths in the family Gracillariidae: *Phyllonorycter, Caloptilia, Parornix, Leucospilapteryx, Aspilapteryx, Callisto*; and from the Nepticulidae, Tischeriidae, Incurvariidae, Heliozelidae, Lyonetiidae, Elachistidae and Momphidae; as well as some non-lepidopterous miners. However, even such generalists tend to be found most frequently on certain species of host and/or certain foodplants.

Godfray *et al.* (1995) studied the parasites of two species of *Phyllonorycter* that invaded Britain recently and found unexpectedly that they had as many species associated with them as did native *Phyllonorycter* species, although their parasite fauna was very much dominated by a few species. Against further expectation, the parasite species involved were not just species with a very wide host range. The most important parasite on *P. platani* was a specialist that invaded Britain with its host, whereas that on *P. leucographella* was a British species that previously used *Phyllonorycter* species with similar ecological preferences.

Parasites do not necessarily respond to distastefulness in larvae and they are often specialists on such larvae. Burnet moth larvae, Zygaenidae, release cyanides from their damaged tissues if attacked by predators, but have parasites that are unaffected by this. Edmunds (1976) suggested that the lack of heavy predation may make such larvae specially favourable as parasite hosts but their rates of parasitism are not necessarily very different from those of palatable larvae.

Askew and Shaw (1986) found that the greatest diversity of parasites seems to be at around latitudes 30–40°, with a decline both towards the equator and the poles and the specialist koinobionts seem to be most affected. This is in sharp contrast to the diversity of their insect hosts but it has been suggested that, although there are more insect species in the tropics, they are more scattered and fragmented in their occurrence and so make less easily located hosts. Taxonomic and sampling problems mean that these data are still open to question and more studies are urgently needed.

As Shaw (1996) stresses, the conservation of parasites is a much more pressing problem than that of their hosts. Parasitoids that are host specific are by definition rarer than their hosts and so the observed decline in moth species (see Chapter 10) must be accompanied by a more severe but unobserved decline in the parasite species. We still know very little of the biology and status of these parasites and Shaw makes a plea for lepidopterists to keep and record all parasites that they breed, rather than throwing them away in disgust when the hoped-for moth does not appear!

PREDATORS OF MOTHS

What feeds on moths?

Almost every predatory animal that is not too large feeds on moths in their various stages at some time or another but the most frequent predators are those set out in Table 23. The precise balance between these will depend on the location and time of year and no attempt has been made to prioritise them. The birds are the most obvious predators, and Atlegrim (1992) found that they dramatically reduced the numbers of larvae feeding in the field layer of a Scandinavian forest, but it is very likely that other types have at least as important a role, even if less often observed.

TABLE 23   *Predators of different stages in the life cycle of moths.*

Stage	Predators
Eggs	Bugs (Hemiptera); beetles (Coleoptera); Earwigs (Dermaptera); small birds
Larvae	Birds; spiders; bugs and other predatory insects; lizards and other reptiles
Pupae	Birds; beetles; small mammals
Adults	Birds; bats; spiders; mantids and other predatory insects; lizards; amphibians

The senses of moth predators

Most of the predators of moths, with the exception of the small mammals that feed mostly on pupae, and bats, which are treated separately below, have colour vision but this is not always linked to a binocular capability. Mantids certainly use binocular vision to help them judge the size of a prey item and its distance from the mantid; the same applies to lizards and some birds (such as owls). However, many predators of moths find it difficult to judge sizes and they may well respond more to movement than to pattern. Consequently, the defensive strategy of the moths may depend as much on the behaviour that accompanies colour pattern and shape, as on precise appearance. Size may well be misjudged by a predator, and an immobile organism, even if its appearance seems a little incongruous to us, may well remain undetected.

Mammals have a keen sense of smell, which will help them detect a buried pupa, and they and owls also hear well, so that rustles of wings or the scraping of legs may give away the presence of a moth or its larva. When we find a moth we judge its defensive capabilities from our own visual perspective but we must remember that the real predators of the moth may literally see things differently.

HOW GREAT IS THE MORTALITY DUE TO PREDATORS?

Analysing mortality using k-factor analysis – Winter moths as a classic example

It is obviously important to know which cause of mortality has the most decisive effect on the overall population of a moth under study. It may be that the most visible cause, perhaps the hungry bird, has much less of an impact than the unnoticed disease. Studies that attempt to distinguish these effects are called key factor analyses. In essence they quantify the effect of each separable mortality factor by arranging them in a table which charts the numbers present in a population, as this proceeds from start to finish (a 'life table'), and then identifies the factor with most effect on the number of animals that survive to breed successfully. This form of analysis, important as one of the basic techniques in population dynamics, was first worked through in full detail by Varley and his co-workers on the Winter moth (*Operophtera brumata*) in Wytham Woods, near Oxford. (These woods and this species have an honourable place in the history of ecology!) Discussion is restricted here to Winter moth studies and a brief account of the Pine Looper (*Bupalus piniaria*).

Winter moth life table

Varley *et al.* (1973) provide a summary of the basic life table analysis of the Winter moth, drawing on the work of many others who laboriously counted eggs, larvae, pupae and

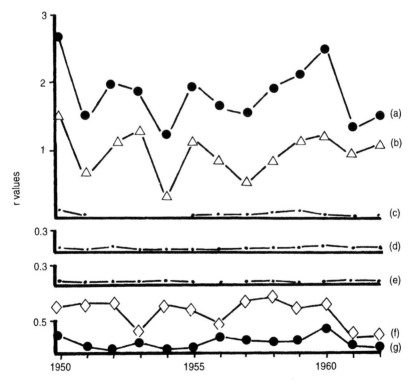

FIG 41   *Year to year changes in mortality (as r values) of Winter moths* (Operophtera brumata) *in Wytham Woods, Oxfordshire between 1950 and 1962. (a) overall mortality; (b) winter disappearance; (c) parasitism by an insect parasitoid* Cyzenis *sp.; (d) other insect parasitoids; (e) microsporidian disease of larvae; (f) predation of pupae; (g) pupal parasitism by* Cratichneumon *sp. (Source: Varley et al., 1973), with permission from Blackwells Scientific.*

TABLE 24 *A classic life table for the Winter moth* (Operophthera brumata) *1955–56.*

Life cycle stage	% of previous stage alive	No. killed per m²	No. alive per m²	Log no. alive per m²	k
Adult female (1955)			4.39		
Egg female × 150			658	2.82	
Larvae					0.84 k1
full grown	86.9	551.6	96.4	1.98	0.03 k2
p. by *Cyzenis*	6.7	6.2	90.2	1.95	0.01 k3
other paras.	2.3	2.6	87.6	1.94	
diseased	4.5	4.6	83.0	1.92	0.02 k4
Pupae					
predated	66.1	54.6	28.4	1.45	
parasitised	46.3	13.4	15.0	1.18	0.27 k5
Adult female (1956)			7.5		

Source: Varley *et al.* (1973).

Notes:

Bold figures were measured, the others were derived.

In this table 'k' refers to the scale of the decline caused by each factor.

k1 (0.84) is winter disappearance and this was the most important 'killing factor' in 1955–56.

adults in Wytham Woods and who spent many hours watching predators feeding on these stages. The adult moths emerge in November/December, the wingless females crawl up trees and attract the winged males to mate, they then lay their eggs in crevices in the bark. In spring, just as the buds of the trees are opening, the larvae hatch and start to feed; they form loosely spun shelters and become fully grown in a matter of weeks; they then let themselves down from the trees on silk threads and burrow into the top layer of the soil, where they pupate. They remain there until they hatch the following winter. Varley and others were able to count the adults; the egg loads of the females; the early and late larvae and how many were parasitised; the pupae; and then the next generation adults, etc. From these counts they made up a life table and quantified the mortality rate between each stage (conventionally this is expressed as a log value). During the intervals between counts, mortality from several causes occurred and so their conclusions were rather generalised. For example, they lumped together all events between the females climbing the trees and the larval counts (called by Varley 'winter disappearance'). Table 24 records the life table for 1955–56.

After several years have been studied, with estimates for the effects of various factors, the relationship between the numbers each year and the magnitude of the various mortality factors can be assessed. It then becomes possible to decide which of the factors is the one that affects the population levels most – the 'key factor' (see Fig. 41). Varley's study of the Winter moth showed that 'winter disappearance' has the most effect. Subsequent studies have divided this into many more specific effects and have clarified the most important. For example, Feeny's studies (see Chapter 6) showed that the mortality caused when larvae hatch out before the buds have opened fits within this time period. For Winter moths it is not the highly obvious bird predation of larvae, or their heavy parasitism, that is usually the most important mortality factor.

DENSITY-DEPENDENT AND DENSITY-INDEPENDENT MORTALITY FACTORS

Studies such as these have now been carried out on many moths, particularly pest species, such as the Spruce Budworm (*Choristoneura fumiferana*), with a view to understanding what controls their population size and therefore what strategy might succeed in reducing it. Such studies have clearly shown that some of the mortality factors are density-dependent. Winter moth pupal predation shows this pattern; as the pupal population increases so does predation on the pupae and this tends to regulate the overall moth population, reducing it most when it is already large. Other factors are independent of density and will not lead to regulation, but some of these may be very variable from year to year. Winter disappearance, the key factor, proved to be density independent in Winter moths and this helps to lead to the very variable moth populations that are observed. Some years when the population is already high, winter mortality is low, allowing an even bigger population to develop, whereas in other years a small population may be driven lower by an unexpectedly high winter disappearance. Of course at higher population levels the density dependent factors begin to assume a greater importance and may even become the key-factors in those circumstances, so that the extent of variation in the populations may be checked. The relative importance of different factors varies from time to time so that the key factor may change over a period of years.

The importance of different mortality factors also varies from place to place, a good example being a parasite of Winter moth larvae *Cyzenis albicans*, which is not a key factor in Wytham Woods, and acts independently of density there, but has had a dramatic effect on Winter moth populations in Canada (Roland and Embree, 1995). Winter moths were accidentally introduced into northern America and *Cyzenis albicans* and a wasp *Agrypon flaveolatum* were brought to Novia Scotia as potential control agents in the 1950s and then later into British Columbia and Oregon. *C. albicans* established well and there was a rapid collapse in Winter moth populations in all areas. The parasite then became very scarce but the Winter moth did not fully recover its numbers and the general pattern seems to be that the parasite has acted to reduce the moth from its peak, but that other causes of mortality (such as predation on pupae) have since kept numbers low.

PINE LOOPER POPULATION CYCLES

The analysis of moth populations has been continued with enthusiasm since Varley's early work, providing further seminal insights into the way that animal populations fluctuate and are controlled. Frequently, cycles of abundance are found, as Barbour (1985) discovered with the Pine Looper (*Bupalus piniaria*).

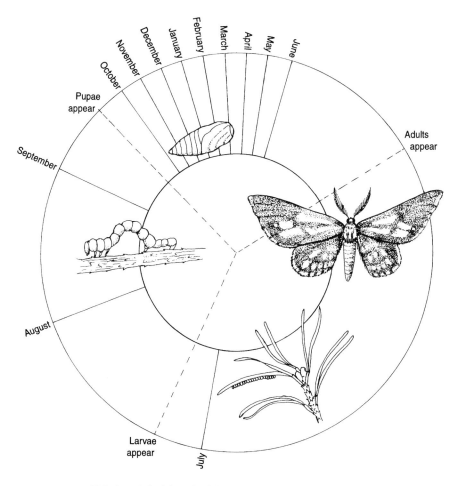

FIG 42   *The life cycle of the Pine Looper* (Bupalus piniaria)

Barbour accumulated data collected over 25 years in several forests in Britain and found that all populations fluctuated, varying around an apparent equilibrium, within a fairly narrow range. He distinguished between those populations where even one year of increased abundance led to a subsequent decline and those where the return swing was delayed for two years. The former showed 'immediate density dependence' and the latter 'delayed density dependence' but they seem to be at either end of a spectrum of response, rather than two distinctly different responses. Examples of each are shown in Figure 43. The causes of these two patterns are difficult to unravel but the delayed density dependence seems to be caused by the action of a parasitoid wasp *Dusona oxycanthae*. If the abundance of the moth and the parasite are plotted together, the parasite variation lags behind that of the moth but is a good predictor of the moth population in the next generation. This sort of result can be regarded as an illustration of the 'classic' model of host/parasitoid interactions and the result is variation about an equilibrium.

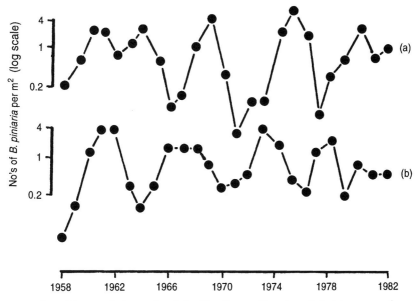

FIG 43   *The population cycles of the Pine Looper* (Bupalus piniaria) *measured as number of pupae per m², between 1958 and 1982 in two nearby forests in Scotland. (a) Roseisle); (b) Culbin. (Source: Barbour, 1990)*

The immediate density dependence pattern cannot be explained by the simple parasitoid model, because the response is too quick, and so less certain causes have to be invoked. In the Netherlands, Klomp (1966) suggested that an interaction between the survival of the young larvae and the effects of parasites could lead to rapidly fluctuating populations and Barbour was able to rationalise this as the explanation of the cycles that he found. He also suggested (Barbour, 1990) that some population cycles were synchronous over wide areas, perhaps because dispersal at times of peak numbers kept the populations in contact.

Berryman (1996) reviews many examples of population cycles in forest Lepidoptera, concluding that some of them are remarkably regular. For example, the Larch Budworm (*Zeiraphera diniana*) goes through 10 000-fold changes in density over a cycle of 8.24 years over a wide area in the Alps. He also reviews the probable causes of these variations and concludes that insect parasitoids are the main causative factor.

HOW DO MOTHS AVOID BEING EATEN?

Many of the defensive strategies of moths are passive; they depend on the avoidance of predators. However, there are some which have poisonous chemicals or irritant hairs and which advertise these features. In all cases the moths use a behavioural repertoire that backs up the appearance adopted. A special case concerns wing scales. These brush off the wings easily and if a moth gets slightly entangled with a spider's web it can escape, leaving some scales behind.

Leather and Brotherton (1987) studied the repertoire of defensive actions taken by the Pine Beauty (*Panolis flammea*). They prodded and poked the different stages of this species and found that the adults responded by violent twists and turns, having fallen to the floor; the larvae dropped away from disturbance on a thread when young; older larvae tended to remain motionless but under prolonged attack they twisted their heads against the attacker and attempted to 'bite' and dislodge it; pupae responded by wriggling and burying into the leaf litter of pine needles.

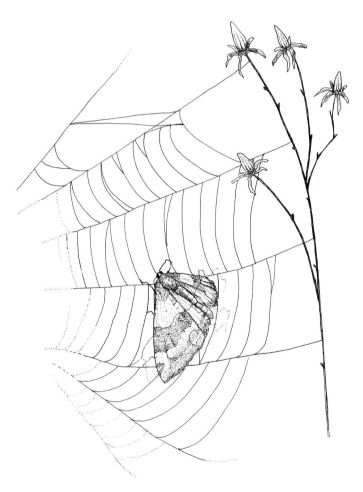

Even a wing-covering of loose scales does not always save moths which blunder into a spider's web.

Protective colours

Most moths are not distasteful or poisonous and have to avoid being recognised by potential predators. In some cases, moths hide in crevices, the soil or other places where they cannot be seen and these moths are usually dull coloured, and their colour plays no functional role in defence. There are surprisingly few examples of adult moths or larvae that use this tactic but many pupae do, even if inside a protective cocoon; the predominant colour of pupae is the brown of the tanned protein that forms their outer shell.

Most moths and larvae sit exposed in the environment and have a disguise. Two forms of camouflage are used to achieve this: in one the moth resembles the general background, so that it is not seen by the predator (crypsis); in the other the moth resembles a specific inedible object and the predator sees it but passes it over as the inedible 'model' (true camouflage) (Cott, 1940). The first of these two tactics results in rather variable colour patterns, for the general background is rarely constant, whereas the second may produce a very specific and invariable pattern, closely matching the inedible object.

Moths that sit exposed on bark or rock, like the Mottled Beauty (*Alcis repandata*) or the Dark Marbled Carpet (*Chloroclysta citrata*), can be very variable, within the limits of having the variegated appearance of a lichen covered surface. In contrast, bird dropping mimics, like the Chinese Character (*Cilix glaucata*) and the tortricid *Apotomis betuletana* are quite invariable. There is a long list of moths and larvae that resemble almost every possible feature of the inedible landscape, and their coloration and shape includes extravagant displays of all kinds. The 'prominent' moths (Notodontidae) and their larvae specialise in odd shaped knobs and bumps; the carpets (Geometridae) have intricate and varied patterns on their broad wings; *Caloptilia* spp. sit with their long thin wings wrapped closely around their bodies, which are set at a sharp angle away from the surface; and the plumes (Pterophoridae) have wings reduced to fine 'fingers', which resemble tiny scraps of twig or feather. The cocoons of the Puss moth and its relatives (*Cerura vinula* and *Furcula* spp.) are covered with chewed fragments from the bark on which they are made, so that they are exactly the same shade as the tree. For many enthusiasts the remarkable array of colour patterns is the chief fascination of moths.

Behaviour must match coloration

In some cases the colour patterns depend on the animals adopting a suitable position. For example the countershading of hawk moth larvae, such as the Eyed Hawk (*Smerinthus occellata*), requires that they sit upside down on the underside of twigs. Some pale coloured moths must sit on equally pale backgrounds, so that they are camouflaged, and the Tawny Shears (*Hadena perplexa*) has a series of colour forms in different parts of its range, each with a ground colour that matches that of the predominant soils and rocks in its area. It is thought that moths detect the tone of their own wings and match this against a background of the same shade. Bark mimics sit on trees, whereas other species nestle amongst ground vegetation and Barbour (*pers. comm.*) believes that the Pine Beauty (*Panolis flammea*) usually sits head down amongst the terminal buds of a pine branch, among which it is beautifully hidden. In all cases, the moths or larvae must remain perfectly still, until actually touched by a potential predator. Twig caterpillars, mostly Geometridae, sit rigid by day, at an angle from a branch and this greatly reduces the time that is available to them for feeding. However, all larvae except those that are internal feeders share this limitation.

Disruptive colours

In disruptive coloration the effect is such that the shape of the moth or larva is broken up by a bold disruptive stripe or pattern, so that the predator does not recognise the shape of the whole moth and misinterprets the signal that it receives. Often there is a clear bar across the wings or a series of scalloped colours around the edge, as for example, the Scalloped Oak (*Crocallis elinguaria*) illustrates.

Flash coloration and eye spots

The Large Yellow Underwing moth (*Noctua pronuba*) and its close relatives have varied but dull coloured forewings and rest by day in low vegetation, where they are well hidden. However, if they are disturbed, they fly off erratically before diving back among plants. As soon as they fly, the forewings are spread, displaying the yellow and black hind wings. This sudden flash of bright colour is startling and when in flight the alternation of light yellow and dull brown makes it difficult to follow the track of the moth accurately. Predators are put off by the sudden colour, giving the moths time to escape, and then cannot easily re-find the moth when it settles again. A number of moths use this defensive device and in some, like the Poplar Hawk (*Laothoe populi*), the 'warning' underwing colour is a round patch. This moth is so large that it has to warm up its wing muscles before it can fly and so its defence has to operate in a static situation. The startling effect has to deter the predator from attacking, even before the moth has flown away. In the Eyed Hawk (*Smerinthus ocellata*) the coloured patch has an extra feature; a concentric pattern resembling a large and bloodshot eye, which has led to speculation that it is mimicking the eye of a fierce animal. The two eyes, separated on the hind wings, imply that the face is large and so small predators decide to leave the moth alone. Such a defence can only work on moths large enough to have well separated and large eye-spot patterns. The Emperor moth (*Pavonia pavonia*) carries this to extremes by having a pair of eyes on both fore and hind wings. These eyes are not flashed from behind the forewings but the moth swings its wings around to face an intruder and perhaps this has the same effect. It may be difficult to appreciate the dramatic effect of the sudden appearance of eyes but Blest (1957) has shown, using captive birds, that they do avoid such signals, showing real signs of alarm.

Some butterflies have an alternative type of eye-spot on their wings. These are small and placed near the wing edge. Peck marks, which have excised pieces from the wing, suggest that the eye-spots are deflecting attack away from the vulnerable body to the wing, where some damage is of no consequence. Although some moths have small round marks on their wings, these do not resemble eyes and moths do not seem to have deflecting spots.

Warning colour and distastefulness

Moths that are distasteful, poisonous or have irritant properties benefit if potential predators recognise and learn their appearance easily; typically such moths are brightly coloured or 'aposematic'. To use such coloration effectively, it is necessary to make it clearly and unambiguously obvious, so aposematic moths tend to rest fully exposed against contrasting backgrounds and to move slowly and deliberately. Usually the universally recognised colours of (pale) red or yellow are set on (dark) black or brown backgrounds, so that there is great contrast even for colour-blind predators. Good examples of this are the Cinnabar moth (*Tyria jacobaea*) (crimson and black adults and yellow and black larvae) and the burnet moths (crimson spots on a black background in the adults and yellow and black larvae). Inexperienced predators can only learn that such colours indicate distastefulness after first trying to eat an example. However, these moths are tough skinned, so they sometimes survive the first tentative attack, before the predator realises that they are evil tasting. Burnet moths exude acrid fluid when attacked and birds have been observed discarding them and wiping their beaks in apparent distress after an attempt to eat them.

Rothschild (1985) provides many examples of aposematic lepidoptera, noting their defensive chemicals and behaviour and making the point that the most poisonous are day-flying. Many distasteful moths are found in the same families, i.e. all of the Zygaenidae and many of the 'tigers' Arctiidae; whereas almost all Noctuidae are edible. However, there are some examples of noxious moths amongst families of edible species. The Magpie moth (*Abraxas grossulariata*) is one of the few poisonous Geometridae. Every stage of this species is warningly coloured: the eggs are laid in obvious yellow clusters; the larvae are creamy yellow and dark brown; the pupae are black with yellow rings (and are formed in very loose weave cocoons, so that the colours show); and the adults are white, yellow and black.

Protective hair

Alternative warning displays are the conspicuous hair tufts of larvae such as the Vapourer moth (*Orgyia antiqua*) or general hairiness of the Fox moth (*Macrothylacia rubi*) whose hairs provide both the warning and the unpleasant experience – such a hairy mouthful would be unpalatable to most predators. Cuckoos are reputed to be able to eat such hairy larvae. The ultimate in distasteful hairs are those of the Brown Tail moth (*Euproctis chrysorrhoea*), for they have barbed ends which make them catch in the skin and they contain histamines and various other irritant chemicals, which cause severe skin rash if the larvae are handled. The females are pure white and obvious, with a tuft of irritant hairs. They spread these on their eggs to protect them. The larvae then grow their own hairs and are gregarious, a common feature with poisonous larvae, and their hairs are incorporated in the cocoon.

Crypsis and warning in one moth

Many species compromise in their defensive appearance, being cryptic at a distance but showing warning coloration close to. Rothschild believes that even the gaudy Cinnabar moth larvae are cryptic on the yellow flowerheads of Ragwort, until close to, when their warning stripes are obvious. The Muslin moth (*Diaphora mendica*) females are pure white with a few black dots. They rest upside down below a leaf but if seen resemble a feather. The male is plain brown but, if attacked, both sexes expose their yellow leg bases and dotted abdomens – clearly a warning signal, if rather a muted one. They belong to the commonly poisonous family Arctiidae. The Garden Tiger (*Arctia caja*) has beautifully cryptic forewings with a disruptive pattern of brown and cream but when disturbed it flashes its scarlet hind wings and body, with bluey-black spots. This species flies at night and is certainly distasteful but less toxic than the day-flying and fully aposematic Scarlet Tiger (*Panaxia dominula*) according to Rothschild (1985). Strangely Rothschild (1967) reports that some species that are consistently cryptic, like the July Highflyer (*Hydriomena furcata*), are nevertheless distasteful to birds and bats and it is difficult to understand why they have not adopted an aposematic appearance. In fact the July Highflyer shows one of the most striking and extraordinary bark mimicking cryptic patterns, with an infinite variety of intricate colours and patterns.

An odd defence is shown by the larvae of *Diurnea fagella*, which live in spun shelters on trees. These have inflated sections on their third thoracic legs with which they can make a scratching and tapping noise by scraping the leaf surface. Hunter (1987a) suggests that this deters spiders and parasitoids from entering the shelters but it seems unlikely that such slight noises would affect birds.

Mimicry – false warning

A minority of moths are apparently edible but have a colour pattern which mimics that of known distasteful or well defended species. These species gain an advantage from false warning or Batesian mimicry (named after the naturalist Bates, who provided many examples of the phenomenon). However, there is a frequent resemblance between different poisonous species which share the advantage of the coloration, so-called Mullerian mimicry. A potential predator may have to test possible prey items before it learns which are edible. If two distasteful species look sufficiently similar that they are confused by the predator, then both species will benefit if the predator needs only one experience from either of them, before it learns what the colour pattern means. If the two species are not equally toxic then in one sense the less toxic species is also a Batesian mimic of the other, rather than being wholly a Mullerian mimic.

The general resemblance between the red and black Cinnabar and burnet moths is an example of Mullerian mimicry. This demonstrates that if the species involved provide a strong deterrent message to shared predators, then the similarity need not be exact. In this case being red and black, regardless of the detail of the pattern, is sufficient. Probably the general resemblance between the various species of tiger moths is another example of Mullerian mimicry.

A very striking example of mimicry concerns the Hornet and Lunar Hornet clearwing moths (*Sesia apiformis* and *S. bembeciformis*), both of which look strikingly like large vespid wasps. These species share with the wasps a lazy buzzing flight and are almost 'super-wasps' in that they are larger and brighter than the real thing. However, Rothschild (1985) reports that she has fed the Hornet Clearwing to naive bird predators and that the birds rejected the moths, with much bill wiping, so that perhaps these are also Mullerian mimics.

Genuine Batesian mimics may be rarer than was once thought but the two Bee Hawk moths (*Hemaris tityus* and *H. fuciformis*) are possible examples. Like most hawk moths they are probably edible to birds but they are very similar in appearance to bumble bees (*Bombus* spp). and have a buzzing day-time flight. However, Jones (1934) put out specimens of an American *Hemaris* species on to a bird feeding tray and they were not eaten, so perhaps even these are slightly distasteful!

Warnings to non-visual predators

This discussion has focused on predators with colour vision similar to our own and this bias must not go unchallenged. To other eyes the appearances may be very different; this applies especially to predators that are not birds. Many will either not have colour vision, or not have binocular vision (so that size is less easily judged), or may not use vision at all. A distasteful moth will presumably have to use a disagreeable smell to signal its inedibility to a mouse, while the signals passed to bats are noted below. Rothschild points out the dangers of according human values to the situation by referring to the Death's Head Hawk moth (*Acherontia atropos*). This species specialises in robbing bee hives of honey, using its short sharp proboscis to pierce the wax caps of cells. It can blow air through its proboscis, producing a breathy squeak, which supposedly resembles the piping of a queen bee, so confusing defending worker bees, and its thorax pattern is similar to the head pattern of a 'super' queen bee, again reducing the aggressive response of the workers. This mimicry is called aggressive mimicry because the resemblance is used to permit an aggressive action. Humans have always interpreted the thorax pattern as a skull and cross bones, as if this could have any significance in the life of a moth!

MELANISM IN MOTHS

The occurrence of black or dark examples of many species of moths has been widely studied, especially the Peppered moth (*Biston betularia*) and its changing response to industrial pollution. Ford (1955) devoted a whole chapter to the subject and there have been many

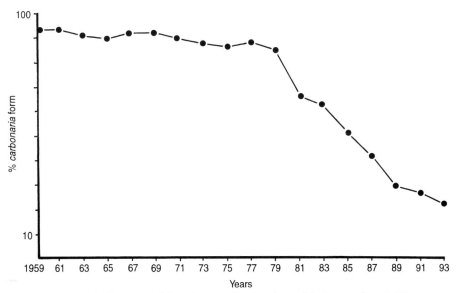

FIG 44   *The frequency of the melanic carbonaria form of the Peppered moth* (Biston betularia) *at Caldy Common, Wirral between 1959 and 1993. (Simplified from Clarke et al., 1994)*

accounts more recently, including Kettlewell (1973). There has been a recent decline in melanism, following the beneficial effects of the clean air acts and this example of evolution in action has had a profound influence on evolutionary biology in general. Perhaps the two most important inter-linked lessons that this has provided have been that evolution can proceed much faster than was previously believed, with major changes occurring over a handful of generations, and that selective pressures can be much greater than was previously thought.

There have been many good accounts of industrial melanism so only a brief discussion is needed here. The normal form of the Peppered moth is pale, with a few black pepperings over the wings but rare dark forms have always been known. In 1848, it was noted that dark forms were becoming more frequent near industrialised Manchester and by 1895 the dark form comprised 98% of the population there. In a series of classic observations from 1953 onwards, Kettlewell released numbers of marked pale and dark forms in a polluted area near Birmingham and in unpolluted Dorset and he found that twice as many light ones as dark ones were subsequently recaptured in Dorset, but that the reverse was true in Birmingham. By careful observation he was able to show that birds were eating moths at rest on tree trunks and that differential predation was causing the differences in recapture rates. In polluted areas the tree trunks were predominantly dark, owing to soot deposits and the lack of lichens, so that pale moths were easier to find than dark ones. Before Kettlewell's studies, very few examples of bird predation had been observed and it was not thought to be a major source of mortality in moths. Since the 1970s, the proportion of melanic Peppered moths has been declining again, throughout industrialised Britain, as the air has become cleaner, although it is by no means sure that this is because tree trunks have become lighter and more lichen covered (Clarke *et al.*, 1994; Grant *et al.*, 1995).

CHANGES IN COLOUR AND PATTERN OVER VERY SHORT DISTANCES

Many moths have occasional dark examples. Presumably most of these are easily found and eliminated by predators and so the proportion of melanics remains low. In species which have several patterns or colour forms, the proportion present must also represent a balance between the relative advantages of the different forms on the usual resting backgrounds. However, this very simplistic account is dramatically extended by the observations of Aldridge *et al.* (1993), who studied the appearance of several polymorphic species in Gloucestershire in September 1991.

They placed three light traps close together; one was 20 m inside a Larch (*Larix* spp.) plantation; one 28 m away in the boundary zone between this plantation and a garden; and the last a further 26 m away in the garden. The boundary zone was mainly Bracken (*Pteridium aquilinum*) and the garden was of mown grass, amongst some trees, shrubs and herbaceous plants. All traps were used for the same seven nights and the appearance of the captured moths noted. Four species were found in sufficient numbers for analysis; the Common Marbled Carpet (*Chlorodysta truncata*), the Grey Pine Carpet (*Thera obeliscata*), the Pine Carpet (*Thera firmata*) and the Large Yellow Underwing (*Noctua pronuba*). All have varied colour forms that can be described as ranging from pale to dark and all showed the same result, as exemplified by the Common Marbled Carpet (see Table 25).

There are statistically significant differences in the proportions of the different forms

TABLE 25   *The numbers of each of four different forms of the Common Marbled Carpet* (Chloroclysta truncata) *taken at different sites on the same nights in September 1991.*

Form	Forest trap	Boundary trap	Garden trap	Total
Typical pale	56	74	36	166
rufescens	47	31	14	92
perfuscata	52	36	6	94
nigerrimata	31	4	0	35
Total	186	145	56	387

(*Perfuscata* is semi-melanic; *nigerrimata* is fully melanic)

Source: Aldridge *et al.* (1993).

taken at each trap, with the palest forms more frequent in the garden and the darkest in the forest and an intermediate position in the boundary zone, despite the traps being only 54 m apart! This finding is most unexpected and deserves attention, for it suggests that selective differences can act with surprisingly high resolution in very small areas. Possibly the differences are caused by differential predation by birds, with the melanic forms at an advantage in the darkest of the three habitats; alternatively it could be that the darkest forms seek out the darkest places in which to rest; finally it could be that some other factor is acting, such as the advantage of being dark in the coolest area, and predation is not important.

Aldridge *et al.* (1993) claim that their data are insufficient to distinguish between these possible explanations but they are unnecessarily dismissive of predation, claiming that this could not be sufficiently intensive to produce the result. Their cautionary message is that differences in morph frequency may have to be assessed and explained at a micro-scale and that differences between general areas cannot be claimed if traps are placed in different types of locations in each area. This questions some of the work on melanism in Peppered moths and sets a different standard for future work.

MOTHS AND BATS

How bats detect moths

Moths have a more sophisticated relationship with bats than with any other of their predators. Although small bats feed mainly on smaller insects like midges (Diptera), many medium and large bats are specialised predators of moths and have a very well developed echo-location system that allows them to track and catch moths. They produce ultrasonic squeaks projected forward from their mouths or specially adapted noses, and they detect the returning echoes from any solid object in range. The range of frequencies used varies between bat species, as does the intensity of the sound, with some being 'whispering' bats and others producing squeaks nearly as intense as smoke alarms. Since most of the frequency of the squeak is typically above 20 kHz, we can hear only a very small proportion of it (Fenton *et al.*, 1987).

Generally, a cruising bat emits calls about 3–10 times a second, in a narrow frequency band, often characteristic for the species, allowing moths to be detected at a range of

5–20 m. Once a moth has been detected, the band width is widened and the rate of calling goes up dramatically to a 'feeding buzz' of up to 200 calls a second. It must be difficult for a bat to detect a moth among all the confusing echoes from waving leaves and branches but there is a characteristic echo from a fluttering moth (Fenton *et al.*, 1987). As the moth's wings move up and down they produce a fluctuating echo that apparently makes their 'signal' very different from that of leaves. The Greater Horseshoe bat (*Rhinolophus ferrumequinum*) can even distinguish flying Noctuidae from Geometridae, apparently on the rate of flutter (Schnitzler, 1987), although other bats may be incapable of such fine distinction.

Some bats, such as the Noctule (*Nyctalus noctula*), can use radar to detect moths sitting on leaves, which indicates the fine resolution of the location system.

A moth being chased by a bat.

How do moths detect the approach of bats?

Many moths, such as the Herald (*Scoliopterix libatrix*), have ears and some Notodontidae (prominents) have complex pinnae that 'point' backwards. Often these ears are connected to very few nerve cells, tightly tuned to the usual range of bat frequencies, typically around 40 kHz. These ears allow the moths to detect bats at 30 m or more, so that the moth hears the bat before the bat detects its presence. It is thought that some bats produce extra high frequencies to avoid being heard by moths (Rydell *et al.*, 1995) but these higher frequencies are not so well propagated through the air and the bats have to squeak very energetically to get a useful range. As Figure 45 shows, most moth-catching bats use frequencies either lower or higher than those detected most easily by moths. Often the night air is full of sounds – cicadas, frogs, bats, wind in the trees and it must be difficult for moths to differentiate the

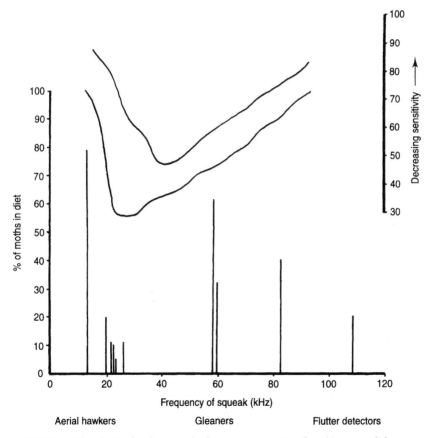

FIG 45   *The relationship between the frequency sensitivity of moth's ears and the pre-dominant squeak frequency of various species of bat, together with the percentage of moths in the diets of the bats. The Barbastelle* (Barbastella barbastellus) *has a squeak frequency of 35 kHz and yet feeds predominantly on moths. However, it seems to spe-cialise on 'deaf' moths, such as Tineidae.* (*Source: Rydell* et al., *1995*)

bats' call, but by comparing the time of arrival of sounds on their two ears, moths even seem to be able to judge direction (Fullard, 1987).

How moths avoid bats in flight

If moths detect a faint squeak from a bat, they turn and fly away. However, if the sound is loud, and the bat is near, they may either close their wings and drop to the ground or fly powerfully downwards. These avoidance strategies are effective, for they reduce the success rate of the bats to approximately half that of their catches of moths without ears (Roeder, 1967).

The use of confusing squeaks

Some moths have another defence strategy. They can produce a squeak or loud click themselves, when they hear a bat nearby. It has been suggested that this may confuse the bat, so that the true echo is mistaken; or that it may act to startle the bats into veering away. The most likely explanation, however, supported by experimental results, is that the clicks are warning sounds produced by moths that are distasteful to bats.

Achrya and Fenton (1992) report work with Red and Hoary bats (*Lasiurus borealis* and *L. cinereus*) and some species of Arctiidae (tiger moths), including the 'Muslin' moth (*Cycnia tenera*), near Ontario, Canada. When a bat approached the moths, they made loud clicks and continued to fly lazily along in a straight line, quite unlike the behaviour of most moth species. The bats then immediately gave up the chase and flew elsewhere. Occasionally a young bat would approach and catch such a moth, which was then rejected; sometimes their intact corpses were found amongst piles of wings at the place where the bats ate the other moths they caught. Dunning *et al.* (1992) also found that noxious moths were preyed on less than edible ones. The clicks and direct flight clearly act as 'warning coloration' does to a visual predator. Overall, the interaction between moths and bats does not seem to be quite as one-sided as it may first appear.

THE WAY MOTH POPULATIONS ARE ORGANISED

In general, the life cycles of moths are arranged to suit small organisms that have little influence over the external environment. They produce abundant offspring as quickly as possible and their numbers grow rapidly when conditions are amenable and crash when they are poor. This type of population dynamic is common to small animals and they are grouped together as 'r-strategists', in the terminology of MacArthur and Wilson (1967).

Reproduction is all – 'r strategy'

MacArthur and Wilson postulated that there are two basic types of animals, with respect to their population dynamics. 'r-strategists' devote their resources to maximising reproductive output, whereas 'K-strategists' emphasise the production of a smaller number of robust offspring, each one well provided by the parents. In real life there is a spectrum of strategies, but the ideas help organise thoughts about the way that many life history characteristics fit together. Small organisms like moths are usually r-strategists, whereas large organisms like whales or elephants are K-strategists.

Once a small organism is recognised as an r-strategist, many facets of its life history fit together. Moths are small and cannot improve their environment, except in some minor ways. Larvae that spin shelters improve their surroundings to a small extent but generally moths have to accept the climate and habitat available to them. Moths produce large numbers of eggs, typically many tens for larger species to several hundreds for the smaller species. Each of these has little stored food and the only 'extra' parental investment is some effort by the female to lay the eggs in a suitable place.

Myers (1978) studied the eggs of Western Tent moths (*Malacosoma californicum*), which are laid in an egg batch, with the first eggs at the top of the group; these are said to have more food reserves than the later eggs. However, she was unable to find any differences in the viability of the eggs, or the growth and survival of the resultant larvae. Subinprasert and Svensson (1988) found a great difference in the fate of eggs of the Codling moth (*Cydia pomonella*). Those laid on the upper surface of leaves survived much better than those on the underside, apparently because the bugs that prey on them search the undersides more assiduously.

Moth eggs hatch to produce tiny and ill-resourced larvae that have to find food quickly. Once they begin to feed they can grow rapidly to their full size, allowing a relatively short generation time (see Chapter 4). Many perish, so that the number of individuals reaching the next generation is variable but often low. A corollary of the low parental investment is that it does not necessarily pay to choose a particularly 'fit' mate. Furthermore, if the population is low, any mate may be very hard to find. Consequently, moths devote much effort to finding a mate (see Chapter 7) but do not trouble much to 'select' a good quality mate – their courtship rituals are brief. K-strategists, for example humans, are the reverse; we need not search to find potential mates but devote great effort to selecting particularly suitable ones!

Easy extinction and quick population increase

This style of reproduction leads to a population size that can increase or decline dramatically in a very short time, although there may be density-dependent mortality factors that act to return the population to an equilibrium level. Such regulation often fails and local populations of moths can become extinct, the decline being rapid and often surprising and unexplained. Alternatively, populations can rise equally fast. Anyone who has run a moth trap for a few years in one location has noticed unlikely rises and falls in the numbers of species that are usually common and regular. In the 1970s and early 1980s the White Ermine (*Spilosoma lubricipeda*) was reliably common in Aberdeenshire, with the fast-crawling, brown, hairy larvae a frequent sight on the roads, but it then declined, so that almost none were present in the late 1980s and early 1990s. Since then there has been something of a recovery, although not yet to previous levels. Farther north in Scotland, the population seems to have remained high throughout all these years.

Populations of pests

A 'boom or bust' population style is an ideal pre-adaptation for a species to become a pest. If the right environment is provided, a field or forest full of high quality foodplant, for example, a moth can rapidly increase to pest proportions. With the recent decline in crop rotation, there may be several successive years of food availability to stimulate such population growth. Our response is usually to try to reduce the moth population with chemicals but the amount of genetic variation represented in the myriad larvae present means that some larvae are likely to be immune to the chemical used. These survive to find themselves among a plentiful food supply but with few competitors, so their offspring can increase dramatically and pesticide resistance is quickly established. Even if the initial pesticide treatment reduces the population level, the good mate-finding abilities of moths ensure that mating occurs and the pest succeeds. A more profitable long-term solution must surely involve control agents, such as parasitoids or predators, that will act in a density dependent fashion and will not give rise to resistance in the pest.

CHAPTER 9

Catching and Studying Moths

THIS chapter aims to provide information on the various methods used to study moths. There are already practical handbooks, such as Dickson (1976) or Smithers (1982); Freidrich (1986) concentrates on the techniques used to rear moths. To avoid too much repetition, this account will concentrate on field methods, rather than those used in the assembly of a collection and it is not designed as a comprehensive guide but as a commentary on the methods in question.

EARLY MOTH HUNTERS AND THEIR APPARATUS

Ford (1945) reproduces the charming frontispiece from Moses Harris's book *The Aurelian*, published in 1765, which shows two lepidopterists hunting for butterflies and moths in some suitably rustic woodland glade. Both are armed with the long style of net called by Harris the 'batfolder' and by others the 'bat-fowler', supposedly because it was used for snaring bats and sparrows out of the tangled vegetation on houses or trees. The bag of the net, made from gauze, was hung from two long curved handles, joined at the tip, and the net was swung at the insects, while the handles were held open, and then the handles were flung shut. These must have been very unwieldy but their sheer size would have partly compensated for this. Apparently more orthodox smaller nets were also in use, as were ones with a 'lid' to prevent the escape of the insects and so Moses Harris would not have been too surprised by the modern 'kite-shaped' net.

Large moths were killed by pinching the thorax under the wings, a quick and effective means but one not possible with smaller species. These were killed in a bottle containing crushed laurel leaves to produce a weak source of cyanide fumes, before being pinned through the thorax and stored in cork lined boxes. The wings were spread in a series of styles, as the years progressed, often on a curved cork board with small card braces or wound cotton thread to keep the wings apart. The Camberwell Beauty butterfly *(Nymphalis antiopa)* that Ford illustrates, which dates from 1793, could have been caught and set yesterday, except for the rather old-fashioned backwards slope of the forewings.

Kirby and Spence (1815–26) produced a book on entomology that for many years was the main source of reference on all matters to do with the study of insects and they provide a wealth of detail and illustration of the apparatus that they recommend. They describe in sober fashion how the serious student should equip himself, including bag nets of very modern sounding design. Most of the succeeding moth books also include a section on techniques for forming a collection and they outdo one another in the extravagance of the net designs and elaborate collecting tins and cases they describe. Often minute details are given as to the correct mode of manufacture of the apparatus, as if digression from the approved design would lead to shameful failure. There were devices for every eventuality, including, for example, nets with circular notches in their frame to allow them to be pressed securely against lamp-posts, or nets with small lanterns hung on an extended pole just above them for 'taking moths from high blossoms' (Furneaux, 1907). In the days when page space was of less importance, such fine detail was obviously appreciated! P.B.M. Allan, who wrote four excellent, light-hearted books on various aspects of the study of moths, includes a very full discussion in *A Moth Hunter's Gossip* (1937) of the old ways and he was obviously full of respect for their ingenuity, if amused by the unnecessary complexity of their techniques. However, the essence of moth hunting – the net of gauze; the pill box or tube; the killing jar; the setting board; the glass framed drawer; and the caterpillar pot are the universal tools of the trade. The two revolutions, that is the use of 'sugar' to attract moths and then the advent of effective light traps, will be described in more detail below. Otherwise little has changed.

COLLECTING AND STUDYING LARVAE

There are compelling reasons why a lepidopterist has to become an expert at finding the larvae of moths. These include the fact that they are the only stage of some species that are findable at all; they are often the stage that most requires study in the field if the ecological requirements of a species are to be understood; they are a source of specimens in immaculate condition for study or a collection; and their capture often needs the use of real ingenuity and skill, the exercise of which is very satisfying! Tutt (1901–05) explains forcefully why you cannot claim to be a true lepidopterist unless skilled at larva hunting.

In some cases larvae are warningly coloured and sit exposed on their foodplant, so that they require little skill to find. Even then care must be taken to collect them in a way that fulfils the needs of the study and does not endanger the population. If a breeding stock is required, larvae must be collected that will provide adults of both sexes in roughly equal numbers and choosing larvae of varying sizes will improve the chance of achieving this. They must be selected to maximise the chance of providing individuals as unrelated and widely representative of the genetic complement of the population as possible. This will increase the chance of successful matings and will optimise the representative nature of the sample. To achieve this it is prudent to collect a few larvae from many widely separated sites in the overall habitat. However, gregarious larvae may not thrive in small groups and it would be wrong to collect so many from one group for it to cease to function as such. Different species differ in this respect; some of the 'processionary' species (*Thaumetopoea* spp.) thrive only in large groups, whereas other species change as they develop. The Kentish Glory (*Endromis versicolora*) feeds in groups when in its first stages but the groups decrease in size as the instars progress, and the older larvae are solitary. Common sense must be applied!

Collect a range of larvae

The need to collect a range of sizes of larvae from a wide set of locations applies if the object is to sample the range of physiological abilities or developmental rates, but it is even more necessary if a study is to made of the rate of parasitism. This aspect of the study of Lepidoptera is often neglected and it is advantageous if full samples of parasites are collected and analysed. Some parasitised larvae may be smaller than their unparasitised siblings and occasionally there is an external sign of their fate, either as the still attached parasitic egg, or as a dark mark or an asymmetric shape. Regrettably, moth collectors or breeders often avoid such larvae, and parasites are under-represented in the sample.

The main predators of large larvae are birds, which generally hunt visually by day. It follows that many larvae hide by day and only become active at night and the older generation of collectors know that the easiest way to find such larvae is to search the food-plant at night using a light (Allan, 1980). The extremely localised Rosy Marsh moth *(Eugraphe subrosea)*, for example, is best found either using a light trap for the adults or by scanning Bog Myrtle *(Myrica gale)* leaves at night in May, when the fully fed larvae are easily seen. A complication is that many larvae are easily disturbed by even dim light and quickly fall back into the undergrowth, so that the use of a red light of medium power may be advantageous. Although it is true that the pool of light is necessarily small, so that searching efficiency is low, it is also true that some larvae seem to show up more clearly in the very unidirectional light of a torch at night, so that they are more easily found than might be thought.

It is rare to search for larvae of a species about which nothing is known. In most cases enough is known of a species for at least its foodplant and approximate time of larval growth to be recorded. These and any other details must be considered and appraised. Regrettably, many standard books repeat information which includes the wrong foodplants or an unhelpful and usually inaccurate statement that a species feeds on 'low plants'. Consequently, it is necessary to consider published data carefully. However, some previous knowledge is usually found to narrow the area of search. Sometimes larvae remain close to their feeding sites when hiding during the day, like the Poplar Hawk *(Laothoe populi)*, but often the larvae crawl away to hide elsewhere. The Merveille-du-jour *(Dichonia aprilina)* larvae climb down oak trunks to rest in cracks of the bark by day.

The clues that larvae leave behind

The reason why larvae may rest away from their feeding site is clear when it is remembered that chickadees spend longer searching on branches which have had their leaves artificially damaged than on branches that have entire leaves (see Chapter 6). For lepidopterists, this is also a very promising clue that can be used in many circumstances. Larvae of the Sand Dart *(Agrotis ripae)* live by day under the surface of sand on the foreshore but their presence is clear from the chewing left on their foodplant Sea Rocket *(Cakile maritima)*. The young larvae of the Narrow-bordered Bee Hawk *(Hemaris tityus)* chew characteristic round holes on either side of the mid-rib of *Succisa* and rest underneath the leaf. These signs are useful but not infallible, for many other insects cause damage to leaves and only freshly made, pale holes are useful. However, especially with micro-lepidoptera, many of which can only be found as larvae, such signs are the main clues available. Good examples are the characteristic transparent patches, with small circular entrance holes, left by the case-bearing larvae of the Coleophoridae.

The presence of droppings or frass are another useful indication of the presence of larvae. However, this applies mainly to the larger species, or in circumstances where the frass can accumulate in easily observable amounts. The Death's Head Hawk *(Acherontia atropos)* has been found in potato fields after its droppings were noticed. More helpful are the accumulations of frass that occur at the entrance of burrows. The micro *Argyresthia glaucinella* feeds as a larva under the bark of oak trees and the only way to detect its presence is to learn to recognise the small piles of pale droppings in the bark crevices. Even though boring beetles also produce external droppings, it is easy to distinguish the two. The Brindled Ochre *(Dasypolia templi)* feeds internally in the lower stems of *Heracleum* and *Angelica* but ejects frass at holes at the stem nodes, so revealing its presence. Similarly, the Goat moth *(Cossus cossus)* ejects strong smelling frass in great quantities from its burrows, making its presence very clear.

Collecting internally feeding larvae

Many micro-lepidoptera live internally in leaves or make constructions within which to hide. The patterns of internal feeding and the precise nature of the shelters may be sufficiently diagnostic to allow individual species to be determined from them. These signs often remain after the shelters have been vacated, allowing a study of the dynamics and preferences of species without the live specimens being present. Members of the genus *Phyllonorycter* live between the leaf surfaces of their foodplants and cause a puckering of the surface. If a larva fails to grow, the juvenile mine remains visible as a slight surface scar. Their larvae also pupate within the mine, often surrounding the pupa with a characteristic pattern of frass. When they emerge they leave the pupal skin trapped at the emergence hole, whereas if a parasite emerges it leaves a small round hole. If a mine is opened by an insectivorous bird this usually leaves a gaping jagged hole. The fate of the individual larva is therefore often obvious. *Phyllonorycter messaniella* feeds in this way on the evergreen Holm Oak (*Quercus ilex*), on which leaves remain for more than one season. Consequently, examination of the tree allows a count of all the mines of two semi-overlapping generations of the moth, with full characterisation of the fate of each larva and its parasites.

Nepticulidae larvae are mostly leaf miners and their characteristic feeding signs are either blotches, or more usually long serpentine mines on leaves of trees, shrubs or, less frequently, herbs. The adults lay their eggs on the outer surface and the first clue to identity is whether the egg is on the upper or lower side, or is set in the vein angles. As the larvae feed they leave a track. The frequency of its turn, the angularity of line and turn, the position of the track in relation to the leaf edge or veins, and the precise pattern in which the frass is laid out within the mine (whether in dispersed, linear or spiral lines) and finally the colour of the larva, especially its head and anal plates, may be important. All of these, taken with the host plant identity and the time of feeding, often lead to identification which is as certain and quick as that for the adult.

Keys to larval feeding signs

Many books provide keys and diagrams to the feeding signs of micro-lepidoptera, for example, Hering (1957), Emmet (1988) and Emmet, Watkinson and Wilson (1985). Most

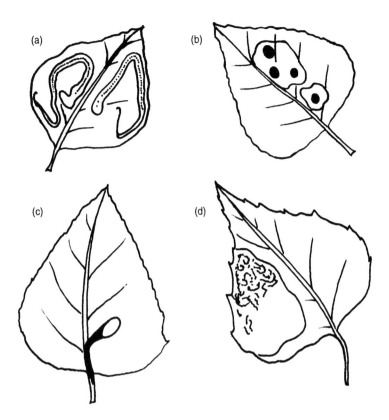

FIG 46   *Some contrasting examples of leaf-mining Lepidoptera on birch.* (*a*)
Stigmella confusella (*Nepticulidae*); (*b*) Ectoedemia occultella (*Nepticulidae*); (*c*)
Heliozela betulae (*Heliozelidae*); (*d*) Eriocrania semipurpurella (*Eriocraniidae*). *The*
dark marks within the mines of (*a*), (*b*) *and* (*d*) *are the frass.*

micro-lepidopterists include a herbarium of preserved leaves in their collections. The cross-
referencing of foodplants against species in Emmet (1991a) makes it possible to make a list
of micro-lepidopterans from a habitat based on the time, style and position of their feeding.
In the autumn, when most of the feeding shelters and mines for the season are in place on
leaves, it is possible to visit a locality and make records of dozens of species from these structures. This can be a very useful guide to relative species richness of different localities.

Beating and sweeping larvae

Searching for larvae is laborious and often apparently inefficient, at least at first until one's
eye is in, but the information gained is great and often leads to priceless insights into the
factors affecting the lives of moth species. In some cases, however, perhaps where a general
knowledge is needed of all the species using a tree host, or present in a meadow, a more
wide-ranging approach is called for. Beating trays and sweep nets fulfil this need. Beating

trays may be as small as a folded net, or as organised as the purposefully designed 'Bignel pattern' tray, or as all-embracing as a spread sheet. In each case, the tray is placed carefully beneath the branch to be sampled and this is then tapped abruptly and forcibly, so that the unexpected jar dislodges the larvae. The sweep net is a stoutly rimmed and tough net that is swept vigorously back and forth through ground vegetation, again to dislodge the larvae. Both suffer several disadvantages. Firstly, the vegetation may be damaged. Secondly, the buffeting may also damage the larvae, especially those that hang on well and have to be roughly torn from their perch. Thirdly, the foodplant of a swept larva from mixed herbage may be unknown. While there is clearly a place for beating or sweeping in general studies or where a collector wants to make a quick collection of larvae, they are very much a second best to specialised searching.

PUPA-DIGGING AND OTHER METHODS OF COLLECTING PUPAE

The pupal stages of Lepidoptera are carefully hidden and it is often impossible to make an effective survey or count of the pupal stage. There are exceptions, such as the conspicuous papery cocoons of the burnet moths, and, if the pupation habits are well known, it is possible to devise an efficient scheme to attract them to pupate in traps. However, the least known stages of the life cycles of the moths are usually pupae.

Many species pupate under the soil or the litter that covers it and different ones go to different depths and to specific locations. Presumably the soil offers a relatively secure hiding place, with lower predation than on the surface (although there are many soil dwelling predators, such as carabid beetles, so that it is not an absolute refuge). Species whose larvae feed on tree leaves often descend to the ground to pupate and so merely let themselves drop off the tree, often steadied by a silk thread, arriving anywhere beneath the canopy, whereas others crawl down the branches and trunk, finding their pupation site at or near the foot of the tree. The Winter moth *(Operophtera brumata)* may be sampled as a pre-pupation larva by setting out trays of known size in arrays beneath the branches of forest trees, so intercepting the larvae as they fall. The Pine Beauty *(Panolis flammea)* is a pest, especially of Lodgepole Pine *(Pinus contorta)* in northern Scotland, and this necessitates sampling its abundance, so as to activate control measures when necessary. This is achieved by taking wide diameter soil cores from beneath the trees, then teasing out and counting the pupae. The practice has been carried out now for many years for the Pine Beauty and the Pine Looper *(Bupalus piniaria)* and has provided excellent data sets which illustrate the variable nature of the population size of the species (Barbour, 1985) (see Chapter 8).

Many species crawl down tree trunks to find a pupation site and there are more pupae near the foot of the tree than on the general forest floor; it is sometimes profitable to search specifically there. This is 'pupa-digging', closely identified with Parson Greene, who wrote a short book on the subject in 1857. He claimed dramatic success, to an absurd degree, as so humorously discussed by Allan (1937), but in certain conditions many pupae can be found. Different species have characteristic places around the tree in which they pupate. Some, like the Nut-tree Tussock *(Colocasia coryli)*, choose the layer of moss that surrounds the trunk above the soil; some, like the Marbled Brown *(Drymonia dodonea)*, merely lie almost loose at the soil surface amongst the root angles; some, like the Lime Hawk *(Mimas tiliae),* dig into the soil close to the tree; whereas others, like the Great Prominent *(Peridea anceps),* move away from the trunk and burrow under vegetation. The general complexity of the forest floor, compared with the base of an isolated tree, means that it is often more profitable to search the isolated tree or on the edge of the wood.

The secret of success in pupa hunting is to learn the precise appearance of the object of search and to define the nature of the pupation site. A successful, specific search can then be carried out. Pupae are also often rather delicate and do not thrive unless kept with the correct type of protection at the right temperature and humidity, so great care is needed to avoid damaging or scratching pupae during their collection and they must then be stored carefully until eclosion of the adults.

CATCHING AND STUDYING ADULT MOTHS

Day-flying moths and butterflies are most often studied by direct observation and may be caught by netting. A kite-shaped net with dark meshed gauze is generally favoured. Once in the net the moths are then transferred to pill-boxes, or for the smaller species, to glass or plastic tubes. In these they will often settle quietly, especially if put into a dark, still and cool place, but some species like the Saxon moth *(Hyppa rectilinea),* are known to be restless, and must be dealt with soon after capture. On no account must the tubes or boxes be put in the sun, to avoid a greenhouse effect; also care must be taken to avoid any moisture, or moisture-producing agent, such as a piece of leaf, being in the tube. If any damp is present the moth will inevitably get caught by the wings and will become unrecognisable. In dry tubes adult moths will survive for many days at around 3–5°C, in the bottom of a domestic fridge.

Many species of moth fly preferentially at dusk and dawn, particularly micro-lepidoptera, which often swarm then. The tiny Elachistidae are well known to have an abundant dawn-flight but dawn is usually cooler than dusk and the dusk flight is greater. For many micro's this flight begins just as the daylight begins to fade, and this is the time to begin searching for them. Such small creatures are not easy to see as true dusk approaches but larger species, especially the Hepialidae or 'swift' moths and the Plusiinae, then begin to take their place. This is well known entomological lore but it is not clear whether the flight of micro's declines as true night appears or whether they are not seen so readily then. Small moths are particularly prone to adverse effects of wind, so sheltered conditions are needed, but they use nectar or plant secretions and so can be found at blossoms or resin, like larger species.

Butterfly enthusiasts quickly recognise days on which butterflies will not be flying and in Britain there are many such days. However, moth collectors are less able to predict precisely whether a night will be productive for moths, so they are more likely to go out and waste their efforts. A few moths may be found on almost any occasion but good moth nights are just as scarce as good butterfly days. Mild, still, humid nights are best, with generous cloud cover, a new moon and rising or stable barometric pressure. In Britain an easterly or northerly air flow is to be avoided and in other parts of the world winds from cool sectors have the same effect. The perfect night is rare but moths often surprise by their unexpected abundance or scarcity.

Smaller species are more easily disturbed by day than larger ones and so judicious tapping of vegetation may well disturb them and they often fall on to the beating tray or the sweep net. A technique that is used for disturbing micro's is that of 'smoking' them out of grass tussocks, witch's broom or thatch. For this a bee-smoker is used to generate the smoke, which is then puffed into the vegetation. A little time will elapse before the moths emerge but surprising numbers may then appear, particularly if there is sufficient breeze to make shelter attractive.

ASSEMBLING MOTHS TO VIRGIN FEMALES

Some moths, such as the dead-white males of the Ghost Swift *(Hepialus humuli)*, attract mates by vision but most use scents or pheromones (see Chapter 7). Some species are particularly known for this, like the Emperor moth *(Pavonia pavonia)* and related Saturniidae, but most female moths use pheromones to attract a mate. This attraction is often used to collect males of a species, either for research, a collection or as part of a pest control programme.

Some species produce an attractive odour immediately they emerge. For example, a Vapourer moth *(Orgyia antiqua)* may emerge, attract a male, mate and lay all her eggs all within three hours. Some burnet moth cocoons attract males even before the female has emerged from the pupa, so that the females have crowds of courting males available before they have even extended their wings. However, this is exceptional and usually females will begin calling only once they can fly to a suitable perch, often on the same night as they have emerged but almost invariably by the second. Almost always if a female moth is found feeding, free flying or attracted to a trap, then she will have already mated.

To attract a mate to a virgin female, she must be put into a cage which allows the breeze to blow gently through and which is sufficiently large to allow her to rest easily from the roof. This must be placed in an airy but semi-sheltered position in the likely habitat at dusk and must be left sufficiently undisturbed for the female to settle. For many species no pre-feeding is needed but some will only call after they have been fed with dilute sugar-water on their first night. The males will appear from downwind and, as long as they cannot actually get to the female, she will continue to call and attract more. Such males are easily caught, for they are intent on the female and are not easily distracted from her. Females will only bother to call on nights when the weather is conducive to flight by the males and so many nights will be blank. If a mating is required, only 2–3 males should be put with the female. She might reject one, if he was for some reason not producing the correct scent or behaviour, but too many would disturb and distract her. Once mating has begun the other males should be removed.

SALLOWING

In Britain, moths begin to emerge from hibernation and from overwintering pupae in early spring. A good guide is that moths will begin to appear when the first blossom begins to open on the sallows and willows *(Salix* spp.). The initial flush of moths declines, before numbers begin to rise again in May to peak in mid-summer. Sallow blossom, both the male 'pussy-willows' and the less showy female flowers, are highly attractive to both day- and night-flying insects. During the day sallows are surrounded by the hum of bees, while on spring nights moths feed avidly on the blossom. Most of the spring night-flying moths, particularly of the noctuid genus *Orthosia* and the hibernating Cucullinae, feed avidly on sallow blossom and are easily collected there. Sallows in full flower should be noted by day and then re-visited an hour or so after dark, by which time the moths will have arrived. They can be inspected by torch light – a red light causes less disturbance. Alternatively, a sheet can be spread beneath the tree and a light set up on it. If the tree's branches are shaken, many of the moths will be dislodged and will fall to the ground. When they then begin to fly again, they will be attracted to the light in great numbers. Usually some of the older blossoms will also be shaken off on to the sheet and many of these will harbour moth larvae, for example, the Slender Pug *(Eupithecia tenuiata)*. Consequently, 'sallowing' can provide a wealth of adults and larvae.

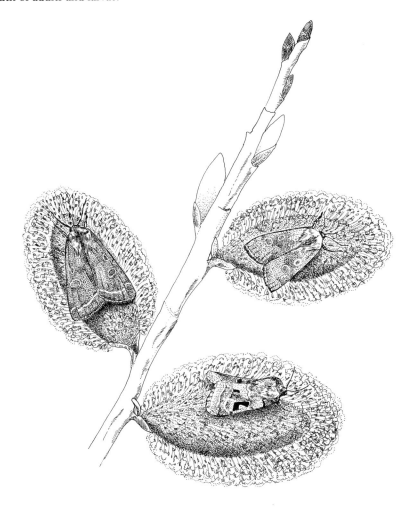

Moths feeding at sallow blossom.

ATTRACTING MOTHS TO SUGAR

Allan (1937) reviews the early history of the method of attracting moths known as 'sugaring'. There is some dispute about who first noticed that moths will visit sweet secretions and used this knowledge to catch them by putting out a sugary mixture, but it seems probable that it was Edward Doubleday, of Epping. He noticed that empty 'hogsheads' of sugar were attractive to moths and in 1832 he wrote an article recommending their use. By 1841 he had substituted a mixture of sugar and water, brushed on to bark, and this is still the essence of the method. Gardiner (1986) reports a published sugar recipe from 1849.

Some species are more attracted to sugar than to any other lure, and female moths, which are scarcer than males at light, are frequent at sugar. The Old Lady moth *(Mormo maura)*, the Sword Grass *(Xylena exsoleta)* and the Red Underwing *(Catocala nupta)* are good examples of 'sugaring' species.

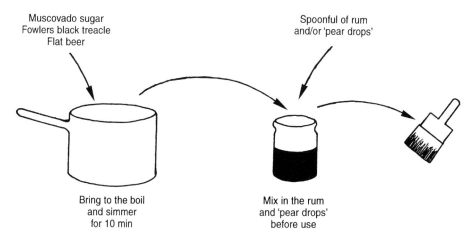

Muscovado sugar
Fowlers black treacle
Flat beer

Spoonful of rum
and/or 'pear drops'

Bring to the boil
and simmer
for 10 min

Mix in the rum
and 'pear drops'
before use

FIG 47   *A basic recipe for 'sugar' for attracting moths.*

Secret sugaring recipes

A folk-lore is attached to sugaring and many lepidopterists guard the secret of their recipe. However, all include the same basic ingredients; dark sugar and black treacle, usually dissolved by boiling in a liquid base of flat beer, and an aromatic attractant, such as fermented bananas, rum or amyl acetate (pear drops). The rich sweet smell attracts the moths and the alcohol makes them drowsy and approachable. The method of application also has many traditions but most lepidopterists paint vertical strips on a series of fence-posts, tree trunks or, if these are not available, then any other surface. A recently revived method uses ropes impregnated with sweetened, fermenting wine. Since the sugar may be said to be imitating either nectar or honey-dew, it is also effective if washed over flower heads, bunches of grass heads or leaves. On sand dunes marram grass heads, which are themselves attractive to moths, are almost the only thing that are paintable, and some species, such as the Orange Sallow *(Xanthia citrago)*, are said to come to sugared leaves more often than to tree trunks. Sugar works best on mild damp nights but it competes poorly with natural blossoms or honey-dew.

The great variation in the effectiveness of sugar in different weather conditions, or when competing with natural attractions, means that it is of no use for taking regular comparable samples but it is essential if an attempt is to be made to complete a list of moths from an area, or to provide the collector with specimens of some species.

LIGHT TRAPS

The mode of action of light traps was reviewed in Chapter 3; they have been used for as long as moths have been studied, initially by putting candles or lamps in windows but later in specifically designed traps. Gardiner (1995) reports the possible first use of a light trap, as well as an early reference to pest control. In 1565, Stevens and Liebault published a method for catching and killing moth pests of bee-hives, using a 'high and narrow mouthed tin-pot, with a burning light at the bottom of it, for presently all the butterflies [sic] will hasten and fly thither into the light and, flying about it, will burn themselves: for they cannot easily, from a narrow bottom, fly right up . . .'. By the 1850s there are several references to more conventional designs using candles to attract moths.

In their general design these traps resemble lobster pots, with easy entrance and difficult exit and with a bright light source in the entrance. The trap design is quite variable but the main revolution in the use of moth traps came when lamps became available that emitted large amounts of ultra-violet light, which corresponds to the part of the spectrum most visible to moth eyes. These bulbs often include mercury vapour in their envelopes and are referred to as MV bulbs.

Three types of portable traps are now most often used in Britain, all named after their inventors. A popular design is the 'Robinson' pattern trap, which is most like a traditional lobster pot, with an inverted cone leading to the main chamber. Recently the 'Skinner' trap has gained in popularity. This has two sloping perspex plates leading to the chamber, instead of a cone, and the base folds up so that the whole is more easily transported. Both of these traps run from the mains supply or from a generator, usually with a 125 W MV bulb and so they are heavy and usually operated close to a house or car. John Heath, who combined an electrical education with a love of moths, designed a truly portable trap, with a collapsible box made from aluminium and a small fluorescent tube light, run from a battery. This may be carried to remote sites and is used very widely. Variations on these basic designs are now found throughout the world, and have been hauled to the canopy of rainforests and left by glaciers in the Arctic. A further advantage of the fluorescent tube traps is that the tube remains cool and is unaffected by rain, whereas the MV bulbs run at very high temperatures and may shatter if cool rain drops fall on to them. To avoid this problem, a 'Pyrex' bowl is often placed over them as a rain shield.

A different design, using a standard tungsten filament bulb and an inverted glass cone arrangement, was adopted by Rothamsted Experimental Station for its country-wide set of traps. This is less efficient than the MV traps and so the catches are smaller, but it is weatherproof and is run every night of the year, to produce comparable annual series of catches. If comparative studies are to be made, the design of each trap must be standardised.

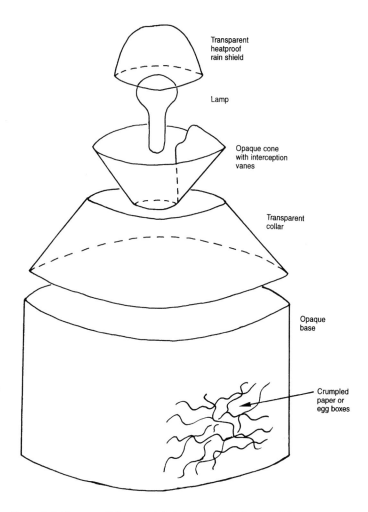

FIG 48   *Expanded diagram of the essential elements of a light trap. There are many variants of each element but the most effective lamps produce much light in the ultra-violet spectrum.*

Using light traps

Light traps work best in a reasonably sheltered position but one where the light shines out over an open area. The ground around the trap should be uncluttered, often a white sheet is put under the trap. An alternative strategy is to run a light without the body of the trap and to place the sheet beneath it or adjacent to it. Moths are attracted towards the light; some fly straight into the trap but the majority settle nearby first, or make a series of fly-pasts before escaping its influence. Many settle in nearby shade or on the ground and if the light is attended they may be examined and released. Even those that enter the trap may find their way out again – their escape can be discouraged by putting old egg boxes or crumbled paper inside for them to settle on. As dawn approaches some will fly off to find a dark, day-time refuge and this is when the largest number escape. It follows that the catch will be greatly increased if the light is attended while in operation, or at least examined at dawn. Moths that settle near the trap are often found and eaten by birds in the early morning, another good reason for visiting it at dawn. If the trap is placed so that the sun shines on it while moths are inside, they will either be killed owing to the heating caused by the 'green-house' effect, or will wake up and try to escape. Moths can be inspected while dormant on the egg trays and should then be released away from the trap site the following evening, after birds have gone to roost. If it is unavoidable that catches should be killed, then it is possi-ble to place a slow release anaesthetic pad in the bottom of the trap, replacing it sufficiently often for it to remain effective. These anaesthetics must be non-inflammable.

If a monitoring programme is in progress, or it is necessary to make consecutive catches, traps may be run in the same location every night but some birds and bats will quickly learn to associate the trap with a source of food and predation may become a problem. Furthermore, the same individual moths may be caught repeatedly, disrupting their mating and egg-laying. This should be avoided if possible by using the trap in different locations and/or irregularly. Despite these problems, there is no evidence of damage being caused by light traps to populations even of rare moths. However, a trap that is found to be capturing many specimens of a potentially vulnerable species should be re-sited.

It is well known that some species are more easily attracted to light than are others and so an inventory for a locality cannot be completed using light traps alone. Because female moths are also either less attracted or fly less frequently they encounter a trap less often. Therefore, sex ratios cannot be assessed using light traps. Nevertheless, their use has revo-lutionised our knowledge of the distribution of moths and their habits and they are among the most necessary pieces of entomological equipment.

MARKING MOTHS FOR RESEARCH

The broad wing area of moths provides opportunities for marking them so that they may be recognised on re-capture but care is required to avoid affecting their flying or survival abilities.

Butterflies have been marked for many years and this has included glueing small paper labels to the wings of the larger species, such as the Monarch *(Danaus plexippus)*, but the commonest method is to use dabs of coloured paint or ink at a series of positions on the wings. This method can also be used for some moths, such as the day-flying burnet moths (Zygaenidae). Specimens are caught, held securely but gently against the fabric of the net and dots of ink applied using indelible felt-tip pens. The aposematic colour of these species, showing that they are designed to be highly visible, means that it does not matter if the spots make them more conspicuous. The obvious advantage is that the marks are then vis-ible without needing to re-catch the specimen, so avoiding the dangers inherent in handling delicate creatures.

Where species are cryptic and/or night-flying, it is important that their visible, coloured surfaces are not altered. Marks can be applied to the underside of the wings or to the upper surface of the hind wing, which is hidden at rest. In both cases a recaptured

FIG 49   *A marked burnet moth. Different colours can be used to represent '100's, '10s' and 'units', so that hundreds of moths can be marked individually by placing the marks at predetermined positions.*

individual must be manipulated in the net, for the marks to be read, and this often causes some damage. With broad winged Geometridae the under-surfaces are exposed in the net and may be marked relatively easily but with Noctuidae this is difficult. Species smaller than medium sized Noctuidae are too small and other methods have to be considered.

Instead of using dye marks, it is possible to use punches to remove small circular or angled pieces of wing. If these are small, the cryptic appearance is not reduced and flying ability should not be compromised – moths fly naturally when their wings are rather tatty! However, one cannot be sure that such holes do not reduce performance and this method must be used with care. As a rough and ready method it works well and the holes may be made so as to be visible without capture, if the specimen is clearly seen feeding or on a sheet.

For some purposes it is not necessary to tell apart each individual but merely to know if a specimen has been found previously. In this case a single simple clip is sufficient.

REARING MOTHS

Friedrich (1986) sets out the general principles for rearing moths and gives specific advice for each main group of species, information which has been added to, with specific reference to the micro's, by Emmet.

Coping with larvae

There are several crucial stages in the life of a larva, when particular care is needed. These are at hatching and when moulting, overwintering and pupating. At each stage success will result from considering very carefully how to mimic the natural conditions for the species; or if modifying them, which features of the natural conditions are crucial to success. Experience is the best guide and it is disappointing how few accounts have been published of successes and failures in rearing moths.

Some species eat all or part of their egg shell on hatching and will not thrive without this. In practice, this is rarely a cause of trouble because the larva is immediately in contact with the egg shell but hatching is eased if conditions are slightly humid at the time and these conditions may also improve the palatability of the eggshell. Consequently, when hatching is imminent (sometimes indicated by a change in egg colour), it helps to include a damp spill of paper in the egg container.

This introduces a recurrent difficulty; while some humidity is essential to almost all stages of moths, providing it by using damp material leads to two major problems. The first is fungal infection and the second is condensation, in which larvae frequently drown. The best solution is to use conditions that allow the normal atmospheric humidity to prevail, with free air flow. This may be impossible either because cut food may wilt in free air flow, or because room heating may reduce natural humidity so that the air is too dry. Although some humidity is essential, more larvae are killed by too much, rather than too little.

Encouraging feeding

For newly hatched larvae the main problem is encouraging the start of feeding. Some larvae, like zygaenid species, wander about before settling to feed – in nature their eggs are often not laid on the foodplant and so this is necessary. Most larvae will feed immediately, as long as food is present in just the correct condition. In nature the female moth will have selected the egg position so that the correct age, size and condition of leaf is available; the lepidopterist has to mimic this. Sometimes eggs may be collected from the wild, so that the type of leaf is indicated, but most often the eggs will have been laid in captivity, perhaps on an artificial substrate, and so the right food has to be introduced at the right time. The newly hatched larva will often show a tendency to crawl upwards, towards light, or along a twig to the end, presumably in nature this would tend to take it to the youngest leaves at the twig tip. In captivity, this tendency may well take the larva away from the food to the top of the container and many losses result from this apparently perverse behaviour. They must be prevented either by surrounding a larva with food so that it cannot avoid it (but this usually leads to excess condensation in the container); or by arranging the food so that the larva's behaviour leads it to a suitable twig tip, or to a leaf at the top of its chamber. Sometimes putting the chamber in the dark reduces the tendency to wander.

Cut food wilts very rapidly and is then less suitable for larvae, especially to newly hatched ones, which are generally incapable of using sub-optimal leaf quality. If food must be cut, it must be changed frequently to avoid deterioration. Wilting will be reduced if the container is kept cool (although this will slow larval growth), or if kept in the dark (although some larvae will feed only in sunshine). If possible, cut food should have the shoot ends placed in water, which will greatly extend the time it remains palatable, but larvae may walk down a twig and drown, unless the water bottle neck is closely sealed. Potted plants provide excellent conditions, as do sleeves on free growing plants. A sleeve is a simple tunnel of netting placed over a growing branch and tied at both ends. In practice, different species need different degrees of care and this is where Friedrich's book (1986) and experience are so useful.

Whatever method is used, larval droppings will collect near the larvae and are a source of infection and fungal attack. They must be cleaned away as frequently as possible, particularly when larvae are kept in groups. If larvae can be kept separately or in small groups this will reduce many difficulties, including losses to diarrhoea and disturbance during feeding or moulting.

Protecting moulting and pupating larvae

When a larva moults it has to rest quietly for a preparatory period, often choosing a sheltered or secluded spot and spinning a pad of silk on which to sit. The actual moult may be quite quick but during it the larva is completely helpless and for a period afterwards it remains soft and vulnerable. During this time it must remain strictly undisturbed. A pre-moult larva may often be recognised by: its quiescence; the choice of a non-standard resting place; the presence of the new larger head capsule pre-formed behind the old one; and a dullness of colour. To avoid disturbance, it is preferable to keep larvae separately and to change food by cutting around a larva, rather than picking it off its leaf.

When pupation nears, the larvae may change colour, become restless and leave the food-plant. It must then be provided with a different set of conditions. Most larvae will not attempt to pupate unless conditions are favourable, until they are so exhausted by searching that they fail to complete the change successfully. Each species has its own characteristic requirements which must be matched, unless experience has shown that an artificial substitute is suitable. If many larvae are being reared, later larvae must not be allowed to disturb earlier ones, particularly since most species have pre-pupation resting phases. Many larvae burrow into soil and later larvae may well destroy the cells of earlier ones, so overcrowding must be avoided.

Overwintering larvae

The most difficult larvae to care for are those that overwinter or aestivate. During this dormant period the larva is particularly liable to predation, disease, desiccation or succumbing to fungal infection. No doubt losses are great in this stage in nature but it is the job of the lepidopterist to improve on this in captivity. If the important factors are identified then modifications may be made to optimise these. Tremewan (1985), for example, advocates the placing of zygaenid larvae in closed plastic boxes in the bottom of a refrigerator for the winter, so providing them with a constant temperature of around 3°C. This mimics the normal cool winter conditions but avoids the potentially lethal sub-zero periods during normal winter weather, as well as the occasional warmer conditions that may induce arousal at an inappropriate time. Because the refrigerator does not provide normal atmospheric humidity this must be provided by using some water drops between the outer of several layers of plastic bags around each box. Some species resist all care; the Fox moth (*Macrothylacia rubi*), for instance, is very difficult to rear over the winter, although Friedrich does provide detailed instructions on the best available advice.

STORING EGGS AND PUPAE AND ENCOURAGING EMERGENCE

Eggs may usually be stored easily in small plastic containers in cool dimly lit places but should not be kept unseasonably warm, or they may hatch before their foodplant is available. Protection from even tiny predators, such as earwigs (Dermaptera) or bugs (Hemiptera: Heteroptera), and parasites such as chalcid wasps, is needed. It is rarely possible to lift eggs off their substrate and so it is better to induce egg laying on a movable surface, rather than allowing a moth to lay eggs on the inside of a pill box.

Pupae may often be left where they form, particularly if this includes a cocoon. However, if the pupae are formed in soil, it is difficult to keep this sufficiently moist and soft and yet well drained. Such pupae can be removed, without scratching their surface, and kept in a cool airy place until they are due to hatch. It may be best to cover them with a thin layer of *Sphagnum* moss to help retain some humidity, because this genus of moss has a disinfectant quality that is beneficial.

When the time for emergence approaches, the pupae should be allowed to experience natural temperatures, or should be brought into a warm room, if some forcing is required. Higher humidity is needed at emergence and may be provided by a very light spray with distilled or boiled water if necessary, preferably on the sides of the container rather than

Red Underwing females (Catocala nupta) *usually lay their eggs in cracks in willow bark but will do so freely in folds of cardboard.*

directly on the pupae. Once the moths have emerged, they will need to dry their wings quickly without disturbance. Therefore, they must be provided with appropriately rough twigs or surfaces on which to climb and hang. Usually they climb to the top of the container, which must also be roughened, otherwise they will repeatedly fall from their perch and fail to expand their wings successfully. If more than one pupa is to emerge, disturbance must be avoided. The fluid accumulated during the pupal stage, the meconium, will be shed after the wings are dry and may damage other individuals, if it comes into contact with them.

THE SUCCESS OF A REARING SCHEME

The final test of successful rearing is the proportion of the eggs that give rise to adults. Anyone can produce a low percentage success but less than 80–90% should be regarded as failure! As Allan (1943) points out, it is often easier to rear most of a small number of eggs than it is to rear some of a very large batch, as more care can be lavished on the smaller number.

KEEPING ADULT MOTHS

Adult moths that are not needed for mating may be kept in small containers in a refrigerator, at 3–5°C. If they are previously fed, this period may extend to a week or even more, during which they will use food reserves. They will then need to be fed if they are to regain full activity. If mating is to be attempted, and if a male has to be kept until a female emerges, feeding is essential. In nature the food would be either nectar, honey-dew or sweet plant secretions and this must be mimicked in captivity. Water is itself necessary to prevent desiccation and sugar is also necessary to provide the fuel for flight. Consequently, the basic food is a weak (5–15%) sugar or honey solution, presented on a damp pad or in an artificial flower to a fully warmed moth in spacious and undisturbed conditions. Really large species, such as the Sphingidae, may be encouraged to feed by extending the proboscis on to the food.

It is now realised that nectar may also contain other food resources, such as essential vitamins, that cannot be mimicked in sugar water. These may be necessary for the full development of eggs but the subject is little studied and no recipes exist for an artificial nectar for moths. However, the formulations used in the popular hummingbird feeders in the USA may well be worth trying for moths!

To lay eggs successfully a female moth requires the correct stimuli, although some species seem to lay indiscriminately on any surface. The Red Underwing (*Catocala nupta*) needs to have a series of rough crevices into which to insert her ovipositor and many species require a twig of the right species of plant on which to lay. Most will also lay only if kept fed with sugar water and if left undisturbed in mild, dark conditions, and so special egg laying containers are needed to achieve full success. In general, however, moths lay eggs fairly readily and this stage in their rearing can be achieved reasonably successfully. If no or few eggs are laid by a captive reared female, it may be due to deficiencies in the larval diet. Even when larvae grow, pupate and produce adult moths, they may have suffered from dietary deficiencies and will fail to mate and produce fertile eggs. The full test of the rearing programme is the next generation.

CHAPTER 10

Conservation of Moths

THE CAUSES OF RECENT REDUCTIONS IN BRITAIN'S MOTHS

IN Chapter 2 reference was made to a number of species of moths that had declined in range in Britain in recent years, in some cases to the point of extinction. Various causes were briefly reviewed there. To help set the rest of this chapter in context, these causes will also be referred to here with some further examples to illustrate them.

Overcollecting

The rapacious collector has frequently been blamed for the decline of moths and butterflies and no-one would ever condone taking many specimens of any species, let alone rare ones. Allan (1943) wonders whether the retreat of the Kentish Glory (*Endromis versicolora*) from England was hastened by the ravages of collectors, who were able to use the technique of assembling to a virgin female to collect scores of males; but on balance it seems more likely that other factors were mainly responsible, particularly loss of habitat (Young, 1991). If collecting is ever to be an important factor, it must be possible for a high proportion of a population to be caught and there are reasons given below why this may be unlikely.

The only species seriously considered to have been exterminated by collectors is the New Forest Burnet (*Zygaena viciae*). This species was first found in Britain in 1869 in open woodland clearings and the edge of heaths in the New Forest but it lasted only 16 years at the first location. Eight more sites were eventually found nearby but at these it also declined and the last specimen was caught in 1927. Tremewan (1966), considers that the habitat changed to some extent at some of the sites but that the ultimate cause of extinction was overcollecting, facilitated by the highly colonial and visible nature of the species. He reports that some professional collectors took all the adults that emerged in a season. Amazingly a new locality was found in 1963 on the coast of Argyll but at this one site it is now critically rare.

Ravenscroft studied the Slender Scotch Burnet (*Z. loti*), which now occurs at only eight sites on the adjacent islands of Mull and Ulva. On two of these it is still abundant, even if very local, and he was able to mark and recapture sufficient to find that even in the complete absence of collecting the average adult lifespan was only one day! The rapid turnover, so that a collector who visited the colony for several days would meet only a very small proportion of the population, combined with a very rapid deterioration in condition, so that specimens soon rendered themselves unattractive to trophy hunters, made him conclude that the species is not vulnerable to collecting, at least at the large populations (Ravenscroft and Young, *in press*).

One or two of the colonies of *Z. loti* are now so small, however, that they may well be at risk from any collecting and this illustrates the general principle that moths are probably not threatened by collecting until they have already declined to very low levels for other reasons. There has been much debate about whether more species than the handful that are currently listed should be given legal protection from collecting. At first it seems obvious – who would condone collecting of rare species? – but there are counter arguments. Almost all the distribution records on which conservation strategies are based, as well as much of the natural history knowledge that underpins our understanding of the ecology of moths, derives from 'collectors', many of whom are genuinely responsible and do not overcollect. If more species were protected, as they are in parts of continental Europe, these collectors would withdraw their co-operation, feeling that their interests were threatened without real need, and this would be seriously counter-productive. Although there are still some rapacious collectors, who do nothing but harm, they are becoming fewer as the climate of opinion progresses and to legislate to defeat these few alone may now be unnecessary.

Pesticides and pollution

Contrary to popular opinion, and with one exception, there seem to be no obvious examples of species of moth that have declined significantly in Britain because of the use of chemicals in the countryside. Even pest species have survived the pesticides used against them and non-target species have apparently shown no effects.

The exception may be the Brighton Wainscot (*Oria musculosa*). The larvae of this species feed in the stems of many different grasses but mainly seem to use commercial cereal crops. However, it has never been a pest species. After its initial discovery near Brighton, its true headquarters were found to be in central southern England, including Salisbury Plain but extending well to the east and north. The species comes to light and so can be recorded reasonably easily but it apparently has not be seen in much of its range recently. It may be that this apparent scarcity is due to under-recording but, if it proves to be genuine, then a different explanation must be sought. Perhaps this lies in recent changes from spring-sown to autumn-sown cereals, or to increased stubble burning, or to new strains of cereal; or it may be that the climate has become unsuitable. However, because cereals are subject to an ever-changing range of insecticides, targeted at stem borers as well as aphids or root flies, it may be that this moth has been adversely affected by the pesticides.

Barbour (1986) suggests that general air pollution is one of the causes of the greater decline in butterfly numbers in the more heavily populated south and east of Britain and the same may apply to moths. Perhaps the Small Eggar (*Eriogaster lanestris*) has been affected, for its larvae occur on hedgerows, where they are exposed to car fumes and drift of agricultural chemicals; however, this species may also have been affected by changing hedgerow management. Overall, Barbour's argument is not universally accepted.

Climate change

World-wide climatic changes have occurred recently and in general these have produced warmer conditions. Several of the warmest years on record have been since the mid-1980s

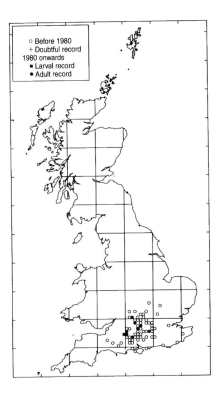

FIG 50   *Distribution changes of the Brighton Wainscot,* Oria musculosa. *Since 1980 this species has only been found at a minority of its previous sites. (Source: courtesy of Waring, National Recording Network for the Rarer British Macro-moths)*

but these have also been accompanied by extreme droughts, floods, gales and cold spells, so that the climatic pattern in any one area may have changed in a variety of significant ways. The climatic requirements of moths are almost completely unknown, with only the suggestion that warmer conditions should favour the northward range extension of southern species and the potential loss of species that are adapted to the climate of the northern mountains. If there have been consequent losses in Britain's moth fauna in recent years the most simplistic effect of the warmer years should have been to cause the loss or reduction of the northern species. However, there is no evidence of this at all and these species seem to be unchanged in their status. Perhaps the change has been too short-term for such changes to be noticeable.

The drought that has generally accompanied the warmth should have affected south-eastern species most but, although there have been some range contractions (as discussed in Chapter 2), they are usually explained by habitat loss, rather than climate change. The exception noted previously was the Buttoned Snout (*Hypena rostralis*), which Waring believes has retreated to the warmest part of its previous range (Waring, 1993b). Overall there are no convincing examples of species that have responded to climatic change.

Habitat loss and change

There is universal agreement that the greatest deleterious effect on Britain's moths has been the loss of habitat. Some extinctions, such as those of the Reed Tussock (*Laelia coenosa*) (last seen in 1879) and the Gypsy (*Lymantria dispar*), were indisputably due to the drainage of the fens (de Worms, 1979). (The latter species was last seen as a resident in 1907 but has been found as an occasional migrant since, including several batches of larvae, apparently deriving from an accidentally introduced female in Essex in 1995; Waring, 1995). Other declines have been attributed to a range of causes (Heath, 1974; Fry and Lonsdale, 1991). That of the White-spotted Pinion (*Cosmia diffinis*) was due to the dramatic loss of its food-plant, Elm (*Ulmus* spp.), caused by Dutch elm disease in the 1970s. The Small Eggar (*Eriogaster lanestris*) may have declined because of severe cutting of hedges and the Currant Clearwing (*Synanthedon tipuliformis*) may have suffered from the grubbing up of old currant bushes and their more regular replacement with new stock. The reduction in the extent of grazed grassland, particularly on the chalk and limestone of the south and east, may have contributed to the general reduction in abundance of species such as the Lace Border

Transparent Burnet moths (Zygaena purpuralis) *rely on grazing to keep vegetation short in their coastal grassland habitats.*

(*Scopula ornata*). This change occurred particularly after the decline of rabbits as a result of myxamatosis, which was followed by scrub invasion of the downlands. Haggett and Hall (1992) report the loss of moths from the sandy heaths of the Breck District of East Anglia, largely caused by extensive planting of pine forests.

The loss of large tracts of ancient deciduous woodland in the south may have contributed to the current scarcity of the Dark Crimson Underwing (*Catocala sponsa*), which is said to need very extensive woodlands in which to thrive (Bretherton *et al.*, 1983). This example illustrates a problem, however, for no-one has studied the habitat requirements of the species and so its needs are merely guessed at. Of all the species of moth that are scarce enough to qualify for inclusion in the British Red Data Book, only about 10 have had any sort of study made of their requirements. This depressing theme is returned to below. Despite this, there is no doubt that habitat change and loss are the main causes of the decline of moths in Britain and the same seems to apply in other countries.

MONITORING THE DISTRIBUTION AND STATUS OF MOTHS

The essential evidence that is needed in the planning of a successful campaign to conserve any animal or plant is reliable and up-to-date information on their distribution and status. Britain has an enviable reputation in this respect, for there are proportionately more British naturalists than any other nationality and there is a long tradition of interest. Moreover the mapping base of Britain is excellent, so that records can be securely located. By the 1960s and 1970s this had been capitalised on to the extent that there were increasing numbers of recording schemes for different groups of animals, after the first authoritative plant atlas (Perring and Walters, 1962). Heath began the butterfly and larger moth recording scheme at the Biological Records Centre (BRC) in 1967 (Heath, 1967), with data provided by an army of enthusiastic amateurs.

However, two factors have led to a dangerous decline in the collection of records. First of all Government money has not continued on the scale necessary to allow the BRC to support the many schemes that had been initiated. On John Heath's retirement in 1982 the moth recording scheme ceased. The new approach has been to provide some background help to a society or group of enthusiasts who were prepared to continue their recording and, although this has worked splendidly in a few cases, such as the water beetle recording scheme of the Balfour-Browne Club, in many cases it has left at best a half-hearted effort in place. The second factor has been that some mapping schemes seemed to lead nowhere and so ran out of steam. The larger moth scheme produced some maps eventually but the Geometridae, for example, have never been mapped and the data have not been used to support conservation efforts. The amateurs lost heart and many large efforts apparently finished without realising their potential. Many lepidopterists still run regular moth traps but the data they collect are not collated effectively.

MAPPING RARE SPECIES AND RECORDING KEY SITES

In 1979, the then Nature Conservancy Council began to accumulate insect records to establish a site-based list, called the Invertebrate Site Register, which allows interesting sites to be identified and which supplies data if any of the sites need defending. By 1992 over 8500 sites were listed on a computer data-base, which allows searches to be made by site or species (Waring, 1992b).

Hadley (1984) compiled a list of nationally rare macro-moths, using the BRC data-base and further comments from experienced amateurs; these lists were used in the preparation of the Red Data Book (see below). Other families of moths are now being covered in a similar way.

The rare species of larger moth are now the focus of a specific record collection effort by Waring, who is running the National Recording Network for the Rarer British Macro-moths, with contract support from the Joint Nature Conservation Committee, routed through Butterfly Conservation (Waring, 1991). The records are aimed directly at selecting those species which need priority conservation action. Waring's own resources are strictly limited and so, despite heroic efforts by many willing voluntary recorders, he is unable to achieve the coverage that he would like and cannot begin to extend his efforts to the species-rich micro-lepidoptera, some of which are certainly as deserving of action. At a time when most Governments have signed 'Biodiversity' treaties and are concerned about the potential effect of climate change, the lack of support for recording schemes is deplorable.

Assessing the true status of moths

Unless constant efforts are applied and are spread equally across the country it is very difficult to be sure of the accuracy of the data that result from recording schemes. The examples of species in decline that were used above are some for which there is no real argument – they certainly have declined or disappeared. For many other species the results are equivocal. The Small Autumnal Moth (*Epirrita filigrammaria*), according to Waring's most recent maps which have pre- and post-1980 records separated, has suffered a recent decline of around 50%. However, the modern records are spread across its full range and it is surely true that the apparent decline is merely a reflection of less recording since 1980.

Furthermore, atlases merely lead to a 'spot' on a map and a single stray will be recorded as equal to a strong colony. To determine the real status of a species, it is necessary for some standardised recording method to be applied. For orchids this is often the yearly counting of flowering spikes, for birds it is the 'Common Bird Census' and for butterflies it is the transect walk (devised by Pollard, 1977). Burnet moths are counted on a few of the butterfly transects but there is no equivalent scheme for nocturnal species, apart from the standardised effort of the Rothamsted trap series. Data from these traps are distinctly under-used but, more importantly, the traps are deliberately sited so that they do not catch rare species regularly and so they do not provide status records for the rarest species. They do give excellent notice of general population changes, however, and are very useful for that. There seems to be no prospect for providing true status data for the rarer species except on a one-off survey basis, when it has already been decided that a species is genuinely rare!

Defining rarity

Rarity is an interesting concept and failure to understand it has led to some problems in the past. Some species are rare, even when at their full extent, in one or both of two ways. They may be either very confined geographically or they may be at low density over a wide area. Rabinowitz *et al.* (1986) have recently produced a matrix of abundance that makes this point well. A similar matrix, with British moth examples, is shown as Table 26.

Where their restricted range and abundance is 'natural', as is probable for the Herald and perhaps the Sweet Gale moth, then these species presumably would not benefit from conservation effort. However, the scarcity (but perhaps not the restricted Scottish range) of the New Forest Burnet is due to man's influence and could be reversed.

TABLE 26   *Different states of rarity and abundance in British moths.*

| | Geographic range | | | |
| | Wide | | Narrow | |
Habitat types	Wide	Narrow	Wide	Narrow
Abundant species	X. xanthographa	A. vestigialis	A. aceris	P. brevilinea
Scarce species	S. libatrix	H. petasites	A. euphorbiae	Z. viciae

Source: After Rabinowitz et al. (1986).

Key to species:

X. (=Xestia) xanthographa Square-spot Rustic – abundant everywhere.

A. (=Agrotis) vestigialis Archer's Dart – abundant, but only on coastal sand dunes around Britain.

A. (=Acronicta) aceris Sycamore – common but only in south-east England.

P. (=Photedes) brevilinea Fenn's Wainscot – common only in coastal reed beds of East Anglia.

S. (=Scoliopterix) libatrix Herald – scarce but very widespread throughout mainland Britain.

H. (=Hydraecia) petasites Butterbur – scarce along river valleys throughout England and southern Scotland.

A. (=Acronicta) euphorbiae myricae Sweet Gale – scarce on coasts and inland in highland Scotland only.

Z. (Zygaena) viciae New Forest Burnet – scarce at one site in Scotland only.

Assessing the most threatened species

Waring's mapping scheme is an attempt to identify those species most threatened by man's activities and in need of conservation action. He has concentrated on species thought to occur in fewer than 100 10-km grid squares. The criteria for 'most threatened' must take note of the types of rarity defined above and must include at least two additional factors. One of these is the current rate of decline and the second is whether there are identifiable threats which apply to a significant part of the remaining population. It is almost impossible to collect sufficient reliable evidence to allow the proper prioritisation of many of the rarer British species. Regrettably, this does not really matter, for so few resources are available for invertebrate conservation in Britain that significant efforts had only been mounted for six species by 1996 (with some recording for a few others). These six species are listed in Table 27.

TABLE 27   *Species of moth for which significant conservation efforts had been mounted in Britain by 1995.*

Species	Conservation effort
New Forest Burnet *Zygaena viciae*	Habitat restoration
Slender Scotch Burnet *Z. loti*	Habitat restoration
Essex Emerald *Thetidia smaragdaria*	Habitat restoration and captive breeding
Barberry Carpet *Pareulype berberata*	Habitat restoration and captive breeding
Black Veined *Siona lineata*	Habitat restoration
Reddish Buff *Acosmetia caliginosa*	Habitat restoration and captive breeding

Only if there is an increase in the resources available will it be necessary to tackle the thorny question of exactly which extra species are really in need of conservation action!

FORMAL NOTIFICATION OF RARITY – THE RED DATA BOOKS

The official method of recording the status of Britain's rarer animals and plants is to include them in a series of Red Data Books that are intended to be regularly updated. The preparation of these has proved to be a useful spur to the assessment of the true status of Britain's fauna and flora but they are only as good as the data available and, since these are very patchy, they are themselves often misleading and inaccurate. Each species is assigned to a category depending on its range and status and these categories are set out in Table 28, which was compiled from Parsons (1993).

The original Red Data Book for insects in Britain (Shirt, 1987) was acknowledged to be incomplete and so there have been a series of reviews, undertaken by the Joint Nature Conservation Committee, to update and complete the task. For example, Parsons (1993) has reviewed the Pyralidae, resulting in a much more realistic and reliable account of this group. Waring's work will achieve the same for the 'macro's'. Even so, it must be stressed that our knowledge of the distribution and status of even the large and obvious species is incomplete and constantly needs updating. Consequently, Red Data Books must never be regarded as the final word. The current British RDB listing for the macro's is as follows, with 82 included, out of the overall British total of around 800.

Category	No. of species
RDB1	17 (of which 5 may be extinct)
RDB2	14
RDB3	47
RDBK	4

Some of the most threatened species have been given formal Government protection by a listing on the Schedules of the 1981 Wildlife and Countryside Act. Schedule 5 of this Act lists those species for which it is a criminal offence to take or harm specimens or their habitats, or to sell either live or dead examples. Only seven moths are included on the schedule (Table 29) and no prosecutions have ever resulted from the Act as far as moths are concerned. Perhaps this is to be expected and maybe the Act has actually deterred some

TABLE 28   *Abbreviated Red Data Book Categories.*

Category	Status
RDB1	In danger of extinction (to include species from one site; and/or from threatened habitat; and/or showing rapid decline; and/or recently extinct but may be re-found)
RDB2	Vulnerable and may become endangered (declining rapidly; and/or from threatened habitat)
RDB3	Rare and at risk (found in fewer than 15 10-km grid squares; and/or highly localised and scarce)
RDB4	Out of danger (formerly in RDB1–3 but recovered)
RDB5	Endemic (not found outside Britain. May be RDB or safe)
RDB Extinct	(Extinct in Britain)
RDBI	Indeterminate (probably RDB1,2 or 3 but unclear which)
RDBK	Insufficiently known (suspected of being RDB but insufficiently known and/or recently discovered)
Notable A	Scarce (not RDB but found in up to 30 10-km grid squares; and/or seven vice-counties and scarce)
Notable B	Scarce (found in 31–100 10-km grid squares; and/or eight to twenty vice-counties and scarce)

Note: for some types of insect the Notable categories are not subdivided and the detailed distribution criteria may be varied.

collectors from taking specimens, but it has certainly not helped prevent damage to habitats. The sheep stocking policy, that led in the 1980s to the extreme restriction of the New Forest Burnet (*Zygaena viciae*) to a part of its one site, was illegal, but the estate owners had not been made aware of the potential deleterious effect and so the listing of this species had no practical benefit.

It could be claimed very fairly that in Britain we should concentrate our conservation efforts on those species that are most endangered throughout their world-wide range and not put efforts into those that are rare in Britain but still secure elsewhere. If a listing were made on that basis, it would exclude such species as the New Forest Burnet (*Zygaena viciae*) (one site only in Britain but still widespread in Europe) but might include others that are

TABLE 29   *Species fully protected in Britain by inclusion on Schedule 5 of the 1981 Wildlife and Countryside Act (at 1995).*

Scientific name	Common name
Zygaena viciae	New Forest Burnet
Thetidia smaragdaria	Essex Emerald (extinct in wild)
Thalera fimbrialis	Sussex Emerald
Pareulype berberata	Barberry Carpet
Siona lineata	Black Veined Moth
Acosmetia caliginosa	Reddish Buff
Hadena irregularis	Viper's Bugloss Moth (extinct in wild)

Note: These seven species make an interesting contrast with the butterflies. Of the 57 resident species, 25 are scheduled, although this only prevents the sale of most of them.

rare elsewhere, even if they are secure in Britain, such as Fenn's Wainscot (*Photedes brevilinea*).

Unfortunately, since 1991 Britain's Government conservation agencies have been split between England, Wales and Scotland and each agency is now developing its own list of priority species. It is to be hoped that these will concentrate only on those species that are rare throughout the UK, rather than those rare in each region. Recently, Bland and Young (1996) have made a preliminary list of those species that may deserve conservation effort in Scotland, based partly on the collated opinions of Scottish lepidopterists, because there is no formal mapping scheme for micro's, and in this they specifically identified those species which, although rare or local in Scotland, are on the edge of their range there and are not in need of Scottish attention. Their categories are shown in Table 30.

The provisional nature of the listings is shown by the fact that seven species that would have been in Category X have been rediscovered since 1979 and continuing efforts are being made to find more. Urgent action is clearly expected to be concentrated on species from Categories X, 1A and 2A, a modest total of 33, for which resources might be available. However, to reiterate a previous point, sufficient ecological knowledge is available for only six or seven of these at most.

It is unsurprising that the degree of threat required before a moth is notified for conservation action is distinctly greater than that for more fashionable animals. Pipistrelle bats, common frogs and adders are protected by law in Britain despite being widespread and common in many places!

COPING WITH SMALL AND ISOLATED POPULATIONS

Random extinctions of small populations

So far it is mainly the *decline* of moths that has been considered, with the implication that removal of the causes of decline will lead to recovery, but there are extra problems associated with small populations and these may prevent recovery, even if the causes of decline are rectified. Caughley (1994) refers to these two paradigms in conservation, the 'small population' and 'declining population', and expresses the belief that they are usually treated

TABLE 30   *Categories used in Bland and Young (1996) for Scottish moths deserving conservation attention.*

Category	Status
X	Species for which it is probably too late!
1A	Scottish species or sub-species with a very restricted distribution and potentially or already in urgent need of protection
1B	Scottish species in urgent need of research into biology and/or distribution; potentially in need of protection
1C	Scottish species for which better distribution data are needed but which seem to be reasonably widespread and secure
2A	British species of very restricted distribution with colonies in Scotland in urgent need of protection
2B	British species, with colonies in Scotland, in urgent need of research into biology and/or distribution
3	Species on the edge of their range in Scotland, not needing immediate protection

Number of species in Category X –   7
                 1A – 18
                 1B – 34
                 1C – 28   Total Scottish list = 1487 species
                 2A –   8
                 2B – 27
                  3 – 22

separately, whereas they should be integrated, and that most conservation efforts have concentrated on the declining population scenario.

All insect populations vary greatly from year to year, sometimes declining to abnormally low levels because of the action of various factors, some of which are random (termed stochastic factors). The vagaries of weather during mating time, or an unexpectedly biased sex ratio in one generation, with few reproducing females, for example, may lead to an unexpected decline. Such variations in population may not matter for a large initial population that can recover quickly in subsequent generations, but it may be terminal for a small population, which may decline below the sustainable limit by chance. If a species becomes dramatically rare in its habitat, it may have extra problems finding mates and this may lead to even greater decline and perhaps extinction. The downwards spiral is termed an 'extinction vortex' and is a potential cause of the unexpectedly rapid decline to extinction observed for some insect species, such as the Chequered Skipper butterfly (*Carterocephalus palaemon*) in England in the 1970s. This species seemed to be secure at several sites in 1965 but was extinct by 1977 (Ravenscroft, 1992).

These random effects on moth populations are potentially much more hazardous than they would be for the inherently more stable populations of large mammals. (In large animals environmental effects are reduced by the capacity of each animal to cope with and modify unusual conditions.) Insects are susceptible to environmental changes and rely on their high reproductive rate to pull them back quickly from low levels.

Isolation and recolonisation

Even quite large populations of moths are likely to become extinct through random variations in population size sooner or later, so that extinction is a normal event in the context of individual populations. Normally this is counteracted by reinvasion from other nearby sites. A series of sub-populations, arranged so that there is sometimes interchange of individuals between them, with recolonisations where needed, is termed a 'meta-population'. It is likely that many (?most) insects have this form of population but little real evidence exists for this in insects generally and even less for moths. In practice, every population will be different in size and some will persist for much longer than others. The larger ones are called 'source populations' and the smaller ones, which more frequently need recolonisation, are called 'sink populations'.

If one site for a moth is lost through habitat change, the prospect for interchange of individuals or recolonisation at other sites is reduced. Hence the loss of one population decreases the chance of others persisting and another extinction vortex begins to apply. This is why it is so important to retain a matrix of conservation areas in the general countryside – in the long term a few isolated nature reserves will not be sufficient.

Isolation, small populations and genetics

Each individual moth will carry only a small sub-set of the genetic variation in the whole population and therefore the small number of individuals left when a population suddenly crashes, or acts as founder of a new colony, will also only include a sample of the full genetic complement. Furthermore, this sample may not be representative of the usual variation found in the full population. This is the basis of the 'founder effect', where a founded population may contain a different range of genes from the parent population and there may be noticeable differences in appearance between them. Consequently, a small population will usually contain less genetic variability than a large one, leading to less adaptability to changing environmental conditions.

This reduces the overall viability of the population and so there is an advantage to retaining as full a genetic complement as possible. Nearby sub-populations, between which individuals can occasionally move, can restore the full genetic potential and this is another reason why it is disadvantageous for isolation to occur. Another problem is that in small populations individuals are likely to be closely related and so to share many of their genes. Consequently, at mating there will be inbreeding, increased homozygosity and reduced fitness, when the homozygous genes are deleterious. Inbreeding therefore leads to a downward spiral of viability, with ever decreasing genetic variation – another extinction vortex.

These factors together point to the importance of retaining the full meta-population structure.

RESEARCHING THE HABITAT REQUIREMENTS OF MOTHS

Once the first essential information about a moth, its distribution and status, has been collected and it is certain that action is required to conserve it, then it is necessary to plan this action. This must be based on a sound understanding of the ecology of the moth, information that is not available for most species. It is necessary to understand what the ecological requirements of the species are, what is causing the decline, and what the likely effects of the current population size may be – in other words both of Caughley's paradigms must be considered together.

Sometimes it is hardly necessary to guess at the cause of the decline. If a meadow has become a motorway then nothing more needs to be said about why a moth has declined. However, if it is suspected that a habitat is changing in a more subtle way, it is necessary to know the precise requirements of the moth, before planning action to return the habitat to a suitable state. There are very interesting parallels here with work that has been carried out on butterflies, which may be presumed to have rather similar general life history strategies and thus might provide clues to the responses of moths.

The precise requirements for butterflies

It has been found for a number of butterflies that many parts of the life cycle are rather undemanding but that often a single stage is very particular, so that providing for its needs can ensure the survival of the population. For example, Thomas *et al.* (1986) found that the Silver-spotted Skipper (*Hesperia comma*) females only lay their eggs on the grass *Festuca ovina* when this is in short turf adjacent to bare ground, for the larvae need the warmth that is not found in longer turf, if they are to digest their food sufficiently quickly. Thomas also found (1977) that the Large Blue (*Maculinea arion*) needs very short turf, to encourage the survival of the only ant species, *Myrmica sabuleti,* that is a suitable host for the butterfly larvae. In this case it is the ant that needs the extra warmth. Dempster *et al.* (1976) found that the single key factor for the Swallowtail butterfly (*Papilio machaon*) was that the larval food-plants (Milk Parsley, *Peucedanum palustre*) had to be vigorous and to emerge strongly above the surrounding vegetation; otherwise the females would ignore them. Other examples also make the point that there may be a simple requirement for a species.

The clues that revealed the butterfly's requirements were gained by watching them and noting their general behaviour. However, for nocturnal moths planning and carrying out the research is much more difficult. Of the very few moth species which have been studied carefully, most are day-flying species! Even if only the Scottish list of deserving species is consulted, there are too many species for the research effort available, which means choices have to be made. Generally, either those on the point of extinction or the most showy and attractive are chosen for attention. The former may be a bad choice because they are already beyond help and the latter may not be a rational choice at all. If a small research effort is to be used best, it should go to species that are certainly in need but which have a realistic chance of survival, and to a range of species from different habitats and with different basic life styles, so that the answers may illuminate a variety of different situations.

EXAMPLES OF RESEARCH ON THE CONSERVATION OF MOTHS

Most conservation research in the past has concentrated on mammals and birds but there are features of the general ecology of moths and other insects that make it likely that they will respond very differently to habitat change. Insects are small and highly specialised, with short generations and no long-term resistant stages. Consequently, they are likely to be

quickly affected by even small changes. Furthermore, the magnitude of the changes in population size will be larger. Overall they will show an exaggerated response and research into
their needs will have to focus on a finer scale (Young, 1992).

The Kentish Glory

The Kentish Glory (*Endromis versicolora*) declined inexorably in England to extinction and
is also very local in Scotland. Marren (1981) reviewed the possible causes for this decline
but was unable to attribute one precise cause to it. Consequently, the species was studied on
Deeside, Aberdeenshire, one of its few strongholds, to try to ascertain its needs. There were
some tentative suggestions amongst lepidopterists that the female may lay eggs only on
twigs on small Birch bushes (*Betula* spp.) and so the research began by observing the
females and the egg sites. This species is partly diurnal and is very large and showy, so it is
rather easier to study than most. Barbour and Young (1993) soon noted that the egg
batches were indeed highly localised, with almost all found at a height of around 1.2 m on
bushes that were themselves no more than 3 m tall and invariably on the outer twigs of side-
shoots. The preferred bushes were also not touching one another but were in areas of active
birch regeneration.

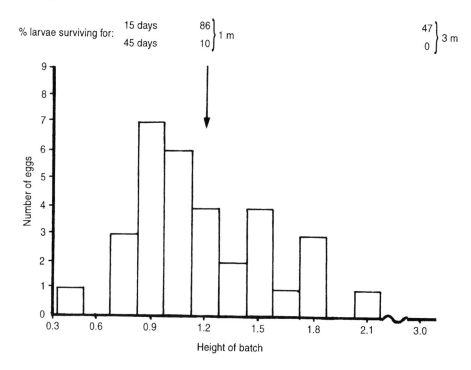

FIG 51   *The height at which egg batches of the Kentish Glory* (Endromis versicolora)
are laid on birch bushes and the survival rate of larvae at 1 m and 3 m above ground.
(Source: Barbour and Young, 1993)

To see if there was a difference in survival of larvae at different heights, some egg batches were transferred to heights of 1 and 3 m on birch twigs and it was found that larvae at the higher position were apparently dislodged from the twigs by the greater wind effects. Although these findings do not explain all the Kentish Glory's requirements, (for example similarly sheltered places could be found on the lower branches of much taller trees but these sites were not used), it is sufficient to suggest a real cause of the contraction in range. Suitable egg sites are only found where there are very extensive areas of regenerating birch (for this large moth needs a large colony site). Such conditions are transient and the only places in Britain to hold large areas of regenerating birch woodlands this century have been in the highland valleys – just where the moth has survived. A conservation plan is easily suggested but not so easily arranged. Large contiguous areas of birch regeneration must be provided.

Problems with the Essex Emerald

The next example illustrates the problems posed by the small population paradigm, for the Essex Emerald (*Theditia smaragdaria*) has become extinct in the wild and has a shrinking captive population in Britain. Many years ago the larvae of this species were reported in hundreds on small patches of their foodplant Sea Wormwood (*Artemisia maritima*), although they have always been very local in Britain, living around the outer Thames estuary area. In 1988, a survey found only a handful of larvae at three of the remaining sites and 56 at the largest. Numbers in the wild then dwindled to zero by 1991, despite Waring's view (Waring, 1993a) that the habitat has not changed in an obvious way. He does not say how close together these four sites were but the species does not fly strongly and so they may well have been effectively isolated. If so, the small population problems referred to above, namely liability to extinction due to random factors, genetic limitation and inbreeding depression, will certainly have applied.

Waring established a captive population in 1987 but even at the beginning there were warning signs. The females rarely laid a full complement of around 80–100 eggs and many laid none at all; furthermore many of the eggs failed to hatch and the males and females seemed reluctant to court and mate, although the few hatched larvae grew normally and survived well. Perhaps these were already signs of inbreeding depression. The stock was kept free from parasites and attempts were made to sterilise the surface of the eggs so as to reduce the likelihood of disease. Various attempts were made to re-establish larvae and to record their mortality but, although a very small number of adults resulted from some attempts, no final success was achieved. Waring also put adults into semi-caged situations on the original sites and other likely areas but males seemed very reluctant to approach the females and the females that had been mated laid very few eggs. Waring notes that it would be useful to introduce a new genetic stock, since his derives from only three females (which may themselves have been related) in 1987. However, Continental Essex Emeralds do not have the same habits as British ones and also have some morphological differences, so that they may either be incompatible with British stock or produce hybrid offspring which do not have the correct response to British habitats. It seems likely that work on this species started too late for success.

The apparently hopeless case of the New Forest Burnet

At first sight the situation for the New Forest Burnet (*Zygaena viciae*) seems hopeless, for it was found to be restricted to one tiny ledge on one site in 1990, with a population of no more than 20 adults, after a period of some years when none was seen at all. For some reason, however, the species has hung on in succeeding years, even with signs that it may now be spreading beyond its ledge back on to the rest of the site, which is now subject to management.

There were too few moths to allow active research but it was clear in 1990 that the difference between the ledge and the main site was that the ledge was ungrazed, whereas increased sheep stocking in the early 1980s had produced a short cropped turf on the main site. Based on this observation, it was decided to exclude sheep and so Scottish Natural Heritage fenced them out in 1991. Although the vegetation composition has not changed much, there is now much more flowering and the turf height is much longer. Furthermore, the larval foodplant, Meadow Vetchling (*Lathyrus pratensis*), has definitely spread. There is no rational reason why such a small population of insects should survive so long and it still seems likely that it will ultimately fail. Population viability analysis, which is a modelling technique for predicting the chance of extinction of a population, based on various measures of its size, reproductive rate and environmental requirements, would suggest imminent extinction in this case.

There is a cautionary tale to this example, for research has also been conducted on other very rare Burnet moths on the west coast of Scotland at the same time. One of these, the Slender Scotch Burnet (*Zygaena loti*), has only eight populations left and is abundant at only two, after a period of dramatic decline. This species feeds as a larva on Bird's Foot Trefoil (*Lotus corniculatus*) but in general seems similar to the New Forest Burnet in its appearance and habits. However, the research has revealed that it can survive only in closely grazed areas, where the turf is short and pock-marked by footprints or erosion gullies and holes. In other words, the conservation requirements of this species are for heavy grazing, the exact opposite of the New Forest Burnet, despite their close taxonomic relationship. Every species of moth needs its own research!

POSITIVE CONSERVATION ACTION

Choosing and managing nature reserves for moths

There are many examples of nature reserves that have been chosen to protect either one or a small group of species but they are almost all concerned with birds, large mammals or charismatic plants like orchids. Generally, this seems to be a short-sighted approach, for it makes better 'economic' sense to use resources to conserve a full community of animals. Actually this is often the case; Caerlaverock reserve on the Solway Firth (for example), which is primarily for geese, also protects the whole saltmarsh and mud-flat ecosystem in the area. So long as the management of such a single purpose reserve does not conflict with that needed for the general interest of the area there is an overall gain. These days even special interest reserve managers, such as the Royal Society for the Protection of Birds (RSPB), do try to make sure that their efforts benefit everything. Does this help conserve moths?

Unfortunately, it is not true that nature reserves established to benefit one group of animals will necessarily benefit others. Prendergast *et al.* (1993) analysed the BRC data base to identify 'hotspots' for birds, butterflies, dragonflies, liverworts and aquatic plants in Britain. They identified those 10 km grid squares that held records for atypically large numbers of species of each group and then asked the questions: do species-rich squares for one group also harbour atypically large numbers of species from other groups?; and do nationally rare species tend to occur in hotspots? There was some overlap between butterflies and dragonflies in southern England, but no more than might be expected from two groups that are mostly southern in their distribution. Otherwise there was no positive correlation – in other words, areas that are good for birds (for example) are not necessarily good for other animals. This counter-intuitive result means that if we wish to conserve moths on reserves, those reserves will have to be chosen and managed specifically for moths. There may be associations between groups of animals that are more closely related in taxonomic or ecological ways than are the groups studied by Prendergast. Perhaps reserves for butterflies might also be good for moths – such an analysis has yet to be done.

Prendergast *et al.* (1993) also found that really rare species did not necessarily occur in species-rich areas, although scarce species did. The hotspots contained large assemblages of common and scarce species but rare species tend to occur in specialised places. Reserves designed to benefit rare species will have to be established specifically for them.

It is an interesting comment on conservation priorities that until 1990 almost no nature reserves in Britain had been established primarily for moths. Even the site of the New Forest Burnet is listed as of special interest for plants and geology and the essential fence that was finally erected there to protect the interests of the moth was originally delayed, in case its construction should disturb a pair of golden eagles. Scarce though these birds may be, they are not in the same category of threat as the moths!

Among the very few reserves which were established for moths is a small area of heathland called the Devil's Race in Sussex, bought by the Sussex Trust for Nature Conservation to secure the habitat of the Lewes Wave (*Scopula immorata*). Unfortunately, no effective habitat management was carried out and the area became shaded and covered in bracken. Scrub control was not started until the mid-1960s, but the last moth was seen there in 1961 and it has not returned. Two of England's best known reserves, Wicken Fen and Woodwalton Fen, were established largely because of their insect fauna (including moths), and several of the UK's Sites of Special Scientific Interest (SSSIs) were declared because they hosted rare moths. The only British habitat of the Marsh Mallow Moth (*Hydraecia osseola hucherardi*) is one, as is one of the sites for the Black Veined Moth (*Siona lineata*).

Managing reserves for insects

The Heath Fritillary butterfly (*Mellicta athalia*) was found by Warren to require very early coppice stages for survival (Warren, 1987). In such open conditions the larval foodplant, Cow Wheat (*Melampyrum pratense*), thrives and the females lay their eggs in sunny positions. Consequently, a number of woodlands in south-east England are coppiced to benefit the butterfly, for example Blean Woods reserve in Kent. Coppice may benefit other species as well but when Sterling and Hambler (1988) studied the leaf mining moths in coppiced woodland they found that these were more abundant in un-coppiced areas and that coppicing, by introducing times when no tree and shrub leaves were available, was deleterious to leaf mining species. Similarly, Housego and Gormally (1993) found a lower overall insect diversity in young coppice, compared with old. However, Harper (*pers. comm.*) believes that coppicing does benefit some woodland moths and that the balance of costs and benefits has not yet been fully assessed.

At Dinnet Muir NNR on Deeside, where the research was carried out on the Kentish Glory moth, the area was open moorland until the 1960s when burning and grazing was stopped and some birch regeneration began. By the 1970s this regeneration was extensive, favouring the moth, but by 1995 most of the moorland area was covered by semi-mature birch and pine woodland. The reserve was declared for many different interests, including archaeology and glacial geomorphology, but also for the botanical interest of the species-rich moor. The rich gravel based soils mean that Bearberry (*Arctostaphylos uva-ursi*) is co-dominant with the heather and that other plants, such as Wintergreen (*Pyrola media*) and Pettywhin (*Genista anglica*), are common. The regenerating woodland was also identified as of interest. The research on the Kentish Glory indicated that there was a need to provide a permanent large area of very young regenerating birch, perhaps by a cycle of burning to prevent the young trees from growing to maturity. At the same time it was found that several scarce moths and one very rare one, the case-bearer *Coleophora arctostaphyli*, which feeds on Bearberry, are found on the species-rich moorland. Despite these findings, the current management plan allows for the great majority of the reserve to progress to mature woodland, with only a small part of the area being managed as moorland and with no provision for the continuity of young birch. The interests of nationally rare moths have been outweighed by the desire for birch regeneration to progress to maturity, despite birch woodland being reasonably common across wide parts of Scotland.

If the most effective general conservation strategy is to conserve habitats by appropriate management, it is essential to investigate how common management practices, such as grazing of chalk grassland, coppicing of deciduous woodland, or cutting fenland, affect moths. Unfortunately, such studies have been very rare.

PRACTICAL CONSERVATION EXAMPLES

Although there have been few studies of the general effect of habitat management on rare moths, a number have been undertaken on single species.

The Netted Carpet (*Eustroma reticulata*) feeds exclusively on Touch-me-not Balsam (*Impatiens noli-tangere*) and has always been very localised in Britain, with its headquarters in the Lake District, where around 25 locations were known in 1980, and one or two sites in north Wales. Hatcher searched all previously known sites in the Lake District in 1990, plus some other possible ones where the foodplant occurred. He found no balsam at seven of the sites and judged that it had either been shaded out or, on sites that had dried out, had been out-competed by bracken. He found evidence of the moth at only 13 locations. In 1991 he visited north Wales and noted feeding signs at two places, one of which was new, but he commented that the numbers of plants at one site had been greatly reduced by a road widening scheme (Waring, 1992a). Clearly some action is needed and the National Trust have agreed to carry out tree cutting at some of the Lake District colonies to try to reduce the shading there, so as to encourage the foodplant. As yet it is too early to assess the success of this plan but it is promising that it has been started.

The unique race of the Sandhill Rustic (*Luperina nickerlii leechi*) in Cornwall has been studied by Spalding (1994) but as yet there has been no habitat management for it. However, some sites for the related subspecies *L. n. gueneei*, which is found on sandhills on the north Welsh and Lancashire coast, have had some scrub clearance by Wallace and others.

The Barberry Carpet

The Barberry Carpet (*Pareulype berberata*) has the misfortune to feed on the wild Barberry (*Berberis vulgaris*), which has been deliberately removed from many hedgerows because it is a host of the wheat rust fungus *Puccinia graminis*. By the late 1970s there was only one known site for the moth and its status was unclear. This locality, in Suffolk, was extensively damaged by a stubble fire in 1991 at a time when the larvae would have been two-thirds grown, with almost 75% of the Barberry bushes badly scorched or destroyed altogether. This illustrates graphically the accidents that can befall single sites and so the need to have several colonies. Waring had established a captive stock in 1988 and used this stock to try a new establishment at an apparently suitable place in 1990. This trial has survived for at least two generations unaided, a possible indication that the requirements of the moth are now sufficiently known to allow further releases. New bushes have also been planted to boost the available habitat at the known sites. However, the finding of two new populations in Gloucestershire and Hampshire in 1990 and 1992, following catches of adults in light traps, illustrates that the true distribution and status is not yet known. Determining this must be a priority, so that conservation can concentrate on existing wild populations (Waring, 1992d).

The Black-veined Moth

The Black-veined moth (*Siona lineata*), which in Britain lives only in a very restricted area of Kent, was originally thought to feed on Tor grass (*Brachypodium pinnatum*), because the larvae were always found sitting on this in the wild. However, it never proved possible to rear the larvae on this grass and various clues, such as seeing chewing marks on nearby plants, led Waring to offer Marjoram (*Origanum vulgare*) instead. This was readily accepted but the larvae seem to find a refuge among the grass. It would seem, therefore, that the species needs both the grass and the herb.

The last two remaining sites for the moth were two nearby, rank meadows, one of which was part of a National Nature Reserve. In the 1980s, part of this reserve became over-grazed, restricting the moth so that it became threatened. However, once its requirements became known, management was begun to produce a mixed sward with Tor grass and Marjoram. By 1991 adult moth numbers on the reserve were as high as during the 1970s, when the moth was regarded as secure. A fire damaged 10% of the other meadow in 1990 but regeneration was swift and the moth re-invaded the area within a year. In 1995, another colony was discovered, surviving on a historical site and it was confirmed that the moth was breeding on a new meadow which had been managed for it (Waring, 1995). Clearly, suffi-cient is known to help the moth; however, the populations are still relatively small and iso-lated and could suffer the problems associated with this. It would be preferable to plan for the establishment of several semi-isolated large colonies, so that the advantages of a func-tioning meta-population can be realised.

Reintroducing the Reddish Buff

The Reddish Buff (*Acosmetia caliginosa*) was not seen after 1984 at its last two known colonies, both of which were ride edges in coniferous plantations. Previously it had been known from several other similar areas, both in Hampshire and the Isle of Wight. Urgent survey work was started and it was rediscovered in 1988 at a location from which it had been last recorded in the 1940s. This site was atypical, being grassy heathland, rather than woodland edge. The larvae feed on Saw-wort (*Serratula tinctoria*), which is most abundant on the edges of woodland and on open ground, whereas at most of the old sites it had been shaded out by encroaching woodland. The management priority was to restore the abundance of the Saw-wort by clearing the scrub and trees. This was carried out around the moth's remaining site in 1991 and has been repeated since. It seems to have been beneficial, for there have been more larvae present in succeeding years and the species has spread on to adjacent areas; however, the site is still small. In the past, grazing and periodic but erratic scrub clearance had maintained more open ground with more abundant foodplant.

Waring established a captive breeding stock in 1987 and latterly this has been maintained at Paignton and Marwell Zoos. In 1989, larvae were released at an experimental site on the Isle of Wight where two clearings had been made to encourage the Saw-wort. This establishment was a success at first, in that some moths were seen up to 1992 but none was found in 1993. This failure seems to have been because the area cleared was far too small and the moth may need quite extensive colonies to thrive. A much larger area was prepared in 1993 in Hampshire, preparatory to a release of 100 adults in 1994, and light trapping in 1995 succeeding in catching two specimens, showing that at least some had bred and survived (Waring, 1995).

Although there is encouragement here, in that success has sometimes followed very simple and quick management, the cautionary tale of the Essex Emerald indicates that it is not always so easy. Conservation success cannot finally be claimed until several self-sustaining colonies have survived for many generations and this has not been achieved so far for any species.

RECOVERY PROGRAMMES AND VIABILITY ANALYSES

In recent years it has been the policy of British conservation agencies to develop 'recovery' programmes, or 'species action plans' for rare and endangered species of animal and plant. These review the status and ecology of each species very briefly but their main purpose is to set out the actions needed to sustain and/or increase the populations of the species, until they can be regarded as no longer threatened. They also set criteria for this successful point, usually couched in such terms as '(five) self-sustaining populations that have survived for (five) years'. The actions needed to achieve these aims are costed in terms of the resources needed and the whole point of these recovery plans is that they should be enacted, rather than just discussed. Waring's work on the moths has latterly been guided by recovery plans. Such plans have been developed for a wide range of organisms and their preparation has stimulated useful action and research. However, they can succeed only if they are based on sound ecological knowledge.

How long will moth populations survive?

Two forms of modelling have recently been developed to help predict the fate of animal populations. 'Population viability analysis' (PVA) is a form of modelling that uses information about the population dynamics of a species, its current abundance and distribution, and characteristics of the environment that the species relies on. These are combined in the model, which is then run many times to see whether future generations are likely to be more or less abundant than the starting generation. The point of running many simulations is to allow a probability to be developed for the population surviving for a set number of generations. For this approach to be useful it is necessary to have reliable information on many aspects of the population dynamics of the species (such as fecundity or length of life), as well as on the environment available to it. Although such data are known for some large mammals, such as the Arabian Oryx, this does not apply to any moths, except in the most general terms. Consequently, this analysis is not yet of use in moth conservation but it is a worthwhile aim to try to collect the data for species which may be threatened, to see if the approach can help to predict future problems before they are otherwise apparent.

What are the smallest populations that will survive?

A related modelling technique is called 'minimum viable population' analysis (MVP). This also uses information on the population dynamics of the species concerned and it then attempts to predict the population size needed to ensure that the population survives for a given number of years (or generations). This helps to plan the size of population that must be achieved in a conservation programme before it is likely that survival for a significant time will take place. Such analysis has helped to produce 'rules of thumb' for mammals. For instance the 50/500 rule indicates that at least 50 reproducing individuals are needed for short-term genetic conservation and 500 for long-term survival of a species (Soule, 1987). These figures might be applied to elephants but clearly have no relevance for a moth and more realistic limits must be set for each species modelled!

The lack of useful information for moth species means that such modelling is not yet possible and so recovery programmes have to be based on common sense and guesswork.

CONSERVATION IN THE WIDER COUNTRYSIDE

It is a conservation truism that conservation cannot work if it is based on a reserve or species strategy alone. The problems of reserve isolation and size, linked with the longer-term problem that, if the climate changes, static reserves cannot move location to track this, means that sooner or later species will become extinct on their reserves. Unless recolonisation or relocation can occur, then such extinction will be final. If there were sufficient reserves for some interchange to occur, or if reserves were linked by 'conservation corridors' or 'stepping stone' reserves, this would be less of a problem. However, it is unrealistic to expect this, at least in the short term. Consequently, it is suggested that general countryside management schemes, presumably including farming practices, should be devised so that animals and plants can find a refuge in the wider countryside and not be dependent on reserves. This might be achievable for species that are undemanding and still widespread and abundant, such as the Large Yellow Underwing (*Noctua pronuba*), but it is difficult to see how it could ever apply to those species that are currently threatened and, almost by definition, have exacting needs. The only sense in which this could work is that space must be found around the edges of commercial forests and farmland for a host of mini-reserves, with motorway and railway verges and golf course and country park roughs added as well. Realistically, such areas cannot be managed in a sufficiently sophisticated way to benefit the rarest species, but they may help the commoner majority.

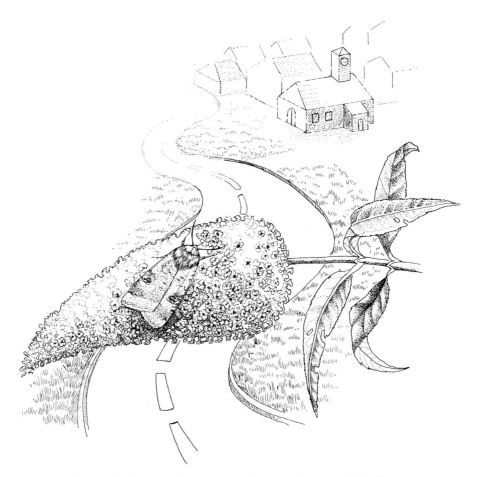

Some moths thrive in urban areas, in this case feeding on buddleia flowers.

THE FUTURE FOR MOTHS IN BRITAIN

A recent encouraging sign for Britain's moths is that they now have a slightly higher profile in conservation than they had even 20 years ago. However, more focused survey work has revealed that many species have declined seriously and apparently continue to do so. There are many candidates for extinction in the short and medium term. To some extent these are countered balanced by the colonists, most of which have taken advantage of the increasing abundance of exotic plants in Britain but the balance sheet still shows a net loss.

There are clear priorities for action. Survey work must be encouraged and co-ordinated, so that the true distribution and status of species are known. On the basis of this information, the most needy species must be selected and realistic recovery programmes prepared and acted upon (as is increasingly being done). The very limited resources for moth conservation must be carefully allocated. Managers of all sorts of nature reserves and more generalised countryside areas must be made more aware of the value and needs of moths, so that they take these needs into account in their own management programmes.

This would be helped if the beauty and fascination of moths could be shown and appreciated more widely. As lepidopterists we all have a valuable part to play in the conservation of these lovely insects. By sharing our enthusiasm, recording, advising and evangelising, we can all make a real and practical contribution to try to ensure that the moths we cherish do not slip inexorably away.

The future may not be rosy but it is not yet hopeless!

References

ACHARYA, L. and FENTON, M.B. (1992). Echolocation behaviour of vespertilionid bats (*Lasiurus cinereus* and *L. borealis*) attacking airborne targets including arctiid moths. *Canadian Journal of Zoology*, **70**: 1292–1298.

AGASSIZ, D.J.L. (1984). Microlepidoptera in Wester Ross. *Entomologist's Record and Journal of Variation*, **96**: 12–13.

AGASSIZ, D.J.L. (1996). *Invasion of Lepidoptera into the British Isles*. In: Emmet, A.M. (ed.) *Moths and Butterflies of Great Britain and Ireland Vol. 3*. Harley Books, Colchester.

ALDRIDGE, D., JONES, C.W., MAHAR, E. and MAJERUS, M.E.N. (1993). Differential habitat selection in polymorphic Lepidoptera in the Forest of Dean. *Entomologist's Record and Journal of Variation*, **105**: 203–214.

ALLAN, P.B.M. (1937). *A Moth-hunter's Gossip*. Watkins and Doncaster, London.

ALLAN, P.B.M. (1943). *Talking of Moths*. The Montgomery Press, Newtown.

ALLAN, P.B.M. (1980). *Leaves from a Moth-hunter's Notebooks*. E.W.Classey, Oxfordshire.

ASKEW, R.R. (1994). *Parasitoids of Leaf-mining Lepidoptera: What Determines their Host Ranges?* In: Hawkins, B.A. and Sheehan, W. (eds) (1994). *Parasitoid Community Ecology*. Oxford University Press, Oxford.

ASKEW, R.R. and SHAW, M.R. (1986). *Parasitoid Communities: their Size, Structure and Development*. In: Waage, J. and Greathead, D. (eds) (1986). *Insect Parasitoids*. Academic Press, London.

ATKINSON, T.C., BRIFFA, K.R. and COOPE, G.R. (1987). Seasonal temperatures in Britain during the past 22 000 years, re-constructed using beetle remains. *Nature*, **325**: 587–592.

ATLEGRIM, O. (1992). Mechanisms regulating bird predation on a herbivorous larva guild in boreal coniferous forests. *Ecography*, **15**: 19–24.

BAKER, R.R. (1972). Territorial behaviour of the nymphalid butterflies, *Aglais urticae* (L.) and *Inachis io* (L.). *Journal of Animal Ecology*, **41**: 453–469.

BAKER, R.R. (1978). *The Evolutionary Ecology of Animal Migration*. Hodder and Stoughton, London.

BAKER, R.R. (1982). *Migration: Paths through Time and Space*. Hodder and Stoughton, London.

BAKER, R.R. and MATHER, J.G. (1982). Magnetic compass sense in the large yellow underwing moth, *Noctua pronuba*. *Animal Behaviour*, **30**: 543–548.

BAKER, R.R. and SADOVY, Y. (1978). The distance and nature of the light trap response of moths. *Nature*, **276**: 818–821.

BALDWIN, I.T. (1995). Pests leave lasting impression on plants. Quoted in: *New Scientist*, 4 March 1995, pp.13.

BALDWIN, I.T. and SCHULTZ, J.C. (1983). Rapid changes in tree leaf chemistry induced by damage: evidence for communication between plants. *Science*, **221**: 277–279.

BALE, J.S. (1993). Classes of insect cold hardiness. *Functional Ecology*, **7**: 751–753.

BALE, J., HODKINSON, I.D., BLOCK, W., WEBB, N.R., COULSON, S.C. and STRATHDEE, A.T. (in press). *Life strategies of arctic terrestrial Arthropods*. In: Woodin, S.

and Marquiss, M. (eds) *Ecology of Arctic Environments*. British Ecological Society Symposium. Blackwells, Oxford.

BALTENSWEILER, W., BENZ, G., BOVEY, P. and DELUCCHI, V. (1977). Dynamics of larch bud moth populations. *Annual Review of Entomology*, **22**: 79–100.

BARBOUR, D.A. (1985). *Patterns of Population Fluctuation in the Pine Looper Moth* Bupalus piniaria *L. in Britain*. In: Bevan, D. and Stoakley, J.D. (eds) (1985). *Site Characteristics and Population Dynamics of Lepidopteran and Hymenopteran Forest Pests*. Forestry Commission Research and Development Paper 135.

BARBOUR, D.A. (1986). Why are there so few butterflies in Liverpool? An answer. *Antenna*, **10**: 75–75.

BARBOUR, D.A. (1990). Synchronous fluctuations in spatially separated populations of cyclic forest insects. In: Watt, A.D., Leather, S.R., Hunter, M.D. and Kidd, N.A.C. (eds) *Population Dynamics of Forest Insects*. Intercept, Andover.

BARBOUR, D.A. and YOUNG, M.R. (1993). Ecology and conservation of the Kentish Glory moth (*Endromis versicolora* L.) in eastern Scotland. *Entomologist*, **112**: 25–33.

BARRETT, C.G. (1892–1907). *The Lepidoptera of the British Isles*. Reeve and Co., London.

BECK, S.D. (1982). Thermoperiodic induction of larval diapause in the European corn borer, *Ostrinia nubilalis*. *Journal of Insect Physiology*, **28**: 273–277.

BEIRNE, B.P. (1952) *The Origin and History of the British Fauna*. Methuen, London.

BELL, C.H. (1976). Factors governing the induction of diapause in *Ephestia elutella* and *Plodia interpunctella* (Lepidoptera). *Physiological Entomology*, **1**: 83–91.

BERENBAUM, M.R. (1995). *Bugs in the System*. Helix Books, Massachusetts.

BERGELSON, J., FOWLER, S. and HARTLEY, S. (1986). The effects of foliage damage on casebearing moth larvae, *Coleophora serratella*, feeding on birch. *Ecological Entomology*, **11**: 241–250.

BERRYMAN, A.A. (1996). What causes population cycles of forest Lepidoptera? *Trends in Ecology and Evolution*, **11**: 28–32.

BIRCH, M.C. (1979). *Eversible Brushes*. In: Heath, J. and Emmet, A.M. (1979).

BJOSTAD, L.B., LINN, C.E., DU, J-W. and ROELOFS, W.L. (1984). Identification of new sex pheromone components in *Trichoplusia ni* predicted from biosynthetic precursors. *Journal of Chemical Ecology*, **10**: 1309–1323.

BLAND, K.P. and YOUNG, M.R. (1996). *Priorities for the Conservation of Moths in Scotland*. In: Rotheray, G.E. and MacGowan, I. (eds). *Conserving Scottish Insects*. Edinburgh Entomologist's Club, Edinburgh.

BLEST, A.D. (1957). The function of eyespot patterns in the Lepidoptera. *Behaviour*, **11**: 209–256.

BOURN, N.A.D. (1995). *The Ecology, Conservation and Population Genetics of Three Species of Zygaenid Moths*, Zygaena lonicerae, Z. purpuralis *and* Z. filipendula, *in North-west Scotland*. Unpublished PhD Thesis, University of Aberdeen.

BOWDEN, J. and CHURCH, B.M. (1973). The influence of moonlight on catches of insects in light traps in Africa. Part II. The effect of moon phase on light trap catches. *Bulletin of Entomological Research*, **63**: 129–142.

BRADLEY, J.D., TREMEWAN, W.G. and SMITH, A. (1973). *British Tortricoid Moths*. *Tortricidae: Tortricinae*. Ray Society, London.

BRADLEY, J.D., TREMEWAN, W.G. and SMITH, A. (1979). *British Tortricoid Moths*. *Tortricidae: Olethreutinae*. Ray Society, London.

BRATTSTEN, L.B., WILKINSON, C.F. and EISNER, T. (1977). Herbivore–plant interactions: mixed-function oxidases and secondary plant substances. *Science*, **196**: 1349–1352.

BRETHERTON, R.F. (1983). *The Incidence of Migrant Lepidoptera in the British Isles*. In: Heath, J. and Emmet, A.M. (1983).

BRETHERTON, R.F., GOATER, B. and LORIMER, R.I. (1983). *Noctuidae: Cuculliinae to Hypeninae*. In: Heath, J. and Emmet, A.M. (1983).

BROWER, L.P. and JONES, M.A. (1965). Precourtship interaction of wing and abdominal sex glands in male *Danaus* butterflies. *Proceedings of the Royal Entomological Society of London*, (A), **40**: 147–151.

BRUIN, J., SABELIS, M.W. and DICKE, M. (1995). Do plants tap SOS signals from their infested neighbours? *Trends in Ecology and Evolution*, **10**: 167–170.

BRUUN, H.H. (1992). *Changes in Species Composition of the Moth and Butterfly Fauna on Houtskar in the Archipelago of SW Finland during the Years of 1954–1989* (*Lepidoptera: Hesperiidae-Noctuidae*). Abo Academy Press, Finland.

BURTON, J.F. (1991). Larval foodplants of *Lithophane leautieri hesperica* Boursin (Lep.: Noctuidae). *Entomologist*, **110**: 81.

CAMPION, D.G., CRITCHLEY, B.R. and McVEIGH, L.J. (1989). *Mating Disruption*. In: Jutsum, A.R. and Gordon, R.F.S. (eds) *Insect Pheromones in Plant Protection*. John Wiley and Sons, Chichester.

CARDE, R.T., BAKER, T.C. and ROELEFS, W.L. (1975). Ethological function of components of a sex attractant system for oriental fruit moth males, *Grapholitha molesta* (Lepidoptera: Tortricidae). *Journal of Chemical Ecology*, **1**: 475–491.

CARDE, R.T. and MINKS, A.K. (1995). Control of moth pests by mating disruption: successes and constraints. *Annual Reviews of Entomology*, **40**: 559–585.

CARTER, D.J., KITCHING, I.J. and SCOBLE, M.J. (1988). The adaptable caterpillar. *Entomologist*, **107**: 68–78.

CAUGHLEY, G. (1994). Directions in conservation biology. *Journal of Animal Ecology*, **63**: 215–244.

CHEN, R.-L., SUN, Y.-J., WANG, S.-Y., ZHAI, B.-P. and BAO, X.-Y. (1995). Migration of the Oriental Armyworm *Mythimna separata* in East Asia in relation to weather and climate. 1. In: Drake, V.A. and Gatehouse, A.G. (1995).

CLARKE, C.A., GRANT, B., CLARKE, F.M.M. and ASAMI, T. (1994). A long term assessment of *Biston betularia* (L.) in one UK locality (Caldy Common near West Kirby, Wirral) 1959–1993, and glimpses elsewhere. *The Linnean*, **10**(2): 18–26.

CLAYTON, D.H. and WOLFE, N.D. (1993). The adaptive significance of self-medication. *Trends in Ecology and Evolution*, **8**: 60–63.

COLEY, P.D. (1980). Effects of leaf age and plant life history patterns on herbivory. *Nature*, **284**: 545–546.

COLLINS, N.M. and THOMAS, J.A. (eds) (1991). *The Conservation of Insects and their Habitats*. RES Symposium No. 15. Academic Press, London.

CONRAD, K.F. and PRITCHARD, G. (1990). Pre-oviposition mate-guarding and mating behaviour of *Argia vivida* (Odonata: Coenagrionidae). *Ecological Entomology*, **15**: 363–370.

COOPE, G.R. (1995). *The Effects of Quaternary Climate Changes in Insect Populations: Lessons from the Past*. In: Harrington, R and Stork, N.E. (1995).

COTT, H.B. (1940). *Adaptive Coloration in Animals*. Methuen, London.

CRAWLEY, M.J. (1985). Reduction of oak fecundity by low-density herbivore populations. *Nature*, **314**: 163–164.

CRAWLEY, M.J. and NACHAPONG, M. (1984). Facultative defences and specialist herbivores? Cinnabar moth (*Tyria jacobaea*) on the regrowth foliage of ragwort (*Senecio jacobaea*). *Ecological Entomology*, **9**: 389–393.

CRAWLEY, M.J. and PATTRASUDHI, R. (1988). Interspecific competition between insect herbivores: asymmetric competition between cinnabar moth and ragwort seed-head fly. *Ecological Entomology*, **13**: 243–249.

CROFT, B.A., KNIGHT, A.L., FLEXNER, J.L. and MILLER, R.W. (1986). Competition between caged virgin female *Argyrotaenia citrana* (Lepidoptera: Tortricidae) and pheromone traps for capture of released males in a semi-enclosed courtyard. *Environmental Entomology*, **15**: 232–239.

DACIE, J. (1985). A home for old ladies in Wimbledon. *Entomologist's Record and Journal of Variation*, **97**: 59–62.

DAMMAN, H. (1987). Leaf quality and enemy avoidance by the larva of a pyralid moth. *Ecology*, **68**: 88–97.

DANDY, J.E. (1969). *Watsonian Vice-counties of Great Britain*. Ray Society, London.

DANELL, K. and HUSS-DANELL, K. (1985). Feeding by insects and hares on birches earlier affected by moose browsing. *OIKOS*, **44**: 75–81.

DAVID, C.T. and BIRCH, M.C. (1989). *Pheromones and Insect Behaviour*. In: Jutsum, A.R. and Gordon, R.F.S. (1989).

DAVID, C.T., KENNEDY, J.S. and LUDLOW, A.R. (1983). Finding a sex pheromone source by gypsy moths released in the field. *Nature*, **303**: 804–806.

DEMPSTER, J.P. (1991). *Fragmentation, Isolation and Mobility of Insect Populations*. In: Collins, N.M. and Thomas, J.A. (1991).

DEMPSTER, J.P., KING, M.L. and LAKHANI, K.H. (1976). The status of the swallowtail butterfly in Britain. *Ecological Entomology*, **1**: 71–84.

DENNIS, R.H.L. (1977). *The British Butterflies – their Origin and Establishment*. Classey, Oxfordshire.

DENNIS, R.H.L. (1993). *Butterflies and Climate Change*. Manchester University Press, Manchester.

DENTON, G.H. and HUGHES, T.J. (1981). *The Last Great Ice Sheets*. Wiley, New York.

DICKSON, R. (1976). *A Lepidopterist's Handbook*. Amateur Entomologist's Society, Middlesex.

DOANE, C.C. and McMANUS, M.L. (eds) (1981). *The Gypsy Moth: Research toward Integrated Pest Management*. USDA Forest Service Technical Bulletin 1584.

DRAKE, V.A. and GATEHOUSE, A.G. (eds) (1995). *Insect Migration: Tracking Resources through Space and Time*. Cambridge University Press, Cambridge.

DUDLEY, R. (1995). *Aerodynamics, Energetics and Reproductive Constraints of Migratory Flight in Insects*. In: Drake, V.A. and Gatehouse, A.G. (1995).

DUNNING, D.C., ACHARYA, L., MERRIMAN, C.B. and DAL FERRO, L. (1992). Interactions between bats and arctiid moths. *Canadian Journal of Zoology*, **70**: 2218–2223.

DUSSOURD, D.E. and EISNER, T. (1987). Vein-cutting behaviour: insect counterploy to the latex defence of plants. *Science*, **237**: 898–901.

EDMUNDS, M. (1976). Larval mortality and population regulation in the butterfly *Danaus chrysippus* in Ghana. *Zoological Journal of the Linnean Society*, **58**: 129–145.

EDWARDS, P.J. and WRATTEN, S.D. (1985). Induced plant defences against insect grazing: fact or artefact? *OIKOS*, **44**: 70–74.

ELKINGTON, J.S. and CARDE, R.T. (1984). Effect of wild and laboratory-reared female gypsy moth (Lepidoptera: Lymantriidae) on the capture of males in pheromone-baited traps. *Environmental Entomology*, **13**: 1377–1385.

EMMET, A.M. (1985). *Phyllocnistidae*. In: Heath, J. and Emmet, A.M. (1985).

EMMET, A.M. (1988). *A Field Guide to the Smaller British Lepidoptera*. British Entomological and Natural History Society, London.

EMMET, A.M. (1991a). *Chart Showing the Life History and Habits of the British Lepidoptera*. In: Emmet and Heath (1991).

EMMET, A.M. (1991b). *The Scientific Names of the British Lepidoptera. Their History and Meaning*. Harley Books, Colchester.

EMMET, A.M. and HEATH, J. (eds) (1991). *The Moths and Butterflies of Great Britain and Ireland*. Vol 7, pt2. Harley Books, Colchester.

EMMET, A.M., WATKINSON, I.A. and WILSON, M.R. (1985). *Gracillariidae*. In: Heath, J. and Emmet, A.M. (1985).

ENGELBRECHT, L. (1971). Cytokinin activity in larval infected leaves. *Biochemica Physiologia Pflanzen*, **162**: 9–27.

ENGELBRECHT, L., ORBAN, U. and HEESE, W. (1969). Leaf-miner caterpillars and cytokinins in the 'green-islands' of autumn leaves. *Nature*, **223**: 319–321.

ENGLISH-LOEB, G.M., KARBAN, R. and BRODY, A.K. (1990). Arctiid larvae survive attack by a tachinid parasitoid and produce viable offspring. *Ecological Entomology*, **15**: 361–362.

FABRE, J.H. (1937). *The Great Peacock, or Emperor Moth*. Reprinted in: *Social Life in the Insect World*. Pelican Books, Middlesex.

FAETH, S.H. (1985). Host leaf selection by a leaf-mining insect, *Stilbosis juvantis*: interactions at three trophic levels. *Ecology*, **66**: 870–875.

FAETH, S.H. (1990). Structural damage to oak leaves alters natural enemy attack on a leafminer. *Entomologia Experimentalis et Applicata*, **57**: 57–63.

FARMER, E.E., JOHNSON, R.R. and RYAN, C.A. (1992). Regulation of expression of pro-teinase inhibitor genes by methyl jasmonate and jasmonic acid. *Plant Physiology*, **98**: 995–1002.

FEENY, P. (1968). Effect of oak leaf tannins on larval growth of the winter moth *Operophtera brumata*. *Journal of Insect Physiology*, **14**: 805–817.

FEENY, P. (1970). Seasonal changes in oak leaf tannins and nutrients as a cause of spring feed-ing by winter moth caterpillars. *Ecology*, **51**: 565–581.

FENTON, M.B., RACEY, P.A. and RAYNER, J.M.V. (eds) (1987). *Recent Advances in the Study of Bats*. Cambridge University Press, Cambridge.

FIELDING, C.A. and COULSON, J.C. (1995). A test of the validity of insect food-plant and life history records: Lepidoptera on heather (*Calluna vulgaris*). *Ecological Entomology*, **20**: 343–347.

FORD, E.B. (1945). *Butterflies*. New Naturalist. Collins, London.

FORD, E.B. (1955). *Moths*. New Naturalist. Collins, London.

FORDER, P. (1993). *Odonthognophos dumetata* Treitscke (Lep.: Geometridae) new to the British Isles with a description of a new form *hibernica* Forder ssp.nov.. *Entomologist's Record and Journal of Variation*, **105**: 201–202.

FOWLER, S.V. and LAWTON, J.H. (1985). Rapidly induced defences and talking trees: the Devil's advocate position. *American Naturalist*, **126**: 181–195.

FRIEDRICH, E. (1986). (Trans. by Whitebread, S.) *Breeding Butterflies and Moths*. Harley Books, Colchester.

FRAIERS, T., BOYLES, T., JONES, C. and MAJERUS, M.E.N. (1994) Short distance form frequency differences in melanic Lepidoptera across habitat boundaries. *British Journal of Entomology and Natural History*, 7: 47–52.

FRY, R. and LONSDALE, D. (1991). *Habitat Conservation for Insects – a Neglected Green Issue*. Amateur Entomologist's Society, Middlesex.

FULLARD, J.H. (1987). Sensory ecology and neuroethology of moths and bats: interactions in a global perspective. In: Fenton, M.B., Racey, P.A. and Rayner, J.M.V. (1987).

FURNEAUX, W. (1907). *Butterflies and Moths*. Longmans, Green and Co., London.

FUTUYAMA, D.J. (1976). Food plant specialisation and environmental predictability in Lepidoptera. *The American Naturalist*, **110**: 285–292.

GARCIA-SALAZAR, C., PODOLER, H. and WHOLAN, M.E. (1988). Effects of tempera-ture on diapause induction in the codling moth, *Cydia pomonella* (L.) (Lepidoptera: Olethreutinae). *Environmental Entomology*, **17**: 626–628.

GARDINER, B.O.C. (1986). The sugaring formula. *Entomologist's Gazette*, **37**: 13–14.

GARDINER, B.O.C. (1995). The very first light-trap, 1565? *Entomologist's Record and Journal of Variation*, **107**: 45–46.

GASTON, K.J., REAVEY, D. and VALLADARES, G.R. (1992). Intimacy and fidelity: inter-nal and external feeding by the British microlepidoptera. *Ecological Entomology*, **17**: 86–88.

GATEHOUSE, A.G. and ZHANG, X.-X. (1995). *Migratory Potential in Insects: Variation in an Uncertain Environment*. In: Drake, V.A. and Gatehouse, A.G. (eds) (1995).

GAYDECKI, P.A. (1984). *A Quantification of the Behavioural Dynamics of Certain Lepidoptera in Response to Light*. Unpublished PhD Thesis, Cranfield Institute for Technology.

GODFRAY, H.C.J., AGASSIZ, D.J.L., NASH, D.R. and LAWTON, J. (1995). The recruitment of parasitoid species to two invading herbivores. *Journal of Animal Ecology*, **64**: 393–402.

GORMAN, M.L. (1979). *Island Ecology*. Chapman and Hall, London.

GOULSON, D. and ENTWHISTLE, P.F. (1995). Control of diapause in the antler moth, *Cerapteryx graminis* (L.) (Lepidoptera: Noctuidae). *Entomologist*, **114**: 53–56.

GRANT, B., OWEN, D.F. and CLARKE, C.A. (1995). Decline of melanic moths. *Nature*, **373**: 565.

GRANT, G.G. and BRADY, U.E. (1975). Courtship behaviour of phycitid moths. I. Comparison of *Plodia interpunctella* and *Cadra cautella* and the role of male scent glands. *Canadian Journal of Zoology*, **53**: 813–826.

GREENE, J. (1857). *Pupa Digging*. Edward Newman, London.

GROOMBRIDGE, B. (1992). *Global Biodiversity*. World Conservation Monitoring Centre. Chapman and Hall, London.

GULLAN, P.J. and CRANSTON, P.S. (1994). *The Insects: an Outline of Entomology*. Chapman and Hall, London.

GUNN, A. and GATEHOUSE, A.G. (1987). The influence of larval phase on metabolic reserves, fecundity and life-span of the African armyworm, *Spodoptera exempta* (Walker). *Bulletin of Entomological Research*, 77: 6451–6660.

HADLEY, M. (1984). *A National Review of British Macrolepidoptera. Invertebrate Site Register*. Unpublished Report 46. Nature Conservancy Council, London.

HAGGETT, G.M. and HALL, M.R. (1992). The effect of pine afforestation on the Lepidoptera of Breckland. *Entomologist's Gazette*, **43**: 3–28.

HAGGETT, G.M. and SMITH, C. (1993). *Agrochola haematidea* Duponchel (Lepidoptera: Noctuidae, Cuculliinae) new to Britain. *Entomologist's Gazette*, **44**: 183–203.

HAGSTRUM, D.W. and SILHACEK, D.L. (1980). Diapause induction in *Ephestia cautella*: an interaction between genotype and crowding. *Entomologia Experimentalis et Applicata*, **28**: 29–37.

HARPER, M.W. and YOUNG, M.R. (1986). *Periclepsis cinctana* [D. & S.] and other Lepidoptera on Tiree in 1984. *Entomologist's Gazette*, **37**: 199–205.

HARRINGTON, R. and STORK, N.E. (1995). *Insects in a Changing Environment*. Academic Press, London.

HARRIS, M. (1755). *The English Lepidoptera: or, the Aurelian's Pocket Companion*. J.Robson, London.

HARTLEY, S.E. and LAWTON, J.H. (1987). Effects of different types of damage on the chemistry of birch foliage, and the responses of birch feeding insects. *Oecologia*, 74: 432–437.

HARTSTACK, A.W., HOLLINGSWORTH, J.P. and LINDQUIST, D.A. (1968). A technique for measuring trapping efficiency of electric insect traps. *Journal of Economic Entomology*, **61**: 546–552.

HARTSTACK, A.W. and WITZ, J.A. (1981). Estimating field populations of tobacco budworm, *Heliothis virescens* moths, from pheromone trap catches. *Environmental Entomology*, **10**: 908–914.

HATCHER, P.E. (1991). The conifer-feeding macrolepidoptera fauna of an English woodland, as determined by larval sampling. *Entomologist*, **110**: 11–23.

HATTENSCHWILER, P. (1985). *Psychidae*. In: Heath, J. and Emmet, A.M. (eds) (1985).

HAUKIOJA, E. (1980). On the role of plant defences in the fluctuation of herbivore populations. *OIKOS*, **35**: 202–213.

HAUKIOJA, E. and NIEMALA, P. (1977). Retarded growth of a geometrid larva after mechanical damage to leaves of its host tree. *Annales Zoologici Fennici*, **14**: 48–52.

HAUKIOJA, E., SOUMELA, J. and NEUVONEN, S. (1985). Long-term inducible resistance in birch foliage: triggering cues and efficacy on a defoliator. *Oecologia*, 65: 363–369.

HEATH, J. (1967). Lepidoptera distribution maps scheme. *Entomologist's Monthly Magazine*, 103: 124–125.

HEATH, J. (ed.) (1970). *Provisional Atlas of the Insects of the British Isles*. Pt 1 Lepidoptera Rhopalocera. BRC, Abbot's Ripton.

HEATH, J. (1974). *A Century of Change in the Lepidoptera*. In: Hawksworth, D.L. (ed.) *The Changing Flora and Fauna of Britain*. Academic Press, London.

HEATH, J. (ed.) (1976). *The Moths and Butterflies of Great Britain and Ireland*. Vol. 1. Blackwells and Curwen Press, Oxford.

HEATH, J. and EMMET, A.M. (eds) (1979). *The Moths and Butterflies of Great Britain and Ireland*. Vol. 9. Curwen Books, London.

HEATH, J. and EMMET, A.M. (eds) (1983). *The Moths and Butterflies of Great Britain and Ireland*. Vol. 10. Harley Books, Colchester.

HEATH, J. and EMMET, A.M. (eds) (1985). *The Moths and Butterflies of Great Britain and Ireland*. Vol. 2. Harley Books, Colchester.

HEGDEKAR, B.M. (1983). Effect of latitude on the critical photoperiod for diapause induction in the bertha armyworm, *Mamestra configurata* (Lepidoptera: Noctuidae). *Canadian Entomologist*, 115: 1039–1042.

HEINRICH, B. (1971). The effect of leaf geometry on the feeding behaviour of the caterpillar of *Manduca sexta* (Sphingidae). *Animal Behaviour*, 19: 119–124.

HEINRICH, B. and COLLINS, S.L. (1983). Caterpillar leaf damage, and the game of hide-and-seek with birds. *Ecology*, 64: 592–602.

HELIOVAARA, K. and VAISANEN, R. (1988). Periodicity of *Retinia retinella* in northern Europe (Lepidoptera: Tortricidae). *Entomologia Generalis*, 14: 37–45.

HELIOVAARA, K., VAISANEN, R. and SIMON, C. (1994). Evolutionary ecology of periodical insects. *Trends in Ecology and Evolution*, 9: 475–480.

HENDRIKSE, A. and VOS-BUNNEMEYER, E. (1987). Role of host-plant stimuli in sexual behaviour of small ermine moths (*Yponomeuta*). *Ecological Entomology*, 12: 363–371.

HENDRIX, S.D. (1979). Compensatory reproduction in a biennial herb following insect defoliation. *Oecologia*, 42: 107–118.

HERING, E.M. (1951). *Biology of Leaf Miners*. 's-Gravenhage.

HERING, E.M. (1957). *Bestimmungstabellen der Blattminen von Europa*. Vol 3. 's-Gravenhage.

HIGASHIURA, Y. (1989). Survival of eggs of the gypsy moth (*Lymantria dispar*) II. Oviposition site selection in changing environment. *Journal of Animal Ecology*, 58: 413–426.

HILTON, D.F.J. (1982). The biology of *Endothenia daeckeana* (Lepidoptera: Olethreutinae); an inhabitant of the ovaries of the northern pitcher plant *Sarracenia p. purpurea* (Sarraceniaceae). *Canadian Entomologist*, 114: 269–274.

HOUSEGO, A.J. and GORMALLY, M.J. (1993). Investigation of the invertebrate communities associated with different ages of hazel coppice at Upper Hamble Country Park, Hampshire. *Entomologist*, 112: 3–9.

HORTON, P. (1977). Local migrations of Lepidoptera from Salisbury Plain in 1976. *Entomologist's Gazette*, 28: 281–283.

HSIAO, H.S. (1972). *Attraction of Moths to Light and to Infra-red Radiation*. San Francisco Press, San Francisco.

HULLEY, P.E. (1988). Caterpillar attacks plant mechanical defence by mowing trichomes before feeding. *Ecological Entomology*, 13: 239–241.

HUNTER, M.D. (1987a). Sound production in larvae of *Diurnea fagella* (Lepidoptera: Oecophoridae). *Ecological Entomology*, 12: 355–357.

HUNTER, M.D. (1987b). Opposing effects of spring defoliation on late season oak caterpillars. *Ecological Entomology*, 12: 373–382.

HUNTER, M.D. (1990). Differential susceptibility to variable plant phenology and its role in competition between two insect herbivores on oak. *Ecological Entomology*, 15: 401–408.

HUNTER, M.D. and WILLMER, P.G. (1989). The potential for interspecific competition between two abundant defoliators on oak: leaf damage and habitat quality. *Ecological Entomology*, **14**: 267–277.

JOHANSSON, R., NIELSEN, E.S., van NIEUKERKEN, E.J. and GUSTAFSSON, B. (1990). The Nepticulidae and Opostegidae (Lepidoptera) of North West Europe. *Fauna Entomologica Scandinavica*, **23**: 1–413.

JOHNSON, C.G. (1969). *Migration and Dispersal of Insects by Flight*. Methuen, London.

JOHNSON, S.J. (1995). *Insect Migration in North America: Synoptic-scale Transport in a Highly Seasonal Environment*. In: Drake, V.A. and Gatehouse, A.G. (eds) (1995).

JONES, F.M. (1934). Further experiments on coloration and relative acceptability of insects to birds. *Transactions of the Royal Entomological Society of London*, **82**: 443–453.

JUTSUM, A.R. and GORDON, R.F.S. (1989). *Insect Pheromones in Plant Protection*. John Wiley and Sons, Chichester.

KAAE, R.S. and SHOREY, H.H. (1972). Sex pheromones of noctuid moths. XXVII. Influence of wind velocity on sex pheromone releasing behaviour of *Trichoplusia ni* females. *Annals of the Entomological Society of America*, **65**: 437–440.

KEARNS, P.W.E. and MAJERUS, M.E.N. (1987). Differential habitat selection in the Lepidoptera: a note on deciduous versus coniferous woodland habitats. *Entomologist's Record and Journal of Variation*, **99**: 103–106.

KENNEDY, C.E.J. and SOUTHWOOD, T.R.E. (1984). The number of species of insects associated with British trees: a re-analysis. *Journal of Animal Ecology*, **53**: 455–478.

KENNEDY, J.S. (1985). *Migration, Behavioural and Ecological*. In: Rankin, M.A. (1985).

KERSLAKE, J., KRUUK, L., HARTLEY, S. and WOODIN, S. (1996). Winter moth (Operophtera brumata lepidoptera: Geometridae) outbreaks on Scottish heather moorlands: effects of host plant and parasitoids on larval survival and development. *Bulletin of Entomological Research*, **86**: 155–164.

KETTLEWELL, B. (1973). *The Evolution of Melanism*. Clarendon, Oxford.

KIRBY, W and SPENCE, W. (1815–1826). *An Introduction to Entomology*. (4 volumes). London.

KLOMP, H. (1966). The dynamics of a field population of the pine looper, *Bupalus piniaria* L. (Lep. Geom.). *Advances in Ecological Research*, **3**: 207–305.

KRIEGER, R.I., FEENY, P.P. and WILKINSON, C.E. (1971). De-toxification enzymes in the guts of caterpillars: an evolutionary answer to plant defences? *Science*, **172**: 579–581.

LAWTON, J. (1986). Surface availability and insect community structure – the effects of architecture and fractal dimensions of plants. In: *Insects and the Plant Surface*. Juniper, B. and Southwood, R. (eds). Edward Arnold, London.

LAWTON, J. (1995). *The Response of Insects to Environmental Change*. In: Harrington, R. and Stork, N.E. (1995).

LAWTON, J and SCHRODER, D. (1977). Effects of plant type, size of geographical range and taxonomic isolation on the number of insect species associated with British plants. *Nature*, **265**: 137–140.

LEATHER, S.R. (1984). Factors affecting pupal survival and eclosion in the pine beauty moth, *Panolis flammea* (D. & S.). *Oecologia*, **63**: 75–79.

LEATHER, S.R. (1990). The analysis of species–area relationships, with particular reference to macrolepidoptera on Rosaceae; how important is insect data-set quality? *Entomologist*, **109**: 8–16.

LEATHER, S.R. (1995). New terms for cold – in support of a re-classification of insect cold hardiness. *Antenna*, 19: 66–67.

LEATHER, S.R. and BROTHERTON, C.M. (1987). Defensive responses of the pine beauty moth, *Panolis flammea* (D. & S.) (Lepidoptera: Noctuidae). *Entomologist's Gazette*, **38**: 19–26.

LEATHER, S.R., WATT, A.D. and FORREST, G.I. (1987). Insect-induced chemical changes in young lodgepole pine (*Pinus contorta*): the effect of previous defoliation on oviposition, growth and survival of the pine beauty moth, *Panolis flammea*. *Ecological Entomology*, **12**: 275–281.

LEATHER, S.R., WALTERS, K.F.A. and BALE, J.S. (1993). *The Ecology of Insect Overwintering.* Cambridge University Press, Cambridge.

LEES, E. and ARCHER, D.M. (1980). Diapause in various populations of *Pieris napi* L. from different parts of the British Isles. *Journal of Research on the Lepidoptera,* 19: 96–100.

LENNON, J.J. and TURNER, J.R.G. (1995). Predicting the spatial distribution of climate: temperature in Great Britain. *Journal of Animal Ecology,* 64: 370–392.

LEONARD, D.E. (1972). Survival in a gypsy moth population exposed to low winter temperatures. *Environmental Entomology,* 1: 549–554.

LEVERTON, R. (1991). Mate competition in *Noctua pronuba* (Lep: Noctuidae) Large Yellow Underwing. *Entomologist's Record and Journal of Variation,* 103: 18.

LEVERTON, R. (1994). Notes on rearing *Acronicta leporina* L. (Lep.: Noctuidae). *Entomologist's Record and Journal of Variation,* 106: 191–192.

LEVIN, D.A. (1973). The role of trichomes in plant defence. *Quarterly Review of Biology,* 48: 3–15.

LOADER, C. and DAMMAN, H. (1991). Nitrogen content of foodplants and vulnerability of *Pieris rapae* to natural enemies. *Ecology,* 72: 1586–1590.

LOEFFLER, C.C. (1996). Adaptive trade-offs of leaf folding in *Dichomeris* caterpillars on goldenrods. *Ecological Entomology,* 21: 34–40.

LUFF, M.L. and WOIWOD, I.P. (1995). *Insects as Indicators of Land-use Change: a European Perspective, Focusing on Moths and Ground Beetles.* In: Harrington, R. and Stork, N.E. (1995).

MacARTHUR, R.H. and WILSON, E.O. (1967). *The Theory of Island Biogeography.* Princeton University Press, Princeton.

McGEACHIE, W.J. (1988). A remote sensing method for the estimation of light trap efficiency. *Bulletin of Entomological Research,* 78: 379–385.

McLEOD, D.G.R., RITCHAT, C. and NAGAI, T. (1979). Occurrence of a two generation strain of the European corn borer, *Ostrinia nubilalis* (Lepidoptera: Pyralidae), in Quebec. *Canadian Entomologist,* 111: 2330–2336.

McNEIL, J.N. (1991). Behavioural ecology of pheromone-mediated communication in moths and its importance in the use of pheromone traps. *Annual Reviews of Entomology,* 36: 407–430.

McNEIL, J.N. and DELISLE, J. (1989). Host plant pollen influences calling behaviour and ovarian development of the sunflower moth, *Homeosoma electellum. Oecologia,* 80: 201–205.

MARREN, P. (1981). Speculative notes on the Kentish Glory. *Entomological Record and Journal of Variation,* 92: 235–238.

MEIJDEN, E. van der. (1979). Herbivore exploitation of a fugitive plant species: local survival and extinction of the cinnabar moth and ragwort in a heterogenous environment. *Oecologia,* 42: 307–322.

MEYRICK, E. (1928). *A Revised Handbook of British Lepidoptera.* Watkins and Doncaster, London.

MIKKOLA, K. (1976). Alternate-year flight of northern *Xestia* species (Lep., Noctuidae) and its adaptive significance. *Annales Entomologici Fennici,* 42: 191–199.

MORRIS, R.K.A. and COLLINS, G.A. (1991). On the hibernation of Tissue moths *Triphosia dubitata* L. and the Herald moth *Scoliopteryx libatrix* L. in an old fort. *Entomologist's Record and Journal of Variation,* 103: 313–321.

MORTON, R, STUART, L.D. and WARDHAUGH, K.G. (1981). The analysis and standardisation of light trap catches of *Heliothis armiger* (Hubner) and *H. punctiger* (Lepidoptera, Noctuidae). *Bulletin of Entomological Research,* 7: 207–225.

MOTHES, K., ENGELBRECHT, L. and SCHUTTE, H.R. (1961). Uber die Akkumulation von Alpha-aminoisobuttersaure im Blattgewebe unter dem Einfluss von Kinetin. *Physiologia Plantarum,* 14: 72–75.

MUIRHEAD-THOMSOM, R.C. (1991). *Trap Responses of Flying Insects – the Influence of Trap Design on Trap Efficiency.* Academic Press, London.

MURLIS, J., ELKINTON, J.S. and CARDE, R.T. (1992). Odour plumes and how insects use them. *Annual Reviews of Entomology*, **37**: 505–532.

MYERS, J.H. (1978). A search for behavioural variation in first and last laid eggs of western tent caterpillar and an attempt to prevent a population decline. *Canadian Journal of Zoology*, **56**: 2359–2363.

MYERS, J.H. (1981). Interactions between western tent caterpillars and wild rose: a test of some general plant herbivore hypotheses. *Journal of Animal Ecology*, **50**: 11–25.

MYERS, J.H. (1985). Effect of physiological condition of the host plant on the ovipositional choice of the cabbage white butterfly, *Pieris rapae*. *Journal of Animal Ecology*, **54**: 193–204.

MYERS, J.H. and CAMPBELL, B.J. (1976). Distribution and dispersal in populations capable of resource depletion. A field study on cinnabar moth. *Oecologia*, **24**: 7–20.

NASH, D.R., AGASSIZ, D.J.L., GODFRAY, H.C.J. and LAWTON, J.H. (in press). The pattern of spread of invading species: two leaf-mining moths colonising Great Britain. *Journal of Animal Ecology*.

NAUMANN, I.D. (ed.) (1994). *Systematic and Applied Entomology*. Melbourne University Press, Melbourne.

NEALIS, V. (1985). Diapause and the seasonal ecology of the introduced parasite *Cotesia* (*Apanteles*) *rubecula* (Hymenoptera: Braconidae). *Canadian Entomologist*, **117**: 333–342.

NEMEC, S.J. (1971). Effects of lunar phases on light-trap collections and populations of bollworm moths. *Journal of Economic Entomology*, **64**: 860–862.

NEWMAN, E. (1874). *An Illustrated Natural History of British Moths*. Hardwicke, London.

NIEMALA, P. and HAUKIOJA, E. (1982). Seasonal patterns in species richness of herbivores: macrolepidopteran larvae on Finnish deciduous trees. *Ecological Entomology*, **7**: 169–175.

NYLIN, S. (1989). Effects of changing photoperiods in the life cycle regulation of the Comma butterfly, *Polygonia c-album* (Nymphalidae). *Ecological Entomology*, **14**: 209–218.

OWEN, D.F. (1984). The geographical distribution of Buddleia-feeding in *Cucullia verbasci* in the British Isles. *Entomologist's Record and Journal of Variation*, **96**: 49–52.

OWEN, D.F. (1987a). Winter breeding by *Cynthia cardui* (L.) (Lepidoptera: Nymphalidae) in Crete and Madeira, and the possible significance of parasitoids in initiating migration. *Entomologist's Gazette*, **38**: 11–12

OWEN, D.F. (1987b). Insect species richness on the Rosaceae: are the primary data reliable? *Entomologist's Gazette*, **38**: 209–215.

PARSONS, M.S. (1993). *A Review of the Scarce and Threatened Pyralid Moths of Great Britain*. Joint Nature Conservation Committee, Peterborough.

PEDGLEY, D.E. (1985). Windborne migration of *Heliothis armigera* (Hubner)(Lepidoptera: Noctuidae) to the British Isles. *Entomologist's Gazette*, **36**: 15–22.

PENNINGTON, M. (1995). *Shetland Entomological Group, Newsletter*. 9. Shetland.

PERRING, F.H. and WALTERS, S.M. (1962). *Atlas of the British Flora*. Nelson, London.

PETERSON, S.C., JOHNSON, N.D. and LEGUYADER, J.L. (1987). Defensive regurgitation of allelochemicals derived from host cyanogenesis by eastern tent caterpillars. *Ecology*, **68**: 1268–1272.

PIERCE, F.N. AND METCALFE, J.W. (1938). *The Genitalia of the British Pyrales with the Deltoids and Plumes*. Oundle.

POLLARD, E. (1977). A method for assessing changes in the abundance of butterflies. *Biological Conservation*, **12**: 115–134.

POLLARD, E. (1979). Population ecology and change in range of the white admiral butterfly *Ladoga camilla* L. in England. *Ecological Entomology*, **4**: 61–74.

PORTER, J. (1995). *The Effects of Climate Change on the Agricultural Environment for Crop Insect Pests with Particular Reference to the European Corn Borer and Grain Maize*. In: Harrington, R. and Stork, N.E. (eds) (1995).

POWELL, J.A. (1980). Evolution of larval food preferences in microlepidoptera. *Annual Reviews of Entomology*, **25**: 133–159.

PRENDERGAST, J.R., QUINN, R.M., LAWTON, J.H., EVERSHAM, B.C. and GIB-

BONS, D.W. (1993). Rare species, the coincidence of diversity hotspots and conservation strategies. *Nature*, 365: 335–337.

PRESZLER, R.W. and PRICE, P.W. (1993). The influence of *Salix* leaf abscission on leaf-miner survival and life history. *Ecological Entomology*, 18: 150–154.

PULLIN, A.S. (1986). *Life History Strategies of the Butterflies* Inachis io *and* Aglais urticae *Feeding on Nettle* Urtica dioica. Unpublished PhD Thesis (CNAA), Oxford Polytechnic.

PULLIN, A.S. (ed) (1995). *Ecology and Conservation of Butterflies*. Chapman and Hall, London.

RABINOWITZ, D.S., CAIRNS, S. and DILLON, T. (1986). *Seven Forms of Rarity and their Frequency in the Flora of the British Isles*. In: Soule, M. (ed) *Conservation Biology*. Sinauer Associates, Sunderland, MA.

RANDALL, M.G.M. (1982). The ectoparasitism of *Coleophora alticolella* (Lepidoptera) in relation to its altitudinal distribution. *Ecological Entomology*, 7: 177–185.

RANKIN, M.A. (ed) (1985). *Migration: Mechanisms and Adaptive Significance*. Marine Science Institute, University of Texas at Austin.

RAVENSCROFT, N.O.M. (1992). *The Ecology and Conservation of the Chequered Skipper Butterfly* Carterocephalus palaemon *Pallas*. Unpublished PhD Thesis, Aberdeen University.

RAVENSCROFT, N.O.M. (1994). The enigma of the Burnet moths of western Scotland. *British Wildlife*, 5: 222–228.

RAVENSCROFT, N.O.M. and YOUNG, M.R. (in press). Population estimates and trends for *Zygaena loti* (the slender Scotch burnet moth). *Journal of Applied Ecology*.

RENWICK, J.A.A. and CHEW, F.S. (1994). Oviposition behaviour in Lepidoptera. *Annual Reviews of Entomology*, 39: 377–400.

RHOADES, D.F. (1983). Responses of alder and willow to attack by tent caterpillars and web-worms: evidence for pheromonal sensitivity of willows. In: Hedin, P.A. (ed) *Plant Resistance to Insects*. American Chemical Society, Washington.

RICKARDS, J., KELLEHER, M.J. and STOREY, K.B. (1987). Strategies of freeze avoidance in larvae of the goldenrod gall moth *Epiblema scudderiana*: winter profiles of a natural population. *Journal of Insect Physiology*, 33: 443–450.

RIDGWAY, R.L., SILVERSTEIN, R.M. and INSCOE, M.N. (eds) (1990). *Behaviour-Modifying Chemicals for Pest Management: Applications of Pheromones and other Attractants*. Marcel Dekker, New York.

RIEDL, H. and CROFT, B.A. (1978). The effects of photoperiod and effective temperatures on the seasonable phenology of the codling moth (Lepidoptera: Tortricidae). *Canadian Entomologist*, 110: 455–470.

RING, R.A. (1982). Freezing-tolerant insects with low supercooling points. *Comparative Biochemistry and Physiology*, 73A: 605–612.

RIVERS, C.F. (1976). *Diseases*. In: Heath, J. (ed) (1976).

ROBERTS, I. (1996). *The efficiency of light traps for moths in relation to meteorological conditions*. Unpublished BSc Thesis, Aberdeen University.

ROEDER, K.D. (1967). *Nerve Cells and Insect Behaviour*. Harvard University Press, Massachusetts.

ROELEFS, W.L., COMEAU, A., HILL, A. and MILICEVIC, G. (1971). Sex attractant of the codling moth: characterisation with electroantennogram technique. *Science*, 174: 297–299.

ROLAND, J. and EMBREE, D.G. (1995). Biological control of the winter moth. *Annual Reviews of Entomology*, 40: 475–492.

ROTHSCHILD, M. (1967). Mimicry, the deceptive way of life. *Natural History Society of New York*, 76: 44–51.

ROTHSCHILD, M. (1985). *British Aposematic Lepidoptera*. In: Heath, J. and Emmet, A.M. (eds) (1985).

ROTHSCHILD, M., APLIN, R., BAKER, J. and MARSH, N. (1979). Toxicity induced in the Tobacco Hornworm (*Manduca sexta* L.) (Sphingidae: Lepidoptera). *Nature*, 280: 487–488.

RUDDIMAN, W.F. and McINTYRE, A. (1981). The north Atlantic ocean during the last de-glaciation. *Paleo*, 35: 145–214.

RYDELL, J., JONES, G. and WATERS, D. (1995). Bat echolocation, moth hearing and the evolutionary arms race: who is the current leader? *OIKOS*, **48**: 1–6.

SAGERS, C.L. (1992). Manipulation of host plant quality: herbivores keep leaves in the dark. *Functional Ecology*, **6**: 741–743.

SATTLER, K. (1991). A review of wing reduction in Lepidoptera. *Bulletin of the British Museum (Natural History) (Ent.)*, **60**: 243–288.

SCOBLE, M.J. (1991). *Classification of the Lepidoptera*. In: Emmet, A.M. and Heath, J. (1991).

SCHNITZLER, H-U. (1987). Echoes of fluttering moths: information for echolocating bats. In: Fenton, M.B., Racey, P.A. and Rayner, J.M.V. (1987).

SCHWEITZER, D.F. (1979). Effects of foliage age on body weight and survival in larvae of the tribe Lithophanini (Lepidoptera: Noctuidae). *OIKOS*, **32**: 403–408.

SCRIBER, J.M. (1977). Limiting effects of low leaf-water content on the nitrogen utilisation, energy budget and larval growth of *Hyalophora cecropia* (Lepidoptera: Saturniidae). *Oecologia*, **28**: 269–287.

SCRIBER, J.M. and FEENY, P. (1979). Growth of herbivorous caterpillars in relation to feeding specialisation and to the growth form of their food plants. *Ecology*, **60**: 829–850.

SEPPANEN, E.J. (1969). Suurperhostemme talvehtimisasteet. *Annales Entomologici Fennici*, **35**: 129–152.

SHAW, M.R. (1994). *Parasitoid Host Ranges*. In: Hawkins, B.A. and Sheehan, W. (eds) (1994). *Parasitoid Community Ecology*. Oxford University Press, Oxford.

SHAW, M.R. (1996). *Hymenoptera in relation to insect conservation in Scotland*. In: Rotheray, G.E. and MacGowan, I. (eds.) *Conserving Scottish Insects*. Edinburgh Entomologist's Club, Edinburgh.

SHAW, M.R. and ASKEW, R.R. (1976). *Parasites*. In: Heath, J. (ed) (1976).

SHIRT, D.B. (1987). *British Red Data Books: 2 Insects*. Nature Conservancy Council, Peterborough.

SHOREY, H.H. (1976). *Animal Communication by Pheromones*. Academic Press, London.

SHREEVE, T.G. (1987). The mate location behaviour of the male speckled wood butterfly, *Pararge aegeria*, and the effect of phenotypic differences in hind-wing spotting. *Animal Behaviour*, **35**: 682–690.

SIDDORN, J.W. and BROWN, E.S. (1971). A Robinson light trap modified for segregating samples at pre-determined time intervals, with notes on the effect of moonlight on the periodicity of catches of insects. *Journal of Applied Ecology*, **8**: 69–75.

SKINNER, B. (1984). *Colour Identification Guide to Moths of the British Isles*. Viking, Middlesex.

SKOU, P. (1991). *Nordens Ugler*. Danmarks Dyreliv Band 5. Appollo Books, Denmark.

SMITHERS, C. (1982). *Handbook of Insect Collecting*. David and Charles, Newton Abbott.

SOMME, L. (1965). Further observations on glycerol and cold hardiness in insects. *Canadian Journal of Zoology*, **43**: 765–770.

SOTTHIBANDHU, S and BAKER, R.R. (1979). Celestial orientation by the large yellow underwing moth, *Noctua pronuba*. *Animal Behaviour*, **27**: 786–800.

SOULE, M.G. (1987). *Viable Populations for Conservation*. Cambridge University Press, New York.

SOUMELA, J., KAITANIEMI, P. and NILSON, A. (1995). Systematic within-tree variation in mountain birch leaf quality for a geometrid, *Epirrita autumnata*. *Ecological Entomology*, **20**: 283–297.

SOUTH, R. (1907–09). *The Moths of the British Isles*. Wayside and Woodland Series. Frederick Warne and Co., London.

SOUTHWOOD, T.R.E. (1961). The number of species of insect associated with various trees. *Journal of Animal Ecology*, **30**: 1–8.

SPALDING, A. (1994). The Sandhill Rustic – the Unanswered Questions. *British Wildlife*, **6**: 37–39.

SPEIGHT, M.R. and WAINHOUSE, D. (1989). *Ecology and Management of Forest Insects*. Oxford Science Publications, Oxford.

STAINTON, H.T. (1854). *The Entomologist's Companion*. van Voorst, London.

STAINTON, H.T. (1857–59). *A Manual of British Butterflies and Moths*. J. V. Voorst, London.

STEPHENS, G.R. (1971). The relation of insect defoliation to mortality in Connecticut forests. *Connecticut Agricultural and Experimental Station Bulletin*, **723**: 1–16.

STERLING, P.H. and HAMBLER, C. (1988). Coppicing for conservation: do hazel communities benefit? In: Kirby, K.J. and Wright, F.J. (eds) *Woodland Conservation in the Clay Vale of Oxfordshire and Buckinghamshire*. Nature Conservancy Council, Peterborough.

STRONG, D.R., LAWTON, J. and SOUTHWOOD, T.R.E. (1984). *Insects on Plants*. Blackwell, Oxford.

SUBINPRASERT, S. and SVENSSON, B.W. (1988). Effects of predation on clutch size and egg dispersion in the codling moth *Laspeyresia pomonella*. *Ecological Entomology*, **13**: 87–94.

TAUBER, M.J., TAUBER, C.A. and MASAKI, S. (1986). *Seasonal Adaptations of Insects*. Oxford University Press, New York.

TAYLOR, L.R., KEMPTON, R.A. and WOIWOD, I.P. (1976). Diversity statistics and the log-series model. *Journal of Animal Ecology*, **45**: 255–272.

TENOW, O. and NILSSEN, A. (1990). Egg cold hardiness and topoclimatic limitations to the outbreaks of *Epirrita autumnata* in northern Fennoscandia. *Journal of Applied Ecology*, **27**: 723–734.

THOMAS, J.A. (1977). *The Biology and Conservation of the Large Blue Butterfly – Second Report*. ITE, Monkswood, Abbots Ripton, UK.

THOMAS, J.A. (1983). The ecology and conservation of *Lysandra bellargus* (Lepidoptera Lycaenidae) in Britain. *Journal of Applied Ecology*, **20**: 59–83.

THOMAS, J.A., THOMAS, C.D., SIMCOX, D.J. and CLARKE, R.T. (1986). The ecology and declining status of the silver-spotted skipper butterfly (*Hesperia comma*) in Britain. *Journal of Applied Ecology*, **23**: 365–380.

THOMPSON, J.N. and PELLMYR, O. (1991). Evolution of oviposition behaviour and host preference in Lepidoptera. *Annual Reviews of Entomology*, **36**: 65–89.

THOMSON, G. (1980). *The Butterflies of Scotland*. Croom Helm, London.

TOWNSEND, M. (1985). *An Investigation of the Mechanisms by which Green Islands are maintained in Senescing Leaves in Autumn in the Presence of Phytophagous Insects*. Unpublished BSc Thesis, Aberdeen University.

TRAGARDHS, I. (1913). Contributions towards the comparative morphology of the trophi of the lepidopterous leaf-miners. *Ark Zoologica*, **8**: 9.

TREMEWAN, W.G. (1966). The history of *Zygaena viciae anglica* Reiss (Lep.: Zygaenidae) in the New Forest. *Entomologist's Gazette*, **17**: 187–211.

TREMEWAN, W.G. (1985). *Zygaenidae*. In: Heath, J. and Emmet, A.M. (1985).

TURNER, J.R.G. (1988). Sex, leks and fechts in Swift moths *Hepialus* (Lepidoptera: Hepialidae) evidence for the hot-shot moth. *The Entomologist*, **107**: 90–95.

TURNOCK, W.J., LAMB, R.J. and BODNARYK, R.P. (1983). Effects of cold stress during pupal diapause on the survival and development of *Mamestra configurata* (Lepidoptera: Noctuidae). *Oecologia*, **56**: 185–192.

TUTT, J.W. (1901–05). *Practical Hints for Field Lepidopterists*. Elliot Stock, London.

TWEEDIE, M.W.F. and EMMET, A.M. (1991). *Resting Posture in the Lepidoptera*. In: Emmet, A.M. and Heath, J. (1991).

VARLEY, G.C., GRADWELL, G.R. and HASSELL, M.P. (1973). *Insect Population Ecology: an Analytical Approach*. Blackwell, London.

WAGNER, D.L. and LIEBHERR, J.K. (1992). Flightlessness in insects. *Trends in Ecology and Evolution*, **7**: 216–220.

WALL, C. (1974). Effect of temperature on embryonic development and diapause in *Chesias legatella. Journal of Zoology, London*, **172**: 147–168.

WALL, C. (1989). *Monitoring and Spray Timing*. In: Jutsum, A.R. and Gordon, R.F.S. (eds) (1989).

WARING, P. (1991). National review of the recording and conservation of the rarer British macro-moths. *Entomologist's Record and Journal of Variation*, **103**: 193–196.

WARING, P. (1992a). Wildlife Report – Moths. *British Wildlife*, **3**: 176–178.

WARING, P. (1992b). Conserving Britain's rarest moths. *Proceedings of the VIIIth Congress on European Lepidoptera*, Helsinki.

WARING, P. (1992c). Wildlife Report – Moths. *British Wildlife*, 3: 240–241.

WARING, P. (1992d). Wildlife Report – Moths. *British Wildlife*, 4: 119–120.

WARING, P. (1993a). Wildlife Report – Moths. *British Wildlife*, 4: 185–188.

WARING, P. (1993b). Wildlife Report – Moths. *British Wildlife*, 4: 256–258.

WARING, P (1993c). Wildlife Report – Moths. *British Wildlife*, 4: 392–394.

WARING, P. (1994). Moth traps and their use. *British Wildlife*, 5: 137–148.

WARING, P. (1995). Wildlife Report – Moths. *British Wildlife*, 6: 393–395.

WARREN, M.S. (1987). The ecology and conservation of the heath fritillary butterfly *Mellicta athalia* III. Population dynamics and the effects of habitat management. *Journal of Applied Ecology*, 24: 499–513.

WARREN, M.S. (1995). *Managing Local Microclimates for the High Brown Fritillary* Argynnis adippe. In: Pullin, A.S. (1995).

WATT, A.D. and McFARLANE, A.M. (1991). Winter moth on Sitka spruce: synchrony of egg hatch and budburst, and its effect on larval survival. *Ecological Entomology*, 16: 387–390.

WATT, A.D., LEATHER, S.R., HUNTER, M.D. and KIDD, N.A. (eds) (1990). *Population Dynamics of Forest Insects*. Intercept, Andover.

WELCH, D. (1992). High altitude limits of *Coleophora alticolella* Zeller (Lepidoptera: Coleophoridae) in 1991 in northern Britain. *Entomologist's Gazette*, 43: 111–113.

WEHNER, R. (1984). Astronavigation in insects. *Annual Reviews of Entomology*, 29: 277–298.

WERNER, R.A. (1977). Biology and behaviour of the spear-marked black moth, *Rheumaptera hastata*, in interior Alaska. *Annals of the Entomological Society of America*, 70: 328–336.

WEST, A.S. (1936). Winter mortality of larvae of the European pine shoot moth, *Rhyacionia buoliana* Schiff., in Connecticut. *Annals of the Entomological Society of America*, 29: 438–448.

WEST, C. (1985). Factors underlying the late seasonal appearance of the lepidopterous leaf-mining guild on oak. *Ecological Entomology*, 10: 111–120.

WILKES, B. (1747–49). *The English Moths and Butterflies . . .*, 8[22], 64[4], London.

WILLIAMS, C.B. (1958). *Insect Migration*. New Naturalist. Collins, London.

WILLIAMS, D.W. and LIEBHOLD, A.M. (1995). *Potential Changes in Spatial Distribution of Outbreaks of Forest Defoliators Under Climate Change*. In: Harrington, R. and Stork, N.E. (eds) (1995).

WILSON, E.O. (1990). *Success and Dominance in Ecosystems: The Case of Social Insects*. Ecology Institute, Oldendorf, Germany.

WINTER, T.G. (1974). New host plant records of Lepidoptera associated with conifer afforestation in Britain. *Entomologist's Gazette*, 25: 247–258.

WOIWOD, I.P. and HARRINGTON, R. (1994). *Flying in the Face of Change: the Rothampsted Insect Survey*. In: Leigh, R.A. and Johnston, A.E. (eds) *Long-term Experiments in Agricultural and Ecological Sciences*. CAB International, London.

WOOD, J.H. (1894). *Nepticula confusella*, a new birch mining species. *Entomologist's Monthly Magazine*, 29: 272.

de WORMS, C.G.M. (1979). *Notodontidae*. In: Heath, J. and Emmet, A.M. (1979).

YEARGAN, K.V. and QUATE, L.W. (1996). Juvenile bolas spiders attract Psychodid flies. *Oecologia*, 106: 266–271.

YELA, J.L. and HERRERA, C.M. (1993). Seasonality and life cycles of woody plant-feeding noctuid moths (Lepidoptera: Noctuidae) in Mediterranean habitats. *Ecological Entomology*, 18: 259–269.

YOUNG, M.R. (1984). Insects recorded on oil platforms in 1982. *Entomologist's Record and Journal of Variation*, 96: 52–53.

YOUNG, M.R. (1991). *Endromidae*. In: Emmet, A.M. and Heath, J. (eds) (1991).

YOUNG, M.R. (1992). *Conserving insect communities in mixed woodlands*. In: Cannell, M.R.G., Malcolm, D.C. and Robertson, P.A. (eds) *The Ecology of Mixed-Species Stands of Trees*. British Ecological Society, Blackwell, Oxford.

YOUNG, M.R. (1995). An American moth in Aberdeen. *Entomologist's Record and Journal of Variation*, 107: 198–199.

Species Index

Subject Index

Page numbers in **bold** are main discussions; *italics* indicate reference to illustrations and tables.